Modelling the Accumulation and Distribution of Wealth

Modelling the Accumulation and Distribution of Wealth

EDITED BY

Denis Kessler and André Masson

CLARENDON PRESS · OXFORD
1988

Oxford University Press, Walton Street, Oxford OX2 6DP

Oxford   New York   Toronto
Delhi   Bombay   Calcutta   Madras   Karachi
Petaling Jaya   Singapore   Hong Kong   Tokyo
Nairobi   Dar es Salaam   Cape Town
Melbourne   Auckland

and associated companies in
Beirut Berlin Ibadan Nicosia

Oxford is a trade mark of Oxford University Press

Published in the United States
by Oxford University Press, New York

British Library Cataloguing in Publication Data
Modelling the accumulation and
distribution of wealth.
1. Wealth
I. Kessler, Denis   II. Masson, André
339.2'2 · HB251
ISBN 0–19–828523–X

Library of Congress Cataloging in Publication Data
Data available

Set by Colset Private Ltd, Singapore
Printed and bound in Great Britain by
Biddles Ltd, Guildford and King's Lynn

Preface

This book contains the revised versions of the papers given at the conference on Modelling the Accumulation and Distribution of Wealth which was held in Paris on the 2nd and 3rd of September 1984.

This conference, organized by the Centre d'Etude et de Recherche sur l'Epargne, les Patrimoines et les Inégalités (University of Paris-X and CNRS), was sponsored by the Centre National de la Recherche Scientifique and the Commissariat Général du Plan, and we wish to thank these institutions for their very helpful and continuing support. The Centre National de la Recherche Scientifique and the University of Paris-X have also provided support for the publication of the conference proceedings.

The topic of wealth accumulation and distribution has received increasing attention throughout the last decade. Our knowledge of household saving behaviour has increased dramatically in recent years. Both theoretical and empirical progress has been made, due to the work of some of our best scholars on this important topic.

A number of topics have been re-examined, such as the importance of bequest in the wealth accumulation process. Others have been explored, such as the role of social security or the introduction of uncertainty in saving behaviour. In all these matters, new ideas and arguments have been proposed, tested, and discussed. This book is intended to add to these ongoing scientific debates on wealth accumulation and distribution. These scientific debates are not sterile: they have important economic and social implications, in relation to both efficiency and equity.

Economics progresses every day. Since this conference, some new theoretical developments have taken place, and some new empirical evidence has become available. However, we are certain that the papers in this volume contribute greatly to a better understanding of the economic and financial behaviour of households and their distributional consequences.

The editors wish to thank all the authors, discussants, and referees, whose names should all be on the cover page since this book is the outcome of their collective work. They wish also to thank the participants in the conference who gave valuable comments and contributed to a very lively discussion.

D.K. and A.M.

August 1986

Contents

Contents

Introduction

DENIS KESSLER and ANDRÉ MASSON

University of Paris-X and Centre National de la Recherche Scientifique

The aim of the conference was to explore the modelling of personal wealth accumulation and transmission, and to assess the role of various factors in wealth distribution.

Household saving behaviour has two main motivations: life cycle accumulation and wealth transmission. Concerning the distribution of income and wealth, two approaches are possible: intragenerational inequality in current net worth or in lifetime income among households or families, and intergenerational mobility dealing with the relation between income and wealth of parents and children, in particular among siblings.

The contributions study various models of life cycle accumulation and bequest behaviour designed to capture the main features of inequality and mobility in income and wealth. We will present successively the following five topics:

life cycle saving vs. intergenerational transfers;
equal vs. unequal estate division;
intergenerational transfers and the distribution of income and wealth;
uncertainty, risk, and the distribution of wealth;
accumulation behaviour and the distribution of wealth.

Life Cycle Saving vs. Intergenerational Transfers

For a long time, the common view was that inherited wealth represents only a small fraction of existing wealth. Most of the assets held at a given time were considered to result from the past saving of the existing cohorts of consumers. The prevailing opinion was that consumers behave according to the basic life cycle model, first proposed by Modigliani in 1954. Life cycle saving — accumulation primarily for future consumption in retirement — was assumed to be the main source of wealth: in other words, bequests were believed to be of minor importance in the accumulation process.

The consensus was broken by the publication of the work of Kotlikoff and Summers in 1981 in which they argued that the bulk of wealth accumulation is due to intergenerational transfers. On the basis of estimates using twentieth century, US data, they claimed that life cycle saving accounts for only one fifth of existing wealth. These results — if valid — have important theoretical consequences since they cast doubt on the life cycle hypothesis of saving

1

behaviour, and lead to a new view where intergenerational transfers play the dominant economic role.

It is worth mentioning that since the early 1970s, intergenerational transfers have received increasing interest. This may be due in part to two debates which stimulated a growing literature — namely the effects of public debt on savings, first analysed by Barro (1974), and the effects of social security on savings, brought to public attention in the same year by Feldstein (1974).

Two opposing positions can now be distinguished. Both of them lead to the 'law of the 20/80'. The traditional position is that life cycle accumulation accounts for roughly 80% of existing wealth, whereas the new position puts forward exactly the opposite view: that bequests account for 80% of existing wealth.

This debate is crucial for all researchers involved in understanding consumer behaviour and also for policy makers. It has implications relating to both efficiency and equity.

In his contribution to the present discussion (Chapter 1), Modigliani defends the traditional position in replying to the Kotlikoff and Summers (1981) paper. He first reviews the existing evidence on the importance of bequests, particularly from various household surveys. He then estimates the share of inherited wealth from the flow of bequests. The objective is to find a relation between the annual flow of bequests and the stock of inherited wealth. To estimate annual bequests and the stock of inherited wealth, three methods exist: (i) the survey method, where respondents are asked the amount of inheritance received in the course of a year, (ii) inference based on the distribution of wealth by age and on the frequency of death by age, and (iii) the use of probate records.

Using these three approaches Modigliani concludes that 'all direct estimates . . . concur in supporting the pre-Kotklikoff and Summers perception that the share of wealth received through inheritance can be placed somewhere between one tenth and one fifth'. This conclusion is also reached by Ando and Kennickell (1985) who estimate the proportion of self-accumulated wealth by the following method. They compute estimates of saving for individual cohorts for given years consistent with the existing data on national saving. Summing up the saving of each cohort yields each cohort's self-accumulated wealth, and then summing up wealth of cohorts present at a given year yields an estimate of the amount of self-accumulated wealth in relation to total wealth.

It seems, therefore, that the outcomes of the different approaches surveyed by Modigliani cast doubt on the validity of Kotlikoff and Summers' arguments. Modigliani then tries to understand the discrepancy between their estimates and his. It is important to note — as Modigliani and Blinder do in their comments — that Kotlikoff and Summers present two estimates of the proportion of inherited wealth in their 1981 paper. They arrive at a first estimate of 52% using the flow of bequests method. But they prefer the figure of 80% (or over) obtained by their other approach of deriving the share of bequests indirectly as the difference between an independent estimate of total wealth and an estimate of aggregate life cycle wealth.

According to Modigliani, the discrepancy between their estimate and those of others arises primarily from differences in definitions, and subsequently from a series of so called 'errors'. The definitional differences concern notably property income and transfer wealth. Kotlikoff and Summers convert inheritance received in the past into a current stock of inherited wealth after capitalizing it to the present, whereas Modigliani considers that the return to inherited wealth is part of property income. As far as transfers are concerned, Modigliani considers that 'minor gifts as well as moneys provided in support of current consumption, typically to relatives, are treated as part of the current consumption of the giver since they do not result in a rise of wealth'. On the other hand, Kotlikoff and Summers treat all income transfers to people aged over 18 as intergenerational transfers.

Regarding the method used by Kotlikoff and Summers for the accumulation of savings, Modigliani considers that their treatment of durable goods expenditure is erroneous, since they measure consumption as inclusive of the purchase of durable goods instead of including only the estimated durable goods depreciation in consumption of the current year.

Correcting for these differences and the so-called 'errors', Modigliani reduces the proportion of inherited wealth in total wealth from the initial Kotlikoff and Summers 52% estimate based on the flow of bequests to 20.7%, and from the 81% figure based on the accumulation of savings to 20%.

Modigliani argues also that one should not consider that the amount of inherited wealth corresponds to a specific bequest motive. He estimates that a large part of bequests corresponds to a precautionary motive, where wealth at old age serves to hedge against the uncertainty of lifetime (see Davies (1981)).

In their reply to the arguments and recalculations of Modigliani (Chapter 2), Kotlikoff and Summers maintain their basic conclusion that 'the pure life cycle model without intergenerational transfers cannot explain the bulk of US wealth'.

They first report some evidence supporting the importance of intergenerational transfers. They recall notably that early in the twentieth century, people saved considerably even though few of them retired. They insist on the fact that a number of studies in the US conclude that the age–wealth profile does not present the hump shape predicted by the pure life cycle model, since the aged do not dissave. They emphasize the fact that the demand for annuities appears very weak whereas the pure life cycle hypothesis leads to a very strong demand for insurance. Kotlikoff and Summers mention also the results of simulation analyses that call into question the pure life cycle model

(Auerbach and Kotlikoff (1985), Atkinson (1971), Oulton (1976)) .

They stress the fact that they prefer the method of calculating directly life cycle wealth and substracting it from available estimates of total wealth rather than the bequests-flow method. They consider the latter too sensitive to steady-state assumptions, and argue that bequests are too narrowly defined, which tends to cause overestimation of life cycle wealth.

When directly computing life cycle wealth, they define it as the sum over cohorts of the accumulated difference between past streams of labour earnings and consumption, and argue that this corresponds to the standard definition referred to in life cycle theory itself. They do not think that the definition proposed by Modigliani — namely the sum of the difference between past streams of income and consumption — is correct, since income may include capital income earned on previously received intergenerational transfers.

Concerning the age of adulthood, Kotlikoff and Summers 'scribe all consumption expenditures and earnings of those 18 and over to those adults who are directly consuming the expenditures and supplying the labor'. In support of this assumption, they argue in particular that it seems right to consider educational services as intergenerational transfers. Concerning consumer durables, they show that their estimate of the proportion of inherited wealth decreases only very slightly (3 percentage points) when substracting durables both from consumption expenditures and from the amount of total wealth.

They justify their main result on the importance of intergenerational transfers by the specific age–income and age–consumption profiles. According to their computations, both profiles have identical shapes and levels before age 45. Therefore, there is very little life cycle saving over this period. The traditional hump pattern is relevant only for the last part of life, and this leads to small aggregate life cycle wealth since younger cohorts are more numerous than older ones.

It seems an almost impossible task to comment on this controversial debate and to evaluate the arguments proposed by the protagonists. However, Blinder, in his comments, appears successful in assessing the definitions, assumptions, and methods of Modigliani and Kotlikoff and Summers in both their theoretical and empirical dimensions. He examines successively four of the main points raised in the controversy: (i) the methods of calculation (and the error made by Kotlikoff and Summers), (ii) the definition of an intergenerational transfer, (iii) the problem of the accumulated interest on inherited wealth, and (iv) the treatment of durables. He carefully shows the effects on the calculated proportion of inherited wealth in total wealth of alternative definitions and assumptions, and searches for explanations for the differences between the estimates. He does not reconcile the two opposite positions, nor does he say who is right or wrong, but helps to understand the true nature of the debate. It is hoped that additional work will be forthcoming on this issue that will deal not only with the measurement problems but also with the economic and social equity and efficiency implications of the two polar conceptions of the role of bequests and life cycle wealth accumulation.

Equal vs. Unequal Estate Division

Patterns of bequest are important in intergenerational models of the distribution of income and wealth. Transfers among family members can reinforce, attenuate, or have a neutral effect on inequality within a family or among families.

The effects on wealth inequality of alternative inheritance rules (and also savings rate and marriage customs) have been studied in analytical models (Stiglitz (1969), Blinder (1973), Atkinson (1983)), and in simulation studies (Pryor (1973), Blinder (1976*b*)). These studies conclude in particular that an assumption of primogeniture leads to more inequality in wealth that the alternative assumption of equal sharing of estates. However, they did not question the rationale behind the alternative inheritance rules, which were supposed to exist for customary or legal reasons.

More recent works have considered the factors explaining the distribution of parental wealth among children. The models by Becker and Tomes (1976) and by Shorrocks (1979) rest upon the assumption that parents are concerned about the lifetime consumption or income of their children. The Becker and Tomes (1976) model, for instance, predicts that parents will use bequests to attenuate differences in earning abilities among children. If this is true, unequal bequests may have an equalizing effect and efforts to restrict the inheritance of wealth (e.g. by taxing it) may therefore exacerbate wealth inequality within the family.

In his contribution to this discussion (Chapter 3), Tomes explores a theoretical model of family bequest behaviour in which intergenerational transfers take the form of both human capital investment and the bequest of material wealth. He states that 'the fact that intergenerational transfers are made both in the form of human capital investment and (unequal) bequests of material wealth provides an additional degree of freedom enabling the family to achieve both efficiency and equity between siblings'.

Tomes then presents an alternative model (the 'separable earnings–bequest model') where he assumes that parental bequest behaviour is independent from their children's earnings, along the lines of the work of Behrman *et al.* (1982) and Menchik (1980). In this model 'parental preferences concerning the inequality of life earnings are assumed independent of preferences regarding the division of material wealth between heirs'. Since survey data on relative earnings inequality is clouded by a large transitory component and by labour supply decisions, the appropriate test to discriminate between the two models is to determine how frequently unequal estate division occurs.

Such a test also helps to evaluate other hypotheses. Besides the two models mentioned above, Menchik cites in Chapter 4 two other cases where the question of the sharing of estates is crucial. The first is the work by Kotlikoff and Spivak (1981) who consider bequests as a deferred payment for an annuity provided to parents by their children rather than as a transfer between generations. If private annuity markets do not exist, it is efficient for parents to insure against 'living too long' by promising a bequest to children in return for support in old age. If children exhibit declining absolute risk aversion, the child with the highest earnings will provide the largest annuity and receive the largest bequest. Here again, the frequency of unequal estate division among children can be used to support or reject such a theory of bequest.

Menchik also cites the approach of Bernheim, Shleifer, and Summers (1985) where the prospect to receiving a bequest might be used by the testator to control and manipulate the behaviour of potential heirs. If this model is accurate, it implies unequal bequest in the more general case where siblings are not alike in all respects.

As we can see, only empirical data on intergenerational transfers may help to discriminate among the various models. All hypotheses but the 'separable earnings–bequest' one imply that unequal sharing is the rule.

In his contribution (Chapter 3), Tomes uses available data from a 5% random sample of 659 probated estates in the Cleveland area in 1964–5 (previously used by Sussman *et al.* (1970)) to analyse the incidence of equal and unequal division, to examine the determinants of inheritance shares, and to estimate the elasticity of substitution between the lifetime incomes of siblings.

His empirical results differ markedly from those obtained by Menchik (1980) using Connecticut data, since he finds that most estates are unevenly distributed among heirs. He also finds that in those families where unequal division occurs, the most favoured heir receives roughly three-quarters of the total bequest to children. He also provides evidence that parental bequests of material wealth are compensatory in that poor children receive larger bequests that their better-off siblings. Therefore the results seem to confirm the validity of the first model developed by Tomes where decisions concerning human capital and material wealth are interdependent. It may be noted that some of his empirical results may also confirm the hypotheses of Kotlikoff and Spivak (1981) or Bernheim, Shleifer, and Summers (1985).

Menchik does not share this point of view. In his contribution (Chapter 4), he argues that the difference between Tomes' results and his own may come from the way in which the data were generated. In the Connecticut data, information about bequest and gifts comes from probate records, whereas in the Cleveland data it comes from interviewee response to a questionnaire. Menchik has doubts about the accuracy of the data set used by Tomes, and questions whether the appearance of unequal division may simply be the result of noise. To check this point, he tries to replicate the Cleveland sample.

Exact matching with Tomes' sample is unfortunately impossible and Menchik has to rely on probate records drawn from a sample with comparable properties. He finds that, as hypothesized, the differences between his 1980 results, where equal sharing is the rule, and the Tomes' (Chapter 3) results is simply a consequence of response error in the data in the Cleveland area.

If this is the case, the question of why parents bequeath equally still remains a puzzling one, and Menchik himself does not seem entirely convinced by the various possible explanations, such as the existence of transaction costs or the public good nature of familial trust.

Intergenerational Transfers and the Distribution of Income and Wealth

The first attempts to derive the distributional implications of wealth transmission from a theory of bequest behaviour can be found in the 1970s, especially in the work of Blinder (1975, 1976*a*, 1976*b*). His focus was on the relation of bequests to lifetime resources. He suggested that bequests were a luxury good with an elasticity with respect to lifetime resources greater than unity. With this assumption, he found that inheritance was a major factor in wealth inequality, but had only a minimal effect on inequality in annual or lifetime income. Moreover, under perfect capital markets, his model generated almost complete intergenerational wealth mobility, even with assortative mating and unequal division of estates: there was almost no correlation between father's and son's wealth. This result is clearly at odds with the facts, since the intergenerational correlation for inherited wealth is around 0.7 in the US and in Britain (see, for example, Harbury (1962) and Menchik (1979)).

Models of 'altruistic' bequest behaviour may be seen as one attempt to resolve this problem. Altruism means that parents' utility function depends on the characteristics of their children. In Becker and Tomes (1979) model of 'compensated' bequest, parents are concerned with their children's lifetime income (see also Shorrocks (1979)). Davies (1982) has shown that this model resolves some of Blinder's difficulties. Notably, strong intergenerational regression towards the mean in income leads to a high elasticity of bequest for the wealthy, since the bequest acts as a buffer against this regression. Blinder's conclusions concerning the distributional consequences of bequest therefore appear reinforced. Indeed, the higher income mobility is — that is, the higher the regression towards the mean in income — the more disequalizing is the effect of bequest on wealth distribution but the less disequalizing it is on income. Indeed, this leads to the counterintuitive view that inheritance may have an equalizing effect on the distribution of (lifetime) income.

Some attempts have been made to resolve this problem. Davies and Kuhn's

(Chapter 5) and Tomes' (Chapter 6) contributions extend this analysis of the distributional consequences of 'altruistic' bequest behaviours. Davies and Kuhn are concerned mainly with the impact of a tax on inheritance or on life-time income on the inequality of income, whereas Tomes deals with the implications of different altruistic bequest behaviours for intergenerational mobility in lifetime income, wealth, and consumption.

Davies and Kuhn study the possibility of perverse effects on income inequality of redistribution through an inheritance or a (lifetime) income tax. In this fashion, their study is an extension of Becker and Tomes' (1979) analysis. They consider the case of a linear tax-transfer scheme with equal sharing, perfect capital markets which allow for negative bequest, exogenous earnings, and a homothetic utility function. The impact of uncertainty and of fertility and mating patterns are not considered.

In a related paper (Davies (1986)) steady-state implications were analysed; in the present paper, transition paths are studied, since, as demonstrated by Shorrocks (1975), convergence to a steady state may require a long period of time (that is indeed up to ten generations in the present model).

.Let us first consider the distributional steady-state consequences of the model. The impact of redistribution on income inequality may be con-veniently categorized into two effects, that we will examine in turn: the first one, for a given level of transfers, depends on the income equalizing role of inheritance; the second concerns the variation in the level of transfers, since the revenue of the tax is used to fund transfer payments: income inequality is, of course, a decreasing function of the importance of transfers.

To understand how the first effect works, let us consider the corresponding case of non-altruistic bequest studied by Bevan and Stiglitz (1979), where the elasticity of bequest is equal to 1. With bequests proportional to parental income, regression to the mean in earnings implies that 'bequests received will on average increase less than in proportion to child's earnings, so that the existence of inheritance is equalizing'. Hence taxing bequest increases income inequality in the long run.

A similar mechanism is at work with compensated bequests. However, in this case, inheritance and lifetime income depend on a weighted sum of all past generations' earnings, the weights being determined by a geometrically-declining distributed lag of the effective intergenerational propensity to bequest, EIPB. Under regression to the mean in earnings, there is thus an averaging of luck of previous generations with the present one and income inequality is lower than earnings inequality. A rise in the inheritance or income tax necessarily decreases the EIPB and leads therefore to less inter-generational averaging and to more income inequality.

Since a tax increase reduces the EIPB in the long run, it is possible that it actually reduces equilibrium transfer payments so that the second effect is also disequalizing. The tax base is crucial here. An inheritance tax is most likely to cause a reduction of equilibrium transfers. An earnings tax leads to an increase in the level of transfers, while an income tax has an ambiguous effect.

It appears therefore, that the resulting steady-state effect of a rising income tax is more likely to increase income inequality. It does not follow, however, that income inequality rises monotonically during the transition period.

Indeed, the authors argue that the initial effect of the tax increase is likely to be equalizing. This is because transfer payments will be at their highest just after the policy change, while the first (always disequalizing) effect is initially quite weak and grows in strength during the transition period. Thus, an attempt at redistribution could well be successful in the short run though unsuccessful in the long run.

This argument is illustrated by some numerical examples which show that the most likely effect of an income tax increase is a continuous reduction of inequality during the first three or four generations followed by a steady increase until the new equilibrium state is reached.

In his comments. Atkinson contrasts the distributional implications of the compensated bequest model with the view of the 'man in the street' that inheritance leads to greater inequality not only in wealth but also in income, since bequest is indeed a luxury good. This view is also shared by Modigliani (1986) who makes 'the share of resources earmarked for bequest' an increasing function of 'the household's relative position in the distribution of life resources of its age cohort'. Moreover, Atkinson emphasizes the fact that the results of the model may depend crucially upon several assumptions, such as the existence of perfect capital markets which allow for negative bequests. In addition, the results should be re-examined in a broader setting where mating and inheritance patterns and fertility differentials are introduced.

Tomes' contribution in Chapter 6 yields further insights into this debate. First he draws several implications concerning intergenerational mobility in income, consumption, and wealth from the Becker and Tomes (1979) model of inheritance. It is found that those three variables exhibit the same pattern of regression towards the mean, which overstates the degree of wealth mobility.

Second he examines the implications for intergenerational mobility of an alternate way to model 'altruistic' bequest behaviour, and where uncertainty, capital market imperfections which prevent negative bequest, differential fertility, and assortative mating are introduced.

In this new model, the parental utility function is dependent not on children's income, as in the previous model, nor on children's consumption as in Shorrocks (1979), but on their level of utility. As noted by Levy-Garboua in his comments, this choice is the more appropriate one from a theoretical point of view.

Children are assumed to have the same tastes as their parents, and parents take into account the fact that their children also make bequests. This is formally equivalent to saying that parents maximize utility over the consumption of all their progeny. With a homothetic utility function it follows that consumption is a constant fraction of the total resources of the household and all its descendents. Moreover, intergenerational mobility in consumption is zero, no matter how high the degree of mobility in income and wealth, since transfers of material wealth are made to offset the regression to the mean in endowments of human capital.

This model is more realistic as far as income or wealth mobility are concerned, but not in regard to consumption. However, the introduction of uncertainty and endogenous fertility are both sufficient to generate regression to the mean in consumption. Moreover, the constraint on negative bequest creates an asymmetry between rich people who can make positive bequest, and poor households so that there is greater social mobility among the poor than among the rich.

As Levy-Garboua emphasizes, these results, as well as those of Becker and Tomes (1986), which introduce different rates of return for human and non-human capital, show the importance of uncertainty and capital market imperfections in evaluating the distributional implications of intergenerational transfers. This conclusion is shared by Atkinson in his comments on Davies and Kuhn's contribution.

All the contributions reviewed up to now, even those which examine the way estates are shared among heirs, devote little attention to a key demographic variable, namely the number of children per family. This parameter appears neither in the analysis of the effects of public and private intergenerational transfers on wealth inequality and mobility, nor in the study of wealth accumulation over time. It appears likely, however, that the number of children has strong implications on the accumulation and distribution of wealth, particularly in regard to social security in a pay-as-you-go system and bequests through the division of estates.

Cremer and Pestieau seek in Chapter 7 to examine the incidence of varying family size on the accumulation of saving and the distribution of wealth through a pay-as-you-go social security scheme and intergenerational transfers based on equal sharing. They first develop a two-period overlapping generations model following Barro (1974), where individuals work in the first period and retire in the second. Parents are assumed to improve the welfare of their children by leaving them bequests. The utility function is assumed to be Cobb–Douglas. All individuals are alike in all respects but for the number of children and the amount of inherited wealth. Equal sharing is the only way estates are divided among heirs. There is a pay-as-you-go social security scheme financed through payroll taxes.

The first result obtained by the authors is that 'on average, both bequests and saving are independent of the current level of public pensions and of the distribution of family size'. Therefore the Barro neutrality results hold for the economy as a whole. Cremer and Pestieau then study the impact of public pension variations on the variance of bequests. In the steady state, they conclude that social security as well as fertility differentials have a disequalizing effect on the distribution of inherited wealth. This is illustrated through various simulations.

The authors then add another demographic variable to fertility differentials, namely an uncertain life horizon. They find that these two demographic factors, when combined with unfunded social security, have opposite distributive implications. The effect of fertility differentials is neutral towards capital accumulation but disequalizing in terms of bequest and utility, whereas uncertain lifetime has a depressive effect on life cycle accumulation and an equalizing one on bequest and utility. The resulting distributional effect of the two demographic factors combined is utility equalizing at low levels of public pensions but disequalizing beyond a certain level of social security. Cremer and Pestieau thus conclude that 'through unfunded social security and debt financing, public authorities discriminate against large families'.

Commenting on the Cremer and Pestieau contribution, Jenkins notes that it is the first paper studying jointly fertility differentials, lifespan uncertainty, and social security in a model with bequest motives. However, he raises questions about the model specification — in particular that the distributional non-neutrality result is due to the use of a Cobb–Douglas utility function that depends on the net bequest per child, but where the number of children *per se* has no effect on utility. Other specifications of the utility function may lead to very different results.

Uncertainty, Risk, and the Distribution of Wealth

As is evident from Sahota's survey (1978), there are a great variety of theories of income distribution. There also exists a large number of theories of wealth distribution, both intra- and intergenerational, which often have a close correspondence with income distribution theories. This is especially the case with stochastic models of wealth distribution which, like those concerning income distribution, have a long history (see Sargan (1957), Shorrocks (1975)). They attribute the skewed shape of the wealth distribution primarily to luck and random occurrences. Their more important result is 'that even if a generation started from a state of strict equality of income and wealth, inequalities of the degree of Pareto distribution could emerge due to stochastic forces' (Sahota (1978)).

However, the modelling of income and wealth is quite different, since wealth is a stock variable, the accumulation of which occurs over time, while income is a flow and is less dependent on individual decisions than wealth. As a result, age plays a specific role in wealth accumulation and a central role in the life cycle hypothesis (referred to below as LCH) as a framework for analysing saving decisions. Indeed, one major critique of stochastic models

of wealth distributions is that they are not explicitly based upon rational individual behaviour or even that they are not consistent with individual accumulation behaviour.

To overcome this weakness, Vaughan offers in Chapter 8 an original
attempt to combine the LCH with the stochastic approach. He tries to build a
more comprehensive stochastic distributional model where the equation
governing the change in the size distribution of wealth is derived from
individual lifetime utility maximization and risk taking behaviour. This
equation depends also upon the value of environmental parameters (such as
the wage rate and the rate of return to assets) and demographic and estate
sharing laws.

The sources of uncertainty concern the exogenous labour and wealth
returns, as well as life duration. All individuals are assumed to be alike in
their (isoelastic) utility function, expected life duration, wage, return to
assets, and other characteristics, except for the realization of the random
elements. It is only the equilibrium distribution of wealth which is found to be
Pareto-like.

The focus of the paper is on the determinants of wealth dispersion. The
Pareto coefficient measures the degree of skewness of the upper tail of the
distribution. Moreover, the equation relating the Pareto coefficient to other
parameters allows an assessment of the effects of different factors on wealth
inequality. Inequality increases with the savings propensity and the importance of the bequest motive, while it decreases with the rate of population
growth and the rate of time preference. The effect of a change in the average
rate of return to assets or in the degree of income inequality depends on the
value of the relative risk aversion relative to one.

Two points deserve special attention in the interpretation of these results.
First, as Malinvaud mentions in his comments, the individual accumulation
behaviour is not really derived from the LCH, since the wage rate and the
probability of death are kept constant over the lifetime. Second, capital
markets are assumed to be perfect. There is however one important exception
to the latter hypothesis, that is the existence of a low boundary for wealth, a
technical condition which is necessary to derive the equilibrium distribution
of wealth. The problems raised by this condition have been underlined during
the discussion, notably by Bourguignon and Malinvaud, and, in his comments, Malinvaud offers one interpretation which could help to solve them.

On the other hand, it appears that the assumption of perfect capital
markets is also questionable for the upper part of the wealth distribution.
Blinder (1976b), for instance, points out that a large number of tax gimmicks
are available for the rich and that the rate of return to assets rises with the
amount of wealth invested due to the fixed elements in transaction costs, the
costs of acquiring information, the advantages of risk pooling through diversification, and related factors.

Shorrocks' model in Chapter 9 is a response to Blinder's recommendations. It envisages sophisticated risk-taking behaviour due to the presence of strong 'indivisibilities' or entry barriers in the capital market. A standard LCH model of consumption behaviour is used. Moreover all individuals are assumed to have identical tastes and the same initial resources. The amount of wealth owned depends partly on random factors and partly on endogenous lifetime resources. At each period the individual has the choice of either working or of becoming an 'entrepreneur', where he undertakes either 'low-budget' or 'high-budget risk'. The key assumption is that 'low-budget risks require only the input of time . . . while high-budget risks need a substantial monetary investment in addition to time and are only accessible to those who have already demonstrated their success as a low-budget entrepreneur'. Moreover the probability of success for each kind of risk is endogeneously determined by the number of participants and whether risk-pooling strategies are allowed among the two types of entrepreneurs.

Rational behaviour under the assumptions of the model requires that the expected return on high-budget risk is positive, but that it is negative for low-budget risk. Individuals are still willing to take the latter risk in order to have access to the high-budget risk. Moreover, low-budget risk takers will adopt complete specialization to have access to the second stage of fortune seeking, whereas high-budget risk takers will choose complete diversification and risk-pooling to protect their access to that kind of risk.

Indeed the kind of capital market imperfection envisaged by Shorrocks leads, to a certain extent, to a two-class model: the workers on the one hand and the high-budget risk takers on the other, with endogenous interclass mobility. Low-budget risk takers are outliers who adopt individualistic strategies to escape the working class while the high-risk class adopts a collective strategy in order to maintain its privileges.

This model could prove a fruitful device for understanding the building of large fortunes if it were linked to other factors of wealth inequality. In his comments, Bourguignon mentions the necessity of introducing dispersion in risk aversion to explain why some individuals will accept risk at the beginning of their life and others not. Also, if endowments differ among individuals, it is possible to look at the condition of accessibility to high-budget risk — namely the success in the other form of risk-taking — as a screening device to discover who are the more able entrepreneurs.

Accumulation Behaviour and the Distribution of Wealth

Although Shorrocks' model can be viewed as a first step towards a two-class model, it is important to note that workers and successful entrepreneurs follow the same logic of action: they adopt different behaviour only because they have different amounts of resources and therefore face different opportunity sets. Indeed, most models of wealth distribution likewise assume that all consumers behave according to the same behavioural rules. In contrast, some authors have developed models of class behaviour where the different classes are assumed to follow different behavioural rules (Pasinetti (1962), Samuelson and Modigliani (1966), Stiglitz (1969), Vaughan (1979)).

In the same fashion, Wolff tries in Chapter 10 to develop a two-class model in order to explain the downward trend in wealth inequality observed in most occidental countries during the twentieth century. Following Pasinetti, he considers two distinct economic classes — the capitalists and the workers. His major innovation is to assume that workers follow a life cycle model of consumption, accumulating wealth for their retirement period, either through saving or through a social security system. On the other hand, capitalists are assumed to save a fixed proportion of their income, independent of their age.

Moreover, workers are divided into two sub-classes — active workers and retired workers. With perfect capital markets, active workers tend to have negative wealth during the first part of their life cycle; the reason is that only productive capital is considered part of wealth, and houses and durables are excluded. With certainty in time of death and no bequests, retired workers dissave from positive net worth at time of retirement to zero net worth at time of death.

Other assumptions have important distributional implications. All capitalists have the same amount of wealth. At a given age, all workers have the same amount of wealth. Finally the proportions of the two classes are fixed and exogenously given and there is no possible interchange of population between them.

As Russell points out in his comments, the last assumption is crucial to an understanding of the equilibrium properties of Wolff's model. In Stiglitz's model, 'everyone is both a capitalist and a worker'; this high potential interclass mobility explains why initial wealth inequality in steady state declines over time and converges to perfect equality. In Wolff's model, the 'impenetrable barrier between capitalists and workers' leads to a Pasinetti-type economy, where the wealth distribution is constant in the steady state and the Pasinetti relation holds between the rate of interest r and the rates of population growth n, technical progress g, and of capitalists' saving m, namely, $r = g + n/m$. This latter relation holds independently of workers' behaviour.

This result allows Wolff, through a comparative static analysis similar to that of Vaughan, to determine the role of various factors on steady-state wealth inequality. Running alternate simulations, he finds that inequality decreases with the rates g and m and with the duration of lifetime, but increases with the rate r, the age of retirement, and the expansion of the social security system. As Vaughan notes, variations in r, g, and m are bound to change other inequality factors if the Pasinetti relation is to be maintained.

The interpretation of the observed decline in wealth inequality is then apparent. In Stiglitz's model it was the consequence of a vanishing class-difference and occurred during the transition leading to steady state. In Wolff's framework, this decline in inequality is attributable to historical changes, which affect the parameters of the steady-state solution. Wolff's conclusion is that the main equalizing forces have been the increases in the life expectancy and in the retirement period: these changes forced workers to accumulate more, while they have no bearing on capitalists' wealth. However, this effect has been somewhat dampened by the growth of the social security system.

To explain the declining wealth inequality trend in industrialized countries, other factors have also been noted. The one most frequently mentioned is a reduction of wealth dispersion among the more affluent — the capitalists in Wolff's model — which often occurs through intra- or intergenerational redistributions within large families. To account for this factor, Wolff could, as he mentions in his conclusion, introduce a dispersion of wealth within the capitalist class and model their behaviour in terms of bequest motives with a variety of estate-splitting patterns.

This extension of Wolff's model will still attribute the changes that have occurred in the bulk of the distribution of wealth to factors which affect the accumulation pattern of workers and are emphasized by the LCH. Indeed, the underlying idea in Wolff's model is that the top wealth groups form a separate social class with specific wealth holdings motives, but that the life cycle model could well account for a large part of the wealth dispersion within the remaining population.

To test this argument, which is shared by many scholars of wealth inequality, Kessler and Masson try in Chapter 11 to ascertain the wealth distributional implications of the LCH. Their point of departure is Atkinson's (1971) paper which shows that in a life cycle framework, age is only a minor factor in the determination of wealth inequality.

A possible interpretation of these results is that the major sources of wealth inequality are found to be differences in lifetime earnings and inheritances among individuals. However, the LCH points as well to other potential factors of wealth dispersion concerning individual differences in endowments, especially in life duration or expectancy, in tastes, including risk aversion and time preference, in opportunities, especially with regard to information and capital markets, and in 'luck' on the various markets.

Most of these factors are not easy to model, since they depend upon unobservable exogenous parameters. Indeed, there is not even much agreement in the literature concerning the mean value of these parameters, let alone their distributions or correlations. Moreover, accumulation behaviour and the resulting age–wealth profile are complex, and sometimes discontinuous, functions of these factors.

Indeed Kessler and Masson demonstrate that the LCH can generate, under plausible assumptions, a large variety of individual age–wealth profiles. This means that the prediction of hump saving which concerns 'average behaviour' is not very representative of individual behaviour. Conversely, a given accumulation profile can nest a lot of various behaviours and situations and may be difficult to interpret without further information.

As a result, the role of the various individual factors other than age or resources on wealth inequality is very difficult to assess, even though their effect can be quite large. The wealth distributional consequences of the LCH appear therefore largely unpredictable on a theoretical basis.

The use of simulation models based on the LCH to assess the role of various factors, especially inheritance, on wealth inequality is somewhat questionable since they are bound to rely upon a specific variant of the theory or to make simplifying assumptions concerning the distribution of tastes and endowments (see Blinder (1976*b*), Flemming (1979) or Davies (1982)). Moreover, their specification of the environment must be quite oversimplified, particularly in regard to market imperfections, uncertainty, and behaviour towards risk.

For these reasons, such models cannot really claim to offer a direct test of the LCH on wealth distribution. Such a test could be based upon an empirical breakdown of wealth inequality based on age and permanent income.

In their comments, Feaster and Danziger advocate such breakdowns as a means to assess the quantitative importance of individual factors besides age and lifetime resources on the distribution of wealth. Indeed, their main criticism of Kessler and Masson's contribution concerns the lack of any empirical estimates of the magnitudes of these distributional effects.

Conclusion

Numerous other issues and questions are raised in the contributions and comments. Most papers emphasize theoretical work and concentrate more on the upper tail of the distribution of income and wealth. For these reasons, we think that the last word should be given to Haveman, whose primary interest is 'in the bottom tail of the distribution'. The appraisal of current research on wealth accumulation and transmission given by this expert in poverty, income distribution, and social transfers is both refreshing and stimulating.

References

Ando, A. and A. Kennickell, 'How Much (or Little) Life Cycle is There in Micro Data? Cases of US and Japan', Paper presented at Istituto Bancario San Paolo di Torino Conference to Honor Franco Modigliani, in Martha's Vineyard, Massachusetts, mimeo, (1985).

Atkinson, A. B., 'The Distribution of Wealth and the Individual Life Cycle', *Oxford Economic Papers* 23 (1971), 239–54.

—— 'Income Distribution and Inequality of Opportunity', in *Social Justice and Public Policy* (Wheatsheaf Books Ltd, London, 1983), 77–92.

Auerbach, A.J. and L.J. Kotlikoff, 'Simulating Alternative Social Security Responses to the Demographic Transition', *National Tax Journal* **38** (1985), 153–68.

Barro, R.J., 'Are Government Bonds Net Wealth?', *Journal of Political Economy* **82** (1974), 1095–1118.

Becker G.S. and N. Tomes, 'Child Endowments and the Quantity and Quality of Children', *Journal of Political Economy* **84**, part 2 (1976), S143–S162.

—— and ——, 'An Equilibrium Theory of the Distribution of Income and Intergenerational Mobility', *Journal of Political Economy* **87** (1979), 1153–89.

—— and ——, 'Human Capital and the Rise and Fall of Families', *Journal of Labor Economics* **4**, part 2 (1986), S1–S39.

Behrman, J., R. Pollak, and P. Taubman, 'Parental Preferences and Provision for Progeny', *Journal of Political Economy* **90** (1982), 52–73.

Bernheim, B.D., A. Shleifer, and L. Summers, 'The Strategic Bequest Motive', *Journal of Political Economy* **93** (1985), 1045–76.

Bevan, D.L. and J.E. Stiglitz, 'Intergenerational Transfers and Inequality', *Greek Economic Review* **1** (1979), 8–26.

Blinder, A.S., 'A Model of Inherited Wealth', *Quarterly Journal of Economics* **87**, (1973), 608–26.

—— 'Distribution Effects and the Aggregate Consumption Function', *Journal of Political Economy* **83** (1975), 447–75.

—— 'Intergenerational Transfers and Life Cycle Consumption', *Papers and Proceedings of the American Economic Review* **66** (1976a), 87–93.

—— 'Inequality and Mobility in the Distribution of Wealth', *Kyklos* **29** (1976b), 607–38.

Davies J.B., 'Uncertain Lifetime, Consumption and Dissaving in Retirement', *Journal of Political Economy* **89** (1981), 561–77.

—— 'The Relative Impact of Inheritance and other Factors on Economic Inequality', *Quarterly Journal of Economics* **97** (1982), 471–98.

—— 'Does Redistribution Reduce Inequality?', *Journal of Labor Economics* **4** (1986) 538–59.

Feldstein, M.S., 'Social Security, Induced Retirement and Aggregate Capital Accumulation, *Journal of Political Economy* **82** (1974), 905–26.

Flemming, J.S., 'The Effects of Earnings Inequality, Imperfect Capital Markets and Dynastic Altruism on the Distribution of Wealth in Life Cycle Models', *Economica* **46** (1979), 363–80.

Harbury, C., 'Inheritance and the Distribution of Wealth in Britain', *Economic Journal* **72** (1962), 845–68.

Kotlikoff, L. and A. Spivak, 'The Family as an Incomplete Annuities Market', *Journal of Political Economy* **89** (1981), 372–81.

—— and L. Summers, 'The Role of Intergenerational Transfers in Aggregate Capital Accumulation', *Journal of Political Economy* **89** (1981), 706–32.

Menchik, P.L., 'Inter-generational Transmission of Inequality: An Empirical Study of Wealth Mobility', *Economica* **46** (1979), 349–62.

—— 'Primogeniture, Equal Sharing and the US Distribution of Wealth', *Quarterly Journal of Economics* **94** (1980), 299–316.

Modigliani, F., 'Life Cycle, Individual Thrift and the Wealth of Nations', Nobel Lecture, *American Economic Review* **76** (1986), 297–313.

—— and R.E. Brumberg, 'Utility Analysis and the Consumption Function: an Interpretation of Cross-Section Data', In K.K. Kurihara (ed.), *Post-Keynesian Economics* (Rutgers University Press, New Brunswick, 1954), 388–436.

Oulton, N., 'Inheritance and the Distribution of Wealth', *Oxford Economic Papers* **28** (1976), 86–101.

Pasinetti, L., 'Rate of Profit and Income Distribution in Relation to the Rate of Economic Growth', *Review of Economic Studies* **29** (1962), 267–79.

Pryor, F., 'Simulation of the Impact of Social and Economic Institutions on the Size Distribution of Income and Wealth', *American Economic Review* **63** (1973), 50–72.

Sahota, G.S., 'Theories of Personal Income Distribution: a Survey', *Journal of Economic Literature* **16** (1978) 1–55.

Samuelson, P.A. and F. Modigliani, 'The Pasinetti Paradox in Neoclassical and More General Models', *Review of Economic Studies* **33** (1966), 269–301.

Sargan, J.D., 'The Distribution of Wealth', *Econometrica* **25** (1957), 568–90.

Shorrocks, A.F., 'On Stochastic Models of Size Distribution', *Review of Economic Studies* **42** (1975), 631–41.

—— 'On the Structure of Inter-generational Transfers between Families', *Economica* **46** (1979), 415–25.

Stiglitz, J.E., 'Distribution of Income and Wealth among Individuals', *Econometrica* **37** (1969), 382–97.

Sussman C.J., N. Cates, and D. Smith. *The Family and Inheritance* (Russell Sage Foundation, New York, 1970).

Vaughan, R.N., 'Class Behaviour and the Distribution of Wealth', *Review of Economic Studies* **46** (1979), 447–65.

Life Cycle Saving vs. Intergenerational Transfers

1   Measuring the Contribution of Intergenerational Transfers to Total Wealth: Conceptual Issues and Empirical Findings

FRANCO MODIGLIANI
Massachusetts Institute of Technology

I   Historical perspective and overview

In the early Keynesian period, when the study of the consumption function first became fashionable, it was quite generally believed that saving was determined by income, with poor people dissaving and only rich people saving throughout their life. Although there was relatively little concern as to what led people to save, whether to increase their income, to increase their power, or to leave bequests, the basic view of the saving process unavoidably implied that all of the accumulation, or nearly all, would finally wind up as bequeathed wealth. This, in turn, implied that all private wealth originated through bequests — that is, either it had been received through bequests or was destined to be bequeathed.

It was to Harrod's great merit (1948) that he pointed out that saving could also be done with a view toward later dissaving — the so-called 'hump saving'. The life cycle model (see Modigliani and Brumberg (1954, 1980)) can be seen as an endeavour to explore systematically this seminal idea, with major focus on to the role of retirement as a cause of hump saving. One of the most significant early results of the life cycle hypothesis was to establish that, even in the absence of bequests, the retirement motive alone could generate an overall amount of wealth in relation to income, of the order of magnitude of that actually observed for the US at that time, and for other countries as well, as data became available later. It was thus at least conceivable that the bulk of wealth might not be acquired by intergenerational transfers but might instead be accumulated from scratch by each household to be consumed eventually by the end of life.

It was, of course, recognized from the very beginning that some portion of existing wealth most likely came from bequests left at least by those in the upper strata of the distribution of wealth (human and non-human) (see, e.g., Modigliani and Brumberg (1954), Modigliani and Ando (1957), and Modigliani (1975)). But just how large was the contribution of self-accumulated hump wealth relative to that of wealth received by bequests?

That was an intriguing question which could, obviously, be answered only through empirical investigation.

It was the interest in this question that was partly responsible for a flurry of empirical studies which took up this issue, together with some others, relating to saving behaviour in the first half of the 1960s. All four of the studies undertaken in that brief period relying on questionnaire survey methods devoted some attention to ascertaining how much wealth had been received through inheritance (with major gifts sometimes explicitly mentioned). There is reason for suspecting the reliability of the information that can be gathered by this method, especially since the inquiry related to events possibly far past. Furthermore, partly in the light of the above consideration, the studies were aiming only for a rough order of magnitude. Yet, it is impressive that all of these studies arrived at surprisingly similar estimates of the share of wealth arising from inheritance and major gifts; they fell in a narrow range around 15%. On these grounds it has been generally accepted since that time that the proportion of inherited wealth could be placed somewhere between one-tenth and one-fifth (cf. Modigliani (1975)), although it was recognized that this estimate rested on somewhat shaky ground.

This perception has been severely challenged by Kotlikoff and Summer's recent contribution, 'The Role of Intergenerational Transfers in Aggregate Capital Accumulation' (hereafter K&S). In this paper they reach the dramatically different conclusion that the bulk of non-human wealth currently held by households in the United States — somewhat over four-fifths — can be traced to intergenerational transfers through gifts and bequests, leaving very little room for the role of self-accumulation implied by hump saving models.

In the following pages, I propose to review briefly the older evidence, to add to it some that has more recently become available, including some provided by K&S, and to show that all of this evidence basically confirms the previously established conclusion that inherited wealth represents a relatively small portion of total household wealth — probably less than one-fifth, and almost certainly less than one-quarter. The very different estimates produced by K&S will be shown to reflect partly a mathematical slip (of moderate consequence), partly a conceptual slip (with sizeable implications), while the rest is accounted for, largely if not entirely, by the fact that they have defined 'life cycle' and 'transfer' wealth in a way which is very different from the customary one underlying the earlier perception and the other estimates referred to above. Thus, once the figures reported by K&S are properly corrected, they too agree with all other estimates on the conclusion that wealth received by inheritance and major gifts represents a modest fraction of the total, and that an exogenous large reduction in the flow of bequests would not have a major affect on the privately held stock of wealth.

II   Review of some earlier investigations on the share of inherited wealth

As just noted, most of the information for the US has come from a number of studies in the early 1960s. These studies provide, in the first place, some interesting data with respect to the importance of the estate motive as a determinant of saving. In the classic 1962 study, *Survey of Financial Characteristics of Consumers*, sponsored by the Federal Reserve, (Projector and Weiss (1964)), respondents were asked to tell 'about your own personal reasons for saving — that is to say, what sort of things you have in mind to accomplish through saving'. Twelve specific motives were offered, plus an open-ended choice of 'other', and 'no reply'. 13% did not respond, while the remaining 87% gave an average of two reasons. Only 3% mentioned 'To provide an estate for family'! In fact, this motive turned out to be among the least mentioned reasons, with only two reasons being offered less, one of which, interestingly enough, was 'to increase income' (2%), which is the other motive that used to be regarded by conventional wisdom as a major reason for saving. All the remaining eight reasons are consistent with the life cycle hypothesis and, more generally,. with hump saving; in particular, 'old age' (41%), 'emergencies' (32%), and 'children's education' (29%).

The proportion of people referring to the bequest motive does increase, as one might expect, with wealth, but even in the top wealth class (half a million 1963 dollars and over), it is mentioned by only one-third of the respondents. Thus, even if the frequency of respondents is weighted by 'dollars of wealth' rather than by 'number of households', the proportion of 'dollars of wealth' whose owner mentioned an estate motive does not even reach 15%. The proportion also increases markedly with income; however, even among respondents with income above $10 000 — roughly the top 10% of income receivers — and weighting the response by dollars of income, one finds that the proportion mentioning bequests is not quite 14%. It is also interesting, and somewhat surprising, that the importance of the bequest motive does not vary significantly with age, at least after 35 — the proportion mentioning it remains consistently around only 4%.

A very similar question was raised in the 1964 survey underlying the Brookings Study *Economic Behavior of the Affluent* (see Barlow *et al.* (1966)), which sampled only the population with income over $10 000. Respondents were given eight specific choices, including 'to bequeath money'. The percentage mentioning this motive, weighted by income, was larger than in the FRB survey, but still modest — some 26%. The more relevant, wealth-weighted reply is not available.

We turn next to information pertaining to the proportion of presently held wealth resulting from bequests (and possibly gifts) which is summarized in Table 1.1. In 1960, in the course of the study *Income and Welfare in the*

TABLE 1.1. Estimates of stock of wealth resulting from transfers

Source	Nature of Data	Nature of Transfers Included	Valuation	Share of Wealth from Transfers (%)
1. *Income and Wealth in the US* (1960)	Response to survey question on size of transfer received	All (?)	At time of receipt (?)	Less than 10
2. *Survey of Financial Characteristics of Consumers* (1962)	Response to survey question on share of wealth from transfer	Inheritance and large gifts from outside family	At time of receipt	(16)[a]
3. *Economic Behavior of the Affluent* (1964)	Response to survey question on fraction of wealth accounted for by transfers. Limited to income $10 000 and over	Inheritance and gifts	At time of receipt	One-seventh
4. Ibid	As above	Inheritance and gifts	At time of receipt, plus capital appreciation to present	Less than one-fifth
5. Kotlikoff and Summers (1974)	Estimated from wealth of those dying: age gap: 25–30 years	Intergenerational bequests	At time of receipt, corrected for price level changes	$15\frac{1}{2}$–17
6. *Survey of Changes in Consumer Finances* (1963)	Response to question on transfer received during year; age gap: 25–30 years	Inheritance and gifts from outside family	As above	14–$15\frac{1}{2}$
7. Menchik and David (1982)	Probate records; age gap: 25–30 years	Intergenerational bequests	As above	14–15
8. Menchik and David (1983)	Probate records: age gap: 22–25 years	All bequests other than interspousal	As above	20–22

[a] Wealth-weighted average of respondents answering that inherited assets were a 'substantial portion' of total assets.

United States (see Morgan *et al.* (1962)), respondents were asked whether they had 'inherited any money or property', and 'what was it worth'. Only 18% reported ever receiving any inheritance (2% did not reply), and only 3% said they had received more than $10 000, at a time when average household wealth, according to the Board of Governors of the Federal Reserve System (1981) estimates, could be placed at around $30 000.[1] The mean amount received is hard to estimate from the published coarse distribution including an open-ended class, but it seems that it must fall short of 10% of average wealth, as reported in Table 1.1, row 1.

In the 1962 Federal Reserve Study cited earlier (Projector and Weiss (1964)), respondents were also asked whether 'anyone in this family ever received an inheritance . . . or a large gift . . . from someone who is not in the family now' and if so whether it represented 'a substantial portion of your family's present assets'. Only 17% reported having received any amount, which is remarkably consistent with the Morgan *et al.* results, cited above, and only 5% reported that the amount received represented a 'substantial' proportion of wealth. There is, however, again, a strong positive correlation between the proportion of households reporting receipt of inheritance, and their net worth; thus, while only some 3% of those with less than $5 000 of wealth indicated that bequests were a substantial portion of their wealth, the proportion rises to 34% for those with wealth above half a million. There is, unfortunately, no way of calculating from these data the proportion of wealth inherited as against the proportion of respondents reporting inheritance. We can, however, get some very crude approximations by making the heroic assumption that 'substantial' can be approximated as 100%, while 'small' can be 'rounded off' to zero. With this assumption, the share of wealth due to bequests comes to 16% (Table 1.1, row 2).

A similar question was posed to respondents in the 1964 Brookings study cited earlier, covering households with income of $10 000 or over. When the respondents were asked where 'most of your present assets are from' (gifts, inheritance, saving out of income, or appreciation), '. . . only 7 percent mentioned gifts and inheritance alone' (p. 87). The authors further conclude that: 'For the entire high income group . . . about one-seventh of aggregate wealth' came from 'inheritances and gifts' (p. 89). A separate question asked: 'Speaking about inheritance, about what fraction of your total assets today does it account for', and similarly for gifts. The authors report that 'The estimates of the proportion of wealth derived from gifts and inheritances, which can be obtained from the replies to these two questions, are within a couple of percentage points of the first estimates made above, except for the highest incomes [over $300 000] where . . . nearly a fifth of total assets were reported as resulting from gifts and inheritances' (ibid).

One further estimate from this study, which includes an attempted correction for appreciation of bequests since they were received, concludes that 'of total wealth, less than one-fifth' was derived 'from gifts and inheritance plus their appreciation' (p. 90) (Table 1.1, row 4). Further, 'even at incomes over

$300 000, the proportion of total assets from gifts and inheritances and their capital appreciation is less than three-tenths' (ibid). The relatively small effect of adjusting for capital gains may be partly a reflection of the notable stability of prices in the 15 years preceeding the survey.

These fairly consistent findings, which concur in suggesting a proportion of inherited wealth (adjusted for inflation) in total wealth below one-fifth but probably above 15%, are, of course, not inconsistent with the unimportance of the bequest motive reported above. In a world in which the date of death is uncertain and, for various reasons, markets for non-pension life annuities are severely limited, people may end up dying with non-negligible wealth due to life cycle cum precautionary motive, as has been pointed out, e.g., by Davies (1981) and Evans (1981).

None the less, these figures might be regarded as open to question because the respondents' replies were largely undocumented and could suffer from serious recall biases. For instance, is it not conceivable that respondents would tend to underestimate, systematically and significantly, the extent to which their wealth was bestowed on them by others, rather than representing the fruits of their own effort?

Fortunately it is possible to check the above estimates by an alternative route which relies on the information on the flow of aggregate bequests. Specifically, one can attempt to measure the annual flow of bequests and then use it, together with an estimate of the average age gap between donor and beneficiary (and other relevant parameters), to estimate the implied stock of wealth, received by bequests, at a given point of time. This method has become more promising with the recent availability of some data discussed below.

III Estimates of the proportion of inherited wealth from the flow of bequests

This method, which is actually one of the two alternatives used by K&S, rests on the annual flow of transfers, say t. As suggested by K&S, this flow can be translated into a stock of inherited wealth by relying on the steady-state assumption that beneficiaries, on average, receive in the form of bequests a constant fraction of their life labour income, and that the average gap between the age of the bequeathers and that of the beneficiaries is a constant, say g. Under these assumptions, if the economy were stationary, the total stock of inherited wealth, say T, would clearly be $T = gt$. However, if population and/or productivity increase at a stable rate, say n, then the transfer flow made and received τ years earlier would be $te^{-n\tau}$ for $0 \leqslant \tau \leqslant g$. Accordingly, the stock of inherited wealth will come to:

$$T^* = \frac{(1-e^{-ng})}{n} t \tag{1.1}$$

There are three possible methods by which one might estimate the annual flow t: one is the survey method and implies asking respondents the amount of inheritance (and major gifts) received in the course of a year; a second method is to build up an estimate of t from information on the distribution of wealth by age and on the frequency of death by age; the third is to estimate t from probate records.

3.1 The K&S method

The second method is that utilized by K&S, relying on data on wealth provided by the two Federal Reserve studies. For reasons that will become apparent presently, they endeavour to estimate 'distant in age' intergenerational bequests transfer flows, and arrive at a figure for 1962 of $11.9 billion. To this they add one-tenth for life insurance death benefits and a very rough estimate, of just over one-fifth, for transfers in the form of newly established trusts (since neither of these items is included in the survey of wealth). These additions raise the estimated flow, t, to $16 billion.

To arrive at an estimate of T, one still needs values for the growth rate, n, and the age gap, g. For n, they suggest 3.5% as a reasonable estimate for the period they are considering, terminating in 1974. For the age gap, on the other hand, there is very little solid information on which to rely. They opt for a value of 30 years 'which allows for significant transfers to grandchildren'. I would regard 25 years as a more reasonable guess. It receives some support from data for the United Kingdom assembled by the Royal Commission on the Distribution of Income and Wealth, which suggests that transfers to the third generation are very infrequent and that the average gap is well below 25 years, through including interspousal transfers.

For a gap of 25 years and a growth trend of 3.5%, equation 1.1 implies that the stock of inherited wealth is 16.7 times the flow (as compared with 25, in the absence of growth). With t estimated at $16 billion per year, T^* comes to $270 billion. Now, in 1962 the stock of household net worth, according to the above mentioned estimate by the Federal Reserve (1981), came to $1.75 trillion. Thus, the estimated proportion of wealth resulting from intergenerational bequests could be placed at $15\frac{1}{2}$%. Using the K&S gap of 30 years would increase this estimate only modestly, to 17% (as reported in Table 1.1, row 5). These figures seem to be fairly consistent with the various estimates, based on surveys, summarized in Table 1.1, though it should be recognized that the K&S measure of transfers is presumably somewhat less inclusive than that used in the surveys.

3.2 The survey method

The type of information needed to carry out the first approach is available, to my knowledge, only in the Federal Reserve 1963 follow-up study, *Survey of*

Changes in Family Finances (Projector (1968)), in the course of which respondents were asked: 'During 1963 did you . . . receive any gifts or inheritance from persons outside the family?'. The answer to this question should provide an alternative estimate of the flow of gifts and bequests. A recent tabulation of this data yields an estimated of the average reported amount received of $205 per household, or a total of $11.6 billion.[2] This estimate appears encouragingly close to K&S's estimate of $12 billion, though this is a bit deceptive since, presumably, it includes life insurance benefits as well as non-intergenerational transfers (except presumably interspousal). Even if we suppose that it does not include transfers through trusts and make the correction suggested by K&S, we get a total estimated flow of 14\frac{1}{2}$ billion, implying a share of wealth of some 14%. This estimate is smaller than that suggested by most other studies, and particularly K&S, but still confirms the order of magnitude.

3.3 The use of probate statistics

A third approach, which is potentially the most promising in terms of the objectivity and quality of the information, is at present becoming feasible through the painstaking efforts of David and Menchik. In one of their recent papers (Menchik and David (1983)), relying on probate records of people who died in Wisconsin between 1947 and 1978, they have provided information from which one can estimate a mean bequest for all decendents of 20 thousand 1967 dollars (table 3). (This figure, as well as all averages cited below, represents the mean for all persons dying in the course of the three decades spanning the years 1947 to 1978. Presumably, in the course of this span of time, bequests have tended to rise with the rise in per capita income. However, since 1962 is right in the middle of the period covered, we will assume that the mean for the entire period is a reasonable approximation to the mean for the years of the early 1960s.)

Unfortunately the above estimate is based on a sample of deceased men only and is therefore likely to be somewhat upward-massed. If we nonetheless accept this figure as representative of both sexes, and multiply by the number of adult deceased in 1962, 1.5 million, we get an (upper) estimate of the total flow of bequests in that year of 29$\frac{1}{2}$ billion 1967 dollars. But, from this figure one should subtract interspousal transfers. One can secure some information on the size of this adjustment from their analysis of once-married couples (David and Menchik (1982, table 5)). For this subpopulation, they have estimated the mean interspousal transfer at 15.8 thousand 1967 dollars. This figure should presumably be multiplied by the number of people who died married in 1962, amounting to some 700 thousand. This yields an estimated aggregate flow of interspousal transfers of 11 billion. There is reason to suspect, however, that once-married couples tend to have more wealth on average than the population of all those married. This conjecture is supported by the consideration that the mean per capita bequest of this group is estimated at 27.2 thousand dollars (ibid., table 5, sum of means of the last two columns divided by two) as compared with the above cited mean bequest for all male decedents of only 20 thousand dollars. This suggests that the above estimate of the interspousal flow should be scaled down by perhaps as much as one-quarter, around 8–9 billion, implying a flow of non-interspousal bequests for 1962 of around 20 billion 1967 dollars. Converting this figure to 1962 dollars and allowing for some two billion of transfers through trusts yields essentially the same estimate.

It may be noted that this estimate is substantially above that of 16 billion arrived at by K&S; but this can be explained, in good measure, by the consideration that our measure of the flow of bequests includes *all* transfers except interspousal ones, whereas the K&S estimate is meant to cover only intergenerational transfers, as this happens to be the measure that is best suited for their definitions.

In their 1982 paper, David and Menchik have presented an estimate of the relative importance of intergenerational in total transfers. Specifically, for their sample of once-married couples they report (table 5) a mean intergenerational bequest per couple of 23.6 thousand dollars versus a mean household bequest (i.e., excluding interspousal) of 39 thousand dollars; a share of just over 60%. Applying this percentage to our estimate of the total flow of bequests implies an intergenerational transfer flow of, say, around 12 billion, which is not altogether inconsistent with the K&S figure, especially since once-married couples may not be fully representative of all deceased.

In converting our estimate of the flow into a stock, we must remember, however, that the average age gap between bequeather and beneficiary must presumably be appreciably lower than for purely intergenerational transfers — though it is hard to say by how much. If we suppose that, for the roughly one-third of bequests that are not intergenerational, the gap is 15 years, then the average gap would be 22 years, implying $T^*/t = 15.3$. Hence, T^* would come to $280–320 billion, or 16 to 18% of total wealth. But, even if the average gap were 25 years, the estimated share of wealth would remain below 20% (row 8).

Summarizing, it appears that all direct estimates, based on four different approaches, concur in supporting the pre-K&S perception that the share of wealth received through inheritance can be placed somewhere between one-tenth and one-fifth. There is some scatter of estimates within this range, though some of it can be accounted for by differences in concept. The share of purely intergenerational bequests is probably closer to 15% or less; that of total bequests, excluding interspousal, which is presumably the relevant concept, may well be closer to one fifth.

IV An alternative estimate of life cycle wealth

Ando and Kennickell (1985) have provided another estimate of 'life cycle' (i.e., non-inherited) wealth, which is similar in conception to the one proposed by K&S, but is much simpler and also has the advantage of relying on standard definitions of income and saving. They start from existing estimates of national saving — basically Goldsmith (1956) — and allocate them by age, using the saving–age profiles derived from the Bureau of Labor Statistics' Consumer Expenditure survey for 1972 and 1973, to obtain estimates of saving for individual cohorts for specified years. By summing up the saving of any given cohort, they can estimate the *self-accumulated* wealth of that cohort up to any given year (except for capital gains and losses — see below). Finally, they arrive at national self-accumulated wealth in a given year by summing over the cohorts present in that year. The result of this calculation, using both the 1972 and the 1973 ages profiles, are reported for every year from 1960 to 1980, together with the actual value of household net worth for the last quarter of each year derived from the Federal Reserve Board (1984).

The proportions of self-accumulated wealth implied by the two profiles are very similar except that the one for 1973 is consistently five percentage points higher. Based on the 1973 profile, one finds that from 1974 to the end of the series in 1980, the proportion of self accumulated wealth falls between 80 and 85% — remarkably consistent with our 'consensus' estimate of the share of inherited wealth. For the earlier years, the proportion is smaller; around 60% until 1968, then drifting up to over 70% by 1973. But the lower figure for the early years may at least partly reflect a downward bias in the Ando and Kennickell estimate arising from the fact that their estimate of self-accumulated wealth omits changes in real wealth arising from capital gains or losses. In the period before 1974, capital gains were, unquestionably, significantly positive, and hence self-accumulated wealth is underestimated. On the other hand, from 1974 to 1980, this effect was, presumably, undone by the very depressed state of the stock market, even though this may have been partly offset by rising real estate values.

On the whole, it is apparent that this latest method of estimation yields results that are not inconsistent with the conclusion from all other methods that the proportion of inherited wealth is most unlikely to be significantly higher than one quarter, at the very most.

It would be interesting to supplement these findings for the United States, and mostly in the 1960s, with estimates for other times and countries. The only relevant information of which I am presently aware relates to the United Kingdom and is the result of the work of the above cited Royal Commission on the Distribution of Income and Wealth. Their method relies on an estimate of the age pattern of recipients of bequests left by decendents of different age and sex, and on information of the flow of bequests for a long stretch of years terminating in 1973 to obtain an estimate of the 1973 stock of inherited wealth. Combining this with data on total wealth in that year (based on the estate duty method) they arrive at an estimate of the proportion of inherited wealth of 20.3%, which rises to 24.7% when gifts ('all forms of transmitted wealth') are included (report no. 5, ch. 9, tables 90 and 91). This figure is of the same order as those found for the US — but it includes inter-spousal transfers. Considering that for the US these seem to represent some-what over one-quarter of the total, the United Kingdom's share appears to be, if anything, a little smaller than suggested by US data.

V Comparison with K&S results — accounting for the discrepancy

These results make quite a contrast with K&S's claim that inherited wealth represents over four-fifths of the total. What accounts for the difference and, in particular, is there any merit in their enormously higher estimate?

In facing this question, one must first recall that they actually present two different figures. The first is a direct evaluation of bequests received by those living, based on the flow of bequests method referred to in the previous section. With this method, they arrive at an estimate of 52%; about midway between all other estimates and their alternative calculation of (at least) four-fifths. Their alternative, and novel, approach derives the share of bequests indirectly as a residual, namely as the difference between an independent estimate of total wealth of households and an estimate of aggregate 'life cycle' wealth. The latter is presented by the authors as their real contribution, and as providing, distinctly, the more reliable measure.

The discrepancy between theirs and other estimates stems, as mentioned earlier, in part from some outright errors and in part from their unusual and arbitrary redefinition of 'life cycle' and 'transfer' wealth. Since the errors are specific to each of the two methods, whereas the definitional difference concerns both, it is useful to begin by exposing the latter.

5.1 Definitional differences

Superficially, their definitions do not seem to differ from the usual ones: life cycle wealth at any given age is the cumulated difference between consumption and income, consisting of labour income and the return on the accumulation; the difference between the amount of wealth held and life cycle wealth, computed as above, must then represent transfer wealth. Summing the life cycle and the residual wealth respectively over all ages, yields aggregate wealth of each kind.

Actually, this measure coincides with the customary one in the elementary kind of Modigliani–Brumberg (1980) model in which the return on capital is zero, and there is a streamlined age at which people begin to earn, at a constant rate until retirement. But once we drop these simplifying assumptions, the K&S definition departs from the customary one and can lead to a rather different and, in particular, much higher measure of transfer wealth. There are two basic sources of difference:

(i) Property income and the definition of transfer wealth

With a non-zero return on wealth, K&S's definition of life cycle income differs from the conventional one because it excludes one portion of property income, namely the return of net wealth received by transfer plus the capitalized interest thereon. Correspondingly, transfer wealth at a given age is not the sum of the amount received by the beneficiary up to that age but, instead, the amount received capitalized to that age. When one remembers that the age gap between bequeathers and beneficiary is of the order of 25–30 years, the difference in the size of transfer wealth implied by the two definitions can be quite large. We can, in fact, get a pretty good notion of that difference by referring back to equation 1.1 which shows the relation between the flow of bequests and the stock of inherited wealth. Under the K&S definition, inheritance received τ period ago enters into the current stock of inherited wealth after being capitalized to the present, i.e., multiplied by $e^{\tau\tau}$. Accordingly, equation 1.1 is changed to:

$$T = \frac{e^{(r-n)g} - 1}{r - n} t \qquad (1.2)$$

where T is their definition of inherited wealth and t their flow. For their estimate age gap, g, of 30 years and interest rate of 4.5%, the stock-flow ratio according to equation 1.2 is 35, very nearly twice as large as the value of 18.6 implied by equation 1.1. An examination of the merits of their definition is best postponed until we have examined the other differences and established their quantitative implications.

(ii) The definition of transfer flow

One customarily thinks of a household's own accumulation as consisting of the change in its wealth, except that resulting from transfers of capital in the form of bequests (or major gifts). This means that minor gifts as well as moneys provided in support of current consumption, typically to relatives, are treated as part of the current consumption of the giver since they do not result in a rise in wealth. By contrast, K&S's definitions imply that these transactions are regarded as part of life cycle saving of the giver, which result in *negative* transfers. This definition has again the effect of producing a measure of transfer and life cycle wealth which can be quite different from the customary one, and rather arbitrary.

These propositions can be clarified with the help of the illustrations in

Table 1.2. Part A describes a very simple economy of the 'overlapping genera-tions' type: life is divided in two periods, the first active and the second retired. In order to concentrate on the relevant issue, we assume no bequests and zero interest. Clearly, the behavior described in Part A is 'life cycle' *par excellence*: households save 40 units during active life, which they use up entirely during retirement. Accordingly, the aggregate wealth of 40 units (the sum of the average amount held in each period which is 20), would be generally recognized as constituting entirely life cycle 'wealth'.

Now consider Part B. Here the behaviour is essentially the same: there is an accumulation of wealth of 40 units during the active period (cf. col. 6) followed by equal decumulation during retirement. The only difference is that the active households use 20 units of their resources to support the con-sumption of the retired, whose resources and consumption are increased accordingly. Once more it would appear that the behavior described in Part B is pure 'life cycle' behaviour and that accordingly 100% of the wealth of 40 should be regarded as life cycle wealth. But by the K&S definition, the

TABLE 1.2. Some implications of K&S's definitions of income and transfers*

	1	2	3	4	5 (2)−(3)	6 (4)+(5)	7	8	9
	Age	Income	Consump-tion	Trans-fers	Life cycle saving	Change in wealth	Life cycle wealth	Trans-fer wealth	Wealth
A. Reference Case — no support payments									
	1	120	80	0	40	40	40	0	40
	2	0	40	0	−40	−40	0	0	40
Aggregates		120	120	0	0	0	40	0	40
Share of wealth (%)							100	0	
B. The young provide some support for the old									
	1	120	60	−20	60	40	60	−20	40
	2	0	60	20	−60	−40	0	0	0
Aggregates		120	120	0	0	0	60	−20	40
Share of wealth (%)							150	−50	
C. Dependent minors treated as independent households									
	0	0	40	40	−40	0	−40	40	0
	1	120	40	−40	80	40	40	0	40
	2	0	40	0	−40	−40	0	0	0
Aggregates		120	120	0	0	0	0	40	40
Share of wealth (%)							0	100	

*Units are arbitrary.

proportion turns out startlingly different, as can be seen from the bottom row: the proportion of the life cycle wealth is 150% and is balanced by a proportion of transfer wealth of − 50%. The reason for this seemingly nonsensical outcome is that life cycle saving of the young as defined by K&S exceed their accumulation of wealth. The difference must, as a matter of a algebra, be offset by a *negative* transfer, equal to the support provided. This negative flow then translates into a negative stock (col. 7) which cumulates into an economy-wide negative transfer stock.

One can readily verify that if, instead, support were provided *by* the older *to* the younger, then that flow would add to the stock of transfer wealth as measured by K&S, reducing, accordingly, the stock of life cycle wealth as ordinarily measured. Indeed, the life cycle wealth could very well turn out to have *negative* value, even in the presence of a positively humped wealth-holding pattern.

Part C illustrates the arbitrary nature of the measure adopted by K&S. There is, in principle, no major problem in identifying wealth received (or given) as a bequest or even a major gift. But, once we try to include in transfers support of current consumption provided to relatives, it becomes quite important, and also quite arbitrary, whether an individual is classified as a member of another household or, instead, as an independent economic unit. For, in the first case, his consumption will be part of that of the household of which he is regarded as a member, while in the second case it will be treated as negative life cycle saving financed by a transfer from an older household. In Part C we illustrate how much difference this can make. Suppose that in the economy of Part A we think of 80 units consumed by the first age group as including the consumption of all 'minors' who are not actually independent units. Now suppose that we adopt K&S's definition and decide that a certain proportion of the minors, say those above a certain age, are to be treated as separate entities, constituting age group 0. After most careful analysis, perhaps based on some minors that are actually independent households, we conclude that the consumption that should be allocated to age zero is 40 units (col. 3, row 0). The implications are exhibited in the bottom row: although the economy is identical to that of Part A in which all wealth was recognized as life cycle wealth, we find that using K&S's definition, there is *no* 'life cycle' wealth at all — all wealth is, instead, transfer wealth.

5.2 Accounting for the discrepancies

Having clarified the definitional differences, we can now endeavour to account for the sources of the higher estimates obtained by K&S:

(i) Estimate based on the flow of inheritances

Table 1.3 provides a reconciliation of K&S's estimate of the proportion of

TABLE 1.3. Reconciliation of K&S with other estimates

	Correction (percentage points)	Corrected share of wealth (%)
A. Estimates based on flow of bequests		
1. K&S estimate		52
2. Error in formula	− 11.5	40.5
3. Elimination of educational expenses	− 9.0	31.5
4. Elimination of capitalization of inheritance	− 14.8	16.7
5. Assuming a smaller age gap	− 1.7	15.0
6. Including non-intergenerational transfer	5.7	20.7
B. Estimates based on cumulation of saving		
1. K&S estimate		81
2. Error in treatment of durable goods expenditure	− 26	55
3. Elimination of capitalization of inheritances	− 26	29
4. Remaining gap	− 9	20

transfer wealth based on their calculations of the flow of bequests, with our own estimate, based on their flow figures, as reported in Table 1.1, row 5. Row 1 reports their estimate of 52%. The subtraction shown in row 2 arises from the fact that K&S happen to have made a mathematical slip in deriving equation 19 (p. 727) which they use to compute the coefficient exhibited in their table 3, to convert the flow of bequests into a stock. The corrected formula is:

$$T = \frac{t}{r-n}\, e^{(r-n)(D-G)} [e^{(r-n)(G-I)} - 1] \qquad (1.3)$$

where D is the age of death, G the age of the donor, I the age of the bene-ficiaries, and hence, $G - I$ is the age gap, g. If we conveniently assume $D = G$, as K&S also do, this formula reduces to our formula 1.2 above. It is apparent from row 2 that, merely correcting this error, brings their estimate in sight of the older ones and out of sight of their preferred figure of four-fifths.

The next two corrections are definitional. They arbitrarily decide that 18 is 'the age of adulthood' (p. 717), and that therefore every individual of either sex of that age or over is an independent unit whether in fact he is an independent household or a member of the family at home or in school. They should, accordingly, estimate all that is spent on such people when they are part of the household — and they actually do just that, or a close approximation thereof in their alternative estimate. For the estimate under review, their adjustment consists in adding to the flow of bequests an estimate of educational expenditure arising from 'financial support during college' (p. 728). By so doing, they reclassify an outlay that is customarily treated as consumption of middle aged parents as the personal consumption of units around 20 with no or little income. They thereby start out these units with a large negative life cycle wealth, which is then carried forward for the rest of their life, and capitalized. Furthermore, the amount involved is quite large, as the annual flow of college related transfers is put by K&S at nearly one-third of the true bequest flow. When this expenditure is eliminated in row 3, the proportion is reduced to 31.5%. (Note that their approach could not be justified on the ground that educational expenditure results in addition to human capital, since they do not include human capital in life cycle wealth. The only justification is that any expense on behalf of someone above 18 is automatically a transfer.)

The adjustment in row 4 results from measuring inherited wealth as the amount received, and not capitalized, as discussed earlier. As we have already seen, this definitional variation makes a large difference; it halfs the proportion, now down to 17%. This figure agrees very closely with that which we derived from their estimate of the flow of intergenerational bequests and reported in row 5 of Table 1.1. If, in addition, the average age gap between bequeather and beneficiary is reduced from 30 to 25 years, as suggested earlier, then the 17% would be reduced by close to 2 percentage points (see row 5).

Summarizing the difference between their estimate of 52% and ours based on their figures of $15\frac{1}{2}$–17% (and similar estimates of all other sources) can be fully accounted for: some 12% reflects an error and 24% results from their adopting a different definition. The last row shows that allowing for non-intergenerational transfers raises their estimate to 21%, again quite consistent with our estimates.

(ii) Estimate based on the cumulation of capitalized 'life cycle saving'

Row 1 of Table 1.3 part B shows K&S alternative estimate of the share — namely 81%. It is based on assigning to each age group of each sex, in every year since 1900, an income from labour and a consumption, cumulating the difference and capitalizing it, in order to arrive at an estimate of the 'life cycle' wealth of each age and sex cohort alive in 1974. Although they present and discuss many variants, the one underlying Table 1.3B (733 billion from their table 2, LCW2, series 2) has been chosen because it is conceptually the most relevant, as it endeavours to include the life cycle accumulation of a deceased spouse into the accumulation of the survivor. Also, it is the one they tend to stress.

The first large correction in row 2 arises from an error in their calculation of consumption and saving. In the figures they present, they measured consumption as inclusive of the purchase of durable goods, instead of treating such goods as a depreciable investment — including only current year estimated depreciation in consumption and the excess of purchases over depreciation as a saving to be cumulated into a stock. They were misled into adopting their erroneous procedure by the consideration that 'there appears very little difference between the consumer expenditure series and the true economic consumption series'. But that consideration is no more valid than the proposition that if saving is small, one can ignore the stock of wealth. What matters, of course, is the accumulation of each age group, and especially in the US, one can expect younger age groups to be significant investors in durables, while older people may be disinvesting in their stock. Their calculations therefore could be expected to produce a large downward bias in the estimate of life cycle wealth.

We have been able to estimate the magnitude of this error, as K&S have kindly made available to us their basic data and helped us in carrying out the necessary, fairly extensive computations. We were unable to match their original calculations exactly, but still closely enough to have confidence in the mechanics of our correction.[3]

The correction was found to increase the estimates of life cycle wealth, as expected, and by a surprisingly large magnitude; it raised that component from 19% of total wealth as reported by K&S to 45%, an increase amounting to 26% of wealth (roughly one trillion compared with wealth of 3.9). Accordingly, as shown in row 2 of Table 1.3B, the proportion of inherited wealth is cut down from 81% to 55%. Of the remaining difference between their 55% and our direct estimate of inherited wealth of 20% based on probate statistics, a large portion can be accounted for by the definitional difference arising from the capitalization of bequests received which is not included in our direct measure of transfers. As we have seen in part A, the effect of eliminating their capitalization (i.e., including the income from bequests in life cycle income and saving) is estimated to reduce the value of bequeathed wealth by 47%, or 26 percentage points. This brings their corrected share of wealth to 29%, a difference of only 9 percentage points from our direct estimate.

However, we must caution that the figures of table 1.3B may tend to overstate the closeness of the agreement between all the other estimates and that derivable from K&S after adjusting for errors and measurable definitional difference. The reason is that the adjustment for durables reported in row 2 appears implausibly large. Since the adjustment was derived entirely from K&S data and methodology, we see the result as confirming the unreliability of their methodology, requiring a large number of assumptions, to which the results are highly sensitive.

It is quite possible, therefore, that the true difference between the two estimates might be closer to, say, 20% than to 9%. But this is still not a large difference compared with a starting gap of over 60 percentage points (81% versus 20%). Much of it can be accounted for, we believe, by remaining conceptual differences plus measurement errors. The major difference is, no doubt, related to the definitional discrepancy arising from not measuring saving as the difference between income and consumption of households (including independent individuals) as is customary, but calculating it, instead, from an imputed labour income and consumption assigned to every *individual* male and female aged 18 and over. From line 3 of Table 1.3A we see that merely treating as family consumption, rather than transfers, the expenses incurred by the family for the college education of this age group has the effect of decreasing the stock of transfer wealth by some 22%. With this adjustment, their share of transfer wealth would be reduced by over 6 percentage points. There can be, thus, little doubt that K&S's inclusion in transfers of *all* consumption — and not merely educational expenses — of dependent children over 18 years of age can account for a good part of the remaining differences, even allowing for some offset from negative transfers to older generations.

The important role of this source of discrepancy in measuring life cycle saving receives strong support from a perusal of figures 1 and 2 in K&S (1981) and of similar graphs in a preliminary version of K&S (1980). It appears from graph 1 that, according to their estimates, the cohort of 1910 had (life cycle) dissaving for the first 50 years of its life, while the cohort of 1940 saved nothing over a similar span. Similar results are reported for other cohorts in the paper cited. These results, which provide the foundations for the negligible accumulation of life cycle wealth, are inconsistent with information from many other sources. First, all available information indicates that households have, on average, substantial savings, at least after age 25; and, second, such saving is consistent with the fact that wealth rises fairly smoothly between age 25 and age 45 (e.g., in the FRB survey (Projector and Weiss (1964)) it rises by roughly one thousand dollars per year of age). This rise in wealth cannot be attributed to inheritance to any significant extent, since, as one would expect, the receipt of important inheritance is rare before age 45 (cf. Projector and Weiss (1964), table A32). For the same reason, the saving of these age groups cannot be reasonably attributed to the return on inherited wealth.

Finally, there is no need not to account for every single point of the difference between the two set of estimates based as they are on entirely different data as well as methodology — for it is obvious that each method is affected by the many auxiliary assumptions that need to be made to carry through — as well as by sheer error of measurement. The K&S study, for all its ingenuity and imagination, is certainly not exempt from these problems, considering the large number of imputations and assumptions it involves, from age profiles, to return on capital, to the treatment of interspousal transfers. Their results are particularly sensitive to errors and assumptions affecting saving in the early years, for a difference in early saving affects wealth at every later age, and increasingly so, as the saving gets capitalized. To their credit, K&S are fully aware of this problem and have provided some information on the sensitivity of their results to variations in the auxiliary assumptions. They report the results of one alternative set of calculations in which consumption was reallocated from young to old. Granted that the calculation was intended to test the outer limit of possible imputations, the results of the experiments are rather dramatic. The share of life cycle wealth increased from the initial 19% underlying table B to 56%, an increase of 37 percentage points! Our attempt at correcting for the omission of investment in durable goods also points to the sensitivity of results to unverifiable assumptions.

Given this evidence of sensitivity, there seems to be little reason for concern with a residual difference of 10 to 20 percentage points in table B. This conclusion is reinforced by the consideration that all the other estimates are also subject to error and our own preferred estimate, based on probate statistics, of around 20% is no exception. It could certainly be too low by a few percentage points.

But even allowing for this possibility, it is apparent that all available estimates, including those based on either of the K&S methods, point to the conclusion that the share of inherited wealth, as long as it is conventionally defined, as *the amount received by all surviving beneficiaries other than spouses*, is 'relatively modest', probably less than one-fifth, almost certainly less than one-quarter.

VI   Are there any particular merits in K&S's definitions?

Two criteria seem relevant in preferring one definition, or measure, to another. One is conformity with the generally accepted and commonly used meaning. The other is helpfulness in thinking about and understanding substantive issues. We can use these criteria to evaluate the two main differences between K&S's definitions and the conventional ones. The first relates to what is included in the flow of transferred wealth, t; the second to how wealth received from transfers should be valued.

6.1   Conformity with generally accepted definitions

With respect to this issue, we have already argued that their definition of transfers, implicit in that of life saving, departs greatly from the customary one by (i) the inclusion of amounts received for current support in addition to inheritance and major gifts, (ii) the treatment of amounts given as 'negative' transfers, and (iii) the replacement of the family as the unit making saving decisions and owning wealth with individual male and female above some arbitrarily chosen age, to whom family income and consumption are somehow imputed. We have also illustrated in Table 1.2 the counterintuitive implications of their definition and arbitrary nature of the resulting measure of transfer wealth.

With respect to the valuation of inheritance and gifts, adding to the (real) amounts actually received, the capitalization thereof is not only different from the definitions used in earlier studies, but it is also inconsistent with the usual definition of income, and of lifetime saving. One would normally view the life saving of a household as the difference between the value of bequests left and received. The K&S measure is inconsistent with this view except in the limiting case of a zero interest rate. When the interest rate is positive, then a household leaving as much as he received, will be counted under their definition as having negative life saving, and the more so the higher the interest rate.

6.2   Fruitfulness

We come next to the question of the fruitfulness of alternative definitions in analysing substantive issues. For present purposes, we may accept K&S's suggestion that the basic substantive issue is how important is the role of the bequest motive in determining total wealth.

In their paper, they have also proposed an interesting operational way of measuring 'importance'. Suppose that the yearly flow, t, of inheritances declined by 1% exogenously (say, as a result of taxation). By what percentage would aggregate wealth decline? In other words, what is the elasticity of wealth with respect to the transfer flow?

In terms of this proposed operational measurement of importance, their departure from the standard measure in terms of what is included in the flow, t, does not seem to be very useful. This is because, while one can conceive of ways to effectively raise or lower the flow of bequests and major gifts, it is hard to imagine a way to interfere effectively with the direct support of relatives, partly living at home, and in good part probably provided in kind. In addition, as pointed out earlier, the effect of such interference is hard to infer. For instance, reducing support payments to the young would, most likely, reduce their consumption and initial life cycle dissaving (in the K&S definitional) while raising the saving of older households, thus leading to an overall rise in saving and wealth despite the decline in the flow of transfers.

As for K&S's definition of the stock of bequeathed wealth, T, which includes the capitalized value of bequests received, we propose to argue that it is inferior to the standard measure, T^*, which omits the capitalization, because the conventional definition of the share comes close to measuring 'importance', while that of K&S very substantially overstates it.

One way to support this conclusion is to take a look at the estimate of importance worked out by K&S in the section on the '. . . reduction in capital intensity arising from a reduction in intergenerational transfer' (pp. 711–16). Although their calculations are based on some very specific and largely arbitrary assumptions about preferences — namely that the utility is *additive, separable* (in consumption and leisure), and *logarithmic* — their results are suggestive. Recall first that their measure of importance is the elasticity of wealth with respect to the transfer flow, t. This can be written as: $\eta = dW/dT \; T/W$, since the transfer flow, t, is proportional to K&S's transfer stock T (for given growth and capitalization rate). Alternatively, it can be measured by $\eta = dW/dT^* \; T^*/W$ because our measure of transfer stock T^* is proportional to theirs. Thus, η is proportional to the share of bequeathed wealth, the proportionality factor being dW/dT^* or dW/dT as the transfer stock is measured by T^* or T respectively. K&S have computed the value of dW/dT implied by their assumptions and find that it depends almost exclusively on the difference $(r-n)$, decreasing with it. This is because $(r-n)$ measures the extent to which the representative household is made better off when he receives an additional dollar of bequests (which, in turn, he must, on the average, pass on, increased by e^{ng}). Hence the larger $(r-n)$, the more consumption increases, i.e., the larger dC/dT, and the smaller dW/dT. For a value of $(r-n)$ consistent with their estimates of r and n, namely 0.01, they find that dW/dT is only 0.7. This means that the share as measured by K&S greatly *overstates* η — or 'importance' — namely, by $1/0.7$, or nearly 45%.

On the other hand, from dW/dT we can compute $dW/dT^* = dW/dT \; dT/dT^* = dW/dT \; T/T^*$ and we have seen that (for $g = 25$) $T/T^* = 28/16.7 = 1\frac{2}{3}$. Thus, $dW/dT^* = 0.7 \times 1\frac{2}{3} = 1.17$ implying $\eta = 1.17 \; T^*/W$. In other words, their measure of the share T/W overstates importance nearly to the extent to which it exceeds our measure T^*/W. As a result, according to their own calculation, our measure of the shares comes pretty close to measuring importance — underestimating it by only 15%, in contrast to their overestimate of 43%. This result implies, in particular, that the importance of inherited wealth (or η) can still be placed not significantly above 1/4.

To summarize, K&S's redefinition of the flow of bequests has nothing to recommend it over the conventional measure, but is, instead, objectionable on many grounds, including its arbitrary nature. The redefinition of the stock of bequeathed wealth to include capitalized bequests serves to increase the proportion of bequeathed wealth and decrease, accordingly, the proportion of life cycle wealth. But the share so measured tends to exaggerate greatly the contribution of bequests to total wealth, while the smaller, conventionally defined, proportion comes close to measuring it correctly.

VII   Is the share of wealth an adequate indicator of the 'importance' of bequests?

Yet, there may be reasons to question the validity and reliability of the above estimates of importance based on the calculations and somewhat arbitrary assumptions of K&S. On the one hand, there are a number of considerations and bits of evidence that suggest that our measure of the share may be too small and/or that the share, as conventionally defined, may not be an adequate measure of importance. But, on the other hand, one must recognize that the importance of *bequests* and the importance of the *bequest motive* are two quite different issues because a significant portion of inheritance left and received presumably does not reflect at all a bequest motive but rather a 'precautionary' motive related to uncertainty of life (Davies (1981)).

Let us start from the first objection, ignoring temporarily the second. If the economy were stationary and with zero interest rate, then bequests received are passed on unchanged, and their presence has no effect on income or consumption and hence on life cycle wealth. Thus, the share of wealth inherited must coincide with wealth held for bequests. But suppose the economy is growing. Then, in addition to the bequests received and held on their way to be bequeathed, there will be a net lifetime accumulation earmarked for bequests. Thus (at least for zero interest) the share of wealth inherited will underestimate 'importance', and the more so the larger the growth.

This shortfall of the inherited share as a measure of importance has been brought out dramatically in an illustration provided by Kennickell (1984). He considers a situation in which households save at a constant rate, say s, throughout their life and *all* of this accumulation is eventually bequeathed (together with any bequest received). If s and growth were both zero, then existing wealth, if any, is entirely inherited, and the share of inherited wealth, namely 1, is a valid measure of importance. But if s is positive and there is steady growth, then, in addition to the wealth inherited and being held for bequests, there will be some additional wealth being accumulated on its way to being bequeathed. Not surprisingly, the portion is found to increase rapidly with growth. For instance, at a 3% growth rate, the proportion of bequeathed wealth is just below 40% even though *all* wealth is, by construction, bequest-related.

To be sure, the illustration relies on extreme, counter factual assumptions. Yet it may be of some relevance in the light of available evidence on the behaviour of wealth by age. Contrary to what might be expected under the elementary LCH, the behaviour of wealth has been found not to be so different from the monotonic increasing pattern assumed in the illustration (e.g., see Fisher (1950), Lydall (1955)). In particular, according to Mirer (1979), wealth actually continues to rise in retirement. (Note, however, that his estimate is biased as a result of including education in his regression. Given the steady historical rise in educational levels, there will be a strong association between age, educational attainment, and socio-economic status *relative* to one's cohort if one holds constant the absolute level of education. Thus, his results could merely reflect the association between bequests, wealth, and relative income discussed below.)

Most other recent analysts have found that the wealth of a given cohort tends to decline after reaching its peak in the 60–5 age range (Shorrocks (1975), King and Dicks-Mireaux (1982), Avery, Elliehausen, Canner, and Gustavson (1984), Bernheim (1984), Diamond and Hausman (1984), and

Ando (1985)), though there are exceptions, e.g., Menchik and David (1983) discussed below. To be sure, the results depend on the concept of saving and wealth used. If one makes proper allowance for participation in pension funds, then the dissaving (or the decline in wealth) of the old tends to be more apparent, and it becomes quite pronounced if one includes an estimate of social security benefits. But, when the saving and wealth measures include only cash saving and marketable wealth, the dissaving and the decline appears weaker or even absent.

However, the latest US study by Hurd (1986) using a very large sample and relying on panel data finds that, at least for retired people, marketable wealth systematically declines, at an appreciable rate, especially if one leaves out the very illiquid asset represented by owner-occupied houses.

In addition, there are several considerations suggesting that wealth survey data may give an upward-biased picture of the behaviour of wealth holdings during old age. First, as Shorrocks has argued (1975), one serious bias arises from the well-known positive association between longevity and (relative) income. This means that the average wealth of successively older age classes is the wealth of households with higher and higher life resources, hence the age profile of wealth is upward-biased. Second, in a similar vein, Ando and Kennickell (1985) have found evidence that aged households which are poor tend to double up with younger households and disappear from the sampled population so that the wealth of those remaining independent is again an upward-biased estimate of average wealth.

While it is difficult to assess the extent of these biases, the slow decumulation, at least of the marketable assets, would seem to cast doubt on our estimate of bequeathed wealth no more than 25%. Is there some more direct way of estimating the proportion of wealth that is bequest-related?

VIII   Some alternative estimates of bequest-related wealth

One possible line of attack has been proposed by Darby (1979). It consists in identifying the 'true' life cycle component of wealth as the amount of wealth that would be in existence in society if households accumulated just enough assets to enable them to finance their observed (average) retirement consumption, with accumulation up to retirement, and decumulation thereafter, occurring at a *constant rate*. Dividing this amount by total observed household wealth yields the share of life cycle wealth, while the remaining must therefore represent the 'bequest portion(s)' (p. 34).

Darby has applied this method to US data around 1966. The rate of consumption to be financed during retirement was estimated from Survey Data (Smith (1977)) and the portion of this to be financed through 'life cycle accumulation' was obtained by subtracting, from consumption, other sources of income, such as labour income and social security. This method yields a share of 'life cycle wealth,' of but 28.5% if the return to capital is estimated at 3%, and is further reduced to 19% if the return were put at 6%. For a rate of return of 4.5% which we have adopted in previous calculations, the share could be placed at but 23%, implying that over three-quarters of wealth is bequest-related. (These figures are close to the upper estimate of K&S, but this has no significance since K&S intend to estimate wealth received through bequests rather than bequest-related wealth.)

But we suggest that Darby's approach, for all its ingenuity, cannot provide much useful information because of the entirely arbitrary nature of the underlying assumptions. Indeed, there is absolutely nothing in the Life Cycle Hypothesis to suggest that accumulation for retirement would occur at a constant rate except in an elementary illustrative model in which income is constant up to retirement and zero thereafter. What one would expect to be 'smoothed' is the rate of consumption per equivalent adult, and even that subject to variations in *consumption* 'needs' such as those arising from changing family size or from college education. Under these conditions one would most definitely not expect the path of wealth accumulated for retirement to rise monotonically and smoothly until retirement, but to follow instead a jagged course, with many humps in the small as well as in the large. Under Darby's assumption instead it is the accumulation for bequests that is jagged and humped (see Darby's figure 12, p. 37); but how can wealth be earmarked for bequests and yet be partly consumed later?

Yet, it would seem that these shortcomings could be avoided by the simple device of replacing Darby's arbitrary procedure with one based on rational behaviour. To this end, we can replace the *ad hoc* assumption that consumers smooth the accumulation of retirement provisions, with the 'rational' assumption of consumption smoothing. Specifically, given the amount to be bequeathed, we can ask how that amount would be accumulated by a person choosing his life consumption path optimally, subject to the constraint represented by available lifetime resources. For the representative household, these resources consist of lifetime earning plus bequests received, less the amount to be bequeathed which must exceed bequest received by the growth factor e^{ng}. Wealth holding due to bequests can then be computed as the difference between the path of wealth with and without bequests.

One can show readily that, as long as the optimal consumption follows a smooth path (a constant rate of growth), accumulated wealth due to bequests will rise smoothly to an amount equal to the difference between the bequest left and those received, capitalized from the date of receipts.

Assuming that the preferred consumption path grows at the rate c, the annual increment to wealth due to bequests in the year τ can be shown to be:

$$\Delta S_\tau = \frac{A e^{c\tau}(r-c)}{1 - e^{-(r-c)L}} \tag{1.5}$$

where L is length of life and A is the present value at the beginning of life of the difference between the bequest received and left. The path of wealth is the cumulant of ΔS_τ plus the amount of the bequests once received (capitalized).

Equation 1.5 describes the path for a single household. To obtain the aggregate amount of bequest-related wealth at a given point of time, we must sum over the wealth of each cohort present, allowing for the fact that the cohorts of age τ can expect to receive and leave bequests which are larger than those left by the currently deceased by the factor $e^{(L-\tau)n}$. National wealth is the summation of wealth over the cohorts adjusted for mortality. Finally, through the steady state condition, one can express bequests received as (bequest left) e^{-ng}. This yields an expression for aggregate bequest-related wealth ΔW, in terms of the flow of bequests left, t, and the parameters c, n, r, g, p_a, and L, where p_a is the force of mortality at age a. Taking as an illustration the case in which mortality is zero until age L and 1 at L, one obtains:

$$\Delta W = \frac{e^{(r-n)g} - 1}{r - n} \left[1 - \frac{e^{-(r-n)L}}{1 - e^{-(r-c)L}} \left(e^{(r-n)L} - 1 - (1 - e^{-(n-c)L}) \right. \right.$$

$$\left. \left. \frac{r-n}{n-c} \right] t. \right. \tag{1.6}$$

This result has a number of interesting implications. First, note that the first factor is precisely the K&S formula for their share. In the limiting case in which both r and n are zero, the second term in the square bracket goes to zero and equation 1.6 reduces to $\Delta W = gt$ which coincides with both K&S and our preferred measure of the share. For $r \neq n$, the second term has the sign of $(r - n)$. This means that our generalized measure of bequest-related wealth will be *smaller* than K&S's measure if $r > n$, a condition usually regarded as empirically valid and which is satisfied by K&S's own estimates of r and n, namely 0.045 and 0.035.

The reason for this somewhat surprising result is that when $r > n$, then, as noted earlier, the receipt of bequests has a favorable income effect which arises consumption throughout life, reducing wealth until the bequest is received. The K&S share, on the other hand, corresponds to the increment in wealth, beginning with the time the bequest is received. In general, the bias of the K&S share grows with $r - n$; our own formula tends to underestimate, and the error is an increasing function of n and decreasing function of r.

Assigning to r and n K&S's own estimates of 0.045 and 0.035, respectively, and taking $g = 25$ and $L = 55$, one finds that ΔW is $19.8t$. This is well below the K&S measure of the share which is $28.4t$, but only some 20% higher than our measure, $16.7t$. Recalling that our estimate of the share is below 1/5, we can conclude that the share of bequest-related wealth can be placed at less and 1/4.[4]

There remains one puzzle. How can one possibly reconcile the fact that the decumulation of wealth after retirement occurs rather slowly with the result that the share of inherited wealth is no more than 25%? Actually, this

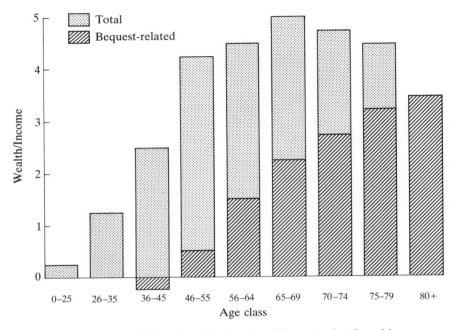

F IG. 1.1.   The life cycle path of total and bequest-related wealth.

apparent puzzle can be readily clarified by means of two considerations. The first is to remember that one of the estimates of the share of bequests is based precisely on the path of wealth of aged households — hence, by construction, there can be no contradiction between the slow decumulation and the small share of bequeathed wealth. The second and more substantive consideration is that, from the observation that bequeathed wealth is not much lower than the peak accumulation, one *cannot* conclude that most of the wealth ever accumulated is finally bequeathed. To see this, one need only realize that if one fixes the path of wealth from peak, around age 65, to death, there is still an infinity of possible paths from, say, age 20 to 65, and each of these paths implies a different amount of aggregate wealth. The earlier the average path approaches the peak value, the larger will be the wealth and hence the life cycle component. The actual path of accumulation, according to family surveys, reveals a far greater accumulation of wealth in the period preceding the likely receipt of bequests — say up to 45 — than is consistent with a pure bequest motive in the absence of life cycle accumulation.

This conclusion is illustrated in Fig. 1.1, which compares the actual path of wealth by age with the path that would correspond to an optimal accumulation. The path of actual wealth scaled by 'permanent' income is represented by the sequence of bars and is computed by averaging two surveys — the 1962 Survey of Consumer Finances and the 1979 Household Pension Survey, as reported in Ando and Kennickell (1985). The optimum bequest accumulation path is shown in Fig. 1.1 by the lower cross-hatched portion of each bar, and is derived from equation 1.5. The difference between the actual and the optimal path is an estimate of life cycle wealth, and it is shown in Fig. 1.2 as the cross-hatched portion of each bar. It has, by and large, the expected path, decreasing rapidly beginning with the retirement age. It is also apparent from these figures that the integral of the actual wealth path is far larger than that of the optimal bequest path — in fact, it is roughly four times larger, as expected from the calculations reported above.

IX The precautionary motive and the importance of bequest motive related wealth

The conclusion reached so far is that the importance of bequests may be a bit larger than the share — but still unlikely to exceed 1/4. But this figure overestimates the importance of wealth-holding related to the bequest motive because a substantial portion of the observed bequest flow undoubtedly

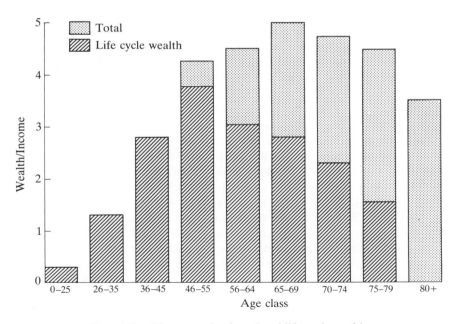

FIG. 1.2. The age path of total and life cycle wealth.

reflects the precautionary motive arising from the uncertainty of the time of death. Indeed, in view of the practical impossibility of having negative net worth, people tend to die with some wealth, unless they can manage to put all their retirement reserves into life annuities. However, it is a well-known fact that annuity contracts, other than in the form of group insurance through pension systems, are extremely rare. Why this should be so is a subject of considerable current interest and debate (see, e.g., Friedman and Warshawsky (1985*a* and *b*)). Undoubtedly, 'adverse selection', causing an unfavorable payout, and the fact that some utility may be derived from bequests (Masson (1986)) are an important part of the answer. In the absence of annuities, the wealth left behind will reflect risk aversion and the cost of running out of wealth (besides the possible utility of bequests).

This point has been elaborated in particular by Davies (1981) (see also Hubbard (1984)) who has shown that, for plausible parameters of the utility function including a low intertemporal elasticity of substitution, the extent to which uncertainty of life depresses the propensity to consume increases with age. As a result 'uncertain life time could provide the major element in a complete explanation of the slow decumulation of the retired' (relative to that implied by a standard LCH model).

It should, of course, be evident that bequests originating from the precautionary motive are, by nature, quite different from those dictated by the bequest motive. Indeed, they belong with pure life cycle accumulation since they are determined by the utility of consumption, and, furthermore, the surviving wealth must tend, on the average, to be proportional to life resources.

This leaves us with the question: how important is the true bequest motive, or, (roughly) equivalently, how large a portion of the flow of bequests can be attributed to it? Unfortunately, we know rather little on this score at present and it is not even clear that we will ever be able to acquire reliable knowledge. Part of the problem arises from the fact noted earlier that the two motives may interact — wealth may produce utility as insurance of consumption against longevity but also as a source of bequests if not used up.

Yet, there is a certain amount of evidence suggesting that the true bequest motive affects a rather small number of households, mostly located in the highest income and wealth brackets. This evidence includes, in the first place, the response to the question posed in the 1962 Survey of Consumers' Finances, cited earlier (Projector and Weiss (1964)) as to whether 'to provide an estate for the family' was an important reason for saving. It will be recalled that only 3% answered affirmatively — though the proportion rose with wealth, reaching one-third for the top class (over half a million 1963 dollars). Thus, the bequest motive seems to be limited to the highest economic classes.

This hypothesis is supported by the finding of Menchik and David that for (and only for) the top 20%, of the distribution of estimated life resources, bequests rise proportionately faster than total resources, something which presumably cannot be explained by the precautionary motive. However, Hurd (1986) presents results which are even more negative about the importance of bequests. It starts from the reasonable hypothesis that if the true bequest motive is an important source of terminal wealth, then retired households with living children should have more wealth and should save more (dissave less) than childless ones. It is found that, in fact, those with children have *less* wealth and, by and large, *dissave* the same fraction of wealth. The first result, as pointed out earlier, is fully consistent with the standard no-bequest LCH, because of the 'cost' of children; but for this reason the test may be biased. But the second result is indeed hard to reconcile with a significant bequest motive.

This evidence suggests that the share of bequests due to the pure bequest motive is unlikely to exceed one-half, and might well be substantially lower. Recalling that the share of all bequests can be put at no more than one-quarter, and taking into account the results of the last section, this would lead to an estimate of the importance of wealth due to such bequests of $\simeq 1/2 \times 1/4 \times 1.2 = 0.15$. To be sure, this figure might underestimate the response of total wealth to measures changing the incentive to leave bequests, e.g., through taxation, because of the possible effect on bequests prevailingly precautionary but influenced also by the utility of leaving bequests. It would be surprising that, even with this correction, the importance (elasticity) could exceed one-fifth.

X   Summary and conclusions

We have shown that the available evidence consistently indicates that the proportion of wealth received by transfer, when measured according to the customary definition, does not exceed one-quarter. This is true whether the inherited wealth is measured directly or through an indirect method, entirely analogous to that used by K&S, based on allocating aggregate saving by age and cumulating. The difference between this figure and the much larger one of 80% reported by K&S, based on allocation by age of income and consumption, has been shown to arise, in part, from some errors, and to a larger extent from differences in definitions — something which, if explicitly acknowledged by K&S, would have greatly reduced the heat produced by their contribution. When their estimates are corrected for errors and for those differences in definitions whose quantitative effect can be pinpointed, we find that the difference shrinks to some 10 to 20%. A good portion of this remaining gap can no doubt be traced to other definitional differences — notably their including expenditures on behalf of any member of the household above 18 years of age in the category of transfers. We have also argued that none of the definitional variations introduced by K&S appear particularly appealing or helpful.

We have next pursued K&S suggestions to bypass sterile definitional disputes, and to measure the importance of the bequest motive in terms of the percentage change in national wealth resulting from a percentage change in the flow of bequests generated by the desire to leave bequests. We have found that this indicator cannot be identified with the share of inherited wealth in either of two definitions. Indeed, to correctly measure importance, as long as the economy is growing, we must take into account not only the wealth received by bequests, but also wealth accumulated as a result of the excess of bequests left over bequests received.

We have endeavoured to estimate the relevant measure of importance by calculations of the optimal accumulation path, carried out with the help of some simplifying assumptions. These calculations lead to the conclusion that the importance of bequests is far less than the share as defined by K&S, and only a little larger (around 20%) than the share as commonly defined. Thus, if all inheritance could be traced to the bequest motive, the measure of importance could be assessed at no more than one-quarter.

However, given the observed absence of effective annuity markets, in reality a large fraction of bequests must be attributed to the precautionary motive. The evidence suggests that only for a small fraction of the population, mostly in the highest income brackets, wealth-holding is significantly affected by a true bequest motive. This leads us to speculate that the importance of the wealth resulting from the bequest motive can be assessed at a rather low value, most probably below one-fifth.

Notes

1. Total estimated net worth of households, non-profit institutions and trusts of $1.88 trillion, less the share of non-profit institutions, estimated at 7% (based on K&S, p. 72), and 58 million households.
2. I wish to express my gratitude to Kim Kowalewski of the Federal Reserve Bank of Cleveland for computing these averages from an edited version of the tape of the 'Survey of Changes in Consumer Finances' (Projector (1968)).
3. To illustrate, our computed value of life cycle wealth for concept LCW2, was 461 for series 1, and 683 for series 2, as compared with their published figures of 502 and 733 respectively (table 2, row 2).
4. Some of the depressing effects of bequests on ΔW can be traced to the 'certainty' assumption that bequests received are known, and result in higher consumption, from the very beginning of the life cycle. However, one can establish that even if one assumes that the effect of the inheritance and, later, bequests begins only upon receipt of the inheritance, ΔW takes the value of 23 t, which is still substantially lower than K&S's formula.

References

Ando, A., *The Savings of Japanese Households: a Micro Study Based on Data from the National Survey of Family Income Expenditure, 1974 and 1979*, (Economic Planning Agency, Government of Japan, 1985).

Ando, A. and A. Kennickell, 'How Much (or Little) Life Cycle is There in Micro Data? Cases of US and Japan', Paper presented at Istituto Bancario San Paolo di Torino Conference to Honor Franco Modigliani, in Martha's Vineyard, Massachusetts, mimeo, (September 1985).

Avery, R. B., G. E. Elliehausen, G. B. Canner, and T. A. Gustafson, 'Survey of Consumer Finances, 1983: a Second Report', *Federal Reserve Bulletin* **70** (1984).

Barlow, R., H. E. Brazer, and J. N. Morgan, *Economic Behavior of the Affluent* (The Brookings Institution, Washington DC, 1966).

Bernheim, B. D., *Dissaving after Retirement: Testing the Pure Life Cycle Hypothesis*, NBER Working Paper No. 1409, (1984).

Blinder, A. S., 'A Model of Inherited Wealth', *Quarterly Journal of Economics* **87** (1973), 608–25.

Board of Governors of the Federal Reserve System — Flow of Funds Section, Division of Quarterly Statistics, *Balance Sheets of the US Economy 1945–1980* (1981).

Darby, M. R., *Effects of Social Security on Income and the Capital Stock* (American Enterprise Institute, Washington DC, 1979).

David, M. and P. Menchik, 'Distribution of Estate and its Relationships to Intergenerational Transfers', In *Statistics of Income and Related Administration Record Research: 1982*, Department of the Treasury, Internal Revenue Service, Statistics of Income Division, (1982).

Davies, J., 'Uncertain Lifetime, Consumption and Dissaving in Retirement', *Journal of Political Economy* **89** (1981), 561–77.

Diamond, P. A. and J. A. Hausman, 'Individual Retirement and Savings Behavior', *Journal of Public Economics* **23** (1984), 81–114.

Evans, O. J., *The Life Cycle Inheritance: Theoretical and Empirical Essays on the Life Cycle Theory of Saving*, (Unpublished doctoral dissertation, University of Pennsylvania, Philadelphia, 1981).

Federal Reserve Board, annual report, (1984).

Fisher, J., *The Economics of an Aging Population, a Study in Income, Spending and Savings Patterns of Consumer Units in Different Age Groups, 1935–36, 1945 and 1946* (Unpublished doctoral dissertation, Columbia University, New York, mimeo, 1950).

Friedman, B. M. and M. Warshawsky, *Annuity Prices and Saving Behavior in the United States*, NBER Working Paper No. 1683, (1985*a*).

—— and ——, *The Cost of Annuities: Implications for Saving Behavior and Bequests*, NBER Working Paper No. 1682, (1985*b*).

Goldsmith, R. W., *A Study of Saving in the United States* (Princeton University Press, Princeton, 1956).

Harrod, R. F., *Towards a Dynamic Economic* (Macmillan, London, 1948).

Hubbard, R. G., *Precautionary Saving Revisited: Social Security, Individual Welfare and the Capital Stock*, NBER Working Paper No. 1430 (1984).

Hurd, M. D., *Savings and Bequest*, NBER Working Paper No. 1826 (1986).

Kennickell, A., *An Investigation of Life Cycle Savings Behavior in the United States* (Unpublished doctoral dissertation, University of Pennsylvania, Philadelphia, mimeo, 1984).

King, M. A. and L. Dicks–Mireaux, 'Asset Holding and the Life Cycle', *Economic Journal* **92** (1982), 247–67.

Kotlikoff, L. J. and L. H. Summers. *The Role of Intergenerational Transfers in Aggregate Capital Accumulation*, NBER Working Paper No. 445, (1980).

—— and ——, 'The Role of Intergenerational Transfers in Aggregate Capital Accumulation', *Journal of Political Economy* **89** (1981), 706–32.

Lydall, H. 'The Life Cycle of Income, Saving and Asset Ownership', *Econometrica* **23** (1955), 131–50.

Masson, A., 'A Cohort Analysis of Wealth–Age Profiles Generated by a Simulation Model in France (1949–1975)', *Economic Journal* **96** (1986), 173–90.

Menchik, P. L. and M. David, 'Income Distribution, Life Time Saving and Bequests', *American Economic Review* **73** (1983), 672–90.

Mirer, T. W., 'The Wealth–Age Relationship Among the Aged', *American Economic Review* **69** (1979), 435–43.

Modigliani, F., 'The Life Cycle Hypothesis of Saving, Twenty Years Later', In M. Parkin and A. Nobay (eds.), *Contemporary Issues in Economics* (Manchester University Press, Manchester, 1975).

—— and A. Ando, 'Tests of the Life Cycle Hypothesis of Saving: Comments and Suggestions', *Bulletin of the Oxford University Institute of Statistics* **19** (1957), 99–124.

—— and R. Brumberg, 'Utility Analysis and the Consumption Function: an Interpretation of Cross-section Data.' in K. K. Kurihara (ed.) *Post-Keynesian Economics* (Rutgers University Press, New Brunswick, 1954), 388–436.

—— and ——, 'Utility Analysis and Aggregate Consumption Functions: an Attempt at Integration', In A. Abel (ed.), *The Collected Papers of Franco Modigliani* (The MIT Press, Cambridge, Ma., 1980).

Morgan, J. N., M. H. David, W. J. Cohen, and H. E. Brazer, *Income and Welfare in the United States* (McGraw-Hill, New York, 1962).

National Center for Health Statistics, US Department of Health and Human Services, *Deaths by Marital Status* (1979).

Projector, D., *Survey of Changes in Family Finances* (The Board of Governors, Federal Reserve System, 1968).

—— and G. Weiss, *Survey of Financial Characteristics of Consumers* (The Board of Governors, Federal Reserve System, 1964).

Royal Commission on the Distribution of Income and Wealth, Report No. 5, Third Report on the Standing Reference, (1977).

Shorrocks, A. F., 'The Age–Wealth Relationship: a Cross-Section and Cohort Analysis', *Review of Economics and Statistics* **57** (1975), 155–63.

Smith, J. P., 'Assets, Savings, and Labor Supply', *Economic Inquiry* **15** (1977), 551–73.

2 The Contribution of Intergenerational Transfers to Total Wealth: A Reply

LAURENCE J. KOTLIKOFF
Boston University and National Bureau of Economic Research

LAWRENCE H. SUMMERS
Harvard University and National Bureau of Economic Research*

Franco Modigliani's (Chapter 1) review of the evidence and analysis in our 1981 paper is the latest salvo in a long running debate on the importance of intergenerational transfers in explaining saving behaviour. We welcome this opportunity to address his criticisms and to place our 1981 results in perspective. While Modigliani corrects an algebraic error of minor consequences in our earlier paper, its correction does not, in our view, call into question the fundamental conclusion that life cycle considerations can account for only a small part of aggregate capital accumulation. Inevitably, it is possible to challenge aspects of any complex empirical calculation. Modigliani's attacks seem to us incorrect in most cases and generally fail to address our primary method of determining the importance of intergenerational transfers. Many considerations at least as important as those raised by Modigliani suggest that our method produces an overestimate of the importance of life cycle wealth. Modigliani is also extremely selective in his reporting of the available evidence from other studies on the importance of intergenerational transfers.

This paper is organized as follows. Section I evaluates the existing empirical evidence on the importance of intergenerational transfers and adduces a number of considerations suggesting the plausibility of our conclusion that life cycle considerations are not paramount in explaining aggregate savings. Section II reviews our principal wealth accumulation method for estimating the importance of transfers and Modigliani's criticisms of this method. While Modigliani argues correctly that a modified treatment of consumer durable expenditures would increase the estimated share of life cycle wealth, our preferred adjustment is quite small. In addition, we find his attack on our definition of life cycle wealth as 'non-standard' unpersuasive both historically and analytically. Indeed, we view our definition as perfectly reasonable given the issue being addressed. Section III examines estimates based on transfer flows, and shows that the available evidence does not permit firm conclusions and provides no reason for doubting the conclusions

* We thank Greg Mankiw, Andrew Myers, Jim Poterba, and Andrei Schleifer for helpful comments. The research reported here is part of the NBER's research program in Taxation and projects in Taxation and Capital Formation and Aging. Any opinions expressed are those of the authors and not those of the National Bureau of Economic Research.

based on our main approach. Section IV concludes the paper and discusses directions for future research.

I   Review of earlier evidence

Modigliani's review of the available empirical evidence includes the assertion that 'all other estimates [agree] on the conclusion that wealth received by inheritance and major gifts represent a modest fraction of the total and that an exogenous large reduction in the flow of bequests would not have a major effect on the privately held stock of wealth.' This assertion is belied by a large number of studies appearing before and after our 1981 paper suggesting the overwhelming importance of bequest and other transfer saving in aggregate wealth accumulation. Here we review five essentially independent types of evidence suggesting the importance of intergenerational transfers. We then argue that the survey evidence cited by Modigliani does not demonstrate the unimportance of intergenerational transfers.

1.1   Historical saving patterns

The essential prediction of life cycle theory is that people save to prepare for their retirement when they must dissave and consume. Without periods of retirement or, at least, significantly decreased labour earnings at the end of life there can be no life cycle motive for savings. Yet substantial positive national saving rates antedate the advent of retirement as an important economic phenomenon. Darby (1979) points out that, although the ratio of expected retirement years to expected life span increased by 67% from 1890 to 1930, aggregate saving rates showed no increase during this period as would be predicted by the life cycle theory. Darby states '. . . the saving income ratio during 1890–1930 was 3 to 4 times higher than can be explained on even a generous reading of the zero-bequest model.' Indeed, Feldstein's (1977) calculations based on the work of Kuznets suggest that the rate of national saving in the United States was substantially greater before World War I than it has been since then. Clearly the incentive to save for retirement was far smaller in the earlier period than it is today.[1] Another type of evidence suggesting that retirement saving may be less important than many think is that the rate of saving today is high in many less developed countries where retirement is uncommon.

1.2   Age–wealth profiles

Decumulation of wealth after retirement is an essential aspect of the life cycle theory. Yet simple tabulations of wealth holdings by age, Mirer (1979) or saving rates by age, Thurow (1976) and Danziger *et al.* (1983), do not support the central prediction that the aged dissave. Mirer reports that wealth holding tends to increase with age. Thurow reports positive saving rates for persons in all age groups, while Danziger *et al.* report that saving rates increase with age with '. . . the elderly spend(ing) less than the nonelderly at the same level of income and (with) the very oldest of the elderly having the lowest average propensity to consume'. A number of questions can be raised about these and other analyses of age wealth profiles including possible selection biases and their failure to take account of the effects of social security. A careful survey of the literature on this issue by Bernheim (1986) concluded that 'while some other studies have found evidence of wealth decumulation after retirement, none have found that it occurs as rapidly as predicted by life cycle models without bequest motives.'

In his own analysis Bernheim (1986) finds '. . . relatively little dissaving among any group of retirees', and his tests of rates of accumulation lead to '. . . empirical refutation of life cycle implications'.

1.3   Evidence from annuity markets

The strict life cycle model without allowance for bequest motives makes strong predictions about the demand for annuities. Since the date of death is uncertain and since bequests provide no utility, life cycle models imply that there should be a very strong demand for annuity insurance. In fact, the demand for annuities appears to be very weak. Friedman and Warshawsky (1985) report that the loads on annuity insurance are no higher than the loads on other frequently purchased types of insurance such as automobile collision insurance or insurance against theft. Yet annuity purchases are a rarity. Friedman and Warshawsky argue that it is necessary to invoke bequest motives to explain this behaviour. While Kotlikoff and Spivak (1981) advance a possible alternative explanation, namely that families will self-insure to a large extent when annuity insurance is only available on very unfavorable terms, this cannot fully account for the widespread failure to purchase annuities. Bernheim, Shleifer, and Summers (1985) review a number of settings where annuities are available on a fair or even subsidized basis and report that even in these cases there is little demand to purchase annuities. They conclude from this evidence that many consumers must have significant bequest motives.

1.4   Wealth and subsequent consumption

An accounting identity holds that the present value of a consumer's future consumption must equal the present value of the income he will receive plus his existing wealth minus any transfers that he will make. This suggests that the importance of transfers may be inferred by looking at the fraction of wealth and future labour income that is devoted to future consumption. Two studies using very different types of data have taken this approach to estimating the importance of intergenerational transfers. Darby (1979) used data on individuals' wealth holding and subsequent labour income and consumption to conclude that at most 29% of US private net worth is devoted to future consumption. White (1978) used aggregate data on the age structure of the population, age earnings profiles, and consumption, along with a wide variety of parametric assumptions to conclude that the life cycle hypothesis can account for only about a quarter of aggregate savings.

1.5 Simulation studies

Simulation analyses also call into question the pure life cycle model. Auerbach and Kotlikoff (1985) show, in a detailed life cycle simulation model, that realistic specification of US demographics, preferences, and fiscal institutions implies a very much smaller wealth-to-income ratio than that actually observed for the US. Their results differ from those of Tobin (1967) because of their inclusion of social security and their more realistic assumptions concerning the growth rate of consumption over the life cycle. In order to generate substantial life cycle savings, Tobin found it necessary to assume that consumption grows at a much faster rate than actually observed.

Other simulation studies by Atkinson (1971) and Oulton (1976) point out the difficulty of explaining wealth inequality on the basis of the zero intergenerational transfer life cycle model. They find that the substantial inequality in wealth relative to earnings can only be explained by bequest behaviour.

1.6 Modigliani's evidence

With Table 1.1, Modigliani attempts to demonstrate an overwhelming preponderance of evidence indicating that intergenerational transfers are not an important aspect of private wealth holdings. Most of his evidence takes the form of the observation, obtained in several surveys, that most people report most of their wealth coming from their own saving rather than from bequests or gifts. There are a number of problems with Modigliani's inference from this evidence. First, as he acknowledges, much of total wealth may arise from intergenerational transfers even if they are unimportant for the vast majority of people who have little wealth and whose parents have or had little wealth. Second, Modigliani's survey evidence fails in many cases to take account of *inter vivos* gifts. Even where gifts are included it is unlikely that respondents report fully 'implicit gifts' such as low interest loans, shares in the family business, or payments of tuition. Third, none of the surveys cited by Modigliani take account of the return earned by recipients on past inheritances or gifts. It is likely that the accumulated value of most transfers substantially exceeds their nominal value. Fourth, the substantial under-reporting of wealth has been documented in the surveys Modigliani cites. It seems plausible that unearned wealth is particularly subject to under-reporting.

Modigliani also attempts in Table 1.1 to provide estimates of the importance of transfers based on 'bequest flow' methods. These suffer from the same difficulties of measurement as his other evidence. Some additional conceptual difficulties are noted in Section 2.3.

We turn next to a review of our method of accounting and Modigliani's criticisms of it. Before plunging into the details of the calculation, it is perhaps appropriate to reiterate that our reading of the evidence is less extreme than Modigliani suggests. Robert Solow (1982) considers much of the same evidence, and states 'My tentative conviction is that (the) view (that intergenerational transfers appear to be the major element determining US wealth accumulation) is essentially right. It is reinforced by general qualitative considerations.'

II Defining and measuring life cycle wealth

In Chapter 1 Modigliani focuses to a very large extent on two issues. The first is 'bequest flow' estimates of the importance of intergenerational transfers to savings, and the second is the proper definition of life cycle versus transfer wealth. Modigliani devotes little space to our main contribution, the direct calculation of life cycle wealth. We devoted most of our paper to the direct calculation of life cycle wealth because, as we stressed, the 'bequest flow' approach overestimates life cycle wealth due to the absence of data on a variety of transfer flows. In addition, unlike the direct calculation, the bequest flow approach requires invoking steady-state and other simplifying assumptions that may not be valid. This section considers the measurement of life cycle wealth while the next section treats the bequest flow calculations.

We address first the issue of properly defining life cycle wealth and then discuss our direct estimates of life cycle wealth, including the proper adjustment for the consumption of durables stressed by Modigliani. This adjustment does not alter the basic conclusion that the pure life cycle model without intergenerational transfers cannot explain the bulk of US wealth. We also point out several reasons why our calculation of life cycle wealth appears to be significantly upward-biased.

2.1 Defining life cycle wealth

Our definition of life cycle wealth is motivated by the following question: Are the US data on labour earnings, rates of return, consumption, and wealth broadly consistent with the view that intergenerational transfers play a negligible role in US wealth accumulation? Stated differently, can one reject the null hypothesis that the life cycle model without intergenerational transfers fully explains US wealth? We defined life cycle wealth according to the theoretical prediction of the zero intergenerational transfer life cycle model, namely as the sum over cohorts of the accumulated difference between past streams of labour earnings and consumption. We defined the difference between actual US wealth and life cycle wealth as transfer wealth. Transfer wealth must equal the sum over cohorts of the accumulated value of past net intergenerational transfers.

While Modigliani asserts that this definition is non-standard and unconventional, it is as standard as the life cycle theory itself; indeed, it is the definition used by Ando and Modigliani (1963), and it is the definition used in the two previous extensive analyses by Tobin (1967) and Darby (1979) of the role of the pure life cycle model in US wealth accumulation. While Modigliani suggests that this definition yields 'nonsensical' results, his example of the use of this definition in Table 1.2 clearly illustrates its ability to distinguish between economies with and without significant intergenerational transfers.

Rather than totalling over cohorts the accumulated difference between labour earnings and consumption, Modigliani would have us total over cohorts the sum of their past saving, where saving is income less consumption. The problem with this definition is that income may include capital income earned on previously received intergenerational transfers. Hence, the sum of saving out of income can not be used to test with maximum power the null hypothesis that the zero transfer life cycle model accounts for essentially all of US wealth, because income may itself reflect intergenerational transfers. Nor can Modigliani's definition be implemented without extremely elaborate adjustments to remove the inflation component of the capital income earned from investing gifts and bequests. Implementing it without inflation adjustments would lead to the unacceptable implication that perfectly balanced inflation would increase the share of life cycle wealth; i.e., transfer wealth defined by Modigliani is the simple sum of past net transfer received by living generations measured in nominal terms. A final limitation of Modigliani's definition is that it does not correspond to an answer to any well-posed behavioural question.

Once one finds that the data are highly inconsistent with the zero transfer life cycle formulation, a natural behavioural question raised is: What would be the impact on US wealth of eliminating all intergenerational transfers? We raised this economic, as opposed to accounting, issue in our paper, indicating how our definition and estimate of life cycle wealth could be used to address this unrealistic, but nonetheless interesting counterfactual. The answer to this economic question is, of course, independent of accounting convention. Our assessment, to which we still subscribe, was that totally eliminating intergenerational transfer would, in partial equilibrium, reduce US wealth by at least 50%. This economic as opposed to accounting statement suggests a much more important role for intergenerational transfers than has generally been thought to be the case.

2.2   The age of adulthood

A second issue of definition discussed in our paper and raised as well by Modigliani is the proper age of adulthood. As Modigliani points out this is an arbitrary choice. At one extreme one could assume that adulthood begins at birth, in which case the accumulated difference between the labour earnings and consumption of young cohorts would be significant negative numbers, and our calculation of 1974 life cycle wealth would be substantially smaller than the figure we report; indeed, this assumption would lead to a negative value for life cycle wealth. At the opposite extreme one could assume that adulthood begins at a very late age, say age 40. In this case all the consumption and earnings of those under age 40 must be imputed to their relatives over age 40, and the value of life cycle wealth would be very much larger than we report.

In our calculation of 1974 life cycle wealth we choose age 18 as the age of adulthood. In our view this age, while appropriate for the post war generations alive in 1974, is probably too old for older cohorts alive in 1974 some of whom were born in the last century. Many of these older generations entered the labour force at younger ages than is currently typical, and they certainly had much shorter lifespans. Hence, it seems reasonable to believe that the generally perceived age of adulthood for the older cohorts in 1974 was less than age 18, and perhaps as young as 16. Indeed, until the 1950s labour force participation rates were calculated relative to the over 14 population. Had we used age 16 for older 1974 cohorts as the age of adulthood we would have reported considerably less life cycle wealth than we did.

Given our choice of age 18 as the age of adulthood, we ascribe all consumption, expenditures, and earnings of those 18 and over to those adults who are directly consuming the expenditures and supplying the labour. Hence, the consumption of a 25 year old graduate student of educational services, as well as food, clothing, etc. is counted as her consumption rather than that of her parents. In contrast, Modigliani argues that the consumption of educational services should be ascribed to the parents when the parents are financing the education. A problem with this line of reasoning is that money is fungible; i.e., there is no reason to treat differently the case of a graduate student whose tuition is directly paid by her parents and the graduate student who pays the tuition from her own check book, but receives an equivalent amount of money from her parents 'for' food, 'for' a car, 'for' a vacation, etc. More importantly, provision of higher education and support during the period of education represents a major form of intergenerational transfers and should be treated as such. In sum, we see no reasonable way to label certain payments from parents to their adult children as 'transfers' and others as 'parental consumption'. From the perspective of the customary view of the life cycle model it would be inappropriate to treat children as adults, but it is equally inappropriate to treat adults as children.

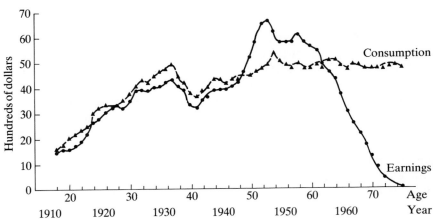

FIG. 2.1.   Sum of male and female longitudinal average earnings and average consumption profiles; age 18 in 1910, age 82 in 1974.

2.3   Consumer durables

In our earlier paper we reported 1974 life cycle wealth of $733 billion compared with 1974 household net worth of $3 884 billion, implying that 1974 life cycle wealth is only 18.9% of 1974 total wealth. The life cycle wealth figure was constructed by accumulating earnings less consumption for each

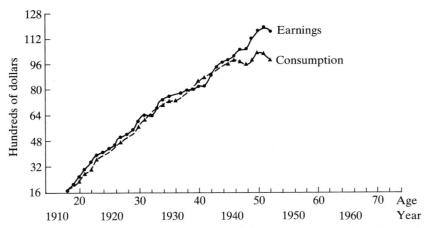

FIG. 2.2.   Sum of male and female longitudinal average earnings and average consumption profiles; age 18 in 1940, age 52 in 1974.

male and female cohort with living members in 1974. The age- and sex-specific levels of consumption and earnings used in this calculation were derived by distributing total consumption and labour earnings in each year beginning in 1900 according to cross-section profiles of relative consumption and earnings by age and sex.

In forming cross-section relative age–consumption profiles we simply used expenditures on durables rather than imputing rent on durables. As Modigliani points out, this treatment of durables has the effect of ascribing too much consumption in a given year to younger individuals and too little consumption to older individuals and biases our calculation towards too little life cycle wealth. In retrospect there is a very easy way to adjust for durables. This is just to exclude the stock of consumer durables from total wealth. Our previous treatment of durables involved treating durables expenditures as consumption for purposes of calculating cohort-specific values of consumption, but, unfortunately, not for purposes of calculating total wealth. Stated differently, our calculation of life cycle wealth really corresponds to life cycle accumulation of wealth excluding durables and should be compared with total wealth excluding durables. Since the stock of durables in 1974 was $530 billion, this correction lowers the total stock of wealth to be explained to $3 349. Since $773 billion is only 21.9% of adjusted total wealth, this adjustment raises our estimate of the life cycle wealth share only trivially, from 18.9% to 21.9%.

In contrast to this correction of 3 percentage points, the correction for the failure to impute rent on durables reported by Modigliani is 26% raising from 18.9 to 44.9% the share of life cycle wealth. Before thinking of the straightforward adjustment procedure described in the preceding paragraph, we assisted Modigliani in using the 1972 Consumer Expenditure Survey to try to estimate both the stock of durables and the implicit rent on durables. This initial crude adjustment for durables involved using the 1972 cross-sectional durables expenditure information and invoking steady-state assumptions to infer past expenditures on durables by households in the 1972 survey. These estimated past purchases of durables were then depreciated to arrive at estimated 1972 stocks of durables, from which rent was then imputed. The calculation turned out to be quite sensitive to the assumed steady-state growth rate. One version of the calculation corresponds to Modigliani's reported 26% adjustment. We place little reliance on this adjustment since, unlike any of the other calculations in our estimation of life cycle wealth, it invokes quite unrealistic steady-state assumptions. These include the assumption that past expenditures on durables at each age equaled the 1972 expenditure of the corresponding age group deflated by a constant growth rate factor.

Modigliani's preferred adjustment raises the estimate of life cycle wealth from $733 billion to $1 743 billion, or 44.9% of total wealth. Note that while this figure is over twice as large as our much more defensible 21.9% adjusted estimate, life cycle wealth is still less than half of total wealth implying an important role for intergenerational transfers.

2.4 Upward biases in our original calculation of life cycle wealth

As we pointed out in our original paper there are several biases in our calculation suggesting that we overestimated life cycle wealth. In order to generate at least some positive value for life cycle wealth we adjusted upwards standard estimates of the labour income of the self-employed by 20%. Since the ratio of self-employed workers to employees was substantially larger in the pre-war period than it is today, the calculated value of life cycle wealth is fairly sensitive to this assumption. Using standard estimates of the labour income of proprietors would reduce estimated life cycle wealth by about $700 billion. We also assumed in the calculation a ratio of average female earnings to average male earnings equal to 0.55, although the data suggest that a ratio closer to 0.45 is more appropriate. Using 0.45 as the ratio would reduce our estimate of life cycle wealth by between $100 and $150 billion. A variety of other biases also increased our estimate of life cycle wealth. These include our assumption that the profile of relative consumption by age is flat after age 75 and our assumption of zero earnings after age 75. In addition, one could argue that for many older 1974 cohorts an age of adulthood younger than 18 is appropriate. This adjustment would lower the estimate significantly. Needless to say, if we adjust for durables simply by excluding the stock of durables from total wealth and make these additional adjustments to our initial $733 billion figure, we would arrive at a negative value of life cycle wealth.

2.5 Explaining our result

It may be useful to repeat our basic explanation for why life cycle wealth is so small in the US. Unlike simple classroom depictions of hump saving in which the consumption profile is flat and the earnings profile rises to retirement, actual age–earnings and age–consumption profiles, such as those in Fig. 2.1 and 2.2 which are reproduced from our paper, have essentially identical shapes and levels prior to at least age 45. Between ages 45 and 60 there is clearly some hump saving in that earnings profiles continue to rise through the early 50s and then decline slowly through age 60 while consumption profiles flatten out, and after age 60 there is clearly dissaving in the sense that the age–consumption profile exceeds the age–earnings profile. However, since this pattern of hump saving and dissaving occurs quite late in the life cycle one would not expect a large accumulation of life cycle wealth in the aggregate because the life cycle wealth of the more numerous generations below age 45 is so small. The simple fact is that consumption does not rise more rapidly through life than labour income.

III   Lower bound estimates of life cycle wealth based on the 'bequest flow method'

The 'bequest flow' method refers to using information on the current flow of intergenerational transfers and assuming the economy is in a steady state to estimate stocks of life cycle wealth. In our original paper we presented estimates for transfer wealth based on this method. Modigliani focuses extensively on this short section of our paper. We stressed that these were lower bound estimates because there are no data sources that systematically report intergenerational transfers made in the form of implicit and explicit gifts. Explicit gifts, which may be in kind as well as in cash, are clearly acknowledged as such by donors and recipients. Implicit gifts, such as making one's son an equal earning partner in a lucrative family business or providing low interest loans to children, may not be viewed as a gift by donors and recipients and would be hard to identify and quantify in a survey. Since the US distribution of wealth is highly skewed, implicit gifts, while perhaps small in number, could be very large in value. Hence, any flow estimates of transfer wealth, including those of Modigliani, should be viewed as potentially seriously downward-biased.

A second concern with the bequest flow method is that it requires invoking steady-state assumptions that may be far from valid. It may be, for example, that the flow of intergenerational transfers in relation to the scale of the economy was much greater in the 1920s than in the 1960s and 1970s, the period for which our transfer flow data is available. Finally, even if one is willing to accept the steady-state assumption, the simple formulae that we and Modigliani examine assume that everyone dies at a given age D, that all transfers are received at a given age I, and all transfers are made at a given age, G. This is obviously unrealistic, and it is not clear exactly what choice of these three ages best approximates reality. As we indicated in the beginning of our earlier paper, the correct approximation depends critically on the steady-state value of the real interest rate, r, and the steady state growth rate, n. For example, when r exceeds n, our measure of transfer wealth depends on the period of accumulation. Hence, if half of transfers are received at age 20 and half at age 60, using age 40 for I would be inappropriate, since transfers received at age 20 should receive more weight in the approximation formula because they are accumulated for a much longer period than transfers received at age 60, and because the accumulation function is a non-linear function of age. In sum, we feel that direct calculation of life cycle wealth is decidedly preferred to using the steady state 'bequest flow' method both because of the nature of available data and the approximations required in the latter approach. This view led to the emphasis in our earlier paper on the direct estimation of life cycle wealth.

Turning to our actual flow calculation, Modigliani points out an algebraic error in our formula relating the stock of transfer wealth, T, to the annual flow of intergenerational transfers, t. The correct formula, which is simply a rewrite of Modigliani's, is:

$$T = \frac{t}{(r-n)} \, e^{(r-n)D} \left[1 - e^{(n-r)(G-I)} \right] e^{(n-r)I}.$$

In the formula in our paper we omitted the last term $e^{(n-r)I}$.

To illustrate the implication of the formula we discussed an example in which D equals 55 (a real-world age of death of 73 if the age of adulthood is 18), $(G-I)$ equals 30, and $(r-n)$ equals 0.01. Because of our algebraic error we did not assume a value for I. In his paper Modigliani uses a value of I equal to 25, which corresponds to a real-world age of 43. We favour a value of I equal to 15 reflecting the fact that the appropriate approximation to I should be smaller if r exceeds n than if r equals n; i.e., since when r exceeds n, transfer wealth depends on the period of accumulation using the simple transfer-weighted age of transfer receipt in the formula would bias downward the estimated stock of transfer wealth. It appears that a similar statement is true of the choice of the age gap factor $(G-I)$; thus, it is likely that our choice of 30 for $(G-I)$ is too small given that we apply the formula to the case that r exceeds n.

In the illustration in our paper we used a value of 45 for the factor multiplying t in the formula for T. Taking I equal to 25 Modigliani calculates a value of 35 for this factor. With our preferred value for I of 15 the factor is 39. Since we reported a *lower bound* estimate for t of $45.4 billion our revised *upper bound* 'bequest flow' estimate for the stock of life cycle wealth, using I equals 15, is $2 113 billion, which is 54% of 1974 household wealth. Note that if we use an age gap $(G-I)$ factor of 45 which may be more appropriate since r exceeds n, the upper bound estimate of life cycle wealth is $1 429 billion, or only 37% of 1974 household net worth.

IV   Implications of our findings for viewing the life cycle model and for future research

The finding that intergenerational transfers are a key feature of US wealth accumulation has not lessened interest in the pure life cycle model. On the contrary, a variety of researchers, including Sheshinski and Weiss (1981), Davies (1981), Eckstein, Eichenbaum, and Peled (1983), and Abel (1983), and Hubbard (1984*a*, 1984*b*) have investigated the potential for unintentional intergenerational transfers within models in which households have pure life cycle preferences, but in which annuity markets do not exist. Kotlikoff, Spivak, and Shoven (1983) and Kotlikoff (1986) also consider non-altruistic life cycle preferences and show that significant intergenerational transfers can arise in a setting of partial annuity insurance provided by family members. Other researchers, such as Bernheim, Shleifer, and Summers (1985) view intergenerational transfers within a pure life cycle model as the implicit payment by parents to their children for material and other types of support. A third view of intergenerational transfers that contains an important role for the pure life cycle model is espoused by Kurz (1984) and others, namely that society is heterogeneous, with a large number of relatively poor households with pure life cycle preferences and a small number of relatively altruistic extended families with significant bequest motives.

Since the short-run and potentially the long-run impact of fiscal policies depends on the relative number of life cycle households in the US economy, a statistic that is unknown, it remains important to understand the impact of fiscal policies within the pure life cycle model. To that end Summers (1981), Auerbach and Kotlikoff (1986), Seidman (1983), Gahvari (1984), Lawrence (1983), and many others have examined fiscal policies within pure life cycle models. These theoretical and simulation studies have been accompanied by a large volume of empirical research testing the implications of the pure life cycle model.

In sum, research on, and interest in the life cycle model has never been greater than in the last few years. Moreover, the nature and heterogeneity of household saving behaviour remains poorly understood. In our view, additional research investigating the nature of saving preferences rather than additional wealth accounting holds the key to understanding the very important role of intergenerational transfers as well as the contribution of pure life cycle saving motives to US wealth accumulation.

Note

1. More recent statistics also point to the inverse correlation between the duration of retirement and the US saving rate. Kotlikoff and Smith (1983) report that since 1950 the expected duration of retirement and other non-working periods for the average adult has almost doubled. This change coincided with a secular decline of over 40% in the rate of US saving out of net national product (Boskin and Kotlikoff (1985)).

References

Abel, A. B., 'Bequests with Uncertain Lifetimes,' Mimeo., Harvard University, (1983).

Ando, A. and F. Modigliani, 'The Life Cycle Hypothesis of Saving: Aggregate Implications and Tests', *American Economic Review* **53** (1963), 55–84.

Atkinson, A. B., 'The Distribution of Wealth and the Individual Life Cycle', *Oxford Economic Papers* **23** (1971) 239–54.

Auerbach, A. J. and L. J. Kotlikoff, 'Simulating Alternative Social Security Responses to the Demographic Transition', *National Tax Journal* **38** (1985), 153–68.

—— and ——, *Dynamic Fiscal Policy* (Cambridge University Press, Cambridge, 1986).

Bernheim, B. D., 'Dissaving after Retirement: Testing the Pure Life Cycle Hypothesis', forthcoming in *Issues in Pension Economics* (NBER Volume, University of Chicago Press, Chicago, 1986).

Bernheim, B. D., A. Shleifer, and L. H. Summers, 'The Strategic Bequest Motive', *Journal of Political Economy* **93** (1985), 1045–76.

Boskin, M. J. and L. J. Kotlikoff, 'Public Debt and US Saving: a New Test of the Neutrality Hypothesis'. (Carnegie–Rochester Conference Volume Series, 1985).

Danziger, S., J. Van der Gaag, E. Smolensky, and M. Taussig, 'The Life Cycle Hypothesis and the Consumption Behavior of the Elderly', *Journal of Post-Keynesian Economics* **5** (1983), 208–27.

Darby, M. R., *Effects of Social Security on Income and the Capital Stock* (American Enterprise Institute, Washington DC, 1979).

Davies, J., 'Uncertain Lifetime, Consumption and Dissaving in Retirement', *Journal of Political Economy* **89** (1981), 561–77.

Eckstein, Z., M. Eichenbaum, and D. Peled, *Uncertain Lifetimes and the Welfare Enhancing Properties of Annuity Markets and Social Security*, mimeo, (1983).

Feldstein, M., 'National Saving in the United States', in *Capital for Productivity and Jobs*, (Prentice–Hall, Englewood Cliffs, 1977), 129–54.

Friedman, B. and M. Warshawsky, *The Cost of Annuities: Implications for Saving Behaviour and Bequests*, NBER Working Paper No. 1682, mimeo, (1985).

Gahvari, F., 'The Optimal Taxation of Housing', *Public Finance* **39** (1984), 213–25.

Hubbard, G., 'Uncertain Lifetimes, Pensions and Individual Saving', NBER Working Paper No. 1363, (1984*a*).

—— 'Precautionary Saving Revisited: Social Security, Individual Welfare, and the Capital Stock', NBER Working Paper No. 1930, (1984*b*).

Kotlikoff, L. J., 'The Impact of Annuity Insurance on Savings and Inequality', *Journal of Labor Economics* (1986).

—— and D. Smith, *Pensions in the American Economy* (University of Chicago Press, Chicago, 1983).

Kotlikoff, L. J. and A. Spivak, 'The Family as an Incomplete Annuities Market', *Journal of Political Economy* **89** (1981), 372–91.

——, J. Shoven, and A. Spivak, 'Annuity Markets, Saving and the Capital Stock', NBER Working Paper No. 1250, (1983).

Kurz, M., *The Life Cycle Hypothesis as a Tool of Theory and Practice*, mimeo, (1984).

Lawrence, E., *Do Transfers to the Poor Reduce Savings?*, mimeo, (1983).

Menchik, P. L. and M. David, 'Income Distribution, Lifetime Saving and Bequests', *American Economic Review* **73** (1983), 672–90.

Mirer, T. W., 'The Wealth Age Relation among the Aged', *American Economic Review* **69** (1979), 435–43.

Modigliani, F. and R. Brumberg, 'Utility Analysis and the Consumption Function: an Interpretation of Cross-Section Data', in K. K. Kurihara (ed.), *Post-Keynesian Economics* (Rutgers University Press, New Brunswick, 1954), 388–436.

—— and ——, 'Utility Analysis and Aggregate Consumption Function: An Attempt at Integration', In A. Abel (ed.), *The Collected Papers of Franco Modigliani* (MIT Press, Cambridge, Ma., 1980).

Oulton, N., 'Inheritance and the Distribution of Wealth', *Oxford Economic Papers* **28** (1976), 86–101.

Seidman, L.S., 'Taxes in a Life Cycle Growth Model with Bequests and Inheritances', *American Economic Review* **73** (1983), 437–41.

Sheshinski E. and Y. Weiss, 'Uncertainty and Optimal Social Security Systems', *Quarterly Journal of Economics* **96** (1981), 189–206.

Solow, R., 'Reflections on Saving Behavior', in *Saving and Government Policy* (Conference Series 25, Federal Reserve Bank of Boston, Boston, 1982).

Summers, L.H., 'Capital Taxation and Capital Accumulation in a Life Cycle Growth Model', *American Economic Review* **71** (1981), 533–44.

Thurow, L., *Generating Inequality*, (Basic Books, 1976).

Tobin, J., 'Life Cycle Saving and Balanced Growth', in W. Fellner *et al.* (eds.), *Ten Economic Studies in the Tradition of Irving Fisher* (Wiley, New York, 1967), 231–56.

White, B.B., 'Empirical Tests of the Life Cycle Hypothesis', *American Economic Review* **68** (1978), 547–60.

Comments on Chapter 1 and Chapter 2

ALAN S. BLINDER*

Princeton University

In a well-known and provocative paper, Laurence Kotlikoff and Lawrence Summers (henceforth, K&S) claimed that a least 81%, and perhaps more than 100%, of US wealth must be accounted for by intergenerational transfers — a number wildly at variance with previous direct estimates of the wealth derived from inheritance. In Chapter 1, Franco Modigliani argues that K&S were wrong and that the true proportion of wealth accounted for by inheritance is closer to 20%. In their reply, K&S defend their earlier conclusion that life-cycle accumulation can account for only a minor share of wealth. I have been assigned the task of adjudicating the dispute. But, before examining the points and counterpoints, let me summarize very briefly what K&S originally found — and explain why.

What K&S found

Distrusting direct measurements of inherited wealth because they are based on scanty data, K&S devised an accounting framework for estimating the life-cycle component of wealth. Since the highest figure they could produce for the life-cycle wealth proportion of total wealth was only 19%, they concluded that inheritance must account for at least 81% of the total. Note that their technique is to estimate life-cycle wealth directly, obtaining inherited wealth as the remainder.

K&S's finding can be explained by noting that the life-cycle profiles of earnings, $E(t)$, and consumption, $C(t)$, coincide closely. (An example is provided in Fig. 2.1 of K&S's reply.) If that is so, then the pure life cycle model with no inheritances or bequests can account for relatively little wealth-holding; only large inheritances can raise the level of non-interest income high enough to generate the observed stock of wealth. The other possibility, of course, is that the life-cycle profile of consumption differs significantly from that shown by K&S's diagrams — which is one way to summarize major portions of the dispute between Modigliani and K&S. (More on this below).

K&S realized, of course, that previous direct measures of inheritances,

* I thank Larry Kotlikoff, Franco Modigliani, and Larry Summers for many stimulating arguments.

generally based on surveys, never came close to the 81% of wealth produced by their residual method. Rather, this evidence, which is summarized by Modigliani, generally gave estimates in the 15–20% range. So K&S made a heroic effort to explain the gap between the two measurement techniques, succeeding in pushing the 20% estimate up to 52%. Thus, as Modigliani's paper opens, we have two 'gaps' to explain:

SHARE OF INHERITANCE IN WEALTH

direct measurements		*K&S residual method*
conventional	K&S	
20%	52%	81% (perhaps over 100%)

Modigliani's paper is devoted to both gaps: he tries to whittle down each of K&S's estimates to numbers closer to the 20% figure derived from the surveys. In the end, he accomplishes this goal to his satisfaction, but not to K&S's. Along the way, he offers many interesting remarks on and insights into life-cycle theory. These alone are worth the price of admission. But, in my remarks, I will limit myself to the issues in dispute between Modigliani and K&S.

Point one: a calculation error

Only one of these issues is easily resolved, and even here the adjudication is not as simple as it may appear. Modigliani notes, correctly, that K&S made an algebraic error in the formula relating transfer flows to stocks of transfer wealth. Correcting it brings the 52% estimate down to 40.5% on Modigliani's assumptions about the typical ages of testators and inheritors, but only to 46% on the assumptions K&S prefer.[1] Splitting the difference, on grounds that arguing about approximations is fruitless, leaves us with:

SHARE OF INHERITANCE IN WEALTH

direct measurements		*K&S residual method*
conventional	K&S	
20%	43%	81%

Note that correcting the error leaves the second gap even bigger than before.

Point two: what is an intergenerational transfer?

Second, K&S use a broader than usual definition of intergenerational transfers, which includes expenditures on dependent children over 18; that is, they count consumption of an 18-year-old living in his parents' household as consumption of the child, not as consumption of the parent. Modigliani prefers a narrower definition restricted to large financial transfers, on the grounds that spending on, say, 18-year-olds living with their parents should be counted as consumption of the parents, not as consumption of the children. Simply reclassifying college expenses as *C* of the middle-aged rather than as *C* of the young reduces the share of intergenerational transfers by 9 percentage points and raises life-cycle wealth by the same amount. Were Modigliani able to estimate expenditures on dependent youths other than those for college, his adjustment would have been larger.

Though debates over definitions are usually sterile, it seems to me that Modigliani is right. K&S argue for their choice on the grounds that money is fungible. What difference, they ask, does it make if a parent pays his child's $12 000 college bill or gives the child a $12 000 cash gift, out of which the child pays the bills? Yet Modigliani's procedure would count the latter, but not the former, as an intergenerational transfer. The answer, of course, is that it makes no economic difference. But it seems to make a big difference to parents. Since parents rarely, if ever, give their children cash and let the kids pay the bills, the K&S argument seems correct in principle but irrelevant in practice.

I side with Modigliani in this dispute over language because the substantive issue at hand is the origin of non-human wealth, while transfers in the form of college expenses presumably build human wealth. If we expand the accounting framework to include human wealth, then many more things should be included — possibly all expenses on child-rearing. Indeed, where human capital is concerned, it can be argued that 100% of wealth is inherited. ('Where would I be today without my genes?')

Putting this issue in Modigliani's column leaves us with:

direct measurements		K&S residual method
conventional	K&S	
20%	34%	72%

Thus most of the first gap is gone (and more would be gone if Modigliani had more information of consumption by youths), but the second gap is even bigger than when we started.

Point three: accumulated interest

If an inheritance of *I* was received *t* years ago, K&S count $I\exp(rt)$ as inherited wealth while Modigliani wants to counts only *I*. This makes a big difference. It reduces the amount of directly measured inherited wealth by 47%, according to Modigliani, reducing its share in total wealth by 16 percentage points. Deducting that from the 34% and 72% figures above would take them down to 18% and 56%,[2] which obliterates the first gap. So resolution of the dispute is important.

Who is right? To answer this question, it is important to distinguish between the accounting question:

(a) How much of existing wealth derives from inheritance?
and the economic question:

(b) By how much would wealth fall if there were no inheritances?
In my view, there is no unambiguous answer to the accounting question because it is not well posed. The economic question is more precisely posed; but it is difficult to answer because it requires empirical knowledge of behavioural responses to changes in inherited wealth. Let me explain.

I begin with two accounting identities for the wealth of a particular individual at age t:

$$\text{(KS)} \quad W(t) = W(0)e^{rt} + \int_0^t (E(a) - C(a))e^{r(t-a)}\,da$$

$$\text{(M)} \quad W(t) = W(0) + \int_0^t S(a)\,da,$$

where $W(a)$ is wealth at age a and $S(a)$ is savings at age a, defined as $E(a) + rW(a) - C(a)$. Each identity is correct. And each has its supporter, as indicated by the names I have attached to them. And each invites us to label the first term 'inherited wealth' and the second 'life-cycle' wealth.[3] Unfortunately, the 'natural' breakdown of wealth into these two categories differs between the two identities. The issue between them can be put starkly as follows. John D. Rockefeller II never earned a penny of labour income, but had a very large flow of property income — so large, in fact, that he was a net saver over his lifetime. Modigliani wants to say that Rockefeller was a life-cycle accumulator. K&S want to say he was a pure inheritor. Futhermore, each protagonist claims that his is the 'standard' answer because it derives from an accounting identity.

I must admit that my preference here lies with K&S. But the issue is largely semantic, and semantics will not dissuade Modigliani. The problem, of course, is that the receipt of inherited wealth changes life-cycle accumulation — as both Modigliani and K&S fully realize. Since the two types of wealth accumulation interact, a pure accounting breakdown is impossible — just as it is impossible to answer the question, 'How much of $V(X + Y)$ comes from X and how much comes from Y?', when X and Y are correlated.

Because inheritance changes life cycle wealth, however defined, only a behavioural economic model can perform the requisite breakdown — by answering the counterfactual economic question: How large would wealth be if there were no inheritances? Let me illustrate the possibilities by an example.

Consider the first three periods (best thought of as decades) in the life of a pure life-cycle saver who earns 10 units in each period. The real interest rate is 20%. With no inheritance, I suppose his consumption would be 8, 10, and 12 units in each of the three periods respectively. Thus we have:

	Period		
	0	1	2
Earnings, E	10	10	10
Opening Wealth, W	0	2	2.4
Interest	0	0.4	0.48
Consumption, C	8	10	12
Saving, S	2	0.4	−1.52

Wealth at end of period 2 = 0.88

Clearly, all this wealth is life-cycle accumulation. No one would question that.

Now suppose he inherits 10 units at the opening of period 0, but changes neither his consumption nor his labour supply behaviour. The new numbers are:

	Period		
	0	1	2
E	10	10	10
Opening W	10	14	16.8
Interest	2	2.8	3.36
C	8	10	12
S	4	2.8	1.36

Wealth at end of period 2 = 18.16

Here wealth has risen by 17.28 units, which is precisely $10(1 + r)^3$. The K&S calculation is exactly correct; 95% of wealth is inherited. Modigliani's method attributes only 10 units (or 55% of the total) to inheritance. Thus, if there is no behavioural response in either E or C, K&S are right.

But it is unreasonable to expect an inheritance to leave the lifetime consumption path unchanged. Suppose it rises by 2 units each period. We get:

	Period		
	0	1	2
E	10	10	10
Opening W	10	12	12.4
Interest	2	2.4	2.48
C	10	12	14
S	2	0.4	− 1.52

Wealth at end of period 2 = 10.88

Here, inheritance has raised wealth by exactly 10 units — precisely the amount inherited. In this case, Modigliani's calculation is exactly correct in attributing 92% of wealth to inheritance. (The books were cooked to make this so.) K&S would attribute too much to inheritance (17.28/10.88 = 159%, leaving − 59% to life-cycle accumulation.) This example illustrates my point: the receipt of 10 units in inherited wealth changed life cycle wealth from 0.88 units to − 6.4 units.

My final example allows for a labour supply response as well. I assume that earnings fall by 1 unit each year. Thus we have:

	Period		
	0	1	2
E	9	9	9
Opening W	10	11	10.2
Interest	2	2.2	2.04
C	10	12	14
S	1	− 0.8	− 2.96

Wealth at end of period 2 = 7.24

Here, inheritance adds only 6.36 units to accumulated wealth. Modigliani would count 10 units. K&S would count 17.28 units. Thus both methods attribute too much to inheritance!

Now comes the hard question: which of these hypothetical examples comes closest to reality? That depends on how large the behavioural responses really are, as is made clear both in K&S's original paper and in Modigliani's contribution to this volume. To provide yet a third way to skin the same cat, I offer the following crude theoretical calculation.[4] In my 1974 book, *Toward an Economic Theory of Income Distribution*, I gave all the formulas needed to compute the effect on $W(t)$ of a rise in $W(0)$, for any age t. The answer depends on the rate of interest and on the parameters of the utility function. I carried out the computations only for a 48-year-old in one simple case (but the formulas are there for any case):

(a) labour supply is inelastic;[5]
(b) the utility function is Cobb–Douglas in consumption and bequests;
(c) adult life lasts 60 years (death at age 78), hence age 48 is half way;
(d) $r = 0.025$, time discount rate $= 0.015$.

With the weight on bequests that I used in the book, the answer is:

$$dW(30)/dW(0) = 0.83.$$

This derivative is very sensitive to age, declining from 1.0 at age 0 to 0.83 at age 30 to 0.03 at age 60. The economywide figure is a weighted average of these, and hence must certainly be below 1.[6] For comparison, the equivalent derivatives in my three numerical examples are 1.73, 1.00, and 0.64 respectively. Note that the last of these comes closest to my theoretical calculation.

Of course, a theoretical model of an optimizing consumer in a perfect capital market is not the right way to learn about behavioural responses. What we need is serious econometric evidence. That is a tall order, given the paucity of data on inheritances. But it is the only way to answer the economic question.

Not knowing what to do about the 15 percentage points that are in dispute leaves me with:

SHARE OF INHERITANCE IN WEALTH

direct measurements		*K&S residual method*
conventional	K&S	
20%	18–34%	56–72%

Point four: the treatment of durables

So far, I have spoken mainly about Modigliani's efforts on the first gap. For the second gap, he offers one very important correction. Or does he?

Due to an oversight, K&S used consumer expenditures rather than true consumption as $C(t)$ in constructing their life-cycle profiles. If durables are important — and they are in the US — this could exaggerate the $C(t)$ of the young and understate the $C(t)$ of the old, leading to an underestimate of the second term in identity (KS) above.

The conceptual issue does not seem to be in dispute; but what to do about it is. Modigliani tells us that when he uses the K&S data, plus some auxiliary assumptions about implicit rental rates on durables, the corrections of the $C(t)$ profiles are enormous. An astonishing 26% more wealth is classified as life cycle wealth. K&S point out that some untested steady-state assumptions must be invoked to do this calculation, and that it 'turned out to be quite sensitive to the assumed steady state growth rate.' So they 'place little reliance on this adjustment'. They offer an alternative estimate of only 3 percentage points.

I too am astounded that the revised consumption profile created by correcting the treatment of durables can account for a 36% change in the estimate of the integral in equation (KS) (from 72% of the total to 46%), especially since expenditures on durables amount to well under 20% of consumer spending. It would be useful to learn more about these calculations, especially about the nonrobustness to which K&S allude. But I am not persuaded by K&S's alternative calculation — which basically changes the question to: What is the share of life-cycle accumulation not held in the form of durables in total wealth exclusive of durable? I think the question they started with is much the more interesting and wish they would stick to it.

Since the gap between 3% of wealth and 26% of wealth is huge, and since controversy seems to swirl around this calculation, this would seem a ripe area for further research — by Modigliani, by K&S, or by someone else. Until this further research is done, I declare this issue nonjudiciable.[7]

Where do we end up?

The two gaps that remain at the end of this attempted reconciliation depend critically on who is right about consumer durables. If Modigliani's 26 percentage point adjustment is accepted, we are left with:

SHARE OF INHERITANCE IN WEALTH

direct measurements		*K&S residual method*
conventional	K&S	
20%	18–34%	30–46%,

depending on how we treat accumulated interest on inheritances. In that case, there is not much left to argue about, given the inherent inaccuracies in each approach. We would conclude, with Modigliani, that life cycle accumulation exceeds inherited wealth.

But if K&S's 3 percentage point adjustment for durables is accepted, we have instead:

SHARE OF INHERITANCE IN WEALTH

direct measurements		*K&S residual method*
conventional	K&S	
20%	18–34%	53–69%.

In that case, the first gap (which started as $(52 - 20 = 32)$ is essentially gone.

But the second gap (which started at $81 - 52 = 29$, or more) is even bigger than when we started. We could then rephrase the nagging question raised by K&S's original paper as follows: if 31–47% of wealth is life cycle wealth and 18–34% is inherited, where does the rest come from?

K&S's 1981 paper suggested that a large volume of intergenerational transfers go unmeasured in survey data. And in this reply they re-emphasize that their 19% estimate for life cycle wealth was the highest of several alternatives. They conclude that 'life cycle considerations can account for only a small part of aggregate capital accumulation.' Modigliani trusts the inheritance data more than K&S's integrals and suspects that life cycle wealth is underestimated. He concludes that 'the available evidence consistently rejects the conclusion of K&S.'

I do not claim to know who is right. But the fact that age–consumption profiles resemble age–earnings profiles makes me hesitant to attribute the entire gap to an underestimate of life cycle saving — especially in view of the troubles the life cycle model has encountered when confronted with longitudinal data, some of which are cited in K&S's reply. Modigliani clearly has no such hesitation. The key question, of course, is whether the resemblance between $C(t)$ and $E(t)$ survives the correction for durables and the reclassification of spending on young people as consumption of their parents.

I am in no position to answer it.

Notes

1. K&S also note that alternative assumptions produce figures as high as 63%.
2. I apply the 47% correction factor only to the direct estimate of inherited wealth. Modigliani applies it also to the residual estimate obtained by subtracting estimated life-cycle wealth from total wealth. His procedure applied to my calculation would take the 72% figure down to 38%.
3. The Ando–Kennickell paper cited by Modigliani uses identity (M).
4. Modigliani's calculation in his Section VIII is similar in spirit. But his is based on a steady-state assumption about bequests while mine is based on optimizing behavior.
5. The time profile of earnings is highly relevant to the time profile of $W(t)$, but it does not effect the derivative $dW(t)/dW(0)$ as long as labour supply is inelastic. Hence no assumption about earnings growth is necessary.
6. K&S raise the possibility that I understated the bequest motive by a factor of four in my book, since I used the survey evidence that inheritances account for no more than 20% of total wealth. If I quadruple the weight on bequests, 0.83 and 0.03 rise to 0.86 and 0.11.
7. Larry Kotlikoff informs me that there are cross-sectional data on holdings of durable goods available for use in such a study.

Equal vs. Unequal Estate Sharing

3 Inheritance and Inequality within the Family: Equal Division among Unequals, or do the Poor Get More?

NIGEL TOMES
University of Western Ontario

> I have made thousands of wills and settlements, and not one in a hundred was based on any principle, but that of equal partition.
>
> Nassau Senior *Fortnightly Review* Oct. 1877

> I am aware that some of my children are more endowed with worldly goods than some of the others, but my love for all of my children is equally great and abiding. In spite of what appear to be disparities in the above bequests and devices, the memory of a fond mother . . . is bequeathed equally to all of you.
>
> The will of Fanny F——, file No. 13-1971,
> Queens County (NY) Surrogate's Court, 1971,
> quoted by Rosenfeld (1979) 53

It has long been recognized that the institution of the family may be an important determinant of inequality in consumption, income, and wealth, and the reproduction of this inequality in successive generations — that is, social mobility (Knight (1921) 374–5). Further, induced changes in the allocation of resources between family members may countervail public policies directed towards reducing inequality and increasing social mobility through redistributive taxation and compensatory health and education programs (Becker and Tomes (1976, 1979)). It is important, therefore, both at the theoretical and empirical levels, to examine the role of the family in the generation and perpetuation of inequality within the existing social order. Conceptually there are two dimensions to this problem: First, between families, higher-income and more educated parents may transmit more income and learning or earning skills to their children; second, within a family, unequal parental contributions to different children may reinforce inequality between siblings if larger transfers are made to the child with greater earning ability, or differential transfers may reduce inequality within the family if low-ability children are compensated in the form of larger transfers than their better-endowed siblings. This paper is concerned with this second intrafamily dimension of inequality which has received less attention in the literature. Specifically, I examine the family decision concerning the size and distribution of inherited material wealth. Theoretical predictions and empirical results are presented relating to the following questions:

1. What determines the inheritance system chosen by decedents? That is,

when do heirs inherit equal shares, when unequal shares are in the parent-donor's estate?

2. When unequal division takes place, do unequal bequests of material inheritance compensate or reinforce differences between siblings in ability and earnings?

The answers to these questions shed light on the underlying parental preferences concerning inequality between their offspring — whether the allocation of expenditures on children's human capital is viewed differently from the allocation of material wealth, and the degree of substitutability between the economic status of siblings — that is the extent of parental aversion to inequality between children.

That the division of the parental estate may have important consequences for inequality is demonstrated in recent theoretical models (Stiglitz (1969), Blinder (1973)) and simulation studies (Pryor (1973), Blinder (1976)), which examined the effects of alternative inheritance rules and also savings rates and marriage customs on wealth inequality. In both approaches alternative inheritance rules governing the division of estates among heirs have powerful effects on the distribution of wealth. Both Stiglitz (1969) and Pryor (1973) demonstrate that in their models under 'plausible' assumptions, equal division of wealth amongst heirs leads asymptotically to an egalitarian distribution of wealth. In contrast a primogeniture rule, whereby all wealth is inherited by the eldest child or son, results in a distribution of wealth displaying marked inequality. A general conclusion of the simulation studies of Blinder (1976) and Pryor is that, given less than perfect assortative mating of spouses, the more unequal the division of inheritance amongst heirs, the greater the inequality in wealth (Blinder (1976) 617). Moreover, Blinder has concluded that the more equally estates are divided the more rapid is wealth equalization on the path to steady-state equilibrium (Blinder (1973) 623–4).

These models are deficient in that alternative inheritance rules, such as equal division and primogeniture have been introduced as a *deus ex machina* due to legal statute or social custom, rather than as the result of explicit utility maximization. Since rules determining the distribution of parental wealth are assumed independent of the circumstances of the heirs, these authors conclude that unequal division increases wealth inequality. Theoretical models recently proposed by Behrman *et al.* (1982) and Menchik (1980), which assume that parental preferences concerning inheritance division are independent of preferences regarding earnings inequality have this implication, and therefore provide a rationale for the earlier simulation studies.

In contrast, Becker and Tomes (1976) and Shorrocks (1979) assume that parents are concerned about the lifetime consumption or income of children and therefore conclude that unequal bequests may reduce inequality in consumption and total (human and material) wealth, since the larger inheritance of the poor child compensates for unequal abilities and human capital investment. Since these alternative models have strikingly different implications for the effects of unequal inheritance shares, it is important to devise empirical tests which discriminate between alternative models. This task is undertaken in the present paper.

Empirical evidence on the division of estates in the contemporary US has been notable by its absence. However, two recent studies have produced striking evidence that equal division is the predominant inheritance pattern. Brittain (1978, 42–6) analysed the division of a sample of estates from the Cleveland, Ohio area in 1964–5. Brittain found some evidence of sex discrimination in favour of sons (p. 45), but concluded that the evidence is 'consistent with generally equal division among siblings' (p. 45, n. 47; see also p. 43, n. 42; p. 44, n. 43).

Menchik (1980) reached the same conclusion from his study of large Connecticut estates probated in the 1930s and 1940s. He concluded that equal division is the rule, regardless of sex or birth order. In these data the incidence of equal division was marked. For example, of the 173 two-child families, in 62.5% of cases both children received exactly equal bequests and in 70.5% of cases equal or almost equal division occurred (Menchik (1980)). Thus it would appear that in the US equal division is the prevailing inheritance practice (i.e., Nassau Senior was right, not withstanding the idiosyncracies of the likes of Fanny F——). This evidence suggests that inheritance does not reduce intrafamily inequality and offers support for the models of Behrman *et al.* (1982) and Menchik (1980) in which parental preferences concerning bequests are independent of the economic status of recipients.

However, in contrast to Brittain and Menchik, other studies of inheritance have reported a considerably lower incidence of equal division. Wedgwood found in his study of large English estates in 1924–5 that 'equal division was not the general rule among rich testators . . . frequently . . . the lion's share of the estate went to one son — usually, but not always, the eldest' (Wedgwood (1929) 148).

More recently, the Royal (Diamond) Commission on the Distribution of Income and Wealth (1977) analysed the pattern of inheritance in a sample of estates in excess of £15 000 probated in England and Wales in 1973. They reported that 'inequality in the division of property among children is a noteworthy feature of the overall pattern of wealth transmission' (p. 179). In over half the cases division was unequal. Moreover the data 'suggest that where inequality of division occurs, its impact is quite pronounced' (p. 179). For example, in *all* two-child families the most favoured child received 62% of the total bequest to children, implying that when unequal division actually occurred, the most favoured child received on average 74% of the total bequest to children, in contrast to the 26% share received by the least favoured child (pp. 178–9).

Evidence of unequal division is not limited to the UK. In an American context two studies conducted by lawyers indicate significant departures from equal division. Ward and Beuscher (1950) analysed a sample of Wisconsin estates for various years 1929–44. In 80% of cases where the decedent was testate, the inheritance pattern deviated substantially from the distribution under the law of intestate succession, which embodied equal division between children. However, little detail is provided on the nature of this deviation.

The findings of Dunham (1963) for a sample of 1953 and 1957 Cook County, Illinois estates are more illuminating. When the decedent left no surviving spouse, Dunham found that 69% of testate cases (40% of all estates) 'avoided the equality principle of the intestate succession laws . . . the modal form is that of varying the shares of children so that they do not share equally' (p. 254). These studies call into question the findings of Menchik and Brittain, that equal division is the predominant inheritance pattern in the contemporary US. This paper re-examines the empirical evidence concerning the incidence of equal division, using the same data set as Brittain and finds that unequal division occurs quite frequently. Evidence is also presented that unequal bequests to children are compensatory in that low-income children receive a larger inheritance of material wealth, than their high-income siblings.

The remainder of the paper proceeds as follows. Section I presents a theoretical model of family bequest behaviour in which intergenerational transfers take the form both of human capital investments and bequests of material wealth. We examine under what conditions parental expenditures compensate or reinforce differences in ability and the 'cross-sib' effects of the ability of one child on parental expenditures on siblings. Section II presents the alternative 'separable earnings-bequest' model and shows how this can be distinguished empirically from the model of Section I. Section III reports empirical results.

I   A model of family bequest behaviour

In order to emphasize the potentially important role of the family in the inter-generational transmission of resources, I make a number of restrictive assumptions:

1. All human capital investment is financed within the family. Capital markets are therefore assumed imperfect in that they do not permit loans on the basis of expected future earnings.
2. The costs of investment in the human capital of the young are borne by parents either in the form of direct expenditures or the foregone contributions of the young to family resources during the investment period.
3. Contracting and enforcement costs are sufficiently high to prohibit loans within the family, both between parents and children and between siblings.[1] Under this assumption both parental expenditures on children's human capital and bequests of material wealth, represent intergenerational transfers.

I assume that parent-child transfers, both of material wealth and human capital, are motivated by altruism in that children's lifetime permanent income (or equivalently wealth) enters, together with own consumption, in the parents' utility function. In general this utility function can be written as:

$$U = U(y, I_1, \ldots, I_n) \tag{1}$$

where y is the lifetime consumption of parents and $I_j (j = 1, \ldots, n)$ represents the lifetime permanent income (wealth) of the jth child. The number of children (n) is assumed exogenously determined and with little loss of generality we set $n = 2$. In order to abstract from preference-induced inequalities between children the utility function (1) is assumed to be characterized by 'child neutrality' — that is the marginal utility of each child's income is the same for all children, when their incomes are equal. Formally, the utility function has the separability property:

$$\frac{\partial U/\partial I_i}{\partial U/\partial I_j} \gtreqless 1 \text{ as } I_i \lesseqgtr I_j. \tag{2}$$

In addition I shall assume that the utility function (1) is 'isoelastic', so that (1) is of the form:

$$U = \frac{y^{1-\lambda}}{1-\lambda} + \frac{I_1^{1-\gamma} + I_2^{1-\gamma}}{(1+\delta)(1-\gamma)} \lambda, \qquad \gamma > 0. \tag{1$'$}$$

This formulation assumes that the elasticity of substitution between the lifetime incomes of heirs is constant. In the special case of $\lambda = \gamma$, the utility function is homothetic with equal elasticities of substitution between all commodities. Finally, if $\lambda = \gamma = 1$ the utility function is Cobb–Douglas.

In equation (1)$'$ $\delta \geq 0$ is the rate of time/generation preference reflecting the degree of parental altruism.

Children's lifetime income (wealth) is derived from human capital (h_i) and inherited material wealth (g_i); that is,

$$I_i = wh_i + (1+r)g_i = \frac{\beta_i x_i^{1-\eta}}{1-\eta} + (1+r)g_i \tag{3}$$

where w is the lifetime wage per unit of human capital. Measuring the stock (h_i) in terms of lifetime income we normalize $w = 1$. $(1+r)$ is the constant lifetime income per unit of material wealth. The human capital production function embodied in the RHS of (3) specifies human wealth as a (constant elasticity) function of a single aggregate input (x_i), exhibiting decreasing returns to scale (i.e., $1 > \eta > 0$). The parameter β_i represents the ith child's 'ability' or efficiency in translating inputs (x_i) into lifetime income. In addition, we also use this parameter to represent differences across families in the ability of parents to produce human capital in their children. Thus greater parental ability in producing, learning or earning skills in their children is represented by a proportional increase in the efficiency parameters for all children in the family.

Assuming that all parent-child transfers of material wealth take the form of parental bequests,[2] the parental lifetime income constraint is:

$$I_p = \begin{cases} y + p(x_1 + x_2) + 2g & \text{(4a)} \\ \\ y + p(x_1 + x_2) + (g_1 + g_2) + C. & \text{(4b)} \end{cases}$$

This constraint captures some essential features of the inheritance process in North America and many other countries. If the parent makes no will, the intestate distribution laws of succession in all 50 states provide for equal division (Wypyski (1976)) (i.e., $g_1 = g_2 = g$ in (4a)). On the other hand, if the donor incurs the cost of creating and executing a will ($C \geq 0$), an unequal division can be achieved (i.e., $g_1 \neq g_2$ in (4b)). In addition we impose the solvency constraint: $g_i \geq 0$ ($i = 1, 2$), that is parents cannot bequeath debt to their heirs. In (4) parental consumption (y) is the numeraire and p is the price of the aggregate input into the production of children's human capital.

Maximizing the parental utility function (1)′ subject to (3) and (4) yields the first-order conditions:

$$\frac{y^{-\lambda}}{\Psi} = 1 \tag{5}$$

$$\frac{I_i^{-\gamma}}{(1+\delta)\Psi} = \frac{p}{\beta_i x_i^{-\eta}} = p_i \qquad (i = 1, 2) \tag{6}$$

$$\frac{I_1^{-\gamma} + I_2^{-\gamma}}{2(1+\delta)\Psi} \leq \frac{1}{1+r} \tag{7a}$$

$$\frac{I_i^{-\gamma}}{(1+\delta)\Psi} \leq \frac{1}{1+r} \qquad (i = 1, 2) \tag{7b}$$

where Ψ is the marginal utility of parental income. The first-order conditions (5) and (6) give rise to three possibilities regarding parental bequests of material wealth: zero bequests to all children if parents are at a corner solution; positive bequest, G, with equal division ($g_1 = g_2 = G/2$); positive bequest $G - C$, with unequal division ($g_1 > g_2$ if $\beta_1 < \beta_2$).

If the donor chooses unequal division, human capital investment will take place up to the point where the marginal cost of investing in each child is equated to the marginal cost of making a bequest: children have the same lifetime income. Alternatively, if the donor makes no will, the estate is equally divided and the marginal rate of substitution between heir's incomes is equated to the marginal rate of transformation via human capital investment (6): equal bequest gives the child with higher ability a higher lifetime income.

I shall now proceed to examine these alternatives.

1.1 Zero bequests

If the inequalities in (7a) and (7b) hold when evaluated at the points $g = 0$ and $g_i = 0$ (all i), respectively, then parental bequests will be zero. In this case all intergenerational transfers occur in the form of human capital. Under these circumstances the marginal rate of substitution between the incomes of children is given by:

$$\left(\frac{h_i}{h_j}\right)^{-\gamma} = \left[\frac{\beta_j}{\beta_i}\left(\frac{x_i}{x_j}\right)^{\eta}\right] = \left(\frac{x_i/h_i}{x_j/h_j}\right) = \left(\frac{p_i}{p_j}\right) \tag{8a}$$

which implies:

$$\ln\left(\frac{h_i}{h_j}\right) = \frac{1}{1-\gamma}\ln\left(\frac{x_i}{x_j}\right). \tag{8b}$$

The relationship between the human wealth of siblings and the inputs to children's human capital depends on the (constant) relative inequality aversion of parents (γ) or stated differently, the elasticity of substitution between children's income in the parental utility function ($\sigma = \gamma^{-1}$). If this elasticity exceeds unity ($\gamma < 1$) relative lifetime incomes (earnings) will be positively related to relative inputs, the converse if the elasticity of substitution is below unity ($\gamma > 1$). Given measures of lifetime earnings and inputs for a sample of siblings who do not inherit material wealth, estimates of the substitution/inequality aversion parameter can be obtained.

The relationship between lifetime incomes and inputs in (8b) results from the response of parents to differences in the ability of siblings. A 'reinforcement' strategy takes place if greater ability of a child is associated with greater parental inputs — expenditures on that child. Conversely, 'compensation' occurs if greater ability is associated with decreased parental inputs, since in this case the effects of lower ability are partially offset by parental investment. The relationship between relative inputs and the relative ability of siblings, which reflects the underlying investment strategy adopted by parents is given by:

$$\ln\left(\frac{x_i}{x_j}\right) = \left[\frac{1-\gamma}{\gamma + \eta(1-\gamma)}\right]\ln\left(\frac{\beta_i}{\beta_j}\right). \tag{9}$$

In general this relationship depends on the parameters of both the utility function and the human capital production functions (η). However, in terms of parental compensation versus reinforcement, the crucial parameter is the elasticity of substitution ($\sigma = \gamma^{-1}$). If this elasticity exceeds unity ($\gamma < 1$) the inequality in parental inputs reinforces differences in ability, since larger human capital inputs are allocated to the more able child. The relative lifetime incomes of high- and low-ability siblings therefore exceed their relative abilities. In the limit when substitutability is perfect, the first-order conditions (6) imply that sufficiently more is invested in the more able child so as to equate the marginal costs of investing in both children — the 'efficient' solution which maximizes the total return to the resources allocated to children. In this special case the investment strategy of the family in the absence of both extra- and intrafamily loans duplicates the perfect capital market solution, which would obtain if either of these types of loans were available at constant cost. However, when such loans are not available and there is less than perfect substitutability, efficiency will be sacrificed for a reduction in inter-sibling inequality.

If the elasticity of substitution is unity — the parental utility function is Cobb–Douglas — inputs are independent of children's ability and parents adopt a 'neutral' strategy of neither reinforcing nor compensating for differential ability. Relative incomes of high to low ability siblings therefore equal relative abilities.

If the elasticity of substitution is less than unity ($\gamma > 1$) low-ability siblings are compensated in the form of greater parental inputs than their advantaged siblings so that the relative income of high- and low-ability siblings are less than their relative abilities. In the limit with fixed proportions (Rawlsian preferences), the incomes of siblings are equalized and unequal inputs fully offset unequal abilities.

The foregoing analysis suggests that in general, when families face imperfect capital markets the lifetime incomes and human capital investment received by individuals will depend not only on their own ability and determinants of 'opportunities' (parental income and family size), but also on the ability of their siblings. The human capital literature, by assuming maximization by an isolated individual and/or perfect capital markets, has neglected this potentially important determinant of human capital accumulation. In contrast, sociologists have occasionally considered such interdependencies through the influence of older siblings as 'role models' for younger kin in the status attainment process (e.g., see Jencks (1972) 296, 346–9). The present model, which places the human capital decision in a family context, allows for reciprocal interactions between siblings through the effects of their abilities on the income-possibility frontier faced by the parents.

The relationship between parental inputs to the human capital of the ith child (x_i) and the abilities of children is given by the expression:

$$\mathrm{d} \ln x_i = \frac{(1-\gamma)}{\theta \Lambda_i} \left[(\Lambda_i - 1) \mathrm{d} \ln \beta_i - \left(\frac{\beta_j}{\beta_i} \right)^{\frac{1-\gamma}{\theta}} \mathrm{d} \ln \beta_j \right] \tag{10}$$

where $\theta = \gamma + \eta(1-\gamma) = \gamma(1-\eta) + \eta > 0$,

and $\Lambda_i = \left[(1-\eta)^{-1} \left(\frac{p}{\beta_i} \right)^{(1-\gamma)/\gamma} \frac{\theta}{\gamma} x_i^{\frac{\theta}{\gamma}-1} + \left(\frac{\beta_j}{\beta_i} \right)^{(1-\gamma)/\theta} + 1 \right] > 1.$

It has also been assumed that $\lambda = \gamma$ in (1)', that is, the elasticities of substitution between the arguments in the utility function (1) are equal. From (10) it can be seen that:

$$\frac{d \ln x_i}{d \ln \beta_i} \gtrless 0 \text{ as } \gamma \lessgtr 1, \qquad \frac{d \ln x_i}{d \ln \beta_j} \lessgtr 0 \text{ as } \gamma \gtrless 1. \tag{10}'$$

If the elasticity of substitution between siblings' incomes exceeds unity ($\gamma < 1$), parents adopt a 'reinforcing' strategy — an increase in own-ability leads to greater inputs into human capital, while an increase in the ability of the sibling results in reduced parental inputs. In this situation it 'pays to have dumb sibs' in that, other things equal, a reduction in the ability of one's siblings leads to a reallocation of parental expenditures in one's own favour. Thus high-ability children gain and low-ability children are penalized by the presence of siblings with differential ability in comparison to a situation where each child had a sibling of equal ability. Since increased own-ability leads to additional parental contributions it follows that if $\gamma < 1$, the elasticity of income with respect to own-ability will exceed unity and income is predicted to be inversely related to sibling's ability.

In the opposite case, if parental aversion to inequality exceeds unity (i.e., $\sigma = \gamma^{-1} < 1$), parental inputs are compensatory. An increase in own-ability leads to reduced human capital inputs and the cross-sib effect is positive. In this context it 'pays to have smart sibs' in that, other things equal, having more able siblings leads to greater parental contributions. In contrast to the previous case, low-ability children benefit, and correspondingly high-ability children are penalized by the presence of siblings with differential ability — as compared to a situation where each child had a sibling of equal ability. When parental inputs are compensatory, children's income will be positively related both to own-ability (with an elasticity less than unity) and sibling's ability.

In the special case of a Cobb–Douglas utility function (1), the level of inputs allocated to each child are independent of their abilities. The level of inputs and the lifetime incomes of children are therefore independent of whether their siblings were of high or low ability, that is, 'cross-sib' effects are zero.

These results are strengthened by isolating the effects of unequal abilities on parental contributions, holding constant the mean income of children. In the present model, when bequests are zero, the allocation of resources between the generations depends in a simple manner on the inequality of ability between children. Specifically, an increase in the inequality of ability between siblings, holding the mean income of children constant, increases (decreases) parental expenditures on children if the elasticity of substitution ($\sigma = \gamma^{-1}$) is less (greater) than unity. This result allows us to state the previous conclusions in a more general manner. If the elasticity of substitution is less than unity (i.e., parental compensation), the high-ability child will be worse off and the low-ability child better off in terms of lifetime incomes, than if all children were of equal ability at a level that would imply the same average level of income for children in the two situations (unequal versus equal abilities). Conversely, if the elasticity of substitution exceeds unity (i.e., parental reinforcement), holding the mean income of children constant, an increase in the inequality of abilities makes the high-ability child better off, and the low-ability child worse off, in terms of their lifetime income. In the special case of Cobb–Douglas preferences, not only the allocation of inputs between children, but also the distribution of family resources between the generations is independent of the distribution of ability between children.

The predicted relationship between parental contributions and the inequality in children's ability, is in principle testable. For example, if the genetic component of ability is significant, inequality in ability would be less for identical (mz) twins than for fraternal (dz) twins or brothers. Conversely, in families containing adopted children, inequality in ability would tend to exceed that of other families. Therefore, if parents compensate low ability children ($\sigma < 1$) we predict that, *ceteris paribus*, families with greater inequality in children's ability (e.g., families with adopted children) will allocate more expenditures to children's human capital and parental consumption will be lower, than in other families. In the opposite case, if parents reinforce differences, greater parental expenditures would be made in families with less inequality in children's ability (e.g., families with identical (mz) twins).

1.2   Positive bequests, equal division

If the marginal rate of substitution between an additional dollar income to each child and \$2 parental consumption (the LHS of (7a)) exceeds the cost of material wealth transfers (the RHS of (7a)) at the point $g_1 = g_2 = 0$, and the utility from a strategy of equal division exceeds that of unequal division, equal bequests will be made to each heir (i.e., $g_1 = g_2 = g > 0$). The magnitude of bequests is determined by the condition (7a) — that the average marginal utility of children's income is proportional to the marginal cost of material wealth transfers: $(1+r)^{-1}$. From (5) this implies: $p_1 + p_2 = 2(1+r)^{-1}$; that is, the average marginal cost of investing in the human capital of heirs is equated to the marginal cost of material wealth transfers. However, in general the marginal utilities of heir's consumption and the marginal costs of human capital investment (p_i) will differ between heirs. The marginal rate of substitution between heirs' incomes is given by (6):

$$\left(\frac{I_i}{I_j}\right)^{-\gamma} = \left[\frac{h_i + (1+r)g}{h_j + (1+r)g}\right]^{-\gamma} = \frac{p_i}{p_j} = \frac{x_i/h_i}{x_j/h_j}. \tag{11}$$

Defining $B_k = (1+r)g/h_k$ $(k = i, j)$ and solving (11) yields:

$$\ln\left(\frac{h_i}{h_j}\right) = \frac{1}{1-\gamma} \ln\left(\frac{x_i}{x_j}\right) + \frac{\gamma}{1-\gamma} \ln\left[\frac{1+B_i}{1+B_j}\right] \tag{12a}$$

$$\simeq \frac{1}{1-\gamma} \ln\left(\frac{x_i}{x_j}\right) + \frac{\gamma(1+r)}{1-\gamma} \cdot \frac{g(h_j - h_i)}{h_i h_j} \tag{12b}$$

where (12b) uses the approximation $\ln(1+B_k) \simeq B_k$ if B_k (the ratio of income from material wealth to income from human capital) is small. Equations (12a and b) give the relationship between lifetime earnings (human wealth), inputs, inherited material wealth, and human wealth inequality, under equal division. These expressions include equation (8b) as a special case since with zero bequests to all heirs, the last term in (12a) and (12b) is zero. This result is intuitive since zero bequests are a special case of equal division in which each heir inherits zero. In both cases of equal division (zero and positive bequests to heirs), the relationship between human wealth, inputs and inherited material wealth yields information concerning parental preferences regarding income inequality among heirs.

When all heirs inherit equal (positive) bequests of material wealth it becomes more difficult to determine when parents will pursue strategies which compensate or reinforce differences in ability. The reason is that the level of human capital investment in each child and bequests are jointly determined. It is possible to show that under these conditions, greater ability is more likely to be associated with greater parental human capital inputs, than when bequests were zero. For example, if parental preferences are Cobb–Douglas, an increase in the ability of the more able child leads to greater human capital contributions to that child. In contrast, when bequests are zero in the Cobb–Douglas case, parental inputs are independent of ability. Thus it appears more likely that own-ability and human capital inputs will be positively correlated (i.e., differences in own-ability are 'reinforced'), when material wealth is bequeathed equally to heirs. The 'cross-sib' effect also differs under equal division. In particular, regardless of the inequality aversion of parents, greater ability on the part of one child will lead to greater human capital investment in other siblings. The reason for this positive 'cross-sib' effect, is the predicted relationship between the parental bequest to each heir and the ability of children. In particular there is a strong presumption that an increase in the ability of either heir reduces the material wealth bequest to both heirs. It can be shown that an increase in the ability of the less able child necessarily reduces bequests. An increase in the ability of the more able child will have the same effect, provided the inequality in heirs' human capital is not 'large'. Since greater ability is expected to be associated with reduced bequests to all heirs, the positive 'cross-sib' effect implies that additional human capital inputs at least partially offset the effects of having higher ability siblings.

Under equal division, the bequest to heirs depends upon the inequality in abilities among children. Holding parental income and the mean income of heirs constant, an increase in the inequality of abilities between siblings will raise the bequest to the next generation if parental aversion to inequality is 'large'. In the special case of Cobb–Douglas preferences, it can be shown that increased inequality in ability will raise parental bequests, if the inequality in siblings' earnings is 'small'. Therefore, with Cobb–Douglas preferences, commencing from an initial position of equal abilities, an increase in inequality unambiguously increases parental bequests. Since bequests are equal to each heir, the increased bequests represent a greater percentage income increase to the heir with lower income and therefore reduce the relative income inequality between heirs. Thus, if either parental aversion to inequality is large, or the inequality in abilities is small (for the Cobb–Douglas case), the response of parents to increased inequality in ability, of increasing bequests to heirs partially offsets the direct effect of unequal abilities on the inequality of lifetime incomes.

1.3 Positive bequests, unequal division

If the marginal rate of substitution between an heir's income and parental consumption exceeds the marginal cost of material wealth transfers (evaluated at the point of zero bequests to that heir) and the utility of a smaller total bequest unequally divided amongst heirs exceeds that of a larger bequest shared equally by heirs, then parents will make unequal bequests.[3] In this case the relevant first-order conditions are (5), (6) and (7b). From (7b) it can be seen that if each heir receives a positive bequest, the marginal utilities of heirs' incomes are equalized, which by the assumption of 'neutrality' (2) implies equality of heirs' incomes. Therefore all differences in ability are offset by unequal parental expenditures, which equalize the incomes of siblings.

The fact that intergenerational transfers are made both in the form of human capital investment and (unequal) bequests of material wealth, provides an additional degree of freedom enabling the family to achieve both efficiency and equity between siblings. Equations (6) and (7b) imply that expenditures on heirs' human capital are determined by the optimum investment criterion that the marginal cost of such investment (p_i) equal the (constant) marginal cost of material wealth transfers. The optimal expenditure on the ith heir's human capital is:

$$x_i = \left[\frac{\beta_i}{p(1+r)} \right]^{1/\eta}. \tag{13}$$

This level of investment is independent of parental income and positively related to the heir's ability — implying that parental human capital expenditures reinforce ability differences. Further, since the marginal cost of investing in the ith heir's human capital is independent of the ability of the jth heir

$(j \neq i)$, the 'cross-sib' effect is zero for human capital investments. Thus we predict that when unequal bequests are made to heirs the human capital of individual children will be independent of the sibling's abilities and the addition of sibling's ability to a lifetime earnings regression should provide no additional explanatory power.[4] This result contrasts with the earlier predictions of such interdependencies for the cases of zero bequests and equal division.

In contrast to human capital inputs, the bequest to the ith heir depends on parental income and the ability of siblings, in addition to own ability. If all commodities in (1) are equal substitutes (i.e., $\lambda = \gamma$), material wealth transfers to the ith heir are given by the expression:

$$g_i = \frac{1}{\phi} \{I_p - c - \tilde{p}[\phi \beta^{1/\eta} - \eta(\beta_i^{1/\eta} + \beta_j^{1/\eta})]\}, (i = 1, 2) \tag{14}$$

where: $\tilde{p} = p^{1 - \frac{1}{\eta}}(1 + r)^{-1/\eta}(1 - \eta)^{-1}$

and $\phi = 2 + (1 + \delta)^{1/\gamma}(1 + r)^{1 - \frac{1}{\gamma}}$

and ϕ^{-1} is the share of each heir's (discounted) lifetime income in 'family resources'. From (14) it can be seen that an increase in own-ability reduces the heir's inheritance — that is, bequests of material wealth are compensatory.

$$\frac{dg_i}{d\beta_i} = \frac{-h_i}{\beta_i(1 + r)\eta}\left(1 - \frac{\eta}{\phi}\right) < 0 \quad \text{since } \phi > 2, \quad 1 > \eta > 0. \tag{14a}$$

The 'cross-sib' effect is positive — that is, other things being equal, the more able one's siblings, the larger the bequest one inherits. These predictions contrast with the reinforcement of own-ability and zero cross-sib effect for human capital inputs. Consequently, the positive relationship between heir's income and ability implied by the reinforcing inequality in human capital investments is partially offset by the inverse relationship between material wealth transfers and ability.

An increase in the ability of the ith child reduces the marginal cost of intra-marginal transfers in human capital form to that child, but leaves the cost of marginal transfers unchanged. Greater child ability therefore implies greater family resources, which increases the demand for all superior commodities — parental consumption and the lifetime income of heirs:

$$\frac{dI_i}{d\beta_i} = \frac{dI_j}{d\beta_i} = \frac{h_i}{\beta_i\phi} > 0 \tag{14b}$$

$$\frac{dy}{d\beta_i} = \frac{(1 + \delta)^{1/\gamma}(1 + r)^{1 - \frac{1}{\gamma}}}{\phi} \frac{h_i}{\beta_i(1 + r)} > 0. \tag{14c}$$

Since greater ability on the part of one heir is predicted to increase the income of siblings and parental consumption, it follows that total parental expenditures on that heir must be compensatory, since resources are reallocated towards other family members.

$$\frac{d[px_i + g_i]}{d\beta_i} = \frac{-h_i}{\beta_i(1+r)}(1 - \phi^{-1}) < 0. \tag{15}$$

Therefore although the parental allocation of investment expenditures reinforce initial ability differences, unequal bequests of material wealth are sufficiently compensatory to dominate this effect and produce a compensatory relationship between total parents expenditures and ability which equalizes the lifetime incomes of heirs. This result — that unequal bequests to siblings reduce the intrafamily inequality in lifetime incomes contrasts with the conclusion of the simulation models referred to earlier (Pryor (1973), Blinder (1976)) in which unequal division increases inequality both within and across families.

From the above analysis (14*b*) it can be seen that an increase in the ability of an heir leads to an equal increase in the incomes of all heirs and therefore leaves income inequality among heirs unchanged. More generally it can be shown that, if all heirs receive positive bequests, the incomes of heirs, parental consumption, and total parental expenditures both on human capital inputs and material wealth bequests are independent of changes in the distribution of siblings' ability which leave the mean income of heirs unchanged. Therefore under unequal division, in contrast to the earlier cases of zero bequests and equal division, both the intergenerational distribution of resources (between parents and children), and the inequality in sibling's lifetime incomes are independent of the distribution of ability among progeny.

II   The separable earnings-bequest model

It is useful to contrast the model presented in the previous section with the 'separable earnings-bequest' model recently proposed and estimated by Behrman *et al.* (1982) and implicit in Menchik's study of inheritance (Menchik (1980)). In that model, rather than being concerned solely with the wealth or lifetime income of children, the lifetime earnings and material wealth of heirs enter separately in the parental utility function. Thus parental preferences concerning the inequality of life earnings are assumed independent of preferences regarding the division of material wealth between heirs. Assuming that the parents utility function is isoelastic and both the earnings branch and the bequest branch are characterized by neutrality (defined equivalently to (2)), this utility function can be written as:

$$U = \frac{y^{1-\lambda}}{1-\lambda} + \frac{h_1^{1-\pi} + h_2^{1-\pi}}{(1+\delta)(1-\pi)} + \frac{[(1+r)g_1]^{1-\mu} + [(1+r)g_2]^{1-\mu}}{(1+\delta)(1-\mu)}. \tag{16}$$

Maximizing this utility function subject to the parental income constant ($4b$) and the human capital production function in (3) yields the first-order conditions for an interior solution:

$$\frac{h_i^{-\pi}}{(1+\delta)\Psi} = \frac{p}{\beta_i x_i^{-\eta}} = p_i \, (i=1,2); \tag{17a}$$

$$\frac{[(1+r)g_i]^{-\mu}}{(1+\delta)\Psi} = \frac{1}{1+r} \quad (i=1,2) \tag{17b}$$

where Ψ is the marginal utility of parental lifetime income. These first-order conditions have a number of implications. First equation ($17a$) implies:

$$\ln\left(\frac{h_i}{h_j}\right) = \frac{1}{1-\pi}\ln\left(\frac{x_i}{x_j}\right). \tag{18}$$

This is identical in form to equation ($8b$) for the earlier model when bequests are zero. Here the parameter π measures the parental aversion to relative life earnings inequality. Second, since preferences regarding bequests are symmetric and independent of earnings, ($17b$) implies that bequests will always be equally divided (i.e., $g_i = g_j = g$), regardless of the relative abilities and life earnings of siblings;[5] that is, the 'poor' (low-ability) sibling does not inherit more. This contrasts with the earlier model which predicts equal division only if the utility loss from the costs of executing a will outweighs the utility gain from doing so, and predicts a 'compensating' unequal division of material wealth if the costs of making a will are sufficiently low. This suggests two tests of the model proposed in Section I against the alternative separable earnings-bequest model. First, the latter model implies that in cases of unequal division the distribution of bequests is independent of the ability and therefore earnings of heirs. In contrast the model of Section I implies that when unequal division occurs bequests to siblings are inversely related to the own-ability and earnings of siblings. Second, the model of Section I implies that when equal division occurs, the relative life earnings of siblings depends not only on relative inputs, but also on the bequest to heirs (($12a$) and ($12b$)). In contrast, the separable earnings-bequest model implies that in cases of equal division, relative earnings depend only on relative inputs and are independent of the bequest to heirs (18). Empirical results of both these tests are reported in the next section.

Before proceeding it is worth noting some additional implications of the separable earnings-bequest model. Although the model predicts that intra-family bequests are independent of ability, interfamily bequests will in general depend on children's ability. For example in the CES case in which all the commodities in (16) are equal substitutes, greater children's ability will increase (decrease) bequests to heirs if the elasticity substitution is less (greater) than unity. More generally, if $\mu \neq \pi$, ($17a$) and ($17b$) imply:

$$\ln g = \frac{-(1-\pi)}{\mu} \ln h_i + \frac{1}{\mu} \ln x_i + \frac{1}{\mu} \ln \left[\frac{p(1+r)^{1-\mu}}{1-\eta} \right] \quad (i=1,2).$$

$$(19)$$

Holding human capital inputs (x_i) constant, bequests will be positively (negatively) related to earnings, if the elasticity of substitution between children's earnings (π^{-1}) is less (greater) than unity. Thus, the observation that *across households*, bequests are inversely related to the recipient's family income (Tomes (1981)) is not necessarily inconsistent with the separable earnings-bequest model. However a similar finding within families would constitute evidence against that model.

Since the relevant elasticity of substitution may lie on either side of unity it follows that across families, differences in bequests may be either compensating or reinforcing. In contrast the model of Section I implies that across families, holding parental income constant, differences in bequests will always be compensatory.

III   Empirical results

The data used in this study derive from a 5% random sample of 659 estates probated in the Cleveland, Ohio area in 1964–5 (Sussman, *et al.* (1970)). Surviving kin and other heirs were interviewed, including 657 sons and daughters of the decedents. Information was obtained on the total estate, usual occupation, education, and other characteristics of the deceased and on the inheritance, income, education, and other characteristics of the surviving kin.

A number of points concerning these data are worth making. First, since the data represent a random sample of probated estates, they are more representative of wealth-leavers than samples drawn from inheritance-tax payers in which only the upper tail of the distribution of terminal wealth is represented. In the present data the mean gross estate of decedents is approximately \$12 000 and the mean inheritance received by each child approximately \$4 000. Second, this sample is (to my knowledge) unique in providing information on the economic status of heirs. Third, although these data have previously been employed by other investigators to estimate cross-section regressions (Brittain (1978), Adams (1980), Tomes (1981)) little use has been made of the family structure inherent in the data, which permits the estimation of intrafamily regressions. In this section we use these data to analyse the incidence of equal and unequal division, to examine the determinants of inheritance shares and to estimate the elasticity of substitution between the lifetime incomes of siblings.

3.1   The incidence of unequal division

Of the 659 estates in the sample, 31.3% were intestate, and under the Ohio statute governing intestate succession were equally divided in cases where the decedent was survived by more than one child. Of the remaining 453 cases, 98 (21.6%) had no surviving children, so that there were 356 testate estates with at least one surviving child. In 81.5% of these cases there was equal division and in only 18.5% of cases unequal division. However this figure is misleading because it includes as equal division cases where all children inherited zero.[6] Excluding cases where all children inherited the lower limit value it is possible to calculate that between 53.2% and 72.4% of testate estates were equally divided and therefore 27.6% to 46.8% were unequally divided amongst heirs.[7] Of course this range is quite wide. Information on the surviving children provides some additional insight. Of the 605 sons and daughters for whom data are available, 25.5% were intestate heirs and therefore, in the presence of other surviving children, would have inherited equally with their siblings. 10.9% of children who would have inherited under the intestate distribution were disinherited under the decedent's will. Of course their siblings may also have been disinherited, possibly in favour of the decedent's surviving spouse.

In order to gain further insight into the incidence of unequal division, the subsample of surviving children was analysed for whom information is available on two or more heirs from the same family. This subsample consists of 346 heirs from 137 families, an average of 2.5 heirs per family. Table 3.1 reports the percentage of heirs inheriting equally and unequally with their siblings. Among all heirs 41.6% inherited exactly equal shares and 63.3% received approximately equal shares — that is, the amounts inherited differed by less than $500 from the mean of heirs (line 1). However, this figure includes cases where all heirs inherited the lower limit value. Excluding such cases, the incidence of unequal division becomes more important (line 2) — only 21% of heirs received exactly equal shares and 78.9% of heirs inherited amounts that differed from their siblings. In about half the cases (49.6%) the amounts inherited deviated from the mean by over $500. Restricting our attention to two-heir families (lines 3–4) leads to a similar picture.

The results for this sample differ markedly from those reported by Menchik (1980). In his sample of large Connecticut estates for two-heir families, 62.5% of heirs inherited exactly equal amounts. In contrast in these data amongst two-heir families, where at least one heir inherited in excess of the minimum, only 22.2% of heirs inherited exactly equal shares.

Table 3.2 reports the shares of heirs in the total bequest to children for two-, three-, and four-heir families. In two-heir families, where at least one heir inherited in excess of the minimum, the 'most-favoured heir' inherited 68.5% of the bequest to children, compared to the 31.5% share of the

TABLE 3.1. The incidence of unequal division
The % of heirs inheriting equally and unequally with their siblings

Sample	Exactly equal division (%)	Unequal division (%)	Approximately equal division (%)	Unequal division (%)
1. All cases with information on multiple heirs ($n = 346$)	41.6	58.4	63.3	36.7
2. As in line 1, excluding cases where all heirs inherited 'zero' ($n = 256$)	21.1	78.9	50.4	49.6
3. As in line 1 for two heir families ($n = 178$)	52.8	47.2	66.3	33.7
4. As in line 2 for two heir families ($n = 108$)	22.2	77.8	44.4	55.6

Notes: 1. Line 2 excludes cases where all heirs received the lower limit value of $250.
2. Approximately equal division includes as equal division cases where the amounts inherited by heirs differed by less than $500 from the mean inheritance of all heirs in the family. Unequal division (in column 4) therefore refers to cases where the inheritances received by children in two-heir families differed by more than $1000.

TABLE 3.2. Inheritance shares

Sample	Mean total amount inherited by heirs ($)	Inheritance shares (%)				G	$\overline{CV}$
		S_1	S_2	S_3	S_4		
1. Two-heir families ($n = 89$)	7 916	61.2	38.8			0.112	0.227
2. Two-heir families ($n = 54$)	8 715	68.5	31.5			0.185 (0.05)	0.374 (0.145)
3. Three-heir families ($n = 28$)	14 840	42.3	33.2	24.6		0.118 (0.097)	0.289 (0.241)
4. Four-heir families ($n = 13$)	8 680	47.3	23.7	16.1	12.9	0.277	0.560 (0.159)

Notes: 1. Line 1 includes cases where all heirs inherit the lower limit value. Lines 2–4 exclude such cases.
2. n is the number of families.
3. S_1–S_4 are the mean inheritance shares received by heirs, ranked from the largest share to the smallest share.
4. G is the Gini coefficient calculated from the average inheritance shares. $\overline{CV}$ is the mean of the intrafamily coefficient of variation for n families.

'least-favoured' heir (line 2). This implies that in those families where unequal division actually occurred, the most-favoured heir received 73.8% of the bequest to children, compared to the 26.2% share of the least-favoured heir. These figures correspond fairly closely to the findings of the UK Royal Commission on the Distribution of Income and Wealth Study. However these results contrast with Menchik's study of large Connecticut estates in which the most-favoured heir in two-heir families received on average 55% of the bequest to children (Menchik (1980) 310).

The final columns of Table 3.2 report two measures of the intrafamily inequality in bequests to children: the Gini coefficient (G) calculated from the average shares of heirs and the mean intrafamily coefficient of variation ($\overline{CV}$). Also presented in parentheses are the corresponding figures reported by Menchik (1980, 311 table 4). In all cases, the inequality measures in this sample are larger than those in Menchik's study. For example, the Gini coefficients for two-heir families in lines 1 and 2 are 224% and 370% of that reported by Menchik (0.05). Similarly the mean intrafamily coefficient of variation for all families which appear in rows 2 to 4 ($n = 97$) is 0.395, compared to the value of 0.178 reported by Menchik (1980, 311 table 4). Thus in the present sample of small estates, the intrafamily inequality in bequests is markedly higher than in Menchik's study. One possible explanation of this difference is that material wealth transfers in the form of *intervivos* gifts are more important among large estates. It is possible that large wealth-holders use unequal gifts to achieve unequal transfers of material wealth, while small wealth-leavers use unequal bequests to achieve this objective. Unfortunately data on gifts are too sparse to permit tests of this conjecture.

3.2 The determinants of inheritance shares

Having examined the occurrence and magnitude of unequal division, we turn to examine the determinants of inheritance shares and to answer the question posed in the title: do the poor inherit more? Table 3.3 reports intrafamily inheritance regressions. Lines 1 to 4 report regressions for all heirs for whom we have data on more than one heir per family. In lines 5 to 8 attention is restricted to the sample of heirs who inherited unequal amounts. The dependent variable is the inheritance received by the heir as a deviation from the mean of all heirs in the family. Several alternative functional forms were estimated using the level or natural log of the inheritance or the inheritance share ($\times$ 100) as the dependent variable. Not surprisingly we lack a comprehensive measure of heirs lifetime earnings or ability. However we do have a measure of the monthly family income of heirs. This measure coded on an annual basis[8] and holding other control variables constant, is used to measure lifetime earnings. The available control variables are the age (AGE), sex (SEX), and marital status of the heir (SINGLE and divorced or separated DIV/SEP), the sex of the principal 'bread-winner' (SEXB), a

TABLE 3.3. Intrafamily inheritance regressions
Dependent variable: inheritance received by heir (\$000s) INH or SHARE

Reg. No.	INCOME	AGE	SINGLE	DIV/SEP	SEX	SEXB	NLABINC	NEMPL	R^2	n
1. INH	−0.815† [4.528]	0.178 [3.296]		−10.218 [2.690]		0.743 [1.564]	−1.258 [1.847]		0.108	346
2. INH	−0.0044 [3.425]	0.168 [3.111]		−10.019 [2.606]		−0.775 [1.611]	−1.141 [1.658]		0.086	346
3. ln INH	−0.042† [1.747]		0.446 [2.823]		−0.172 [2.275]				0.063	346
4. SHARE	−1.556† [2.077]		12.433 [2.528]	−27.204 [1.737]	−5.609 [2.361]	−5.208 [2.343]		−3.761 [1.877]	0.090	346
5. INH	−0.994† [3.808]	0.285 [3.239]		−11.513 [2.327]		−1.816 [2.349]			0.140	202
6. INH	−0.005 [2.874]	0.296 [3.326]	3.793 [1.712]	−11.299 [2.263]		−1.836 [2.351]			0.128	202
7. ln INH	−0.051† [1.474]		0.940 [3.165]		−0.200 [1.563]	−0.160 [1.553]			0.102	202
8. SHARE	−1.865 [1.725]		22.706 [2.473]		−8.092 [2.042]	−9.173 [2.455]		−5.868 [1.728]	0.123	202

Notes:
1. All variables entered as deviations from the family mean.
2. Constant omitted from all regressions.
3. Absolute value of t-statistic reported in parentheses below coefficients.
4. INCOME: level coded in \$, † indicates ln INCOME in \$00's.
5. INH inheritance coded in \$000s, <\$500 coded as 0.250; SHARE = (bequest to heir/total bequests to all children) × 100.
6. SINGLE coded 1 if heir's marital status single, 0 otherwise; DIV/SEP coded 1 if heir's marital status divorced or separated, 0 otherwise. SEX (sex of heir), SEXB (sex of principal 'bread winner' in heir's family): 1 if female 0: if male.

dummy variable for the presence of non-labour income (NLABINC) and the number of family members employed (NEMPL). All variables are entered as deviations from the family means. The regression results, after eliminating variables which are not close to significance at the 10% level, appear in Table 3.3.

In these regressions the significance of the control variables is influenced by the functional form of the dependent variable and whether the INCOME variable is entered as level or natural log. However, regardless of the specification, the income variable enters with a negative coefficient and, with few exceptions, is significant at the 5% level. The income coefficient is smaller than might have been expected, since it implies that a $5000 difference in the family income of siblings in a two-heir family leads to a $400 difference in bequests (line 1) or less than a one percentage point difference in shares (line 4). One possible explanation is that parents are at a 'corner' bequeathing zero to one (or more) heirs. Another is that if the transitory income component is sizeable, the correlation between the income measure employed here and life earnings will be substantially below unity, leading to smaller estimated coefficients.

The regressions for the subsample of heirs who received unequal inheritances (lines 5 to 8) require little additional comment, except to note that the income coefficients tend to be slightly higher than in the corresponding equations in lines 1 to 4. Also, introducing a 'lambda' variable (Heckman (1976)) to allow for possible sample selection bias, left the coefficients unaffected and the lambda variable was never significant — suggesting that sample selection bias is not a problem in the present context.

These regressions provide evidence that parental bequests of material wealth are compensatory in that poor children receive larger bequests than their advantaged siblings. Thus within the family, unequal bequests reduce the inequality in post-bequest incomes as compared to the pre-bequest income inequality. This provides evidence in favour of the model of Section I and leads us to reject the separable earnings-bequest model of Behrman *et al.* (1982) and Menchik (1980).

3.3 Estimates of the elasticity of substitution

Under the maintained hypotheses concerning the constant elasticity functional forms of the utility function (1)' and the production functions, the elasticity of substitution/relative inequality aversion parameter can be estimated from the subsample where heirs inherit equally. Table 3.4 presents 2SLS estimates of equation (12a), which incorporates equation (8b) as a special case, when bequests to children are zero. Lines 1 and 2 report regressions using all cases of equal division, including cases where all heirs received the minimum bequest. Lines 3 and 4 introduce the lambda variable to take

TABLE 3.4. Estimates of the elasticity of substitution within the family Equation (12a) sample: heirs inheriting equally with their siblings

Reg. No.	ln SCH	Z	ln AGE	SEX	NEMPL	NLABINC	LAMBDA	n
1. ln INC	−1.984	−79.483	0.425	0.166	−0.313	−0.149		144
	[0.829]	[2.465]	[0.445]	[0.925]	[1.619]	[0.579]		
2. ln INC	−1.845	−76.926	0.469	0.162	−0.302	−0.158	−0.020	144
	[0.783]	[2.443]	[0.498]	[0.910]	[1.585]	[0.617]	[0.100]	
3. ln INC	−6.296		0.263	−0.025	−0.433	−0.745		90
	[1.835]		[0.192]	[0.079]	[0.926]	[0.847]		
4. ln INC	−6.298		0.263	−0.026	−0.433	−0.744	−0.005	90
	[1.824]		[0.190]	[0.080]	[0.921]	[1.834]	[0.021]	

Notes: 1. All regressions included a constant, not reported.
2. Absolute value of *t*-statistic reported in parentheses below coefficients.
3. All variables (except Z and LAMBDA) entered as deviations from the family mean.
4. $Z = \ln[1 + B_i)/(1 + \bar{B})]$ where $B_i = (1 + r) \mathrm{INH}_i/\mathrm{INC}_i$, $\bar{B} = (1 + r)\overline{\mathrm{INH}}/\overline{\mathrm{INC}}$ where INH_i and INC_i are the inheritance and income of the *i*th heir. $\overline{\mathrm{INH}}$, and $\overline{\mathrm{INC}}$ are the family means.
5. LAMBDA computed variable from an auxiliary probit regression (see Heckman 1976).
6. All equations estimated by 2SLS with ln SCH (years of schooling) and Z as endogenous variables. Exogenous variables: SINGLE, DIV/SEP, SEB and various interaction terms between exogenous variables. Additional exogenous variables in equations (1) and (2) are the exogenous variables used in the probit regressions in Table 3.5.

account of possible sample selection bias; however, once again this variable is not significant.

In lines 1 and 2 the schooling variable is negative, but not significant. The inheritance variable Z which measures the relative importance of material wealth to human wealth, also enters with a negative sign and is significant by conventional standards. The significance of this variable offers additional evidence in favour of the model specified in Section I, since in the alternative separable earnings-bequest model, the relative earnings of siblings are predicted to be independent of the bequest to children (equation (18)).

Although the value of γ implied by the coefficient on Z depends on the value imputed to the rate of return on material wealth (r), the negative coefficients on the schooling and inheritance variables both imply that the relative inequality aversion parameter exceeds unity — that is, the elasticity of substitution between siblings' lifetime incomes is less than unity.

In the regressions for the subsample in which all heirs have received the minimum inheritance (lines 3 and 4) the schooling variable enters with a negative coefficient which is significant at the 7% level. The negative coefficient implies that the relative inequality aversion exceeds unity and is of the order of 1.16, or stated differently, the elasticity of substitution between siblings' incomes is approximately 0.86.

The finding that the elasticity of substitution between siblings' incomes is less than unity implies that amongst families making no material wealth bequests, parental expenditures on children's human capital are compensatory in that more able siblings receive smaller parental transfers. In this case also the 'cross-sib' effect is positive so that high-ability children are penalized and low-ability children gain from the presence of siblings of differential ability, in comparison to a situation in which each had a sibling of equal ability. In addition, it implies that holding the mean income of children constant, parental contributions to children are positively related to the inequality in children's ability.

IV Conclusion

A simple model of human and non-human bequest behaviour where parents take into account only the total lifetime income (earnings and inheritance) of children is shown to lead to three alternate solutions: no material bequest, positive bequest with equal division among heirs, and positive bequest with unequal division. The model takes into account the fact that unequal division can occur in the US only if parents make a will at a certain cost.

In each of the three cases, the model has specific predictions concerning the determinants of human and material transfers and their effect on the income inequalities of children: a crucial question is whether they reinforce or compensate initial differences in the abilities of siblings. The answer often depends on a key parameter, the relative inequality aversion of parents.

These predictions are compared with those of a separable earnings-bequest model where parents care independently for the earnings and the bequest of their children. Reinvestigation of the Sussman *et al.* (1970) Cleveland sample shows ample evidence in favour of the first model based upon childrens' total lifetime income. This result and an estimated value of the relative inequality aversion of parents superior to 1 characterize a situation where total parental transfers have a *compensatory* influence on children income both *within* and *across* families.

One additional result in favour of the new model relates to the choice of equal division versus unequal division. An interesting finding of Table 3.5, consistent with the program of equations (4) to (7) is indeed that, other things being equal, the greater the inequality in siblings incomes (measured by the squared deviation from the family mean) the lower the probability that heirs will inherit equally.

Notes

1. If the investment period of specialization in the acquisition of human capital by the young extended until the decease of parents, this would rule out repayment by the young of parental loans. I further exclude the possibility of intersibling loans and transfers of the type considered by Becker and Tomes (1976).
2. Elsewhere I have shown that in the context of uncertainty and imperfect annuity markets, parental lifetime gifts to children may well be zero for the majority of households, whereas 'contingent' bequests motivated by altruism would still occur (Tomes, 1981). Also, Ishikawa (1974) has shown that in the presence of imperfect capital markets, individual making small transfers of material wealth would prefer a regime of bequests at decease to one of gifts at some specified date during their lifetime.
3. I assume throughout this section that there is an interior solution in which positive bequests are made to *all* heirs.
4. In the absence of omitted variables.
5. Of course dropping the assumption that the bequest-branch of the utility function is symetric and introducing differences in 'tastes' would result in unequal division. See Shorrocks (1979).
6. Because the inheritance data is coded to the nearest $1000 it is not possible to distinguish between inheritances of zero and < $500. I have followed Brittain in recoding a 'zero' inheritance as $250 (i.e., 0.250) the midpoint of the interval [0, $500].
7. The original investigators reported that equal division occurred in 57% of cases in which a testate decedent was survived by adult children (Sussman *et al.*, 98–101).
8. The reported monthly family income which was originally coded in categories was recoded on an annual basis using interval midpoints for the closed intervals and using the (estimated) mean of a Pareto distribution for the open-ended interval.

TABLE 3.5. Probit regressions: the probability of equal division
Dependent variable: probability heir inherited equally with his/her siblings 1: if equal, 0: unequal

Reg. No.	Inequality Variables				Characteristics of decedent							L	n
	lnINCS$_q$	SINGLES$_q$	lnAGE·SEX	SINGLE·SEX	MARRIED	AGE	ORIGINWE	KNIDS	SCH	lnINC	TOTEST		
1.	−0.045	2.214	3.414	4.996	0.161	−0.022	−0.695	0.193	−0.065			57.218	346
	(−0.018)	(0.856)	(1.321)	(1.933)	(0.062)	(−0.009)	(−0.269)	(0.074)	(−0.025)				
	[−1.970]	[2.465]	[1.834]	[3.520]	[1.018]	[−2.387]	[3.271]	[3.821]	[2.047]				
2.	−0.044	2.150	3.450	4.823	0.202	−0.020	−0.688	0.184		−0.129		57.911	346
	(−0.017)	(0.832)	(1.335)	(1.866)	(0.078)	(−0.008)	(−0.266)	(0.071)		(−0.050)			
	[1.893]	[2.401]	[1.851]	[3.412]	[1.248]	[2.201]	[3.242]	[3.637]		[2.187]			
3.	−0.047	1.749	3.090	4.650	0.124	−0.017	−0.647	0.181			−0.012	61.017	346
	(−0.018)	(0.663)	(1.172)	(1.764)	(0.047)	(−0.006)	(−0.245)	(0.069)			(−0.005)		
	[1.982]	[1.959]	[1.629]	[3.275]	[0.798]	[1.786]	[3.042]	[3.557]			[2.023]		
3.	−0.051				−0.589		−0.801	0.156	0.215	−0.595		50.502	256
	(−0.012)				(−0.139)		(−0.189)	(0.037)	(0.057)	(−0.141)			
	[1.659]				[2.698]		[2.693]	[2.195]	[1.990]	[2.826]			

Notes: 1. All regressions included a constant, not reported.
2. ( ): partial derivative evaluated at the mean of independent variable.
3. [ ]: absolute value of *t*-statistics.
4. $L = (−2)$ ln Likelihood Ratio.
5. Sample lines 1–3 all heirs, line 4 all heirs receiving inheritance in excess of minimum.
6. lnINCS$_q$ is the squared deviation of lnINC from mean of heirs. SINGLES$_q$ squared deviation of SINGLE from mean of heirs. SINGLE·SEX: interaction between SINGLE and SEX (both in within family deviation form).
7. MARRIED 1: decedent survived by spouse, 0 otherwise; ORIGINWE 1: decedent's origin western Europe, 0: otherwise; NKIDS Number of decedents surviving children; lnINC: ln of constructed measure of decedent's annual income ($00s) (see Tomes 1981); TOTEST: Total Gross Estate of decedent ($000s).

References

Adams, J. D., 'Personal Wealth Transfers', *Quarterly Journal of Economics* **95** (1980), 159–79.

Becker, G. S. and N. Tomes, 'Child Endowments and the Quantity and Quality of Children', *Journal of Political Economy* **84** Part 2 (1976), S143–S162.

—— and ——, 'An Equilibrium Theory of the Distribution of Income and Intergenerational Mobility', *Journal of Political Economy* **87** (1979), 1153–89.

Behrman, J., R. A. Pollack, and P. Taubman, 'Parental Preferences and Provision for their Progeny', *Journal of Political Economy* **90** (1982), 52–73.

Blinder, A. S., 'A Model of Inherited Wealth', *Quarterly Journal of Economics* **87** (1973), 608–26.

——, 'Inequality and Mobility in the Distribution of Wealth', *Kyklos* **29** (1976), 607–38.

Brittain, J. A., *Inheritance and the Inequality of Material Wealth* (Brookings, Washington, 1978).

Dunham, A., 'The Method, Process and Frequency of Wealth Transmission at Death,' *University of Chicago Law Review* **30** (1963), 211–56.

Ishikawa, T. J., 'Imperfections in the Capital Market and the Institutional Arrangement of Inheritance', *Review of Economic Studies* **41** (1974), 383–404.

Jencks C., *Inequality: a Reassessment of the Effect of Family and Schooling in America* (Basic Books, New York, 1972).

Heckman, J. J., 'The Common Structure of Statistical Models of Truncation, Sample Selection and Limited Dependent Variables and a Simple Estimator for Such Models', *Annals of Economic and Social Measurement* **5** (1976), 475–92.

Knight, F. H., Risk, Uncertainty and Profit, (1921; Reprint: Kelley and Millman, New York, 1957).

Menchik, P. L., 'Primogeniture, Equal Sharing and the US. Distribution of Wealth', *Quarterly Journal of Economics* **94** (1980), 299–316.

Pryor, F., 'Simulation of the Impact of Social and Economic Institutions on the Size Distribution of Income and Wealth', *American Economic Review* **63** (1973), 50–72.

Royal Commission of the Distribution of Income and Wealth, Report No. 5, Third Report on the Standing Reference, (1977).

Sheshinski, E. and Y. Weiss, 'Inequality Within and Between Families', *Journal of Political Economy* **90** (1982), 105–27.

Shorrocks, A. F., 'On the Structure of Intergenerational Transfers Between Families', *Economica* **46** (1979), 415–25.

Stiglitz, J. E., 'Distribution of Income and Wealth among Individuals', *Econometrica* **37** (1969), 382–97.

Sussman, M. B., J. N. Cates, and D. T. Smith, *'The Family and Inheritance'* (Russell Sage Foundation, New York, 1970).

Tomes, N., 'The Family, Inheritance and the Intergenerational Transmission of Inequality', *Journal of Political Economy* **89** (1981) 928–58.

Wedgwood, J., 'The Influence of Inheritance on the Distribution of Wealth: Some New Evidence', *Economic Journal* **38** (1929), 38–55.

Wypyski, E. N., *The Law of Inheritance in all Fifty States* (Third edition, Dobbs Ferry, Oceana Publication, New York, 1976).

4   Unequal Estate Division: Is it Altruism, Reverse Bequests, or Simply Noise?

PAUL L. MENCHIK
Michigan State University

The purpose of this paper is to report some new evidence on estate division, and draw out some of the implications of the evidence for both the modelling of the wealth distribution and the testing of alternative hypotheses of the bequest process. In addition the paper shows how seemingly disparate results may not in fact be different but rather may be rationalized by response error. This second point is shown using a replicate probability sample that points to a significant difference between the pattern of answers concerning what people say they inherited compared to what the administrative records show they were bequeathed.

The results presented here are inconsistent with (a) one version of an altruist model, (b) the family as an annuity model, and (c) a 'manipulative' model of bequests. The results however, are not inconsistent with a separable earnings-bequest model that has recently been advanced. The paper starts with a discussion of the importance of bequeathing patterns in distributional modelling and in some recent theorizing about the bequest process. Next the recent evidence is presented. Thirdly, the new data and their implications are presented and discussed, and a concluding section follows.

I   The importance of estate division

1.1   Distributional modelling

Economists interested in understanding the determinants of the distribution of wealth have constructed rather elaborate intergenerational models (see, e.g., Blinder (1973), Pryor (1973), Meade, (1964 and 1976), Atkinson (1983)). The results of these models are sensitive to assumptions about marital choice, fertility, saving behaviour, and inheritance patterns, specifically estate division among children. An assumption of primogeniture, in which one child (not necessarily the oldest male) inherits the entire parental estate, generally results in more wealth inequality than an assumption of more equal division.

As elaborate as these models are, however, they neglect the reality that since sibling's earnings vary, unequal estate division may in fact result in *less* wealth inequality than equal division. The insight provided by Becker (1974) and Becker and Tomes (1976) (see also Behrman, Taubman and Pollak,

(1982), and Sheshinski and Weiss, (1982)) is that parental transfers, in the form of gifts and bequests, can be either attenuating, reinforcing, or have a neutral effect on wealth inequality within a family and in an economy. If parents bequeath more to their less able children (where ability is earnings ability) unequal estate division may result in a more equal wealth distribution than would result under equal division. The Becker and Tomes (B–T) model explicitly predicts this compensating behaviour by parents, 'differences in parental contributions would fully compensate for differences in endowments' (Becker and Tomes (1976), S153). Indeed, the model predicts that gifts and bequests would be used to perfectly equalize the income of siblings (p. S154).[1] If B–T are correct, the disequalizing effect of unequal estate sizes might be less than previously thought. For example, Davies' (1982) simulation study shows that compensatory bequeathing behaviour would, if practiced, reduce the disequalizing effects of bequests. Given, however, the highly skewed distribution of estate wealth and the positive correlation of earnings across generations (Taubman (1978)), inheritance would still disequalize *among* families in the same generation (see Menchik (1979)).

Inherited wealth should also influence intergenerational mobility as well as intragenerational equality. Inheritance should tend to hamper the wealth mobility that *would* occur due to the partial regression to the mean in labour earnings across generations. A second paper by Becker and Tomes (1979) makes the point that if parents have a collection of offspring that is less able than they, the parents will spend less, and bequeath more than they otherwise would in order to dampen the intergenerational regression to the mean in lifetime resources or consumption. Also, the model presented by Menchik and David (1983) shows that those children who earn more by virtue of their length of schooling, would also be more likely to receive a financial inheritance. Hence bequests are received by children whose parents could afford the optimal (with regard to the children) investment in schooling, while children from poorer families would receive fewer years of schooling and no bequests. This process also implies that inheritance augments the degree of intergenerational immobility as well as adding to the degree of intragenerational inequality. In this paper the evidence presented is confined to the finding of facts regarding estate division. The estimation of parameter values in this field is an important topic that has been neglected,

While it may be possible to make plausible guesses about the likely ranges of coefficients, the microeconometrics of the distribution of income and wealth is an underdeveloped field.

Atkinson (1983), 195.

1.2 Distinguishing between alternative models of bequests

In recent years there has been an increase in interest in understanding the bequest process, perhaps due to research suggesting that bequest saving constitutes the major share of total savings (Kotlikoff and Summers (1981)[2] or due to the great social security debate (Barro (1978)). Evidence on estate division may be useful in attempting to distinguish among alternative theories of the bequest process. As mentioned above, the Becker–Tomes model predicts bequests to be an equalizing factor within families, a result that, if true, might have important implications for death tax policy purposes. The B–T model also has some rather far-reaching implications in another vein. Compensatory education programs, they claim, would be 'failures' (p. S156) since parents would respond to their compensated child's public benefits by withdrawing the parental time and money he/she would have received, giving it to other children or consuming it themselves, leaving only an increase in family income to show for the program.

According to Becker and Tomes, decisions about childrens' schooling, (which constitute a major determinant of earnings) are based solely on grounds of efficiency — an investment in a child's education is made if and only if the increase in the students lifetime earnings exceeds the marginal cost of the schooling. There is no attempt on the parents part to incorporate equality, or distributional, considerations into parental decisions regarding the schooling (and therefore earnings) of their children. Distributional adjustments are made by employing unequal bequests, with (assuming parents show equal concern among children) lower earning children receiving larger bequests than higher earning children.

A competing model has been presented by Behrman, Pollak, and Taubman, B–P–T (1982). In their separable earnings-bequest model, parents are permitted to make schooling decisions on their children's behalf based on both efficiency *and* equity considerations. B–P–T use twin data to determine if equity matters in schooling decisions. They find that equity does matter, parents will sacrifice some aggregate child earnings for a more equal distribution of earnings between siblings. After employing an assumption of separability in the bequest decision they analytically derive the result that equal concern implies equal estate division among children. Hence, the B–P–T model stands in sharp contrast to B–T since equity considerations are taken into account in schooling decisions and equal estate division is employed. In the B–T model only efficiency matters in schooling decisions and equity adjustments are relegated to differential bequests, with equal concern for children implying compensatory bequeathing practices.

A direct test of B–T requires data both on bequests to children and their lifetime relative earnings abilities. At the moment no data set that rich exists. An indirect test would be simply to determine how frequent unequal estate division is. Since earnings inequality among brothers is nearly as large as it is among non-related males (see note 1), the B–T model would require different sized bequests to children as the rule.

Evidence on estate division should allow us to test other theories of bequests. Suppose individuals do not derive utility from bequeathing, only from their own consumption. Risk-averse individuals, uncertain about the date of their own death, have an incentive to purchase annuities to insure themselves against the risk of living 'too long' and becoming penniless. Such an arrangement will allow them to consume all their wealth instead of dying with an 'unintended' bequest due to their risk aversion. Let us assume, however, that the annuity market is imperfect due to asymmetric information and adverse selection. Kotlikoff and Spivak, K–S (1981) argue that the family will construct its own annuity market. Parents will 'purchase' annuities from their children with the price, a bequest at death, paid in return for lifetime support of the elderly parent. A possible problem with this theory is that selfish parents will cheat on the deal, i.e., they will consume both their own wealth and their children's annuity, leaving them nothing at death.[3] Let us assume, however, that non-altruistic parents will behave honestly. The prevalence of this family annuity behaviour should be observable from estate division data. Suppose a widowed parent has more than one child. Is there anything in the model that predicts the children would offer equal sized annuities and receive equal benefits (take equal sized gambles)? On the contrary, if children had unequal earnings (or unequal lifetime wealth) and exhibited decreasing absolute risk aversion — a very weak condition,[4] the wealthier child would be more willing to engage in a gamble of a fixed size than a less wealthy child (Arrow (1970), 96). Consequently, the wealthier child would provide greater support to the parents, and receive a larger bequest as payment, than the poorer siblings. Hence, the K–S model predicts unequal bequests to children, with the wealthiest child systematically receiving more.

It is possible, of course, that children may support their parents with contributions of time as opposed to money. If so, the theory of comparative advantage would suggest that the low-wage child would spend the bulk of the time with the parent. Again, unequal division is implied, this time with the low-wage child receiving the largest share of the bequest, and should be observed in the data. The evidence shows that the overwhelming majority of children caring for elderly parents are daughters and should therefore inherit more than their brothers.[5] Only in the knife-edge case, a coincidence really, in which the wealthy child contributes money and the low-wage child contributes time of equal value would the observation of equal estate division fail to belie the K–S hypothesis.

A third theory of bequests might also be tested using estate division data. It has been argued that the prospect of receiving a bequest might be used by the testator to control and manipulate the behaviour of potential heirs (see the 'power' model of Thurow (1975), and the 'merit good' model of Becker (1981)). The most recent embodiment of this approach is in Bernheim, Shleifer, and Summers, B–S–S (1985). According to their model, parents will use the threat of disinheritance, playing off one potential heir against another, to acquire the attention and 'services' from the beneficiaries. By playing this game the testator can 'appropriate all the surplus generated from the testator–beneficiary interaction'. Once again the testator has an incentive to cheat the heirs, since the testator is indifferent to the heirs' welfare. Let us again assume honest testator-parents. In the B–S–S model there is no reason to expect equal bequests (unless children are identical). Indeed, if disinheritance were a credible threat, one might expect to see it exercized against wealthier (or less manipulable) children. Consequently, the observation that estates are generally divided equally among children (especially since we know that daughters do more for their parents than sons) would tend to belie the B–S–S model as well as the B–T and K–S models. In addition, the explanations of estate division presented in wills may help us to test the relevance and prevalance of the above theories. What does the recent evidence show?

II Patterns of estate division — the recent evidence

Two recent studies appear to come to different conclusions regarding the frequency of unequal estate. Research by this author (Menchik (1980)) examines 379 large Connecticut estates in which (a) there were two or more children and, (b) bequests were made to at least one child. Family size was determined both by probate and inheritance tax data, and cross-checked with obituary column information. It was found that parents bequeathed equally by sex and by birth order. Since males earn more than females and first-born children have higher IQs and subsequent achievement than later-born siblings (Zajonc (1976), Zajonc and Marcus (1975), and Lindert (1977)) this is inconsistent with all three of the hypotheses discussed above. Estate division overall reveals a strong tendency toward equal division. For example, among two-children families (173 cases), 62.5% received exactly equal estates and 70.5% received almost equal (within one percent of equality) estates. A similar degree of equality is found when *intervivos* gifts are included in the bequest definition (p. 311). The coefficient of variation of intrafamily bequests is quite small, 0.178. Hence it was concluded that equal division among children is the rule.

Nigel Tomes (1981) using the data on Cleveland estates generated by sociologists Sussman, Cates, and Smith (1979), reports very different results for the 137 families in which information for more than one child is available (see also Tomes, Chapter 3, in this volume which offers greater detail on the results obtained from the Cleveland sample). He reports that exactly equal division is observed in 41.6% of the cases. However, this sample includes many 'corner solution' cases in which all children received a zero bequest. Excluding such cases equal division is observed in only 21.1% of the cases. (Tomes does report however that in about 50.4% of the cases approximate — here defined as within $500 of the mean — equality is observed). To contrast his results with mine, Tomes reports that among two-children families equality is observed in 22.2% and approximate equality in 44.4% (my figures were 62.5% and 70.5%). In addition, Tomes reported measures of intrafamily inheritance inequality, e.g. the coefficient of variation, that are significantly larger than those found in the Connecticut sample. Tomes states that at least in Cleveland equal estate division is *not* the rule.

Why do these studies come to such different conclusions? One possible explanation is the way in which the data were generated. The Connecticut study reports bequests (and gifts) made as recorded in the probate records. The Cleveland study records interviewee responses on the amount the subject *recalls* receiving. Using the names and family addresses obtained from the probate court, researchers sent questionnaires to the heirs, or contacted them in other ways, to inquire about the amount they recalled inheriting. If siblings were bequeathed the same amount but their responses contain some recall or response error, an equally divided estate will *appear* to be divided unequally. Consequently, the appearance of unequal division may simply be noise.[6] Another reason for suspicion regarding the response accuracy of this data set is suggested by an important internal inconsistency regarding intestacy.

When decedents fail to leave a will explicitly detailing the distribution of their estate among heirs they are said to have died intestate. In such a case, in the United States, the estate is divided according to the laws of intestacy that are in force in the decedent's state of residence. In Ohio, as in every state in the US, the fraction of the estate passing to children is divided equally among all living children. Hence in any subsample of estates, the proportion of cases in which equal division among children occurs must be greater than or equal to the proportion of intestate cases. [Equality could only occur if *every* testate estate employed unequal division.] In the Sussman *et al.* sample, it was determined from administrative records that 68.7% of all estates were testate implying an overall intestacy rate of 31.3%. Tomes (1981 and Chapter 3), relying upon response data, reports that in only 21% of a subsample of estates (in which there were two or more children and at least one child inherited a nonzero amount) was equal estate division among children followed. If the intestacy rate in this subsample is at all similar to (no more than ten percentage points below) the overall intestacy rate, Tomes' result could not be correct even if every testate estate was divided unequally, but would be a specious finding resulting from response error. Although it is plausible that the intestacy rate used in Tomes' subsample may be lower than the overall intestacy rate, the difference based upon other information in the Sussman book and upon my own research, is likely to be small, in the neighborhood of at most several percentage points.[7]

In order to confirm my suspicion that the difference between the Menchik and Tomes results is simply a consequence of response error in the Sussman data, I attempted to replicate the Cleveland sample.

III Replication and reconsideration of the Cleveland sample

To check the reported results on estate division in Cleveland, I travelled to Cleveland and drew a random sample of probate records over the same period as the Sussman sample, 9 November 1964 to 8 August 1965.

At first an exact match was planned, e.g., compare John Doe's questionnaire response on inheritance received to the amount his parent bequeathed to him as revealed in probate. However, an exact match was impossible since the original data, linking name to data record number, was destroyed. As a second best, I employed a strategy of an independent random sample of estates containing 269 cases in which the decedent had more than one child.[8]

Of the 269 estates in the replicate study, equal division was observed in 251, or 93% of the cases, as compared to 41.6% of cases reported by Tomes based on the Sussman data. The appropriate statistical hypothesis test concerning the difference between two proportions is the *t*-test.[9] The proportions are significantly different at a 0.99 level of significance level. Many cases, however, contained the corner solution of zero bequests to any child. These were composed of cases in which the bulk of the estate was left to the spouse or there was no wealth left after all debts were settled. If we only consider the 115 cases in which a positive amount was bequeathed to children, 84.3% of the cases exhibited exactly equal division and 87.8% approximate equality using the Tomes definition. These proportions are significantly greater than those he reported at the 0.99 confidence level for his sample size of roughly 100 cases. The intestacy rate of all sampled estates was computed to be 37.1% with an intestacy rate among the subsample of 115 computed to be 36.4%. Among those testate cases exactly equal division happened 75.3% of the time with approximate equality observed in 80.8% of the cases. Next it was found that estates were divided equally by sex, as they had been in the Connecticut sample. There were only seven estates in which a daughter was favoured over a son, and five in which a son was favoured over a daughter. Finally I examined estate division among two-child families in the replicate sample. While Tomes reported equal division in 22.2% of the estates in the Sussman sample, I found 87% of the 54 estates in the replicate sample (in which one or two children inherited anything) exhibited exactly equal division. In addition 88.8% in the replicate sample exhibited approximate equality, as compared to 44.4% in the Sussman sample. These differences are all statistically significant at the 0.99 level for the subsample size of 54 cases.

A person's will can be considered for his or her last exercise in preference revelation, and I read these results as saying that middle class testators in Cleveland prefer equal division even *more* strongly than the wealthy in Connecticut.

Although equal division was found in most of the replicate Cleveland sample, it may be useful to try to examine departures from equality to see how often, if at all, the B–T, K–S or B–S–S hypotheses are supported. To do this I read the wills. When parents bequeath unequally they often say why. (They never say why they bequeathed equally.) One testator left more to one child than others, stipulating that he was providing for his grandson. Another bequeathed less to one son who was a 'mental incompetent' confined to a State Mental Hospital. A third bequeathed equal amounts of cash to two daughters but left one a ring and the other silverware of unequal value. There was, however, a shred of support for the K–S or B–S–S hypotheses (in five out of 115 cases).

In one case the parent bequeathed the most to the child who, the parent says, supported him. In another case the favoured beneficiary was a daughter who lived with the decedent. In a third case a daughter was favoured 'for the kindness and care which she extended to me during my stay at her home.' In a fourth case two children were favoured 'In consideration of the care and companionship shown to me and my deceased wife.' In the fifth case two children were favoured because they 'furnished me a home' and were 'close in times of stress.' Information contained in the wills did not clearly reveal any evidence supporting the B–T hypothesis of compensating bequests.[10]

IV   Why equal division?

In this paper we have discussed a number of theories which, in general, predict that bequests made to children will not be equal. We have argued that a correct reading of the empirical evidence fails to support these theories. At this point it is fair to ask the author what he thinks might explain parents propensity to bequeath equally to children who are likely to be very different. I will supply several possible reasons for this behaviour, none of which, unfortunately, I find terribly convincing. The first reason ventured is one based upon cost, the cost of making an unequal bequest. This reason, also discussed in Tomes (Chapter 3), makes the case that parents would like to bequeath unequally (for altruistic or other reasons) but the high cost of leaving a will leads them not to since the additional benefits of bequeathing optimally (e.g. unequally) is less than the disbenefits of paying the transactions costs (legal fees) engendered when drawing up a will. Hence people die intestate, and since intestacy laws *mandate* (for unspecified reasons) equal division among children, estates are divided equally among children even though parents would rather not have it that way. The big problem with that argument is that the cost of having a will is negligible. The legal fees of having a will drawn up range from $15 to $35 (Sussman *et al.* (1970), 220) for an individual, a sum dwarfed by a mean gross estate of $12 000. In fact, the law does not even require a lawyer to write a will, the testator can write a will which, if witnessed, is legally valid. An economist observing that a minority of people die intestate must confront the prospect that intestate decedents essentially agree with the state's allocation of the estate among heirs. While it is certainly true that many people leave wills that mimic the intestate allocation to their children there are some additional good reasons for not dying intestate e.g. the allocation of the estate if the testator and the children are jointly killed in an accident.

One possible reason for equal division stems from the assumption that altruistic parents are not simply concerned with the welfare of their children but rather the collective welfare of entire family dynasty extending on forever. A parent may have two children whose relative ability can be ascertained. However, given imperfect assortative mating, luck, forces for regression to the mean, and the like, it may be impossible for parents to know even for a few generations into the future which child's line will be more needy. Risk-averse parents, facing an impossible task of predicting relative dynastic success will 'hedge' their bets by making equal bequests, just as risk-averse investors would hedge by diversifying investments.

A somewhat related theory would have it that the testator is concerned with endowing his line, his genes really, and will try to allocate his wealth to minimize the probability that his wealth will be held by a non-reproducing branch of his family tree. The idea is that as long as a carrier of the testator's genes lives he has a claim on immortality. If the testator knew which, if any, of his children's lines became defunct (did not reproduce) the testator would not bequeath to that child, giving that share to the others. The problem however, is that once again the testator may not know which child's line will end, so as in the previous case the risk-averse testator 'hedges' by bequeathing equally.

A possible problem with both of these 'uncertainty' models is that readily observable behaviour is in conflict with predictions from the model. For example, suppose a testator has a son with a large family and a childless daughter forty-five years of age. Since there is little question as to which line will end first the previous theory would predict a larger bequest to the son, but equal bequests is what is observed in these cases.

The only reason for equal division which to me seems even semi-plausible is one based upon non-pecuniary transaction costs. Only equality dispells the notion of favouritism among the children, a notion that may reduce the trust and cohesion found among siblings. Economists may liken this familial trust to a public good that can be dissipated by the suspicion of preferential concern. Parents recognize the benefits of intrafamily trust and cohesion, realize that unequal division may endanger its existence, and as a consequence strict neutrality in bequest behaviour becomes a firmly ingrained practice.

To sum up, I find that parents divide their estate equally in Cleveland, the reported finding to the contrary being a likely consequence of response error to questions about what heirs recall inheriting. A finding of generally equal division is important in modelling the dynamics of wealth distribution across generations. This finding is not consistent with the prediction of compensating bequests predicted by the Becker–Tomes model. It also is not consistent with the family annuity model of Kotlikoff and Spivak or the manipulative model of Bernheim, Schleifer, and Summers. There is a shred of support, based upon statements made in wills for the latter two hypotheses, but such behaviour is quite rare. The evidence in this paper is consistent with the separable earnings-bequest model of Behrman, Taubman, and Pollak. Lack of support for the Becker–Tomes hypothesis does not negate the possibility of altruism *across* generations, as Tomes (1981) correctly notes. Parents may choose to consume less and bequeath more if their children are *on average* low earners, but they bequeath equally to their children even if they are unequals.

Notes

1. If this was true the amount bequeathed would have to be enormous to equalize lifetime income since the average difference in earnings between brothers is 87% as large as the difference between random individuals (Olneck (1977)), and lifetime earnings dwarfs inheritance received for most people.
2. This result is vigorously disputed by Modigliani ((1983) and Chapter 1).
3. They might do this surreptitiously by taking a loan from a bank, using their house for collateral, and default on the loan at death. Since the bank has the prior legal claim to the house, the children will have been cheated. If the children legally purchase their parents' home, there will be no bequest that can be explained by the K–S model.
4. An attribute of the frequently used isoelastic utility function.
5. In one study of 96 elderly people being cared for by other family members, in 24 cases the 'caregiver' was a daughter or daughter-in-law, in *zero* cases the caregiver was a son or son-in-law, and in the remaining 72 cases the caregiver was the spouse (Chang (1984)).

   In a second study of over 100 cases of an elder living with an adult child, in which the child was 'responsible' for the household, it was reported that 94% of the caregivers were women (Steinmetz and Amsden (1983)). The sample care recipients included 86 mothers or fathers and 22 mothers or fathers-in-law.
6. Tomes (1981, n. 34) offers two alternative explanations for the difference in results. First, *intervivos* transfers more likely to occur with large estates, may be unequal so that total transfers (as opposed to bequests) would be unequal. Second, Sussman *et al.* report that estate redistribution was fairly common (e.g., 27% among the intestate estates (but *not* common in testate cases). Hence this *ex-post* redistribution would result in less equality among siblings than probate records show.

   The response to the first point is that one of my definitions of inheritance *includes* gifts that appear in the probate records, as required by Connecticut law. Measured inequality is no greater using this inclusive definition of inheritance than one counting only the amount bequeathed. Indeed the coefficient of variation using the inclusive definition is smaller, not larger, which suggests that some of the observed bequest inequality represents a final adjustment for unequal life-time treatment, an interpretation that is opposite of Tomes' suggestion.

The idea that voluntary redistribution among heirs, though an interesting finding if true, could explain the differences in our findings is not correct since the respondents were asked what they *inherited*. Hence the coded respondences on inheritance received is prior to any redistribution that may have occurred among heirs.

7. Sussman *et al.* report (p. 72) that the intestacy rates for decedents with only lineal kin surviving them and with a surviving spouse and lineal kin are 27.2% and 29.3% respectively. In the Cleveland probate data I have generated myself (see Section III of this paper), I computed both the overall intestacy rate and the intestacy rate among cases in which there is (a) more than one child and (b) a positive bequest to at least one child. I found a higher intestacy rate for the first group than for the second group, but the difference was less than one percentage point.

8. Ohio law requires a listing of next of kin in probate records, whether or not the decedent had a will, and this information was used to determine family size.

9. The test statistic is

$$t = \frac{\hat{p}_1 - \hat{p}_2}{\sqrt{\dfrac{\hat{p}_1 \hat{q}_1}{N_1} + \dfrac{\hat{p}_2 \hat{q}_2}{N_2}}}$$

with $\hat{p}_1$ and $\hat{p}_2$ the sample proportions of equal division in the two subsamples, $\hat{q}_1$ and $\hat{q}_2$, their respective additive complements to unity and N_1 and N_2 the sub-sample sizes.

10. This was true even in case number 665 361, in which the widow bequeathed equally to two sons, one of whom was the senior US senator from Ohio.

References

Arrow, J.K., *Essays in the Theory of Risk Bearing* (North Holland, Amsterdam, 1970).

Atkinson, A.B., *Social Justice and Public Policy* (MIT Press, Cambridge, Ma., 1983).

Barro, R.J., *The Impact of Social Security on Private Saving: Evidence from the US Times Series*, (American Enterprise Institute, Washington DC, 1978).

Becker, G.S., 'A Theory of Social Interactions', *Journal of Political Economy* **82** (1974), 1063–93.

——, *A Treatise on the Family* (Harvard University Press, Cambridge, Ma., 1981).

—— and N. Tomes, 'Child Endowments and the Quantity and Quality of Children', *Journal of Political Economy* **84** part 2, (1976), S143–S162.

——, 'An Equilibrium Theory of the Distribution of Income and Intergenerational Mobility', *Journal of Political Economy* **87** (1979), 1153–89.

Behrman, J., R. Pollak, and P. Taubman, 'Parental Preferences and Provision for Progeny', *Journal of Political Economy* **90** (1982), 52–73.

Bernheim, B.D., A. Shleifer, and L.H. Summers, 'The Strategic Bequest Motive' *Journal of Political Economy* **93** (1985), 1045–76.

Blinder, A., 'A Model of Inherited Wealth', *Quarterly Journal of Economics* **87** (1973), 608–26.

Chang, T. M., Support for Natural Caregiving. Report No. 3, Office on Aging, Bureau of Human Resources, Division of Community Services, Wisconsin Department of Health and Social Services, (1984).

Davies, J., 'The Relative Impact of Inheritance and Other Factors on Economic Inequality', *Quarterly Journal of Economics* **97** (1982), 471–98.

Kotlikoff, L. J. and A. Spivak, 'The Family as an Incomplete Annuities Market', *Journal of Political Economy* **89** (1981), 372–81.

—— and L. H. Summers, 'The Role of Intergenerational Transfers in Aggregate Capital Accumulation', *Journal of Political Economy* **89** (1981), 706–32.

Lindert, P., 'Sibling Position and Achievement', *Journal of Human Resources* **12** (1977), 198–219.

Meade, J., *Efficiency, Equality and the Ownership of Property* (Allen and Unwin, London, 1964).

——, *The Just Economy* (Allen and Unwin, London, 1976).

Menchik, P. L., 'Intergenerational Transmission of Inequality: an Empirical Study of Wealth Mobility', *Economica* **46** (1979), 346–62.

——, 'Primogeniture, Equal Sharing and the US Distribution of Wealth', *Quarterly Journal of Economics* **94** (1980), 299–316.

Menchik, P. L., and M. David, 'Income Distribution, Life Time Saving and Bequests', *American Economic Review* **73** (1983), 672–90.

Modigliani, F., 'The Life Cycle Hypothesis and National Wealth — A Rehabilitation', MIT, mimeo, (1983).

Olneck, M., 'On the Use of Sibling Data to Estimate the Effects of Family Background, Cognitive Skills and Schooling', in P. Taubman (ed.), *Kinometrics: The Determinants of Socioeconomic Success within and between Families* (North Holland, Amsterdam, 1977).

Pryor, F., 'Simulation of the Impact of Social and Economic Institutions on the Size Distribution of Income and Wealth', *American Economic Review* **63** (1973), 50–72.

Sheshinski, E. and Y. Weiss, 'Inequality Within and Between Families', *Journal of Political Economy* **90** (1982), 105–27.

Steinmetz, S. K. and D. J. Amsden, 'Dependent Elders, Family Stress and Abuse', in T. Brubaker (ed.), *Family Relationship in Later Life* (Sage Publications, Beverly Hills, 1983).

Sussman, C. J., J. N. Cates, and D. Smith, *The Family and Inheritance* (Russell Sage Foundation, New York, 1970).

Taubman, P., *Income Distribution and Redistribution* (Addison–Wesley, Reading, Ma., 1978).

Thurow, L., *Generating Inequality* (Basic Books, New York, 1975).

Tomes, N., 'The Family, Inheritance and the Intergenerational Transmission of Inequality', *Journal of Political Economy* **89** (1981), 928–58.

Zajonc, R., 'Family Configuration and Intelligence', *Science* **192** (1976), 227–36.

—— and G. Markus, 'Birth Order and Intellectual Development', *Psychological Review* **82** (1975), 74–88.

Comments on Chapter 3 and Chapter 4

DENIS KESSLER
University of Paris-X

ANDRÉ MASSON
Centre National de la Recherche Scientifique

The papers by Tomes and Menchik try to test the predictions of intergenerational models of bequest behaviour, and both focus on the role of estate division. Though information on this subject may seem easy to obtain, the evidence appears confusing, especially in the US. Some economists and lawyers find that unequal division is the rule in testate cases, while others find that unequal sharing is the exception.

In this respect the two contributions do not settle the empirical debate. From interviews of a Cleveland sample of heirs, Tomes concludes that unequal division is more common. Menchik on the other hand concludes from Connecticut and Cleveland probate records, that equal sharing is more common. Indeed, Menchik actually collected new probate records in the Cleveland area to check if the Sussman *et al.* (1970) evidence was reliable. According to Menchik, the contradictory empirical evidence comes mainly from errors in the interviewees' answers. However, this new piece of evidence does not close the debate, since Menchik's results still do not adequately explain why American lawyers stress the importance of unequal estate division.

In any case, the debate raises very interesting questions, particularly for French observers. In France equal sharing is enforced by law since Napoleon's 1804 Civil Code, despite the existence of explicit wills. In France, there is very limited freedom to bequeath. In the US, equal sharing is required by law only in intestate cases when there is no surviving spouse.

Menchik's results are interesting. If he is right, it means that whether forced to share estate equally, as in France, or not, as in the US, the outcome appears identical. One might believe that equal sharing is the rule in the US because people do not make wills. This is not the case, since according to Menchik and Tomes, about two thirds of people leaving estates do write wills, and according to Menchik only, 75% of them choose in these wills to divide their wealth equally. Menchik argues that parents bequeath equally in order to prevent disputes among heirs, to avoid the selling of certain assets, or to allocate certain assets to given children.

These comments will focus primarily on three points: (i) Which analytical models of bequest behaviour lead to equal sharing? (ii) Can we reconcile the differences between data coming from a questionnaire survey (Tomes' evidence) and data coming from probate records (Menchik's evidence)? (iii) What are the foundations of the separable earnings-bequest model which implies equal sharing?

Menchik draws a useful distinction between forward-looking altruistic models of wealth accumulation and transmission (such as Becker and Tomes (1979) model or the Behrman, Pollack, and Taubman (1982) model) on the one hand, and reverse bequests models based upon exchanges between parents and children (such as Kotlikoff and Spivak (1981) model and the Bernheim, Shleifer, and Summers (1985) model) on the other. He argues that both the reverse bequests models and the Becker and Tomes model are invalidated if the evidence indicates that equal estate division occurs most often. However, in the latter model, as Tomes mentions, equal sharing may occur due to the high transaction costs of making a will. However, the evidence that families with a will, usually divide their estate equally contradicts the prediction of the Tomes model. Therefore only the Behrman, Pollack, and Taubman model appears compatible with Menchik's results.

Menchik stresses the importance of response errors when explaining the discrepancies between interviews and probate records. Two other explanations are possible. The first explanation tends to support Tomes. When interviewed, heirs do not only consider recorded gifts and inheritance but may also take into account 'undeclared' gifts. Those transfers may not be declared to the IRS in order to avoid taxation. They may even be concealed to other siblings. Besides, heirs may take into account financial loans from parents, or various kinds of help (such as the loan of a dwelling or cash transfers). These transfers may not appear in probate records but may be considered as gifts and inheritances by children. These unrecorded intergenerational transfers may represent sizeable amounts when cumulated over the lifetime (see Kessler and Masson (1979) for data relative to France).

The second explanation is more favourable to Menchik. Interviewees may feel that they are disadvantaged with respect to their siblings, although they receive their fair share of their parents' estate. Some psychological studies carried out in France show that according to the subjective value given by children to certain assets, they may consider to have been disadvantaged although the objective value of their share is fair.

If equal sharing were the normal rule, it would be worth having a close look at the Behrman, Pollack, and Taubman separable earnings-bequest model. This model implies that the efficiency-equity trade off concerns only the parental distribution of human capital investment to their children, since material bequests are evenly distributed.

The rationale for the separable earnings-bequest model may lie in the fact that parental decisions concerning bequest allocation and human capital investment are usually taken at very different ages. In the same line of reasoning, human capital decisions are usually taken by the two parents, whereas the bequest allocation is usually decided by only one parent.

More analysis of the relationship between generations are needed. Factors such as the true nature of parental altruism, the perception and measure of individual characteristics of children such as their differential ability to gain from human capital investment or material wealth ownership, the psychological valuation of parental assets, and relative intrafamily discrimination feelings, need to be explored, and they might cast more light on the troubling contradictory evidence available on estate division.

References

Kessler, D. and A. Masson, *Les translerts intergénérationnels: l'aide, la donation, l'héritage*, (Rapport pour le CNRS, Paris, 1979).

Intergenerational Transfers and the Distribution of Income and Wealth

5 Redistribution, Inheritance, and Inequality: An Analysis of Transitions

JAMES B. DAVIES and PETER KUHN*

University of Western Ontario

As a result of the work of Stiglitz (1978a), Laitner (1979a and b), Atkinson (1980), Ioannides and Sato (1982), Ioannides (1983), and others, it is now well known that inheritance may have an equalizing impact on the steady-state intragenerational distributions of income and consumption. This somewhat surprising result is derived in models with a variety of forms of bequest behaviour, but with the common element of fresh stochastic shocks to income in each generation. Bequests may become an equalizing force by dampening these shocks through the sharing of luck across the generations of a family.[1,2]

Given the possibility of an equalizing role for inheritance, the question arises whether it is necessarily inequality-reducing to tax inheritances, with the revenues (perhaps) being used to fund transfer payments. Using a model with fixed factor prices, regression to the mean in earnings ability, and inter-generational saving in proportion to income, Stiglitz (1978a) argued that although a carefully selected rate of inheritance tax might reduce inequality, there is considerable scope for an excessive rate to increase it by disrupting the equalizing role of inheritances. A similar result was obtained by Becker and Tomes (1979) in a model with 'compensatory bequests' inversely related to children's 'endowed' earnings capacities. Atkinson (1980) pointed out that redistribution is more likely to be successful in cases where either (a) inequality is not initially in steady state but is continually increasing (see also Atkinson (1971)) or (b) there is very unequal division of estates, e.g., under a system of primogeniture.

Both Stiglitz and Atkinson have also considered models which endogenize factor prices and/or human capital accumulation. Stiglitz (1978b), for example, sets up a model in which the attempt to redistribute inheritances turns out to be disequalizing when the reduction in saving and physical capital accumulation induced produces a decline in labour's share of national income. (This is the case with an elasticity of substitution between capital and labour less than unity.) Note, however, that this result depends on inherited wealth exerting a disequalizing force[3] so that the effect of endogenizing

* We would like to thank the editors of this volume, an anonymous referee, and the discussant Tony Atkinson, for their valuable comments and suggestions. We are responsible for any errors or omissions.

factor prices in models where inheritance is equalizing is not clear. A further mechanism tending to produce a perverse effect of redistribution may occur where taxation of inheritances induces a substitution toward transfers in the form of support for education. (See, e.g., Stiglitz (1978*a*) 276–8 and 291–3, and Atkinson (1980) 57–63).

Despite the perverse possibilities pointed out by several authors, many continue to share the traditional view that redistributing inherited wealth is likely to reduce inequality successfully (and at little cost in economic efficiency). Support for this view may be found, e.g., in the alternative models discussed by Atkinson (1980). However, it should be noted that even in the models where a disequalizing effect of redistributing inheritances can arise, it is merely a *possibility*. Our research originates in the observation that it might be worth re-examining closely why a perverse effect of redistribution can occur in these models, and asking whether such effects are likely with real-world parameters.

Davies (1986) analysed the steady-state impact of redistributing inheritances in an intergenerational model with regression to the mean in earnings, fixed factor prices, and compensatory bequests. It was found that an attempt at redistribution has two effects. In this type of model inheritances depend on a geometrically-declining distributed lag of past generations' earnings. One important effect of redistribution is on the structure of this lag. The tax on inheritances always reduces the effective rate of intergenerational accumulation. This reduction leads on average to smaller inheritances and a re-weighting of the lag toward the earnings of more recent ancestors, which are more closely related to the current generation's earnings than are the incomes of more remote predecessors. This first effect is always disequalizing: a higher rate of tax leads to less averaging of the luck of past generations with the present, which increases inequality.

The other effect of redistribution is on the level of government transfer payments. Equilibrium transfers 'normally' rise with the tax rate, which is equalizing. This may more than offset the disequalizing lag structure effect. However, it is possible for a higher tax rate to produce lower government revenue and therefore reduced transfer payments. (In the popular terminology it is possible to be beyond the peak of the 'Laffer curve'.) This is especially true if the elasticity of substitution between parent's consumption and child's income in the parent's utility function (the 'intergenerational elasticity of substitution') is high. When equilibrium transfer payments actually fall, both impacts of redistribution are disequalizing and the new steady-state level of inequality is unambiguously higher.[4]

Calculations with an example in Davies (1986) indicated that with a wide variety of parameterizations the attempted redistribution of inheritances generated an increase in inequality. Even with quite low values of the intergenerational elasticity of substitution, taxation of bequests reduced the rate of intergenerational saving, and therefore the tax base, so sharply that the equalizing impact of transfer payments was swamped by the disequalizing 'lag structure' effect discussed above.

Although redistribution of inheritances was generally unsuccessful in the example considered by Davies (1986), when earnings were added to the tax base with many reasonable combinations of parameters increases in redistribution were generally successful in reducing inequality, even at high tax rates. Thus it appeared possible that even in a class of models — with equal division of estates, identical preferences across social classes, etc. — highly conducive to a disequalizing effect of redistribution, the attempt to increase equality by means of a linear tax-transfer scheme could be successful if properly designed.

The results of Davies (1986) are confined to a comparison of steady states. As demonstrated by Shorrocks (1975), stochastic models of income or wealth distribution may take a long time to converge close to the steady state. It is therefore interesting to examine the *transition* from an initial situation to a new steady state with an increased rate of tax and a greater attempt at redistribution. The purpose of this paper is to study this transition.

In this paper we discuss what happens when there is a pre-announced change in the tax rate characterizing a redistributive scheme based on the taxation of lifetime wealth. It is argued that whatever the steady state to which the society will eventually converge, the initial effect of this change is likely to be equalizing. This is so partly because government transfer payments will be at their highest (relative to mean earnings) in the period in which the policy change occurs. In addition, the disequalizing effect grows in strength during transition, so that it is initially relatively weak compared with the transfer payment effect. Thus, if we are unconcerned about the distant future the possibility of greater redistribution leading to increased steady-state inequality may not be as worrisome as it previously appeared.

The paper proceeds as follows. Section I briefly sets out the model and reviews the results of Davies (1986). Then, in Section II we present analytical results, and conjectures, on the transition process. The analysis and conjectures of Section II are then illustrated in an example of the model in Section III. Transition paths under a variety of alternative parameterizations are examined.

I   The model

We examine a society where reproduction is asexual. A dynasty consists of a series of single individuals who belong to successive generations indexed by t. Calendar time is indexed by τ. Each individual has a lifetime of N years, gives birth to a single child at age m, and retires at age R. His parents die when he is $n = N - m \gtrless R$ years of age, leaving him an inheritance of i_t. While each dynasty gives birth only every m years, it is possible that a number of 'unsynchronized' dynasties may coexist at the same time, such that some dynasty is giving birth (and another dying) in every year. Thus the model can be interpreted as one, not simply of overlapping generations, but of 'overlapping dynasties' as well. Parents are assumed to be fully informed of their child's characteristics at the time their bequest decision is being made.

Simple assumptions are made about factor incomes. The before-tax annual rate of return to capital, ρ, is exogenous and constant for all time. Earnings and the retirement date are also exogenous. Their size distribution is invariant across generations, except for scale. Mean earnings increase at a constant proportional rate, $q - 1$. The earnings of successive generations in a dynasty may either be independent, or (more attractively) imperfectly positively correlated. In the latter case, since the size distribution of earnings is stationary (except for scale) we generally have the important phenomenon of 'regression to the mean' in earnings ability: on average children of low-earning parents will have greater earnings ability than their parents, while children of high-earning parents will have less. This regression is an important force reducing inequality when generations share their luck via bequests.

These assumptions make it straightforward to define, for a dynasty that experienced a birth in year $\tau = 0$:

$$C_t = \int_{\tau = tm}^{tm + N} c_t(\tau) e^{-\rho(\tau - tm)} \, d\tau$$

$$B_t = b_t e^{-\rho N}$$

$$E_t = \int_{\tau = tm}^{tm + R} w_t(\tau) e^{-\rho(\tau - tm)} \, d\tau$$

$$I_t = i_t e^{-\rho n}$$

where $c_t(\tau)$ is the consumption stream of a member of generation t, $w_t(\tau)$ is his earnings stream, b_t is the bequest he leaves, and i_t the inheritance he receives. C_t, B_t, E_t, and I_t are the present values of all these magnitudes as of this individual's birth date. In the following pages, we shall focus on an individual dynasty such as the one described above.

In the absence of government, a member of generation t would have lifetime income, L_t, composed of earnings and inheritances, E_t and I_t respectively. This income could be expended on consumption C_t, or bequest, B_t. Since $i_{t+1} = b_t$ and therefore $I_{t+1} = B_t e^{-\rho m}$, the budget constraint of a member of generation t can be written:

$$C_t + \frac{L_{t+1}}{r} = L_t + \frac{E_{t+1}}{r} \tag{1}$$

where $r = e^{-\rho m}$, which can be thought of as one plus the 'intergenerational' interest rate.

Under the linear redistributive tax-transfer scheme imposed each family receives a basic transfer, or 'demogrant', G_t, which together with E_t and I_t, is taxed at the constant proportional rate u. Thus, lifetime income before tax, L_t^b, is given by:

$$L_t^b = E_t + I_t + G_t \tag{2}$$

and lifetime income after-tax, L_t, is:

$$L_t = (1 - u)L_t^b = (1 - u)(E_t + I_t + G_t). \tag{3}$$

For the tax-transfer scheme to be self-financing *within* each generation we must have[5]

$$G_t = u\overline{L}_t^b = u(\overline{E}_t + \overline{I}_t + G_t) = \left(\frac{u}{1-u}\right)\overline{L}_t. \tag{4}$$

Thus:

$$G_t = \left(\frac{u}{1-u}\right)(\overline{E}_t + \overline{I}_t) \tag{5}$$

Note that (4) and (5) together imply:

$$\overline{L}_t = \overline{E}_t + \overline{I}_t. \tag{6}$$

All parents maximize the same utility function, defined on parent's consumption and child's after-tax lifetime income:

$$U_t = U(C_t, L_{t+1}) \tag{7}$$

U is strictly quasi-concave and homothetic.[6] Denoting the discounted resources of parent and child combined as 'family wealth', W_t:

$$W_t = L_t + \frac{\underline{L}_{t+1}}{r(1-u)} \tag{8}$$

where $\underline{L}_{t+1} = (1 - u)(E_{t+1} + G_{t+1})$, i.e., the 'endowed' after-tax income of the child, (7) is maximized subject to the constraint:

$$C_t + \frac{L_{t+1}}{r(1-u)} = W_t. \tag{9}$$

Since the interest rate is the same for all, and U is homothetic and identical across families, all parents appropriate the same fraction, $(1 - \theta)$, of family wealth for their own use:

$$C_t = (1 - \theta)W_t \tag{10}$$

and the child receives the rest, so that

$$L_{t+1} = r(1-u)\theta \, W_t$$

or

$$L_{t+1} = \delta \, W_t \tag{11}$$

where $\delta = r(1-u)\theta$.

From (10) and (11) it is possible to sign $\dfrac{\partial\theta}{\partial u}$ and $\dfrac{\partial\theta}{\partial r}$. Let the elasticity of substitution between C_t and L_{t+1} be σ. Then:

$$\frac{\partial\theta}{\partial r} \le 0, \quad \frac{\partial\theta}{\partial u} > 0 \qquad ; \sigma < 1 \tag{12a}$$

$$\frac{\partial\theta}{\partial r} = \frac{\partial\theta}{\partial u} = 0 \qquad ; \sigma = 1 \tag{12b}$$

$$\frac{\partial\theta}{\partial r} > 0, \quad \frac{\partial\theta}{\partial u} < 0 \qquad ; \sigma > 1. \tag{12c}$$

Davies (1986) points out that a prior on σ might be formed by analogy to the intertemporal elasticity of substitution in consumption over the life cycle. This suggests that $\sigma < 1$ is the 'leading case'.[7] Thus an increase in the tax rate may well *increase* the fraction of family wealth passed on to children.

From (11) it is easy to show that:

$$L_t = \theta \sum_{i=0}^{\infty} \delta^i \underline{L}_{t-i} = \theta \sum_{i=0}^{\infty} \delta^i (1-u)(E_{t-i} + G_{t-i}). \tag{13}$$

Thus, current lifetime income is simply a geometrically-declining distributed lag of the after-tax endowments of all generations up to (and including) the present. Another way of looking at this is that (using (3) to rearrange (13)):

$$(1-u)\, I_t = (\theta-1)\underline{L}_t + \theta \sum_{i=1}^{\infty} \delta^i \underline{L}_{t-i}. \tag{14}$$

From (14) net inheritances, $(1-u)I_t$, add to $(\theta-1)\underline{L}_t$ an 'average' of all past $\underline{L}_{t-i}$s — that is an average of the luck of all previous generations. Intuitively, the more mobility there is from generation to generation in earnings the greater will be the reduction in current inequality as a result of this averaging. Also, the higher is θ the greater is the importance of past $\underline{L}_{t-i}$s in determining L_t. Or, the higher is δ the more equalizing is the impact of inheritance. In fact, as shown in Davies (1986), if the E_{t-i}s and G_{t-i}s in (13) are fixed, an increase in δ reduces inequality in L_t according to all scale-independent inequality measures which obey the Lorenz partial ordering.

Now $\delta = r(1-u)\theta$ represents what might be called the effective strength of intergenerational accumulation. (A fraction θ of some $\underline{L}_{t-i}$ may be put aside for bequest but the resulting increase in the after-tax income of the next generation is $r(1-u)\theta\underline{L}_{t-i}$ not $\theta\underline{L}_{t-i}$.) Under homotheticity it turns out that δ must always decline when u rises, even though $\dfrac{\partial\theta}{\partial u} > 0$ when $\sigma < 1$.[8] Thus if the G_{t-i}s stayed fixed when u was increased, an attempt at redistribution would always increase inequality in L_t.

But the point of raising u is, of course, to increase the G_{t-i}s. If equilibrium G_{t-i}s *do* rise, this offsets the disequalizing 'lag structure' effect, so that the net change in inequality from one steady state to another is not clear. However, it is possible for the equilibrium G_{t-i}s to fall, guaranteeing an overall disequalizing impact of redistribution. The reason is that equilibrium $\overline{L}_t$, which we can find by taking the expectation of (13) and substituting in $G_{t-i} = \left(\dfrac{u}{1-u}\right)\overline{L}_{t-i}$:

$$\overline{L}_t = \frac{\overline{E}_t}{1 - \dfrac{r}{q} + \dfrac{r(1-\theta)}{\delta}} \tag{15}$$

must fall with u.[9] Clearly, $\overline{L}_t$ will be more sensitive to u the higher is σ. In the example developed in Davies (1986), and extended here in the next section, this effect is very strong, so that with, e.g., $\sigma = 1\frac{1}{2}$ redistribution is typically disequalizing (in steady-state comparisons).

Davies (1986) also found that a less equalizing effect of redistribution in the model was obtained with higher r or lower q. The reason is that both higher r and lower q increase the relative importance of past endowments in determining current income. (Higher r increases δ, making past endowments more important by (13); lower q means, for a given $\overline{E}_t$, larger past $\overline{E}_{t-i}$s.) Thus both produce a more equalizing role for inheritance. Taking the argument a step further, a given increase in u is more disequalizing when r is higher or q is low since the *decline* in the relative weight placed on past endowments is greater with such parameter values.[10]

Finally, in the example studied in Davies (1986) it was found that the degree of intergenerational mobility in the earnings distribution was an important determinant of the efficacy of redistribution. The higher is this mobility, the more effective are bequests in reducing the degree of inequality in current incomes. In consequence, when earnings mobility is high the reduction in bequests induced by taxation tends to increase inequality more: the more important is intergenerational averaging in reducing inequality the more self-defeating it is in this model to tax inheritances.

II Transition: theory

The above analysis considers only steady-state, within-cohort, inequality in lifetime income. In the example of Section III it typically takes from 5 to 10 generations for convergence to within 1% of new steady-state values when a pre-announced change in u takes place in a society initially in steady-state equilibrium. Since a generation (i.e., the time between births, $m = N - n$) lasts about 25 years 'transition' thus lasts something like 125–250 years. Hence an analysis of transition is a necessary complement to the study of steady states if the model is to have much real-world relevance.

If an unannounced tax change occurs at some point, the resulting time-path of inequality is difficult to characterize analytically. Consumption plans of both the first generation in each dynasty that is taxed and of its parents (if they are still alive) are disrupted: $c_t(\tau)$ before the tax increase is fixed; thus individuals cannot achieve the lifetime consumption streams they would have planned if they had known the tax change was to take place. The simple formulation $U(C_t, L_{t+1})$ breaks down. Because of this problem we consider only the case of a pre-announced tax increase in the remainder of the paper.

Pre-announcement is assumed to be implemented as follows. Assume that generation t^* of a particular dynasty is born at time $\tau = 0$. Then at time $\tau = -m$ (the year that generation $t^* - 1$ of that dynasty is born) the following announcement is made: Starting with individuals born at time $\tau = 0$ the lifetime incomes of all individuals will be taxed at the new rate. All individuals born at or before $\tau = -1$ continue to be taxed at the old rate. This 'phasing in', or 'grandfathering', completely eliminates the possibility of 'surprising' people with a tax at any point in their lifetime.

Our pre-announcement scheme has at least two effects on the time-path of inequality. The first is that the parents of the first generation affected are given an opportunity to react. Their intergenerational accumulation falls below the level it would have achieved if the old steady state had continued. This effect reduces the initial equalizing impact of redistribution, and perhaps also the deepness of the 'trough' in inequality that is reached before the long period of ascent to the new steady-state level of inequality.

A second effect of our pre-announcement scheme would arise if we were examining inequality among all members of a population consisting of 'unsynchronized' overlapping dynasties (i.e. a situation where a new cohort is born every year). Because only the youngest cohorts would be affected during the first few years after the tax change, the impact on inequality for the population as a whole would be small. In fact, in the following discussion we confine our attention to inequality among the members of specific cohorts, so that this effect does not show up. It is important to keep in mind, however, when thinking how one might check the predictions of the model: empirical verification would ideally focus on estimates of intra-cohort inequality, rather than the more readily available aggregate statistics.

Under pre-announcement the $t* - 1$ generation uses a new tax rate $\hat{u}$ (rather than the old u) to make its plans. In particular it uses a $\hat{\theta}$ determined by $\hat{u}$, rather than the old θ, to decide how much to bequeath. Hence, using (8) and (11):

$$L_{t*} = \hat{\delta}L_{t*-1} + \frac{\hat{\delta}\underline{L}_{t*}}{r(1-\hat{u})} \tag{16}$$

and

$$L_{t*+j} = \hat{\delta}^{j+1} L_{t*-1} + \sum_{i=0}^{j} \frac{\hat{\delta}^i}{r(1-\hat{u})} \underline{L}_{t*+j-i}. \tag{17}$$

Substituting in from (13) for L_{t*-1} and noting that $\dfrac{\hat{\delta}}{r(1-\hat{u})} = \hat{\theta}$ we get L_{t*+j} as a function of after-tax endowments:

$$L_{t*+j} = \theta\,\hat{\delta}^{j+1} \sum_{i=0}^{\infty} \hat{\delta}^i \underline{L}_{t*-1-i} + \sum_{i=0}^{j} \hat{\theta}^i \underline{L}_{t*+j-i}. \tag{18}$$

Clearly, as j increases, the first term becomes relatively less important. If $\hat{\delta}$ is not too high, the decline in this term will be rapid. In that case L_{t*+j} would soon be close to the value it would have had if the society had been in steady-state equilibrium with $\hat{u}$ forever, assuming the $\underline{L}_{t*+j}$s were fixed.

In fact the $\underline{L}_{t*+j}$s are not fixed since they depend on the G_{t*+j}s, given by

$$G_{t*+j} = \left(\frac{\hat{u}}{1-\hat{u}}\right) \bar{L}_{t*+j}$$

and the $\bar{L}_{t*+j}$s are not fixed, but are evolving toward their new steady-state value relative to $\bar{E}_{t*+j}$. As noted in the previous section this will be lower than the value of $\bar{L}_{t*-1}$ relative to $\bar{E}_{t*-1}$. Hence the $\bar{L}_{t*+j}$s will tend to be above their equilibrium values since the $\underline{L}_{t*+j}$s contain higher than steady-state values of the G_{t*+j}s.

What happens to inequality during transition? First consider the lag structure effect. As transition proceeds, and j rises, as already noted the second term in (18) begins to eclipse the first. Since the second term uses the accumulation factor $\hat{\delta}$, instead of the higher δ, there is a progressive change toward the less equal lag structure of the new steady state. While the picture is slightly more complicated than this suggests, this appears to be the essential lag structure effect during transition.[11] Less and less relative weight is placed on the endowments of previous generations in determining current income, so that the equalizing effect of inheritance is eroded and current inequality tends to rise.

The other effect of redistribution operates via changes in transfer payments. While in principle it appears possible under pre-announcement of the increase in u for transfers to be smaller (relative to earnings) for generation $t*$, than for the last generation under the old regime ($t* - 1$), this does not appear to be a likely outcome. Mean lifetime income, and therefore transfers, will decline (relative to mean earnings) during transition. Hence even if the eventual impact of higher u is for $\bar{L}_{t*+j}$ to fall so much (relative to $\bar{E}_{t*+j}$) that G_{t*+j} declines (again relative to $\bar{E}_{t*+j}$) the initial impact of an increase in u on $G*$ seems likely to be positive.

Although transfer payments will almost certainly jump in the impact generation, producing a strong equalizing effect, their decline (relative to earnings) on the path to the new steady state implies a weakening of the equalizing impact of redistribution. We would expect a generally rising pattern of inequality during transition, *a fortiori*, in view of the fact that the lag structure in (18) becomes steadily less equalizing as transition proceeds.

III   An example

In this section we extend an example set up in Davies (1986) to compare steady states to look at transition paths. The utility function (7) is given the explicit form:

$$
U_t = \begin{cases} \dfrac{C_t^{1-\gamma}}{1-\gamma} + \beta \dfrac{L_{t+1}^{1-\gamma}}{1-\gamma}, & \gamma \neq 1 \\[2ex] \ln C_t + \beta \ln L_{t+1}, & \gamma = 1 \end{cases}
\tag{7'}
$$

and the elasticity of substitution between C_t and L_{t+1} is $\sigma = \dfrac{1}{\gamma}$ and is therefore constant. We also assume that earnings have a stationary distribution and regress toward the mean across the generations.

It is convenient to express the regression to the mean in earnings in terms of changes in human capital, H_t, related to E_t by:

$$
E_{t-i} = w_{t-i} H_{t-i} = w_t q^{-i} H_{t-i}
\tag{19}
$$

where w_{t-i}, the wage rate, grows at the constant rate q. If H_{t-i} has a stationary distribution, then that of E_{t-i} will be stationary except for scale. The regression mechanism is:

$$
H_{t-i} = (1-v)\bar{H} + v H_{t-i-1} + \epsilon_{t-i}
\tag{20}
$$

where ϵ_{t-i} is independent of H_{t-i-1}, and has zero mean and constant variance, $V(\epsilon_{t-i}) = V(\epsilon)$. The parameter, v, determines the degree of intergenerational correlation in earnings ability. For stationary variance in the H_{t-i}s, $V(H)$, we require:

$$
V(\epsilon) = (1 - v^2)V(H).
\tag{21}
$$

The Appendix shows how the transitional coefficients of variation of lifetime income, $CV(L_{t^*+j})$ can be derived.[12] Tables 5.1 and 5.2 show how transition occurs in a central case which uses apparently plausible parameter values. Then in Table 5.3 the sensitivity of the result to alternative parameterizations is investigated.

The central case parameters are the same as used in Davies (1986). They are set as follows: the growth rate, q, is given the moderate value of 1.01 per annum. Popular estimates of the mean household rate of return in the US place r at about 1.04 on an annual basis. (See, for example, Boskin (1978) 19; and Feldstein, Green, and Sheshinski (1978) 64.) A generation is assumed to span 25 years, so that the annual q and r of 1.01 and 1.04 respectively correspond to values per generation of 1.28 and 2.67. By analogy to the evidence on the *intra*generational intertemporal elasticity of substitution in consumption to which we have already referred, σ is set at 0.5. A best-guess for v^2 appears to be about 0.4.[13] Finally, there is no empirical evidence on β. It was set in Davies (1986) by experimenting with alternative values to see which would give a realistic $\dfrac{\bar{I}_t}{\bar{L}_t}$. Blinder (1976) and Davies (1982) both find this ratio is quite small — in fact less than 0.1. If the tax rate that corresponds to the real world is 0.2, then $\dfrac{\bar{I}_t}{\bar{L}_t}$ of about the right size is obtained with $\beta = 0.8$.[14]

Table 5.1 shows the central case transitions from initial steady states with $u = 0.0$ and 0.2 alternatively to new steady states with a variety of $\hat{u}$s. In this central case, increases in the tax rate always lead to a new steady state with a lower CV.

One of the most striking things shown in Table 5.1 is that a large part of the eventual reduction in inequality to be obtained in the new steady state has already taken place in the impact generation (t^*). For example, if we raise u from 0.0 to 0.2 the CV falls 7.6% from $t^* - 1$ to t^*, a drop equal to more than half the fall to the new steady state. In transition to the extreme values $\hat{u} = 0.6$ or 0.8 (starting either at $u = 0.0$ or 0.2) the CV actually falls *more* in the impact generation than in the new steady state.

A second interesting phenomenon shown in Table 5.1 is the considerable overshooting. Again using the transition from $u = 0.0$ to 0.2 as an example, the great-grandchildren of the impact generation ($j = 3$) exhibit a CV 13.9% below the old equilibrium value — significantly lower than the eventual new steady-state CV which is only 10.9% below the former level. Thus, with a moderate tax rate, redistribution has a strong equalizing impact over three or four generations. This is followed by a long period of slowly rising inequality.

A final point to note from Table 5.1 is that the greater the jump in the tax rate, the sooner is the maximum equalizing effect felt, and the sooner do we have convergence to the new steady state.

Some light is thrown on the trends in Table 5.1 by the transition paths of

TABLE 5.1. $CV(L_{t^*+j})/CV(L_{t^*-1})$ — Central Case

j	Transition from							
	$u = 0.0$ to $\hat{u} = \ldots$				$u = 0.2$ to $\hat{u} = \ldots$			
	0.2	0.4	0.6	0.8	0.0	0.4	0.6	0.8
−1	1.0	1.0	1.0	1.0	1.0	1.0	1.0	1.0
0	0.924	0.834	0.722	0.560	1.082	0.903	0.781	0.606
1	0.881	0.755	0.618	0.463	1.126	0.866	0.720	0.550
2	0.864	0.737	0.623	0.513	1.146	0.863	0.734	0.603
3	0.861	0.747	0.655	0.562	1.152	0.872	0.761	0.645
4	0.865	0.763	0.682	0.588	1.151	0.881	0.782	0.667
5	0.870	0.777	0.700	0.600	1.148	0.889	0.795	0.676*
6	0.876	0.787	0.710	0.605*	1.143	0.895	0.802	0.680
7	0.880	0.794	0.716*	0.607	1.139	0.898*	0.806*	0.681
8	0.883*	0.799*	0.719	0.608	1.135	0.901	0.808	0.682
9	0.886	0.802	0.720	0.608	1.132*	0.902	0.809	0.682
10	0.887	0.803	0.721	0.608	1.130	0.903	0.810	0.683
15	0.891	0.806	0.722	0.608	1.124	0.904	0.811	0.683
25	0.891	0.806	0.722	0.608	1.122	0.905	0.811	0.683
∞	0.891	0.806	0.722	0.608	1.122	0.905	0.811	0.683

☐ = minimum or maximum value.
* Convergence to within 1% of new steady-state value.

$\overline{L}_{t^*+j}/\overline{E}_{t^*+j}$ illustrated in Table 5.2. When the policy change is an increase in u the transition path of $\overline{L}_{t^*+j}/\overline{E}_{t^*+j}$ is in each case convex. The drop from $\overline{L}_{t^*-1}/\overline{E}_{t^*-1}$ to $\overline{L}_{t^*}/\overline{E}_{t^*}$ ranges from 32 to 59% of the total drop from the old steady state to the new steady-state value. This considerably reduces the equalizing impact of redistribution in the first period. However, when the initial u is 0.0 we, of course, must have $G_{t^*} > G_{t^*-1}$ and in the experiments with initial $u = 0.2$ there is no case in which transfers do not rise in the impact generation.

Beyond the impact generation, from (4) $G_{t^*+j}/\overline{L}_{t^*+j}$ is constant, producing no upward or downward pressure on inequality. It is therefore the decreasing weight placed on previous generations in the lag structure of (18) which must be responsible for the CV climbing throughout most of transition.

While redistribution produces a decline in steady-state inequality in the 'central case', with a moderate increase in the interest rate or the intergenerational elasticity of substitution this is no longer the case. The equilibrium level of mean inheritances is quite sensitive to changes in these parameters. (In particular, raising r or σ leads to very large increases in $\overline{I}_t$.) Alternatives to the central case were therefore developed in which r and σ were raised to higher values, but offsetting changes were made to other parameters to keep $\overline{I}_t$ in the apparently realistic range. Table 5.3 presents such experiments for the transition path between $u = 0.0$ and $\hat{u} = 0.2$.

TABLE 5.2. $\left(\dfrac{\overline{L}_{t^*+j}}{\overline{E}_{t^*+j}}\right)\bigg/\left(\dfrac{\overline{L}_{t^*-1}}{\overline{E}_{t^*-1}}\right)$ — Central Case

j	Transition from							
	$u=0.0$ to $\hat{u}=\ldots$				$u=0.2$ to $\hat{u}=\ldots$			
	0.2	0.4	0.6	0.8	0.0	0.4	0.6	0.8
-1	1.0	1.0	1.0	1.0	1.0	1.0	1.0	1.0
0	0.929	0.842	0.727	0.556	1.076	0.906	0.782	0.598
1	0.881	0.744	0.581	0.374	1.132	0.848	0.666	0.434
2	0.848	0.683	0.503	0.300	1.174	0.812	0.604	0.367
3	0.825	0.645	0.461	0.270	1.204	0.789	0.571	0.339
4	0.809	0.622	0.439	0.257	1.226	0.775	0.553	0.328
5	0.799	0.608	0.427	0.252	1.243	0.767	0.543	0.324
6	0.792	0.599	0.420	0.250*	1.255	0.762	0.538	0.322*
7	0.787	0.593	0.417*	0.249	1.264	0.758*	0.535*	0.321
8	0.783*	0.590*	0.415	0.249	1.270	0.756	0.534	0.321
9	0.781	0.588	0.414	0.249	1.275	0.755	0.533	0.320
10	0.779	0.586	0.414	0.249	1.279*	0.754	0.533	0.320
15	0.777	0.585	0.413	0.249	1.286	0.753	0.532	0.320
25	0.776	0.584	0.413	0.249	1.288	0.753	0.532	0.320
∞	0.776	0.584	0.413	0.249	1.289	0.753	0.532	0.320

* Convergence to within 1% of new steady-state value.

Table 5.3 shows that high values of r or σ do not necessitate an increase in steady-state inequality. It is only in the third column, where $\sigma = 1.5$ is combined with $\beta = 0.56$, that equilibrium inequality rises as a result of raising u from 0 to 0.2. On the other hand, the case illustrated in the third and fourth columns indicate that the trough in inequality may come a generation earlier with a higher σ. However, Table 5.3 provides assurance that even when the eventual steady-state inequality is higher, or only slightly lower than the initial inequality, there is a long period over which inequality is significantly reduced by the attempt at redistribution. To those who believe the type of intergenerational model considered here is of some relevance this may be reassuring — redistribution can be mounted without the fear of perverse disequalizing consequences, except in the remote future.

IV Conclusion

This paper has extended the analysis of earlier authors, including Davies (1986), by examining the transition paths between steady-state income distributions generated under different levels of linear redistribution in an intergenerational model with altruistically-motivated bequests. A central case example indicates that the equalizing effect of increased redistribution does

TABLE 5.3. Alternative Parameterizations — Transition from $u = 0.0$ to $\hat{u} = 0.2$**

j	$CV(L_{t\bullet+j})/CV(L_{t\bullet-1})$				$\left(\dfrac{\overline{L}_{t\bullet+j}}{\overline{E}_{t\bullet+j}}\right)\Big/\left(\dfrac{\overline{L}_{t\bullet-1}}{\overline{E}_{t\bullet-1}}\right)$			
	$r=1.06$		$\sigma=1.5$		$r=1.06$		$\sigma=1.5$	
	$\beta=0.5$	$\sigma=0.25$	$\beta=0.56$	$r=1.026$	$\beta=0.5$	$\sigma=0.25$	$\beta=0.56$	$r=1.026$
-1	1.0	1.0	1.0	1.0	1.0	1.0	1.0	1.0
0	0.945	0.945	0.924	0.906	0.919	0.958	0.810	0.834
1	0.905	0.908	0.878	0.862	0.856	0.926	0.680	0.732
2	0.884	0.886	0.869	0.859	0.806	0.901	0.591	0.670
3	0.876	0.876	0.890	0.874	0.767	0.882	0.531	0.632
4	0.880	0.874	0.925	0.893	0.713	0.867	0.489	0.608
5	0.889	0.875	0.962	0.909	0.695	0.856	0.461	0.594
6	0.901	0.878	0.995	0.921	0.680	0.847	0.442	0.585
7	0.913	0.882	1.021	0.928	0.669	0.840	0.429	0.580
8	0.924	0.886	1.042	0.933*	0.660	0.835	0.420	0.577*
9	0.935	0.889	1.056	0.937	0.653	0.831	0.414	0.575
10	0.943	0.892	1.067	0.938	0.647	0.827	0.410	0.573
15	0.968	0.900*	1.087*	0.941	0.634*	0.820*	0.402*	0.572
25	0.978*	0.902	1.090	0.942	0.628	0.817	0.401	0.571
∞	0.979	0.903	1.090	0.942	0.628	0.817	0.401	0.571

☐ = minimum or maximum value.
* Convergence to within 1% of new steady-state value.
** Parameter values: $r = 1.06$, $v^2 = 0.4$, $\beta = 0.8$, and $\sigma = 0.5$ except as indicated.

not begin to wear off immediately after the tax rate is increased, but actually increases for three or four generations with moderate tax rates. The reduction in inequality overshoots, however, and after three or four generations inequality begins to increase gradually as it converges to its new steady-state level. Sensitivity testing indicates that with alternative parameterizations the trough in inequality may, however, come a generation or so earlier.

There are alternative ways of interpreting these results. In our view they indicate that as far as models of the type examined are concerned it would be a mistake to worry too much about the possible perverse impact of redistribution on inequality in steady-state analysis. Even in the cases where steady-state inequality rises as a result of an increase in the tax rate there is a long period — 100–200 years — over which inequality is lower than in the previous steady state. Since an increase in inequality over the initial level occurs only, it might be argued, in the distant future, it can effectively be ignored. Also, at least in the central case example, redistribution leads to cumulatively declining inequality for three or four generations.

Pessimists may reply that although there is typically a long period over which inequality is lower in transition than it was initially, the period over which inequality is *falling* only lasts a few generations with some parameter values. Therefore, the fear expressed by Becker and Tomes (1979, 1178) that the equalizing force of the welfare state has already been spent may not necessarily be groundless according to this model. After all, the welfare state has been in force now for about two generations (50 years) in most countries, and longer in some. If the scale of redistribution is not increased, it might be suggested that we can look forward to a long period of slowly rising inequality. This might be characterized by increased social and/or political strain, and perhaps intensified efforts at redistribution. A 'vicious circle' leading to ever more ambitious redistribution might be anticipated.

Appendix

This appendix shows how the example set up in Section III is solved.

First, it is easy to see how mean lifetime income, $\bar{L}_{t \cdot + j}$, will evolve. From (8) and (11):

$$L_{t \cdot + j} = a_0 L_{t \cdot + j - 1} + a_1 \underline{L}_{t \cdot + j}; \quad \begin{cases} j \leq -1: & a_0 = \delta, a_1 = \dfrac{\delta}{r(1-u)} \\[2ex] j \geq 0: & a_0 = \hat{\delta}, a_1 = \dfrac{\hat{\delta}}{r(1-\hat{u})} \quad \text{(A.1)} \end{cases}$$

Taking the expectation of (A.1), and noting that (see (4)):

$$G_{t \cdot + j} = b \bar{L}_{t \cdot + j} \quad ; \quad \begin{cases} j \leq -1: & b = \dfrac{u}{1-u} \\[2ex] j \geq 0: & b = \dfrac{\hat{u}}{1-\hat{u}} \quad \text{(A.2)} \end{cases}$$

we obtain:

$$\bar{L}_{t \cdot + j} = c_0 \bar{L}_{t \cdot + j - 1} + c_1 \bar{E}_{t \cdot + j} \quad \begin{cases} j \leq -1: & c_0 = \dfrac{\delta}{1-\theta u}, c_1 = \dfrac{\theta(1-u)}{1-\theta u} \\[2ex] j \geq 0: & c_0 = \dfrac{\hat{\delta}}{1-\hat{\theta}\hat{u}}, c_1 = \dfrac{\hat{\theta}(1-\hat{u})}{1-\hat{\theta}\hat{u}}. \end{cases}$$
$$\text{(A.3)}$$

We can compute the entire transition path for mean lifetime income from (A.3) if we know $\bar{L}_{t \cdot - 1}$ and $\hat{\theta}$. $\bar{L}_{t \cdot - 1}$ is the initial steady-state value, and can be calculated from (15) (given θ), while $\hat{\theta}$ can be obtained by maximizing (7′) subject to (9) (appropriately modified), yielding:

$$\hat{\theta} = \frac{1}{1 + \beta^{1/\gamma} [r(1 - \hat{u})]^{\frac{1-\gamma}{\gamma}}} \tag{A.4}$$

from which it is straightforward to confirm that (12) holds $\Big($recalling that $\sigma = \dfrac{1}{\gamma}\Big)$. (Note that θ can be calculated from (A.4) by replacing $\hat{u}$ by u.)

In order to compute the variance of $L_{t^{\bullet}+j}$, note first that, from (20):

$$H_{t^{\bullet}+j-i} = \bar{H} + \sum_{k=0}^{\infty} v^k \epsilon_{t+j-i-k} \tag{A.5}$$

Substituting this into (18), and recalling the definition of $\underline{L}_{t^{\bullet}+j-i}$:

$$L_{t^{\bullet}+j} = \theta \, \hat{\delta}^{j+1} \sum_{i=0}^{\infty} \delta^i(1-u) \left(\frac{w_{t^{\bullet}-1}}{q^i}\right) \left(\bar{H} + \sum_{u=0}^{\infty} v^k \epsilon_{t^{\bullet}-1-i-k}\right)$$

$$+ \hat{\theta} \sum_{i=0}^{j} \hat{\delta}^i(1-\hat{u}) \left(\frac{w_{t^{\bullet}+j}}{q^i}\right) \left(\bar{H} + \sum_{k=0}^{\infty} v^k \epsilon_{t^{\bullet}+j-i-k}\right)$$

$$+ \mathscr{C} \tag{A.6}$$

where $\mathscr{C}$ is a term which depends only on the $G_{t^{\bullet}+j-i}$s and other parameters constant across families and is therefore fixed; and $w_{t^{\bullet}-1-i} = \dfrac{w_{t^{\bullet}-1}}{q^i}$ and $w_{t^{\bullet}+j-i} = \dfrac{w_{t^{\bullet}+j}}{q^i}$. Letting $d = \dfrac{\delta}{q}$ and $\hat{d} = \dfrac{\hat{\delta}}{q}$, separating the terms involving $\bar{H}$ into ω (like $\mathscr{C}$ fixed across families):

$$L_{t^{\bullet}+j} = \phi_{1j} \sum_{i=0}^{\infty} \sum_{k=0}^{\infty} d^i v^k \epsilon_{t^{\bullet}-1-i-k}$$

$$+ \phi_{2j} \sum_{i=0}^{j} \sum_{k=0}^{\infty} \hat{d}^i v^k \epsilon_{t^{\bullet}+j-i-k}$$

$$+ C + \omega \tag{A.7}$$

where $\phi_{1j} = \theta \, \hat{\delta}^{j+1}(1-u) w_{t^{\bullet}-1}$ and $\phi_{2j} = \hat{\theta}(1-\hat{u}) w_{t^{\bullet}+j}$.

Now the various terms in (A.7) can be simplified as follows. First:

$$\sum_{i=0}^{\infty} \sum_{k=0}^{\infty} d^i v^k \epsilon_{t^{\bullet}-1-i-k} = \sum_{i=0}^{\infty} \sum_{l=0}^{i} d^l v^{i-l} \epsilon_{t^{\bullet}-1-i} = \sum_{i=0}^{\infty} \left(\frac{d^{i+1} - v^{i+1}}{d-v}\right) \epsilon_{t^{\bullet}-1-i} \tag{A.8}$$

Also, the second term in (A.7) can be split up as follows:

$$\sum_{i=0}^{j} \sum_{k=0}^{\infty} \hat{d}^i v^k \epsilon_{t^*+j-i-k} = \sum_{i=0}^{j} \left\{ \sum_{k=0}^{j-i} \hat{d}^i v^k \epsilon_{t^*+j-i-k} + \sum_{k=j-i+l}^{\infty} \hat{d}^i v^k \epsilon_{t^*+j-i-k} \right\}$$

$$= \sum_{k=0}^{j} \sum_{l=0}^{k} \hat{d}^l v^{k-l} \epsilon_{t^*+j-k} + \sum_{i=0}^{\infty} \sum_{k=0}^{j} \hat{d}^k v^{j+1+i-k} \epsilon_{t^*-1-i}$$

$$\tag{A.9}$$

Simplifying the first term:

$$\sum_{k=0}^{j} \sum_{l=0}^{k} \hat{d}^l v^{k-l} \epsilon_{t^*+j-k} = \sum_{k=0}^{j} \left(\frac{\hat{d}^{k+1} - v^{k+1}}{\hat{d} - v} \right) \epsilon_{t^*+j-k} \tag{A.10}$$

The second term on the RHS of (A.9) can also be simplified. Letting $m = j+1+i$, note that

$$\sum_{k=0}^{j} \hat{d}^k v^{m-k} = \sum_{k=0}^{j} \hat{d}^k v^{j-k} v^{m-j}$$

$$= v^{m-j} \sum_{k=0}^{j} \hat{d}^k v^{j-k}$$

$$= v^{i+1} \left(\frac{\hat{d}^{j+1} - v^{j+1}}{\hat{d} - v} \right).$$

Thus:

$$\sum_{i=0}^{\infty} \sum_{k=0}^{j} \hat{d}^k v^{j+1+i-k} \epsilon_{t^*-1-i} = \sum_{i=0}^{\infty} v^{i+1} \left(\frac{\hat{d}^{j+1} - v^{j+1}}{\hat{d} - v} \right) \epsilon_{t^*-1-i} \tag{A.11}$$

Now, substituting (A.10) and (A.11) into (A.9), and (A.8) and (A.9) in turn into (A.7), and re-arranging:

$$L_{t^*+j} = \phi_{1j} \sum_{i=0}^{\infty} \left[\left(\frac{d^{i+1} - v^{i+1}}{d - v} \right) + \frac{\phi_{2j}}{\phi_{1j}} v^{i+1} \left(\frac{\hat{d}^{j+1} - v^{j+1}}{\hat{d} - v} \right) \right] \epsilon_{t^*-1-i}$$

$$+ \phi_{2j} \sum_{k=0}^{j} \left(\frac{\hat{d}^{k+1} - v^{k+1}}{\hat{d} - v} \right) \epsilon_{t^*+j-k} + \mathcal{C} + \omega. \tag{A.12}$$

The variance of L_{t^*+j} can then easily be found since the ϵ_{t^*-1-i}s and ϵ_{t^*+j-k}s are all independent:

$$V(L_{t^*+j}) = \left\{ \phi_{1j}^2 \sum_{i=0}^{\infty} \left[\left(\frac{d^{i+1} - v^{i+1}}{d - v} \right) + \frac{\phi_{2j}}{\phi_{1j}} v^{i+1} \left(\frac{\hat{d}^{j+1} - v^{j+1}}{\hat{d} - v} \right) \right] \right.$$

$$+ \phi_{2j}^2 \sum_{k=0}^{j} \left(\frac{\hat{d}^{k+1} - v^{k+1}}{\hat{d} - v} \right)^2 \right\} V(\epsilon). \tag{A.13}$$

Once the variance has been computed it is straightforward to calculate the coefficient of variation:

$$CV(L_{t^*+j}) = \frac{\sqrt{V(L_{t^*+j})}}{\bar{L}_{t^*+j}}. \tag{A.14}$$

Notes

1. The relevant portion (pp. 37–54) of Atkinson (1980) does not explicitly consider the distributions of income or consumption. The discussion is confined to the distribution of inherited wealth. However, Atkinson's modelling is formally similar to that applied in a number of cases by the other authors cited. Atkinson has two sources of inequality in inheritances. These lie in the passing forward of (a) some multiple of the inheritance of the previous generation and (b) a (possibly different) multiple of parents' random luck. The role of the latter could alternatively be played by a non-degenerate distribution of earnings i.i.d. across the generations. Thus the model is formally equivalent to one of lifetime income, rather than simply inheritances, similar to some of those considered by other authors. Since steady-state inequality of total inheritances is less than that of the component due to luck in a variety of the formulations studied by Atkinson, in a formal sense his work agrees with the finding of others that inheritance may equalize the intragenerational distribution of income.
2. The presence of stochastic shocks in each generation rules out situations where there is a tendency for inequality to disappear over time as a result of higher saving rates among the poor (Stiglitz, 1969), or assortative mating combined with estate division (Blinder, 1973).
3. Stiglitz (1978*b*) formulates a model where bequests increase inequality since (a) stochastic shocks to income are absent, and earnings of children are identical to their parents', and (b) bequests are a luxury.
4. Inequality is higher according to all inequality measures which obey the Lorenz partial ordering.
5. With taxes based on *lifetime* income this appears to be the only reasonable budget-balancing criterion available: the present value of taxes collected over the lifetime of any generation must equal the present value of transfer payments received. This of course rules out transfers between generations such as occur in social security schemes.
6. Utility can be written as a function of C_t only (without considering explicitly the entire time path of consumption, $C_t(\tau)$) because of the assumption of perfect capital markets: given a fixed 'consumption fund' C_t, the individual is assumed to allocate it optimally over his own lifetime. (See, e.g., Shorrocks (1979) 417.) Note also that interest on savings (borrowing) used to reallocate consumption *within* an individual's lifetime is not subject to tax (tax credits) here, since the tax base is lifetime income.

7. For summaries of the evidence that $\sigma < 1$ in the life-cycle context, see Davies (1981, 573–4) or Auerbach *et al.* (1983, 89). A 'best guess' value appears to be $\sigma \approx \frac{1}{2}$.

8. If $\sigma \geq 1$, from (12) $\dfrac{\partial \theta}{\partial u} \leq 0$ so that $\delta = r(1-u)\theta$ will fall when u rises. From (10) and (11) $\dfrac{L_{t+1}}{C_t} = \dfrac{\delta}{1-\theta}$. When u rises, by homotheticity $\dfrac{L_{t+1}}{C_t}$ must fall. But when $\sigma < 1$, $\dfrac{\partial \theta}{\partial u} > 0$ and $\dfrac{\delta}{1-\theta}$ will *rise* unless δ falls sufficiently. Hence whether the 'propensity to bequeath', θ, rises or falls, the parameter governing the strength of intergenerational accumulation, δ, must always fall in reaction to an increase in u.

9. As pointed out in the previous note, by homotheticity the ratio $\dfrac{L_{t+1}}{C_t} = \dfrac{\delta}{1-\theta}$ must fall with the tax rate u. Thus the last term in the denominator of (15) must rise with u, and an increase in u therefore must reduce $\bar{L}_t$. The unambiguous decline in bequests and lifetime wealth as a result of the taxation of inheritances here, although arising in a somewhat different model, echoes the results of Atkinson (1971).

10. For example, if $\delta = \frac{1}{2}$ the sum of the weights applied to the earnings of all generations is 2. Half of this total weight is applied to current earnings and half to past. If the tax rate rises from 0 to 0.5, with θ constant δ would fall to $\frac{1}{4}$. The total weight placed on the earnings of past generations would decline to $\frac{1}{3}$. Thus the decline in the relative weight placed on the earnings of earlier generations would equal $1 - \frac{1}{3} = \frac{2}{3}$.

If δ were initially higher the relative weight placed on past earnings would be much greater. With, e.g., $\delta = 0.9$, the total weight on past earnings would be 9. Raising u from 0 to $\frac{1}{2}$ would reduce this weight to 0.818 — a spectacular decrease in weight relative to that placed on current earnings of $9 - 0.818 = 8.192$. Thus the decline in relative weight placed on the earnings of past generations produced by any given increase in the tax rate is very sensitive to the initial value of δ and therefore of r.

The influence of q operates in precisely the same way as that of r, mathematically. In terms of our analysis, however, the effect shows up somewhat differently. A lower q means that past earnings were larger relative to present. Hence the importance of past earnings bulks larger, just as if q were held constant and a higher r had been used.

11. Consider a generation $t^* + \tilde{j}$. The weight placed on the endowment of generation $t^* - 1 - i$ in determining $L_t^* + \tilde{j}$ is $\theta \, \hat{\delta}^{j+1} \, \delta^i$ whereas the weight placed on generation $t^* - 2 - i$'s endowment in determining $L_t^* + \tilde{j} - 1$ was $\theta \, \hat{\delta}^j \, \delta^{i+1}$. Since $\hat{\delta} < \delta$ the weight placed on the endowment of a generation a fixed period back from the present (say 10 generations back) thus declines with j, as long as the generation that fixed interval back was one of those prior to t^*.

There is another change in weighting when $\sigma \neq 1$, and $\dfrac{\partial \theta}{\partial u} \neq 0$. This reinforces the disequalizing effect identified in the previous paragraph when $\sigma > 1$, and $\hat{\theta} < \theta$. As we move from generation $\tilde{j} - 1$ to $\tilde{j}$, the weight placed on the endowment $\bar{j}$ generations back switches from $\theta \,\hat{\delta}^j$ to $\hat{\theta} \,\hat{\delta}^j$. When $\hat{\theta} < \theta$ this reduces the weight placed on the endowment of one of the previous generations, which is again disequalizing. However, when $\sigma < 1$, $\hat{\theta} > \theta$ and this effect is reversed. Whether the weight on the endowment of the $\bar{j}$th generation back is ever sufficient to more than offset the disequalizing influence of the decrease in weight for all generations prior to that is not clear. Since this possible equalizing effect involves only one generation, and the disequalizing effect involves an infinite series of ancestors it may be conjectured that the disequalizing effect usually dominates.

12. The coefficient of variation is the ratio of the standard deviation to the mean. It has the special characteristic of equal sensitivity to transfers of fixed amounts between individuals differing in income by a given amount at different points in an income distribution. For a discussion of its properties see e.g., Sen (1974, 27–8), or Hoy and Davies (1985).

13. Blinder (1976, 621) argues that the proportion of the variance of earnings explained by 'family background' may be viewed as an estimate of v^2, and surveys four studies with average R^2 of 0.248, suggesting $v^2 \approx 0.25$. Griliches (1979, 559) concludes that about 30% of the variance in log earnings is explained by family background in studies using sibling data. Taubman (1976, 867) obtains upper and lower bounds of 0.3 and 0.55 for the combined influence of genetics and family environment using data on identical twins. All these studies use annual earnings, producing a downward bias due to transitory earnings. Griliches suggests that correcting this bias could raise R^2 as high as 0.5.

14. Note that $\beta = 0.8$ is not far from 'perfect altruism' ($\beta = 1$). On an annual basis the implied intergenerational rate of time preference is 0.9%.

References

Atkinson, A. B., 'Capital Taxes, the Redistribution of Wealth and Individual Savings', *Review of Economic Studies* **38** (1971), 209–28.

——, 'Inheritance and the Redistribution of Wealth', In G. M. Heal and G. A. Hughes (eds.), *Public Policy and the Tax System* (Allen and Unwin, London, 1980).

Auerbach, A., L. J. Kotlikoff, and J. Skinner, 'The Efficiency Gains from Dynamic Tax Reform', *International Economic Review* **24** (1983), 81–100.

Becker, G. S. and N. Tomes, 'An Equilibrium Theory of the Distribution of Income and Intergenerational Mobility', *Journal of Political Economy* **87** (1979), 1153–89.

Blinder A. S., 'A Model of Inherited Wealth', *Quarterly Journal of Economics* **87** (1973), 608–26.

——, 'Inequality and Mobility in the Distribution of Wealth', *Kyklos* **29** (1976), 607–38.

——, *Toward an Economic Theory of Income Distribution* (MIT Press, Cambridge, Ma., 1974).

Boskin, M. J., 'Taxation, Saving and the Rate of Interest', *Journal of Political Economy* **86** (April 1978 Supplement), S3–S27.

Davies, J. B., 'Uncertain Lifetime, Consumption and Dissaving in Retirement', *Journal of Political Economy* **89** (1981), 561–77.

——, 'The Relative Impact of Inheritance and Other Factors on Economic Inequality', *Quarterly Journal of Economics* **47** (1982), 471–98.

——, 'Does Redistribution Reduce Inequality?', *Journal of Labor Economics* **4** (1986), 538–59.

——, F. St-Hilaire, and J. Whalley, 'Some Calculations of Lifetime, Tax Incidence', *American Economic Review* **74** (1984).

Feldstein, M.S., J. Green, and E. Sheshinski, 'Inflation and Taxes in a Growing Economy with Debt and Equity Finance', *Journal of Political Economy* **86**, 2, Part 2, (1978), S53–S70.

Griliches, Z., 'Sibling Models and Data in Economics: Beginning of a Survey', *Journal of Political Economy* **87** (October 1979 Supplement), S37–S64.

Hoy M. and J.B. Davies, 'Comparing Income Distributions under Aversion to Downside Inequality', University of Western Ontario, CSIER Working Paper No 8521C, (1985).

Ioannides, Y.M., 'Heritability of Ability, Intergenerational Transfers and the Distribution of Wealth', School of Management, Boston University, mimeo, (February 1983).

——, and R. Sato, 'A General Equilibrium Theory of the Distribution of Wealth and Intergenerational Transfers', School of Management, Boston University, mimeo, (March 1982).

Laitner, J.P., 'Household Bequest Behavior and the National Distribution of Wealth', *Review of Economic Studies* **46** (1979*a*), 467–84.

——, 'Household Bequests, Perfect Expectations, and the National Distribution of Wealth, *Econometrica* **47** (1979*b*), 1175–93.

Sen, A.K., *On Economic Inequality* (Clarendon Press, Oxford, 1973).

Shorrocks, A.K., 'On Stochastic Models of Size Distribution', *Review of Economic Studies* **42** (1975), 631–41.

——, 'On the Structure of Intergenerational Transfers between Families', *Economica* **46** (1979), 415–25.

Stiglitz, J.E., 'Distribution of Income and Wealth among Individuals', *Econometrica* **37** (1969), 382–97.

——, 'Equality, Taxation and Inheritance', in W. Krelle and A.F. Shorrocks (eds.), *Personal Income Distribution* (North Holland, Amsterdam, 1978*a*).

——, 'Notes on Estate Taxes, Redistribution, and the Concept of Balanced Growth Path Incidence', *Journal of Political Economy* **86** Part 2, (1978*b*), S137–S150.

Taubman, P., 'The Determinants of Earnings: Genetics, Family and Other Environments: a Study of White Male Twins', *American Economic Review* **66** (1976), 858–70.

Comments on Chapter 5

ANTHONY B. ATKINSON
London School of Economics

To the man in the street, it seems self-evident that inheritance leads to greater inequality of incomes. He thinks of the Rockefellers, the Rothschilds, and the Dukes of Westminster. In the same way, most people expect that a tax on inheritances would be equalising even if the revenue were used in a neutral way. One finds support for higher bequest taxes on the left, not the right, of the political spectrum.

As Davies and Kuhn point out in their interesting paper, there are a variety of distributional models in which the 'man in the street' view is not borne out. Inheritance has, in these models, an *equalising* effect on the distribution of income; and taxes on bequests may have a perverse impact. The reason for this is explained clearly by the authors in their first paragraph. These models are driven by fresh stochastic shocks each generation. The role of bequests is to dampen the effect of these shocks, by sharing out luck across generations. The large fortunes of today's self-made millionaires are, in part, offset by the comfortable amounts owned by the great-grandchildren of last century's tycoons.

The situation described in these models does not seem to accord with reality, certainly not with that recorded in the United Kingdom in the work of Harbury and Hitchens (1979). Davies and Kuhn are right, in my judgement, to be sceptical about the possibility of perverse results from inheritance taxation. They are also right to emphasize the out-of-steady-state behaviour, for the reasons given by Shorrocks (1975). In this, their paper represents a valuable contribution. The numerical findings are of interest, although I would hesitate before drawing any of the possible conclusions described at the end of the paper.

My own feeling is however that, rather that further analysis of the properties of the models, what is needed now is a re-examination of the basic ingredients. This applies to relatively small-scale issues, like the treatment of negative bequests. From (8) and (11) in Davies and Kuhn's paper, we have in the absence of taxation

$$I_{t+1} = \delta L_t - (1 - 1/r)E_{t+1} \tag{A}$$

for the level of wealth inherited by the $(t + 1)$th generation. This may well be negative: for example, where the child has much higher earnings than the parent. Presumably such negative bequests would take the form of the child supporting the parent. However, if we now introduce taxes, it is not clear that negative bequests would receive symmetric treatment. There may well not be 'offsets' where the inheritance is negative. For this reason, it would be useful if the authors commented on the role of negative bequests in their calculations.

More generally, there is the question of modelling the distribution of wealth as an equilibrium phenomenon. Davies and Kuhn take for granted the existence of a unique steady state, and convergence to this steady state, yet it may be that what we are observing is a diverging path. Since $L_t = I_t + E_t$ (in the absence of a transfer), we can see from (A) that this is possible where $\delta = r\theta > 1$, a case that the authors ignore (e.g. in writing (13)). In the model of Stiglitz (1969), where the rate of return is determined endogeneously, general equilibrium considerations ensure that r adjusts such that $\delta < 1$. This is not however necessarily the case in other models, as is discussed in Atkinson (1980).

There are indeed a number of important considerations which need to be incorporated into our model of the distribution of wealth: eg. the pattern of inheritance, the distribution of wealth between the sexes, differential fertility, marriage, and divorce. Until that is done, the man in the street's view of inheritance, and inheritance taxation, will retain its plausibility.

References

Atkinson, A. B., 'Inheritance and the Redistribution of Wealth', in Heal, G. M. and G. A. Hugues (eds.), *Public Policy and the Tax System* (Allen and Unwin, London, 1980).

Harbury, D. C. and D. M. W. N. Hitchens, *Inheritance and Wealth Inequality in Britain* (Allen and Unwin, London, 1979).

Shorrocks, A. F., 'On Stochastic Models of Size Distribution', *Review of Economic Studies* **42** (1975), 631–41.

Stiglitz, J. E., 'Distribution of Income and Wealth Among Individuals', *Econometrica* **37** (1969), 382–97.

6 The Intergenerational Transmission of Wealth and the Rise and Fall of Families

NIGEL TOMES
Western Ontario University

Economists have devoted considerable attention to the distribution of income and wealth among individuals and families. Surprisingly little attention has been devoted to intergenerational mobility — the relation between the incomes and wealth of parents, children, and later descendents — the rise and fall of family fortunes. In contrast, the problems of occupational and social mobility, both over the lifetime and across the generations have been studied extensively by sociologists. However, the numerous empirical studies of mobility by sociologists have lacked a theoretical framework or model to provide predictions and aid the interpretation of results.

This sharp division of labour is unjustified. The close relationship between inequality and mobility in the distribution of wealth suggests sizeable returns from an analysis which considers both dimensions simultaneously. This relationship can be illustrated by means of a simple example. Suppose the incomes of parents and children are related by the linear Markov equation:

$$I_{t+1} = a + bI_t + \epsilon_{t+1}$$

where I_{t+1} and I_t represent the incomes of children and parents, respectively, a and b are constant parameters and ϵ_{t+1} represent stochastic determinants of child's income. Inequality would continue to grow over time if $|b| \geq 1$, but would approach a steady state equilibrium level if $|b| < 1$. The magnitude of b also determines the degree of intergenerational social mobility; the extent to which the income advantages and disadvantages of parents are transmitted to children. Stated differently $(1 - b)$ measures the extent of regression to the mean, provided $0 \leq b < 1$. The need for a unified treatment of inequality and social mobility has been the guiding principle in my research on the intergenerational transmission of inequality (Becker and Tomes (1979), (1986), Tomes (1981), (1982)).

In the Becker–Tomes model (Becker and Tomes (1979)) parent-child transfers arise from utility-maximizing behaviour by parents who are concerned about the welfare of their progeny, as measured by the children's lifetime income or wealth. The intergenerational allocation of resources is determined subject to opportunities which incorporate the possibility that the cultural and genetic endowments of parents are automatically transmitted to ('inherited by') children. Two crucial parameters determine both the equilibrium distribution of income and the degree of intergenerational mobility: the

147

'inheritability' of endowments and the marginal propensity to transfer. The latter parameter reflects the degree of parental altruism and the rate of return on parental investments.

Although this model yields valuable insights, it has a number of short-comings: (i) parental utility depends on the income or wealth of children rather than the consumption of descendents in all subsequent generations as in many overlapping generations models (Laitner (1979), Bevan (1979), Shorrocks (1979), Barro (1974)); (ii) transfers in the form of human capital are not distinguished from bequests of material wealth; (iii) perfect foresight eliminates any role for uncertainty regarding the abilities of descendents; (iv) capital markets are assumed sufficiently 'perfect' to permit both positive or negative transfers; (v) marriage is ignored, or partners are assumed to be identical (perfect assortative marriage); (vi) family size is exogenously fixed, so that there is no 'quality-quantity tradeoff' (Becker and Tomes (1976)). Although some of these factors have been incorporated in simulation models (eg., Blinder (1973), (1976), Pryor (1973), Bevan (1979)) usually they enter in a purely mechanistic way, rather than being incorporated in the utility-maximizing calculus of economic actors.

The present paper reports the results of relaxing these assumptions in the context of a utility-maximizing framework. Interestingly, it turns out that incorporating the factors outlined above can drastically change the implications regarding inequality and the rise and fall of families. Since a comparison paper (Becker and Tomes (1986)) emphasizes implications regarding human capital, this paper concentrates on the role of material wealth.

The paper is organized as follows. The following section presents a brief review of the Becker–Tomes model. Section II presents an alternative overlapping generations model and contrasts the predictions with those of the Becker–Tomes model. Section III discusses extensions to the alternative model. Finally, the paper concludes with a short summary.

I   The Becker–Tomes model

In the Becker–Tomes model (Becker and Tomes (1979)) parental contributions are motivated by altruism — a benevolent concern by parents for the well-being of their offspring as measured by their children's lifetime income. Society is supposed to be composed of one parent–one child families in which the utility function of the generation t parent is iso-elastic:

$$U_t = \frac{C_t^{1-\theta}}{1-\theta} + \delta \, \frac{I_{t+1}^{1-\theta}}{1-\theta} \tag{1}$$

where C_t is the parents' consumption, I_{t+1} the child's lifetime income, δ is the intergenerational discount factor, $\delta = (1+\rho)^{-1}$ and θ is the inverse of the elasticity of substitution. If $\theta = 1$ the utility function is Cobb–Douglas.

The adult income of the child depends on parental investments which yield a constant rate of return (r). No distinction is made between investments in human capital and transfers of material wealth. In addition the income of children depends on 'endowments' determined by the reputation and 'connections' of their families; the genetic constitutions of their parents and the learning, skills, and goals acquired through belonging to a particular family culture. Finally, random 'luck' in the market for incomes may affect children's income. These three components are assumed to determine income in an additive fashion:

$$I_{t+1} = y_t + e_{t+1} + u_{t+1} = (1+r)x_t + e_{t+1} + u_{t+1} \qquad (2)$$

where y_t represents child's income due to parental contributions $(x_t)^1$, e_{t+1} and u_{t+1} represent the child's endowment and market luck, respectively. Parental income is allocated between own consumption and transfers to children:

$$I_t = c_t + x_t = c_t + \frac{y_t}{1+r} \qquad (3)$$

Solving (2) for y_t and substituting into (3) yields a combined constraint for the two-generation family:

$$S_t = c_t + \frac{I_{t+1}}{1+r} = I_t + \frac{(e_{t+1} + u_{t+1})}{1+r} \qquad (4)$$

Family income S_t — the combined resources of the two-generation family — is raised if parents' income increases; it is also raised if the child has greater endowments or market luck. Parents are assumed to know the endowments and luck of children when they allocate resources between the generations. When children become parents they solve a similar problem.

The first-order conditions define demand functions for child's income, parental consumption, and intergenerational transfers:

$$I_{t+1} = \alpha(1+r)S_t = \alpha(1+r)I_t + \alpha(e_{t+1} + u_{t+1}) \qquad (5a)$$

$$c_t = (1-\alpha)S_t = (1-\alpha)I_t + \frac{(1-\alpha)}{(1+r)}(e_{t+1} + u_{t+1}) \qquad (5b)$$

$$y_t = \alpha(1+r)I_t - (1-\alpha)(e_{t+1} + u_{t+1}) \qquad (5c)$$

where $\sigma^{-1} = \left\{ 1 + (1+\rho)^{1/\theta}(1+r)^{1-\frac{1}{\theta}} \right\}$.

α indexes the degree of parental altruism. It is a decreasing function of the discount factor (ρ) and an increasing (decreasing) function of the rate of return if the elasticity of substitution is greater (less) than unity.

Equations $(5a)$–$(5c)$ imply that an increase in parents' income will raise parental consumption and also increases descendent's income via greater parental contributions. The magnitude of this intergenerational effect depends on $\beta = \alpha(1+r)$: the 'marginal propensity to invest' in children. Children's endowments and luck are also important. Other things being equal, an increase in either endowments or luck raises the child's income and parental consumption. This increased parental consumption is 'financed' through reduced transfers (5c), so that child's income rises less than \$1 for every \$1 increase in child's endowments. In the presence of intergenerational transfers, 'shocks' to the resources of either generation are smoothed by the offsetting response of transfers.

The evolution of income over the generations is described by equation (5a). If the parameters α and β and endowments were the same for all families, the differential incidence of market luck would produce income differences between families. If the propensity to invest β is less than unity — as implied by plausible parameter values — the differentials resulting from shocks to previous generations would ultimately be eliminated as elapsed time increases. In the absence of new shocks, incomes would regress to the mean with a velocity determined by $(1 - \beta)$.

An equation similar to (5a) can be derived describing the consumption levels of successive generations of the family:

$$c_{t+1} = \beta c_t + \frac{(1-\alpha)}{(1+r)} (e_{t+2} + u_{t+2}) \tag{6}$$

With constant endowments, the propensity to invest also determines the degree of intergenerational mobility in consumption. In the Becker–Tomes model the degree of intergenerational mobility in consumption equals that of income. Hence estimates of the degree of intergenerational income mobility have immediate implications for consumption mobility.

The incomes and consumptions of parents and children are linked not only by intergenerational transfers, but also by the inheritance of ability, knowledge, skills, goals, reputation, and other characteristics. For simplicity, the transmission of endowments is assumed to be linear:

$$e_{t+1} = (1-h)\bar{e} + he_t + v_{t+1}, \quad 0 \leq h \leq 1 \tag{7}$$

where $\bar{e}$ is the average for the group or society, h is the 'inheritability' of endowments and v_{t+1} represents the stochastic 'luck' component of endowments which is assumed to be observed by parents prior to their investment decisions. If the inheritability coefficient is less than unity, the effects on future generations of random luck in the endowments of a particular generation will diminish as endowments regress towards the mean.

The two processes of transmission — parental investments in children and the 'direct' inheritance of parents' endowments — interact in determining intergenerational mobility in income, consumption, and investments. This can be seen in the stochastic difference equations which describe the motion of these characteristics over the generations:

$$I_{t+1} = \alpha(1-h)\bar{e} + (\beta+h)I_t - \beta h I_{t-1} + \alpha u^*_{t+1} \tag{8a}$$

$$c_{t+1} = \left(\frac{1-\alpha}{1+r}\right)(1-h)\bar{e} + (\beta+h)c_t - \beta h c_{t-1} + \left(\frac{1-\alpha}{1+r}\right)u^*_{t+2} \tag{8b}$$

$$y_{t+1} = (\alpha+\beta-1)(1-h)\bar{e} + (\beta+h)y_t - \beta h y_{t-1} - (1-\alpha)u^*_{t+2} + \beta u^*_{t+1} \tag{8c}$$

where $u^*_{t+i} = [v_{t+i} + u_{t+i} - hu_{t+i-1}]$ $i=1,2$

Equation (8a) describes the effects on subsequent generations of an increase in the income of generation t. An increase in the endowment luck of generation t (v_t), which raises I_t by one unit, will raise the income of children both directly via the inheritance of endowments and indirectly via increased parental contributions. The total effect on I_{t+1} is $(\beta+h)$, which will exceed the increment in I_t, if the sum of these parameters exceeds unity. More generally, the effect on subsequent generations is given by:

$$\frac{dI_{t+i-1}}{dI_t} = \frac{dI_{t+i-1}}{dv_t} = \begin{cases} \dfrac{\beta^i - h^i}{\beta - h} & \text{if } \beta \neq h \\ i\beta^{i-1} & \text{if } \beta = h \end{cases} \tag{9}$$

This effect ultimately diminishes if $\beta, h < 1$, so that eventually incomes regress to the mean. If $\beta+h > 1$, incomes will regress *away* from the mean for a number of generations. For example, if $\beta = h = 0.72$, incomes would regress away from the mean for three generations before the process of convergence begins. On the other hand, if $\beta + h < 1$, regression towards the mean would be monotonic. Moreover, convergence would be quite rapid if both parameters were small. For example, if $\beta = h = 0.125$ the income of children would increase by only 25% of the increment to the parents' income and the effect on grandchildren would be less than 5% of the initial increase. In this case families could go from riches to rags in three generations.

The path of consumption and investments is governed by the same pair of parameters (see equations (8b) and (8c)), so that the predictions regarding income mobility apply equally to consumption and intergenerational transfers.

II   An alternative overlapping generations model

The results reported in the previous section are based on a model in which parents are concerned about the lifetime income or wealth of children. In many overlapping generations models of altruism, the utility of children or the consumption of all subsequent generations appears as an argument in parental preferences (e.g. Barro (1974), Bevan (1979), Laitner (1979)). Becker and Tomes (1979) deal briefly with this case in an appendix. They conclude that 'utility functions that depend on the welfare of children imply exactly the same intergenerational mobility as do functions that depend on the income of children and have similar implications for the distribution of income within a generation' (p. 1185; see also Becker (1981), 171). However, this conclusion depends critically on assumptions regarding uncertainty and foresight as we demonstrate in this section.

Let us now examine the implications of a model in which parents are concerned about the utility of their offspring and have perfect foresight regarding the abilities and handicaps of their descendents in all future generations. It turns out that this formulation yields predictions regarding regression to the mean, the existence of a steady-state equilibrium, and the relation between earnings mobility, wealth mobility, and consumption mobility, which are strikingly different from the Becker–Tomes model outlined in the previous section.

In this section we assume that children's utility, rather than their income, enters parental preferences, in an additive fashion. Using $t + i$ to index the generations $(i = 0, 1, \ldots, T)$

$$U_t = u(c_t) + \delta U_{t+1}, \quad 0 < \delta < 1 \tag{10}$$

where c_t is the lifetime consumption of adult members of the family (parents) in generation t, and δ is the intergenerational discount factor which indexes the degree of parental altruism. We assume, until later, that all families consist of one adult and one child, so that marriage and fertility decisions can be ignored. Childhood consumption is also ignored. U_{t+1} represents the utility of the child when he (she) attains adulthood.

If the preference function (10) characterizes all generations, then the utility of parents in generation t depends indirectly on the consumption of family members in all succeeding generations. By substitution

$$U_t = \sum_{i=0}^{T} \delta^i u(c_{t+i}) \tag{11}$$

Although parents are affected by the consumption of all succeeding generations, they will be more concerned about children and grandchildren, than about more distant descendents if $\delta < 1$. For example, if $\delta = 0.4$ the utility of children's consumption enters with a weight of 0.4, grandchildren with a weight of 0.16 and great grandchildren 0.06. Hence (11) needs not imply that generation t gives an inordinate weight to distant descendents.

The budget constraint faced by generation t is:

$$I_t = H_t + A_t = c_t + \frac{A_{t+1}}{1 + r} \tag{12}$$

Total wealth equals the sum of human wealth (H_t: taken as exogenous) plus material wealth (A_t). This is allocated between consumption and bequests to the following generation. Perfect foresight and certainty are assumed and financial markets are supposed to allow both positive and negative (debt) transfers. The interest rate r is assumed constant for all time.

Succeeding generations maximize a function equivalent to (11) subject to a constraint analogous to (12). Since the resources of adjacent generations are linked by transfers, substitution yields a constraint defined by the resources of the dynasty:

$$A_t + \sum_{i=0}^{T} \frac{H_{t+i}}{(1+r)^i} = \sum_{i=0}^{T} \frac{c_{t+i}}{(1+r)^i} = R_t \tag{13}$$

Dynastic resources equal the value of initial assets, plus the present value of the human capital of present and all succeeding generations of the family.[2]

2.1 Consumption

Given the dynamic consistency of this problem, the consumption of succeeding generations is determined by the first-order conditions:

$$\frac{U'(c_t)}{U'(c_{t+1})} = \delta(1+r) \tag{14}$$

If the utility function is of the constant elasticity form: $U'(c_t) = ac_t^{-\sigma}$ $(\sigma > 0)$ equation (14) becomes:

$$\frac{c_{t+1}}{c_t} = \left(\frac{1+r}{1+\rho} \right)^{1/\sigma} = g \tag{15}$$

where $\delta^{-1} = 1 + \rho$. The consumption of family members will rise or decline at the rate $g - 1$, depending on whether $r \gtreqless \rho$.

If the intergenerational discount factor δ is independent of the level of consumption, equation (15) implies that the consumption of children is proportional to that of their parents. Interfamily inequality in dynastic resources (R_t) due to differences in initial assets or the present value of the dynasty's human wealth, would be reflected in permanent differences across families in the consumption *levels* of family members in all generations. However, the *relative* consumption of adjacent generations would be the same for all families provided families have identical discount factors. Thus equation (15) has strong implications for intergenerational mobility. Under perfect foresight and perfect capital markets, the consumption of successive generations *exhibits no regression to the mean* — social mobility is zero. If families differ only in their resources, the consumption of family members in successive generations would be perfectly rank correlated. This can be seen by writing equation (15) as:

$$\ln c_{t+1} = \frac{1}{\sigma} \ln \left[\frac{1+r}{1+\rho} \right] + \ln c_t \tag{16}$$

Regression towards the mean in consumption requires an elasticity of child's consumption with respect to parents' consumption of less than unity. On the contrary, equation (16) implies an elasticity of unity — if parents' consumption exceeds the average by 1%, the child's consumption will exceed the mean by 1%. Furthermore, notice that (15) and (16) contain no stochastic terms. Given perfect foresight all the relevant information regarding the resources of all future generations is utilized by generation t in determining the consumption path for the entire dynasty. The inequality across families in dynastic resources at 'time zero' determines the inequality in consumption of the initial generation and this inequality is reproduced in all subsequent generations, scaled by the growth factor g. Hence, relative inequality in consumption across families is constant in perpetuity and there is zero social mobility. This is a perfect caste society.

Introducing permanent differences across families in the degree of altruism — the discount factor: δ — influences regression to the mean. Comparing families with equal dynastic resources, more altruistic families (with higher δ) would choose lower consumption for initial generations and a higher growth rate of desired consumption, compared to less altruistic families. Consequently, although initial generations would exhibit regression towards the mean, ultimately there would be regression *away* from the mean as later generations of altruistic families enjoy successively higher consumption levels compared to less altruistic families. In the long run, therefore, permanent heterogeneity in preferences generates regression *away* from the mean and ever-increasing inequality.

The prediction of no regression to the mean is consistent with any degree of earnings mobility across the generations. If the intergenerational transmission of human capital 'endowments' obeys a first-order Markov process similar to equation (17):

$$H_{t+1} = (1-h)\overline{H} + hH_t + v_{t+1}, \quad -1 < h < 1 \tag{17}$$

where $\overline{H}$ is the mean and v_{t+1} represents the random 'luck' of generation $t+1$. The coefficient of 'inheritability': h may be positive, zero, or even negative. Zero intergenerational mobility in the consumption of successive generations implied by equation (16) could occur, while at the same time the human capital (earnings) of successive generations exhibits complete mobility ($h = 0$). Therefore this model implies that the extent of earnings mobility may seriously overestimate the degree of mobility in terms of consumption.

The relationship between the consumption levels of successive generations is depicted in Figure 6.1. If $g < 1$ (i.e. $r < \rho$) the consumption of successive generations will be declining $\hat{c} \rightarrow \tilde{c} \rightarrow \bar{c}$. Conversely if $g > 1$ (i.e. $r > \rho$) consumption will be rising $\bar{c} \rightarrow \tilde{c} \rightarrow \hat{c}$ over time. If $g = 1$, consumption will be constant over the generations.

The path of consumption is constrained by the resources of the dynasty. In the constant elasticity case using (15) and allowing $T \rightarrow \infty$ implies

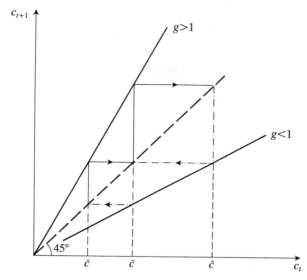

FIG. 6.1. The consumption of successive generations.

$$c_t = \left[1 - \frac{(1+r)^{\frac{1-\sigma}{\sigma}}}{(1+\rho)^{1/\sigma}} \right] \left[A_t + \sum_{i=0}^{\infty} \frac{H_{t+i}}{(1+r)^i} \right] = \mu R_t \qquad (18)$$

assuming $g < (1+r)$, i.e. $r - \rho < r\sigma$.

According to (18) the consumption of generation t is proportional to the resources of the dynasty evaluated at time t: R_t. The factor of proportionality — the marginal propensity to consume out of dynastic resources (μ) — depends positively on the rate of time preference and negatively on the rate of interest (if $\sigma < 1$).

The consumption function (18) is strongly reminiscent of permanent income hypothesis (PIH), as the astute reader will have realized. The present model is, in fact, the PIH applied with a vengence. The permanent income (wealth) of the family encompasses not only the present and future income of generation t, but also all subsequent generations. The family acts to smooth out 'transitory' variations in the resources of particular generations of the family to achieve the desired path of consumption. As with the PIH holding dynastic resources constant, the marginal propensity to consume out of the lifetime income of generation t is zero. If taken seriously, equation (18) implies that the usual measures of permanent income are deficient in failing to incorporate the endowments of subsequent generations.

2.2 Material wealth

Using the expression equivalent to (18) for generation $t+1$ together with equation (15) yields a linear equation for intergenerational wealth transfers:

$$A_{t+1} = g[A_t + H_t] - \widetilde{H}_{t+1} \left[1 - \frac{g}{1+r} \right] \tag{19}$$

where $\widetilde{H}_{t+1}$ represents the (present value of the) human wealth of all succeeding generations. Material wealth transfers are an increasing function of the assets and human capital of generation t and a decreasing function of the human wealth of *all* succeeding generations. This overlapping generations model of dynastic accumulation implies a 'forward looking' intergenerational savings function in which transfers are equalizing in that, *ceteris paribus*, the larger descendents' wealth the less they inherit. Tomes (1981) presents empirical evidence of this 'compensatory' element of bequests.

A linear intergenerational savings function similar to (19) has been derived by Shorrocks ((1979) equation (16), p. 418) and Bevan ((1979) equation (10), p. 386) using overlapping generations models of family altruism. Shorrocks in particular argues that even though the model may generate bequests of debt it provides a realistic description of the real world because: 'Negative transfers are not as absurd as they may appear at first sight, since financial support by children of their aged parents is not uncommon; and this phenomenon is likely to occur exactly in the circumstances predicted by the model' (Shorrocks (1979) 419). However, both Shorrocks and Bevan fail to emphasize the important implications of this model for intergenerational mobility; in particular, zero social mobility in consumption.

Equation (19) describes the behaviour of material wealth over successive generations. To examine its properties suppose that capital was the same for all generations (i.e. $H_{t+k} = H$ for all k). In this case equation (19) becomes:

$$A_{t+1} = gA_t + (g-1) \frac{H(1+r)}{r} \tag{20}$$

Figure 6.2 depicts the path of material wealth over succeeding generations for various values of g.

Equation (20) implies that individuals transfer to their heirs an amount proportional to their inheritance plus (or minus) an amount which depends on the human capital of the family. If $g > 1$, a generation with zero initial assets would donate material wealth of A^* to its descendent (see Fig. 6.2). The heir in turn would leave a larger amount (A^{**}) to the subsequent generation. There is no stable steady state; material wealth grows continuously. This rising path of material wealth finances the desired growth of consumption implied by (15).

If $g < 1$ material wealth transfers decline $\hat{A} \to \widetilde{A} \to \overline{A}$ approaching the

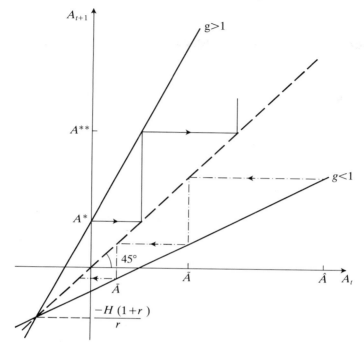

FIG. 6.2. The material wealth of successive generations.

steady state value of $A_s = \dfrac{-H(1+r)}{r}$. In this steady state parents bequeath a debt to their children equal to the present value of dynasty's human capital over all future generations.[3] If $g < 1$ this is the unique steady-state equilibrium and it is stable. If $g = 1$, given constant human wealth, each generation would pass on to its heirs a bequest exactly equal to the wealth it inherited. Each generation would act as if they had 'usufruct' rights to family wealth.

The path of material wealth over the generations is also described by the relationship

$$A_t = g^t[A_0 + \widetilde{H}_0] - \widetilde{H}_t = g^t R_0 - \widetilde{H}_t \tag{21}$$

where R_0 represents the dynastic resources of the initial generation of the family. According to this equation the material wealth of generation t depends on the initial resources of the dynasty and the human wealth of generation t and all succeeding generations. Initial differences in family resources result in differences in material wealth which are magnified over successive generations if $g > 1$. If $g < 1$, the influence of initial differences diminishes as families converge to the steady state. Equation (21) raises the possibility of social mobility in terms of material wealth. Material wealth depends not only on initial family resources, but also the human capital endowment of future generations. Among families with equal initial resources, these families with a larger present value of endowments in generation t will transfer less in the form of material wealth. Hence the rank of families in the distribution of material wealth would tend to change over the generations, producing intergenerational mobility in material wealth. However, since the resulting mobility in material wealth merely 'compensates' for mobility in human capital, this produces zero mobility in consumption — the result described earlier in this section.

If families differ in altruism (δ) with $g > 1$ for some families and $g < 1$ for others, the former would accumulate increasing material wealth and the latter would decumulate, giving rise to regression away from the mean and ever-increasing wealth inequality.

The intergenerational savings function (20) or (21) is of limited value in guiding empirical work, since it contains the human wealth of all succeeding generations — an unobservable. Fortunately, however, if the structural parameters remain constant, this unobservable can be eliminated to yield:

$$\frac{A_{t+1}}{1+r} = \left[1 + \frac{g}{1+r}\right] A_t + H_t - g[A_{t-1} + H_{t-1}] \tag{22}$$

In this formulation the bequest received by generation $t+1$ depends on the material wealth and human wealth of generation t and the lifetime resources of grandparents (I_{t-1}). Given data on these components the structural parameters g and r could be estimated. This relationship can also be written as:

$$\frac{A_{t+1}}{1+r} = \frac{g}{1+r} A_t + \{I_t - g I_{t-1}\} \tag{23}$$

In this formulation, bequests depend on material wealth plus the mobility of parents relative to grandparents in terms of lifetime income, adjusting for growth (g). Other things being equal, upwardly mobile parents are predicted to make larger bequests of material wealth. Put differently, equation (23) implies that wealth mobility follows income mobility with a lag of one generation.

This model also implies that material wealth will tend to run in families. Since in (22) the marginal propensity to bequeath out of material wealth exceeds the propensity to bequeath out of human wealth, families with a larger fraction of lifetime resources in the form of material wealth will make larger transfers of material wealth. Thus the concentration of the dynasty's 'portfolio' in the form of material wealth will tend to be perpetuated in subsequent generations.

2.3   Income

Lastly, we consider the implications of this model for intergenerational mobility in terms of lifetime incomes. This relationship is given by:

$$I_{t+1} = gI_t + H_{t+1} - \mu\widetilde{H}_{t+1} = gI_t + \frac{g}{1+r} H_{t+1} - \mu \frac{\widetilde{H}_{t+2}}{1+r} \qquad (24)$$

where $\widetilde{H}_{t+i}$ is the present value (at $t+i$) of the human capital endowments of generation $t+i$ and all subsequent generations. The lifetime income of generation $t+1$ is positively related to the income of the preceding generation and to its human capital endowment, but negatively related to the human capital endowment of subsequent generations. For a dynastic family with constant human capital endowments, lifetime incomes will be rising (falling) continuously over the generations if $g > 1$ ($g < 1$). The only steady-state solution is $I = -H/r$. This equilibrium is stable if $g < 1$. These properties may be illustrated with a diagram similar to Fig. 6.2.

The evolution of income over successive generations can also be described in terms of the incomes and human capital endowments of past generations:

$$I_{t+1} = [g + (1+r)]I_t - g(1+r)I_{t-1} + H_{t+1} - gH_t \qquad (25)$$

This equation can be compared to the relationship for material wealth transfers (22).

This relationship appears superficially similar to the equation linking the incomes of successive generations in the Becker–Tomes model (8a). However, notice that human capital endowments appear in (25), whereas endowments have been eliminated from (8a). Moreover, the inheritability coefficient (h) does not appear in (25). Assuming human capital endowments are transmitted according to (17) we derive the relationship:

$$I_{t+1} = (1-h)(1-g)\overline{H} + [g + h + (1+r)]I_t - [(g+h)(1+r) + gh]I_{t-1}$$
$$+ gh(1+r)I_{t-2} + v_{t+1} - gv_t \qquad (26)$$

In contrast to the Becker–Tomes model (equation (8a)), the lifetime income of generation $t+1$ depends on the incomes of the *three* preceding generations, with alternating positive and negative signs. In addition, there are now three important parameters: g, h, and $(1+r)$, rather than two: β and h.

III Extensions to the model

The foregoing section developed an alternative to the Becker–Tomes model and examined its implications regarding social mobility in terms of consumption, material wealth, and income. We now examine the impact of changing various assumptions regarding foresight and certainty; capital markets, fertility, and marriage. Rather than relaxing all these assumptions simultaneously, we analyse them one at a time.

3.1 Uncertainty

The discussion in the previous section assumed perfect certainty. However the luck of children in their adult careers and the abilities and endowments of all subsequent generations are unlikely to be known by parents. Moreover, due to moral hazard problems these risks are not fully insurable or diversifiable and must be borne, for the most part, by the family.

If parents maximize expected utility, the expected marginal utility of their children's utility will be proportional to the marginal utility of own consumption:

$$E_t U'(c_{t+1}) = \frac{U'(c_t)}{\delta(1+r)} \tag{27}$$

where E_t represents the expectation based on the information set at time t. Taking a second-order approximation to the L H S of (27) using the constant-elasticity function:[4]

$$E_t U'(c_{t+1}) \simeq a\hat{c}_{t+1}^{-\sigma} + \frac{a\sigma(1+\sigma)}{2} \hat{c}_{t+1}^{-(2+\sigma)} \sigma_\epsilon^2 \tag{28}$$

where $\hat{c}_{t+1}$ is the expected value of c_{t+1}, σ is the coefficient of relative risk aversion, σ_ϵ^2 is the variance in children's consumption.

Substituting this into (27) yields

$$\frac{\hat{c}_{t+1}}{c_t} = g \left\{ 1 + \frac{\sigma(1+\sigma)\sigma_\epsilon^2}{2\hat{c}_{t+1}^2} \right\}^{1/\sigma} \tag{29}$$

In the absence of uncertainty ($\sigma_\epsilon^2 = 0$) this reduces to (15). The introduction of uncertainty raises the desired rate of growth of consumption above g, by an amount that depends positively on the degree of risk aversion (σ). Note, however, that under uncertainty the growth rate of consumption is inversely related to the level of child's consumption; families with a high level of consumption will choose a lower rate of consumption growth. Consequently, the elasticity of child's consumption with respect to parents' consumption is less than unity, implying regression to the mean in relative consumption. The introduction of uncertainty with constant relative risk aversion is therefore sufficient to generate regression to the mean.

However, the impact of uncertainty depends critically on the functional form of the utility function. With constant, *absolute* risk aversion, the introduction of uncertainty does not imply regression to the mean[5] (Becker and Tomes (1986)). More generally, the effect of uncertainty on regression toward or away from the mean depends on the signs and magnitudes of second- and higher-order derivatives of the utility function; parameters we know little about.

3.2   Capital markets

A second crucial assumption employed in the preceding section is that capital markets are sufficiently perfect to permit the transfer of debt across the generations. Essentially this permits current generations to borrow against the human capital endowments of future generations. As a description of the real world this is highly implausible. Bevan (1979) in particular, has emphasized the importance of constraints on the transfer of debt.

Incorporating such a constraint results in two groups of families. Those families with substantial initial assets or relatively high human capital endowments, anticipating regression to the mean in the endowments of their descendents will be unaffected by the constraints. Such families can use bequests of material wealth to offset the declining human wealth of their children, resulting in little regression to the mean in consumption. Conversely, families with low (zero) initial assets and low human capital endowments, would like to borrow against the human wealth of future generations, but are prevented from doing so. Consequently, children's consumption will exceed that of parents. The net outcome is a non-linear (convex) relationship between the consumption of successive generations. Borrowing constraints generate an asymmetry in mobility between the rich and poor. Ascent out of poverty is likely to be quite rapid due to the inability of poor parents to 'tax' their well-endowed children. However, once a family has accumulated significant material wealth, the consumption of family members can be maintained for a substantial period of time via the transmission of material wealth. Hence social mobility among the rich and super-rich is predicted to be lower than among the poor. This scenario is also consistent with the observed skewness in the distribution of material wealth.

3.3   Fertility

Differential fertility can be introduced into the model in a variety of ways. One simple approach is to suppose that parents are concerned about the aggregate consumption of their descendents in future generations

$$U_t = \frac{c_t^{1-\sigma}}{1-\sigma} + \frac{\delta(n_t c_{t+1})^{1-\sigma}}{1-\sigma} + \frac{\delta^2(n_t n_{t+1} c_{t+2})^{1-\sigma}}{1-\sigma} + \dots \tag{30}$$

where n_t is the number of children born to adults of generation t. $n_t n_{t+1}$ is the number of grandchildren, etc. All family members in a given generation are assumed identical in terms of endowments, inheritance, consumption, and fertility.

The budget constraint needs to be modified

$$I_t = H_t + A_t = c_t + \frac{n_t A_{t+1}}{1+r} + \frac{n_t^{1+\beta}}{1+\beta} \tag{31}$$

The final term reflects the cost of producing children. It is assumed that children are produced subject to increasing marginal cost ($\beta > 0$). Successive substitution yields a constraint defined over the resources of all future generations of the dynasty.

The first-order conditions imply:

$$\frac{n_t c_{t+1}}{c_t} = [\delta(1+r)]^{1/\sigma} \tag{32}$$

The *aggregate* consumption of children, relative to parental consumption depends on the interest rate relative to the 'discount' rate. The first-order conditions regarding optimal fertility imply

$$n_t = \left(\frac{H_{t+1}}{1+r}\right)^{1/\beta} \tag{33}$$

Surprisingly, in this formulation, optimal family size is independent of the utility function and depends only on economic costs and returns to producing children. This independence arises from the fact that the number of children and their consumption enter multiplicatively in both the utility function and the budget constraint. Utility considerations determine the *aggregate* consumption of children. The choice between numbers of children and per capita consumption is determined by other factors. Here each child born receives an exogenous endowment of human capital, the present value of which represents the marginal benefit of producing a child. Optimal fertility is determined by equating marginal cost to the marginal benefit. In this model children are purely an investment good.

Given the level of fertility determined by (33) the rate of growth of per capita consumption is determined by:

$$\frac{c_{t+1}}{c_t} = [\delta(1+r)]^{1/\sigma} \left[\frac{H_{t+1}}{1+r}\right]^{-1/\beta} \tag{34}$$

Since endowments are expected to differ across families and across generations (34) implies that rates of growth in per capita consumption would also differ. Consequently, the rank of families in the distribution of consumption could change from generation. Therefore the introduction of endogenous fertility generates intergenerational mobility in per capita consumption.

3.4 Marriage

Imperfect assortative marriage has frequently been introduced in simulation models of income and wealth distribution (e.g. see Pryor (1973), Blinder (1973) (1976)). However, almost without exception marriage is introduced mechanistically — parental transfers are assumed independent of the matching of children in the 'marriage market'. In contrast, theoretical models suggest such a response. Just as parents can adjust transfers to offset the tendency of their children's human capital endowments to regress to the mean, they can do the same with respect to adverse or advantageous marriage, by their progeny. Therefore imperfect assortative marriage need not imply regression to the mean in consumption.

IV Summary and conclusions

This paper has examined theoretical models of the transmission of resources from parents to children and later descendents. The Becker–Tomes (1979) model was reviewed and an alternative model presented. Both models are based on utility-maximizing behaviour by parents concerned about the well-being of their children. The degree of social mobility — the rise and fall of families in the distributions of wealth and consumption were shown to depend on the interaction between utility-maximizing behaviour and the resources of different generations.

Alternative formulations yield strikingly different implications regarding social mobility in terms of income, wealth and consumption. In particular, given plausible parameter values, the Becker–Tomes model generates a stable equilibrium distribution, characterized by regression to the mean across the generations. Moreover, social mobility in terms of consumption mirrors intergenerational mobility in income.

In the alternative characterization, parents, endowed with perfect foresight are concerned about the utility of children, rather than their income. In this model there is no intergenerational mobility in consumption. Differences across families in consumption are perpetuated in each succeeding generation, due to parental transfers of material wealth (assets or debt) which offset the regression to the mean in endowments of human capital. Moreover, if the rate of interest exceeds the discount rate, there exists no stable steady state distribution of income and wealth. Inequality will increase with each succeeding generation.

The final section focused on the set of factors which may produce regression to the mean and stable steady state distributions of income, wealth, and consumption. The introduction of uncertainty and endogenous fertility are both sufficient to generate a significant degree of intergenerational social mobility in consumption. Finally, it was argued that capital market imperfections which limit the transmission of debt to progeny generate a non-linear relationship between the consumption of successive generations. This relationship is characterized by greater social mobility among the poor than among the rich. Hence, the ascent out of poverty should be relatively rapid, whereas the dissipation of sizeable family fortunes is predicted to be a more gradual process.

Notes

1. Parental contributions/investments may be either positive or negative (i.e., y_t, $x_t \geqq 0$), the latter case representing transfers of debt from parents to children.
2. Although transfers of debt are permitted, we assume that family members in any generation cannot borrow in excess of the present value of the human capital of all future generations. That is the resources of the dynasty: R_t are constrained to be non-negative in all generations: $R_t \geq 0$, for all t.
3. This prediction is consistent with simulation results reported by Bevan, who reports that for parameter values implying $g < 1$, '*most* people bequeath the maximum debt' (Bevan (1979) 373, emphasis in original).
4. Equation (28) differs from the one presented by Hall (1978) in that Hall presents a first-order approximation to (27). Taking account of the second-order term turns out to be important in determining the extent of regression to the mean.
5. With constant absolute risk aversion, the introduction of uncertainty merely influences the constant term: a on relationships of the form:

$$c_{t+1} = a + c_t + \epsilon_{t+1}$$

References

Barro, R. J., 'Are Government Bonds Net Wealth?', *Journal of Political Economy* **82** (1974), 1095–1118.

Becker, G. S., *A Treatise on the Family* (Harvard University Press, Cambridge, Ma., 1981).

—— and N. Tomes, 'Child Endowments and the Quantity and Quality of Children', *Journal of Political Economy* **84** Part 2, (1976), S143–S162.

—— and ——, 'An Equilibrium Theory of the Distribution of Income and Inter-generational Mobility', *Journal of Political Economy* **87** (1979), 1153–89.

—— and ——, 'Human Capital and the Rise and Fall of Families', *Journal of Labour Economics* **4** Part 2, (1986), S1–S39.

Bevan, D. L., 'Inheritance and the Distribution of Wealth', *Economica* **46** (1979), 381–402.

Blinder A. S., 'A Model of Inherited Wealth', *Quarterly Journal of Economics* **87** (1973), 608–26.

—— 'Inequality and Mobility in the Distribution of Wealth', *Kyklos* **29** (1976), 607–38.

—— *Toward an Economic Theory of Income Distribution* (MIT Press, Cambridge, Ma., 1974).

Hall, R. E., 'Stochastic Implications of the Life Cycle-Permanent Income Hypothesis — Theory and Evidence', *Journal of Political Economy* **86** (1978), 971–87.

Laitner, J. P., 'Household Bequests, Perfect Expectations, and the National Distribution of Wealth', *Econometrica* **47** (1979), 1175–93.

Pryor, F., 'Simulation of the Impact of Social and Economic Institutions on the Size

Distribution of Income and Wealth', *American Economic Review* **63** (1973), 50–72.

Shorrocks, A. F., 'On the Structure of Intergenerational Transfers between Families', *Economica* **46** (1979), 415–25.

Tomes, N., 'The Family, Inheritance and the Intergenerational Transmission of Inequality', *Journal of Political Economy* **89** (1981), 928–58.

—— 'On the Intergenerational Savings Function', *Oxford University Papers* **34** (1982), 108–34.

Comments on Chapter 6

LOUIS LEVY-GARBOUA

Université de Paris-I

Life-cycle theory has had a major influence upon the description of inequality by shifting from static measures of inequality to the lifetime inequality and intragenerational mobility. Models of overlapping generations now permit the incorporation of the question of intergenerational mobility whose role in explaining different types of societies — caste, class, or meritocratic societies — has been usually emphasized by sociologists.

Tomes presents two models for explaining intergenerational mobility: the Becker–Tomes model (1979) where interactions between only two successive generations have been considered, and a new model where a complete set of present as well as future generations are introduced (chapter 6, section II). Inspite of their apparent similarities, these two models often arrive at strikingly different conclusions, particularly in the context of consumption mobility. In fact, according to the first model, the latter will systematically follow income mobility whereas, according to the second model, it may be nil. In this comment, I try, first, to evaluate the sociological significance of these two models, and second, to look into the differences, real or imagined, between the two models.

I: The persistence of some degree of intergenerational social inertia, after adjustment for growth, has long been puzzling contemporary sociologists. The 'genetic' and 'culturalist' views which they have put forward to explain this fact emphasize the automatic transmission — through genetic or cultural mechanisms — of part of human capital from one generation to the next. Both models presented here take these mechanisms without attempting to separate them, which no one has yet succeeded to do in a convincing way.

The mechanism of hereditary transmission of human capital has been incorporated in both models by a constant parameter, namely, the degree of inheritability. It adds to the mechanism of voluntary acquisition of human capital. The novelty of these two models, *vis-à-vis* sociological literature, is twofold. First, novelty lies in its ability to show that if the mechanism of hereditary transmission is imperfect, like all other mechanisms found in real-life, there will be regression toward the mean between successive generations (and, to a lesser extent, within generations). Second, the novelty lies also in their suggestion that family decisions interact with endowments and luck to generate earnings, income, consumption, and the accumulation of human and material wealth.

In both models, a crucial role is played by the degree of inheritability and

166

hence one would like its value to be more explicitly linked with social organization. For example, it is evident that in a society where children are secluded from their parents and are brought up by specialists (schooling?), the hereditary transmission will be lesser compared to other societies where division of labour is less developed. Given this fact, a rise in schooling of children may have had a positive effect on intergenerational mobility which is not mentioned in these analyses. On the other hand, since the endowment is measured in terms of income, an estimation of the degree of inheritability may incorporate the direct effects of all kinds of hereditary economic discrimination and privileges. In case of segmented capital markets, children's access to the capital of parents itself may be analysed as an additional endowment associated with rich families or with non-wage earning families. It follows from these remarks that the degree of inheritability must be higher in discriminating societies than in democratic societies and in the traditional, highly agrarian and artisanal societies than in a modern society with developed labour market.

II: The difference between the two models lies mainly in their restrictive presentation of parental preferences. Becker and Tomes (1979) represent parental utility function as:

$$U_t = U(C_t, I_{t+1}) \tag{1}$$

where C_t is parents' lifetime consumption (generation t) and I_{t+1} is their children's lifetime income. I_{t+1} is an index of their children's 'quality'. But, it follows from the theory of social interaction (Becker (1974)) that an altruistic head of family, for whom a 'family utility function' exists, will generally behave differently. Indeed he will be directly concerned neither by any particular characteristic of his children, nor even by their 'income', but by their utility. Generally, the two behaviours would not be identical since children, like their parents, arbitrate between consumption and the utility of their progeny. Tomes' (section II) family utility function is alone compatible with the social interaction theory, that is to say, with the consequences of the hypothesis of altruism, when successive generations overlap:

$$U_t = U(C_t, U_{t+1}) = U(C_t, U(C_{t+1}, U(C_{t+2}, \ldots))) \tag{2}$$

The author limits himself, however, to an additively separable function:

$$U_t = U(C_t) + \delta U_{t+1} = \sum_{t=0}^{+\infty} \delta^i U(C_{t+i}) \tag{3}$$

by assuming, perhaps unduly, that every generation has the same preferences.[1] The coefficient δ, lying between 0 and 1, measures the degree of parental altruism.

The achievement of the present article is, then, to demonstrate, that a change in the specification of parental preferences has profound consequences on intergenerational mobility. This result has significant theoretical implications, but its empirical relevance is, perhaps, more limited. In fact, it highlights which assumptions regarding uncertainty and constraints in the capital market are needed for bringing closer the conclusions of the two alternative models. However, the exercise appears to be tricky for two reasons. First of all, the model's conclusions are highly sensitive to the types of uncertainty and to attitudes towards risks about which little is known so far. Indeed, it is difficult to deny that uncertainty is important in the context of intergenerational choices. Moreover, the stationary equilibrium income under perfect capital markets is negative, and therefore unrealizable as it will never permit the descendents to repay the debts contracted by their ascendents. This will imply that the capital market must be imperfect and that the credits will be limited by the borrower's repayment capacity and by the lender's aversion to risks. Credits may be rationed also if the borrowing rate of interest is prevented from adjusting itself to the risks specific to any given borrower.

An essential prerequisite for applying Tomes' (section II) model to real data is to explicitly take into account the hypotheses of uncertainty and imperfection of capital markets. But, as it is pointed out in the present paper, this brings closer the conclusions of the new model and that of the Becker–Tomes' model (1979). It is hardly surprising since the earlier model implicitly assumes that parents ignore everything in their descendents which is not hereditary, and that they cannot leave behind any debt for their children (This last assumption, as pointed out by Becker and Tomes (1986), plays a determining role in 'parents' propensity to invest in their children'). In other words, a realistic model of overlapping generations may finally be more similar than what it appears here, to the first Becker–Tomes model (1979). And this is what the future analyses should make clear.

If the consequences of the change in utility functions, from equation (1) to equations (2) or (3), when uncertainty and imperfection of capital markets are taken into account turn out to be really important, theories of human capital and fertility, in turn, should be reconsidered in the framework of an overlapping generations model.

Notes

1. The hypothesis about constant preferences for all successive generations may appear to be in slight contradiction with the hypothesis of imperfect hereditary transmission of personal characteristics.

7 The Joint Impact of Fertility Differentials and Social Security on the Accumulation and Distribution of Wealth

HELMUTH CREMER
Université de Liège and CORE

PIERRE PESTIEAU
*Université de Liège and CORE

The influence of mandatory retirement, saving, and intergenerational transfers on both the accumulation and distribution of physical wealth is now relatively well established. Both are closely linked to fertility: social security through the pay-as-you-go system in which taxes on the currently working persons are used to finance the pensions of their parents and bequests through the traditionally assumed equal division of estates.

Most analyses assume that all families have an identical number of children. As this is not the case in reality, this paper seeks to examine how fertility differentials affect the incidence of social security on the accumulation of saving and the distribution of wealth in an equal-estate-shares setting.

In the next section, the general features of the paper are presented. Then, within an extremely simple model of overlapping generations and random fertility individuals' saving and bequest behaviour is examined in section 2. It then appears that social security is neutral a la Barro in aggregate terms but not towards the personal distribution of bequests. The third section considers the dynamics of the model which is shown to converge towards a steady-state distribution of wealth under some assumptions. This section also studies the long-run effect on this distribution of changes in social security benefits and variations in the distribution of family size. The following section is devoted to a simulation exercise in which another demographic factor is considered besides fertility differentials, that is, uncertainty over the duration of life.[1] These two factors combined with social security are shown to have diverging effects. A final section provides the conclusions.

I The issue

The social security system, such as in vogue in most developed countries, operates on a pay-as-you-go basis; that is, payroll taxes are levied on workers

* We wish to thank J. Hamilton and S. P. Jenkins for very helpful comments. Financial support of the FNRS is also gratefully acknowledged.

to cover the cost of pensions that retirees are eligible to receive. There is thus no direct link between tax contributions and pension benefits within one's life cycle as in fully funded social security.

Because of this feature, social security may serve a double redistributive function. Within generations, expected pension benefits and taxes paid can be set to equalize life-time incomes. Between generations, pay-as-you-go social security implies some redistribution to earlier generations from later ones. So far, most of the empirical research on this matter has been addressed to the intragenerational aspect, and on this the evidence is quite mixed. Surveying a number of studies on the redistributive effects of social security, Danziger *et al.* (1981) reach the conclusions that it overall reduces poverty and increases income equality. On the other hand, Aaron (1977) finds the opposite result by focusing on demographic and life-time variables. It is now widely admitted that for both statistical and conceptual reasons, it is extremely difficult, if not impossible, to correctly measure the progressivity of social security between and within generations (see Kotlikoff (1985)). In that respect, the aim of this paper is merely conceptual. Starting off with a model a la Barro, it analyses the intergenerational effect of social security schemes in the case of fertility differentials on the intragenerational distribution of inherited wealth.

Barro's (1974) seminal paper points out that social security or any other intergenerational transfer scheme has no impact on the distribution of welfare over time if families exhibit the appropriate altruism. One of the main qualifications of this proposition is that the redistributive scheme is kept within the family or, alternatively, that the number of children is constant across families. Otherwise, it is clear, as alluded to by Barro (1981, 233) himself later on in a footnote[2], that individuals without children as compared to those with children and thus with ties to future generations will be made better off by pay-as-you-go social security. They indeed receive benefits they do not have to pay for through higher bequests to heirs they do not have. The introduction of fertility differentials in Barro's setting modifies the redistributiveness of social security in two ways. First, the distribution of resources over time can now be modified; namely, neutrality does not hold anymore. Second, the distribution of welfare within generations with varying family size can also be affected to the benefit of persons with a below-average number of children. In the analytical part of this paper, the model is specified so that aggregate neutrality still holds, thus stressing the intragenerational distribution of wealth.

In the simulation part, variations in family size but also in duration of life are jointly considered. One knows from Sheshinski and Weiss (1981) that, in general, with uncertain duration of life, social security and private bequest cannot be neutrally substituted for each other and therefore imposed changes in pension benefits will affect the allocation of resources over time. Moreover, one can expect that by acting as an annuity up to a certain level social security tends to decrease the inequality of (unplanned) bequests due to this type of uncertainty. In the opposite way, with fertility differentials, social security increases this inequality. The purpose of the simulation is precisely to assess through simple numerical examples the comparative incidence of these two conflicting demographic variables.

Fertility differentials across families have been observed at all times (see Festy (1979)) and, though slightly decreasing in many (developed) countries, they are still important. There is however no good explanatory theory of fertility differentials. There clearly exists a tendency among demographers and particularly economists to endogeneize the number of children along with choice variables such as savings, bequests, leisure, etc. . . . (see Becker (1981)). This approach is indeed very tempting and there is no doubt that families can exert some control over their fertility rate. It remains that a large fraction of family size differences cannot be accounted for by considerations of individuals' choice. It should instead be attributed to background factors such as religion, customs, . . . or random factors such as infecundity, infant mortality . . . which both have to be taken as exogenous.

In this paper, fertility differentials are thus assumed to escape individuals' control. It is also supposed that before making choices about saving, bequests, . . . households already know their number of heirs. The alternative assumption of having saving and bequest decisions made prior to their knowing of the exact number of children seems less realistic and clearly more difficult to deal with analytically.[3] Finally, it is supposed that family size at one point of time is not only independent of economic variables but also of the family sizes of one's ascent or descent. This assumption seems also better founded in empirical terms. Besides, were family size correlated over time, in the long run only large family dynasties would survive.

II   The model

The model used here is quite simple. Following Barro (1974) and Diamond (1965), it consists of a two-period overlapping generation setting in which individuals work in the first period of their life and retire in the second. Individuals are assumed to have perfect foresight. They are also assumed to care about the welfare of their children by leaving them bequests. Members of a generation are identical in all respects but two: the number of children and the inherited wealth.

2.1   Individual's choice

Each individual born at the beginning of period t is said to belong to generation t; he thus works in period t and retires in period $t + 1$. Let c_{1t}^i and c_{2t}^i be the consumption flows in the first and second periods of life of a member i of generation t. Let b_{t+1}^i be the level of bequests he is going to leave to each of his n^i children, belonging to the next generation $t + 1$. As we consider the case in which individuals care about their descendents, we include as an argument in their utility function net bequests per heir, h_{t+1}^i, that is, gross average bequests minus any transfer a_{t+1} imposed on the next generation to the benefit of the present one.[4] This approach in fact implies a specification a la Barro in which for each individual the maximum utility obtainable by his heir is included as an argument in his utility function. For analytical convenience, each individual is assumed to have a Cobb–Douglas utility function:

$$u_t^i = \alpha \log c_{1t}^i + \beta \log c_{2t}^i + \gamma \log h_{t+1}^i \tag{1}$$

where $h_{t+1}^i \equiv b_{t+1}^i - a_{t+1}$ and $\alpha + \beta + \gamma = 1$. His levels of consumption are:

$$\left. \begin{array}{l} c_{1t}^i = w_t + b_t^i - a_t - s_t^i \\[2mm] c_{2t}^i = r_{t+1} s_t^i + p_t - n^i b_{t+1}^i \end{array} \right\} \tag{2}$$

where s_t^i denotes holding of real assets; a_t is the payroll tax and p_t, the pension; w_t is wage income; r_{t+1} is the one-period gross rate of return on capital purchased in period t.

While n^i denotes the variable number of children, $\bar{n}$ is one plus the population growth rate. Let $y = f(k)$ be the per capita production function with the usual properties and with y for per capita output and k for the capital-labour ratio. One can express the rates of wage and interest as:

$$r_t = \frac{\partial f(k_t)}{\partial k_t} + 1 \quad \text{and} \quad w_t = f(k_t) - k_t \frac{\partial f(k_t)}{\partial k_t}.$$

Further, capital accumulation is equal to the previous period's total savings. In per capita terms, this yields:

$$k_{t+1} \equiv \bar{s}_t / \bar{n} \tag{3}$$

where $\bar{s}_t$ stands for average saving.

In each period t, the working generation which is $\bar{n}$ times more numerous than the retired generation pays a contribution of a_t for financing a pension p_{t-1} so that:

$$p_{t-1} = \bar{n} a_t.$$

One can thus rewrite the budget constraints (2) as:

$$c_{1t}^i + \frac{c_{2t}^i}{r_{t+1}} + \frac{n^i}{r_{t+1}} h_{t+1}^i = w_t + h_t^i + \frac{p_t}{r_{t+1}} \left(1 - \frac{n^i}{\bar{n}} \right) \tag{4}$$

where the RHS can be interpreted as 'full income' a la Becker.

Let us now solve the problem for an individual i of generation t who knows that he will have n^i children ($n^i \leq \bar{n}$). From the first order conditions for a maximum of the utility function (1) subject to (4), one derives the various demand functions and in particular those concerning bequests and savings. One indeed obtains the following expressions:

$$h_{t+1}^i = \frac{\gamma \, r_{t+1}}{n^i} \left[w_t + h_t^i + \frac{p_t}{r_{t+1}} \left(1 - \frac{n^i}{\bar{n}} \right) \right], \tag{5}$$

$$s_t^i = (1 - \alpha) \, [w_t + h_t^i] + \frac{\alpha p_t}{r_{t+1}} \left(\frac{n^i}{\bar{n}} - 1 \right). \tag{6}$$

Equations (5) and (6) indicate that for a given inherited wealth h_t^i and a given family size n^i, the net bequests an individual is going to leave to each of his heirs and the savings he is going to accumulate are a function of two terms:

(i) non-pension income made of wage earnings and net inheritance;
(ii) the wedge between average family size and his own.

It appears that in the particular case considered here bequests per child are inversely related to family size.

2.2 Aggregate level

If we now turn to the overall economy and look at the average level of bequest and capital accumulation, one gets the following expressions:

$$\bar{h}_{t+1} = \frac{\gamma}{\bar{n}} \, r_{t+1} [w_t + \bar{h}_t] \tag{7}$$

$$\bar{s}_t = (1 - \alpha) \, [w_t + \bar{h}_t] \tag{8}$$

where the bar is used for the mean values within a generation. In that respect $\bar{h}_{t+1}$ is defined over the population born in $t + 1$ whereas $\bar{s}_t$ is defined over the population born in t (see Pestieau (1984)). Note that we have in fact calculated the expected values of these variables and thus this approximation is only valid for large populations.

It thus appears that, on average, both bequests and savings are independent of the current level of public pensions and of the distribution of family size. In other words, Barro's neutrality results hold for the economy as a whole. Two remarks are needed on this. First, these results are uniquely due to the use of a Cobb–Douglas utility function which implies that the loss in savings incurred by above average families is offset by the gain made by below average families. Second, neutrality holds for average values but not for their distribution as is shown below.

2.3 Distribution of bequests

In this paper, wage earnings are the same for all within a generation, the emphasis is thus put on differences in accumulated and inherited wealth which are closely related; see (5) and (6). Among the various measures of inequality, we use the coefficient of variation because its derivation is particularly easy in the present setting. As the average bequest is independent of the level of social security, it suffices to look at the impact of public pensions variations on the variance of bequests.

From (5), one can indeed derive the variance of h_{t+1}^i; that is,

$$
\begin{aligned}
\text{Var } (h_{t+1}) = \gamma^2 \, r_{t+1}^2 \, \Bigg\{ & \frac{E(1/n)}{\bar{n}} \left[w_t^2 + E(h_t^2) + \left(\frac{p_t}{r_{t+1}} \right)^2 \right. \\
& \left. + 2 \, w_t \bar{h}_t + 2 \, w_t \frac{p_t}{r_{t+1}} + 2 \frac{p_t}{r_{t+1}} \bar{h}_t \right] \\
& - \frac{1}{\bar{n}^2} \left[w_t^2 + \bar{h}_t^2 + \left(\frac{p_t}{r_{t+1}} \right)^2 \right. \\
& \left. + 2 \, w_t \bar{h}_t + 2 \, w_t \frac{p_t}{r_{t+1}} + 2 \frac{p_t}{r_{t+1}} \bar{h}_t \right] \Bigg\}.
\end{aligned}
\tag{9}
$$

It follows by Jensen's inequality that an increase in public pensions p_t increases that variance and thus the inequality of net bequests:

$$
\frac{\partial \, \text{Var } (h_{t+1})}{\partial \, p_t} = \frac{2 \, \gamma^2 \, r_{t+1}}{\bar{n}} \left[\frac{p_t}{r_{t+1}} + w_t + \bar{h}_t \right] \left[E(1/n) - \frac{1}{\bar{n}} \right] > 0.
\tag{10}
$$

III   Long run equilibrium

3.1 Steady state solutions

We have here a dynamic system made of the three following first-order difference equations in $\bar{h}_t$, k_t and Var (h_t):

$$
\bar{h}_{t+1} = \frac{\gamma}{\bar{n}} \, r_{t+1} [w_t + \bar{h}_t]
\tag{7}
$$

$$
k_{t+1} = \frac{\gamma + \beta}{\bar{n}} \left[w_t + k_t \frac{\gamma}{\gamma + \beta} r_t \right]
\tag{11}
$$

and

$$
\text{Var } h_{t+1} = \gamma^2 \, r_{t+1}^2 \frac{E(1/n)}{\bar{n}} \text{ Var } h_t + \gamma^2 \, r_{t+1}^2 \left[\frac{E(1/n)}{\bar{n}} - \frac{1}{\bar{n}^2} \right].
$$

$$\left[w_t^2 + \bar{h}_t^2 + \left(\frac{p_t}{r_{t+1}} \right)^2 + 2 w_t \bar{h}_t + 2 w_t \frac{p_t}{r_{t+1}} + 2 \frac{p_t}{r_{t+1}} \bar{h}_t \right]$$

(12)

where $w_t = w(k_t)$ and $r_t = r(k_t)$ from the assumption of marginal productivity factor pricing and (11) is obtained from (3), (7) and (8).

If this dynamic process were to converge, its solution would be:

$$\bar{h} = \frac{w}{(\bar{n}/\gamma r) - 1}$$

(13)

$$k = \frac{\gamma + \beta}{\bar{n}} w \left(1 - \frac{\gamma r}{\bar{n}} \right)$$

(14)

with $\qquad \bar{n}/\gamma r > 1$

(15)

and

$$\text{Var} (h) = \left[1 - \gamma^2 r^2 \frac{E(1/n)}{\bar{n}} \right]^{-1} [E(1/n) - 1/\bar{n}] \gamma^2 \frac{r^2}{\bar{n}}$$

$$\left[w^2 + \frac{w^2}{(\bar{n}/\gamma r - 1)^2} + \left(\frac{p}{r} \right)^2 + \frac{2 w^2}{(\bar{n}/\gamma r - 1)} + 2 \frac{wp}{r} \right.$$

$$\left. + \frac{2 pw}{r(\bar{n}/\gamma r - 1)} \right]$$

(16)

with $\qquad \bar{n}/E(1/n) \gamma^2 r^2 > 1.$

(17)

One can easily check that (17) is implied by (15), a condition which is normally satisfied.

One can now verify that in the steady state, social security has a disequalizing incidence on the distribution of inherited wealth. Indeed, differentiating (16) with respect to p yields the following:

$$\frac{\partial \text{Var} (h)}{\partial p} = \left[1 - \gamma^2 r^2 \frac{E(1/n)}{\bar{n}} \right]^{-1} \left[E(1/n) - \frac{1}{\bar{n}} \right] 2 \gamma^2 \frac{r^2}{\bar{n}}$$

$$\left[\frac{p}{r^2} + \frac{w}{r} + \frac{w}{r(\bar{n}/\gamma r - 1)} \right] > 0.$$

It is also clear that an increase in the degree of fertility differentials as measured by $[E(1/n) - 1/\bar{n}]$ which approximates the variance of n^i (see Crama and Pestieau 1982)) also has a disequalizing impact.

3.2 Stability analysis

The stability analysis of capital accumulation epitomized by the average values k_t and $\bar{h}_t$ and of wealth distribution described by the variance of bequests Var (h_t) is relatively simple here. Indeed, to the extent that the accumulation process is independent of wealth distribution, one can just prove the (local) stability of the former and then of the latter. In other words, one is dealing with a recursive system which can be solved separately. We proceed here by first providing the conditions for the local stability of k and hence $\bar{h}$ and then, for a given value of k implying fixed rates of interest and wage, by looking at the stability of Var (h_t).

Equation (11) can also be written as:

$$k_{t+1} = \frac{1}{\bar{n}} \left[f(k_t)(\gamma + \beta - \beta\theta_t) + \gamma k_t \right] \tag{18}$$

with $\theta_t \equiv \dfrac{(r_t - 1) k_t}{f(k_t)}$ denoting the share of capital in production. In the steady state, one has:

$$\frac{f(k)}{k} = \frac{\bar{n} - \gamma}{\gamma + \beta - \beta\theta}. \tag{19}$$

For this equilibrium to be locally stable, one needs to have:

$$\frac{\partial k_{t+1}}{\partial k_t} = \frac{r}{\bar{n}} \left[\gamma - \beta \frac{k}{r} \cdot \frac{\partial r}{\partial k} \right] < 1$$

in the neighbourhood of the steady-state value k. This expression can also be expressed in terms of the elasticity of substitution σ; that is:

$$\frac{\partial k_{t+1}}{\partial k_t} = \frac{1}{\bar{n}} \left[r\gamma + (r - 1) \frac{\beta(1 - \theta)}{\sigma} \right] < 1$$

or, in view of (19):

$$\frac{(r-1)}{f(k)/k} \frac{\gamma + \beta(1 - \theta)/\sigma}{\gamma + \beta(1 - \theta)} < 1.$$

As $f(k)/k > \dfrac{\partial f}{\partial k}$ for all values of k, one can see that the stability condition is satisfied for $\sigma \geqslant 1$. This is clearly a sufficient but not a necessary condition. It is also quite intuitive; were σ very small, capital accumulation would imply a decreasing share of profits and thus, from (15) a possibly increasing rate of saving. Indeed, in this model the rate of capital accumulation depends on the share of wages $1 - \theta$.

Assuming that this condition holds and that thus k is a locally stable equilibrium, one can also state that the equilibrium value of h is equally stable. As to the variance of h, from (12), it is locally stable if, in the vicinity of the equilibrium values, condition (17) holds.

To sum up this section, we have shown that the process of wealth accumulation and distribution has a locally stable steady state, in which an increase in public pension has a disequalizing effect. We now turn to some numerical examples which serve two purposes. They illustrate the present analytical model and they allow for the introduction of an additional demographic variable, the uncertainty of lifetime which has an effect opposite to that of fertility differentials when combined with unfunded social security.

IV Simulations of the distributive effects of fertility differentials and uncertain lifetime combined with unfunded social security[5]

In the subsequent simulations, we basically follow the model of the previous section with a Cobb–Douglas utility function and a CES production function: $y = A[(1 - \alpha) + \alpha k^{-\rho}]^{-1/\rho}$ where $\sigma \equiv 1/1 + \rho$ is the standard elasticity of substitution. There is a single modification: lifetime is uncertain. To allow for a constant population without too many childless families, marriages are introduced though restricted to class mating: that is a man can only marry a woman next to him on their lifetime income scale. Other mating rules were also tried but deleted as they did not add anything relevant to the analysis at hand.

Couples either live one or two periods with a probability π and $(1 - \pi)$ respectively. In the former case, they are likely to leave some unexpected bequests. Each couple maximizes its expected utility given by: $\log c_1^i +$
$\pi \log c_2^i + \pi \log h_\pi^i + (1 - \pi) \log h_{1-\pi}^i$ where $h_\pi^i \equiv \dfrac{r s^i + p - c_2^i}{n^i} - a$ and
$h_{1-\pi}^i \equiv \dfrac{r s^i}{n^i} - a$ stand for the net bequests in case of retirement and premature death respectively. Saving and bequest decisions are made by the couple *per se* on the basis of its joint bequests and earnings and given the interest rate of the current period as perfect foresight is assumed here. Couples may have 1, 2, or 3 children with an equal probability.[6]

Each simulation starts with 400 unmarried people and an average capital stock of 200, the personal distribution of which may be arbitrary as the model converges to a steady state with respect to all its key variables. The evolution and the long run equilibrium values of these variables are presented in Tables 7.1 and 7.2 and Figures 7.1–7.5.

In Table 7.1, we present for various levels of public pensions the long-run values of $\bar{h}$, k, the coefficient of variation of h, and the average utility for three settings of uncertainty: only fertility differentials, only variable lifetime, combination of uncertain lifetime and family size. The production function is Cobb–Douglas: $\sigma = 1$, $A = 40.57$, and $\alpha = 0.25$; the probability for a couple to survive its retirement period is 0.8. In all simulations, the convergence is rapid.[7] However, because of the two sources of randomness, the convergence is only oscillatory (see Figs. 7.3–7.5). Therefore, the

TABLE 7.1. Long-run Values of Key Variables
$\sigma = 1$; $\alpha = 0.25$; $A = 40.57$

1. *Fertility differentials*

Payroll Tax	Pension	$\bar{h}$	Coefficient of variation	k	Average utility
0	0	74.98	0.5285	116.63	4.7014
20	20	75.48	0.5755	116.64	4.6970
40	40	74.97	0.6224	116.65	4.6908
60	60	74.97	0.6694	116.66	4.6826

2. *Uncertain lifetime* ($\pi = 0.8$)

Payroll Tax	Pension	$\bar{h}$	Coefficient of variation	k	Average utility
0	0	98.3	0.3908	129.02	4.5086
20	25	93.64	0.2869	125.05	4.4985
40	50	89.44	0.1727	121.79	4.4902
60	75	85.93	0.0497	119.61	4.4782

3. *Fertility differences and uncertain lifetime* ($\pi = 0.8$)

Payroll Tax	Pension	$\bar{h}$	Coefficient of variation	k	Average utility
0	0	97.08	0.7081	128.01	4.5096
20	20	92.82	0.6904	124.38	4.4989
40	50	89.02	0.6912	121.52	4.4843
60	75	86.24	0.7144	120.2	4.4665

long run values which are given in Table 7.1 are averaged over the 10th to the 30th period.

In Table 7.1 part 1, one clearly sees that in case of fertility differentials social security is neutral towards capital accumulation but disequalizing in terms of bequests or utility. Table 7.1 part 2 shows that with uncertain lifetime and in the absence of private life insurance market, social security decreases average welfare as it has a depressive effect on capital accumulation. Part 3 combines these two factors: as public pensions are raised, average utility diminishes but the coefficient of variation first decreases and then increases. This indicates that beyond a certain level of social security, the equalizing effect of insuring uncertain lifetime is offset by the disequalizing effect of discrimination against large families.

In Table 7.2, we consider different elasticities of substitution between labour and capital and we adopt a lower probability of survival. Comparing Table 7.2 part 2 and Table 7.1 part 3 shows that with a lower probability of survival, the depressive effect of social security on capital accumulation is stronger but the qualitative nature of the results is unchanged. Similarly, the degree of substitution does not seem to affect the conclusions.

TABLE 7.2.   Long-run Values of Key Variables
Fertility Differentials and Uncertain Lifetime
$\pi = 0.5$

1. $\sigma = 2$; $\alpha = 0.03$; $A = 79.5$

Payroll Tax	Pension	$\bar{h}$	Coefficient of variation	k	Average utility
0	0	136.95	0.7949	143.72	4.2068
20	40	122.35	0.7521	133.04	4.1807
40	80	111.63	0.736	126.76	4.1508
60	120	105.62	0.7594	125.75	4.1170

2. $\sigma = 1$; $\alpha = 0.25$; $A = 40.57$

Payroll Tax	Pension	$\bar{h}$	Coefficient of variation	k	Average utility
0	0	135.46	0.7839	144.61	4.2064
20	40	121.62	0.7447	133.76	4.1814
40	80	111.33	0.7312	127.41	4.1522
60	120	105.42	0.7557	126.42	4.1189

3. $\sigma = 0.5$; $\alpha = 0.975$; $A = 4.437$

Payroll Tax	Pension	$\bar{h}$	Coefficient of variation	k	Average utility
0	0	113.74	0.7657	145.22	4.1987
20	40	119.25	0.7315	134.18	4.1762
40	80	109.83	0.7229	127.69	4.1484
60	120	104.18	0.7495	126.86	4.1156

Figure 7.1 in fact illustrates Table 7.1; that is, the incidence on the coefficient of variation of bequests of various levels of social security contributions under the three demographic hypotheses. One clearly sees that when the two variability factors are combined, the inequality first decreases and then increases. If one looks at the effect on the average utility (Fig. 7.2), one sees that in all cases, it decreases with the cost of social security. In other words, even when the inequality decreases, the drop in capital accumulation is so significant that average welfare diminishes. Figures 7.3–7.5 then illustrate the evolution over time of the capital stock, the mean of net bequests and the wage rate.

V   Concluding remarks

This paper shows using an intentionally simple model that unfunded social security combined with fertility differentials may increase inequality in a world of intergenerational family transfers. With a Cobb–Douglas utility

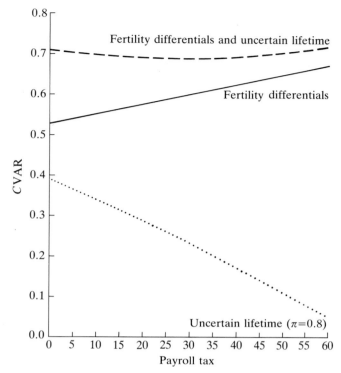

F IG. 7.1.   Steady-state coefficient of variation as a function of payroll taxes.

function, this disequalizing effect occurs even though the aggregate stock of capital is kept unchanged. It should be clear however that it would be observed as well with a more general utility function implying changes in capital accumulation. It is also clear that this unequalitarian effect is due to the pay-as-you-go rule of financing public pensions. With a funded social security regime, payroll taxes and private saving are perfect substitutes and an increase in public pension is thus not going to be shifted to higher bequests. In fact, the same disequalizing mechanism could be observed with debt financing of public spending to the extent that those who benefit from the expenditures allowed by the increased budget deficit are not the same as those who have to pay off the debt (see Cremer *et al.* (1987)).

It thus appears that through unfunded social security and debt financing, public authorities discriminate against large families. Do they so act purposely? Does that mean that large families are paying more than their share? One can in fact doubt that both social security and debt financing are vehicles consciously chosen by the government to redistribute resources from large to small families. In any case, to assess the net incidence of public policy

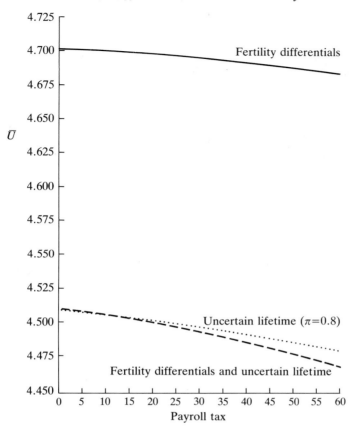

F IG . 7.2. Average level of individuals' steady-state utility as a function of payroll taxes.

towards families, one has to take into account other aspects, probably more important, such as the tax treatment of the family, the possible subsidization of day care, education . . .

Notes

1. If we only consider here these two factors, fertility and length-of-life uncertainty, and not, say, different mating or estate division patterns, it is to keep the paper within reasonable limits and because they are the only factors with which social security interferes directly.
2. Dealing with the question of the neutrality of debt finance, he writes: 'complication to the analysis arises when some taxpayers have more or less than the average

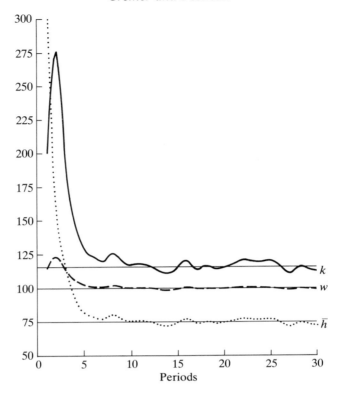

FIG. 7.3.   Convergence process of k, w, and $\bar{h}$ with fertility differentials.

number of descendents. For example, individuals without children may have no
ties to future generations and are therefore made better off by debt issue, although
such individuals must be matched by other persons with an above-average number
of children who are likely to be made worse off by debt issue. A second-order
wealth effect from debt issue would arise if these individual effects do not cancel
out through aggregation. Another second-order effect is the stimulus of debt issue
toward reduced family size, which would be motivated by the corresponding
reduction in family liability for the stream of future taxes.' See also Tobin (1980),
pp. 54–66, for an critical assessment of Barro's argument.

3. See Carmichael (1982). In any case, one could argue that most saving for retire-
    ment and inheritance comes after childbearing.
4. In such a specification people do not get any utility for having children; in fact,
    larger families have lower levels of utility. In an alternative specification used e.g.
    by Sheshinski and Weiss (1981) utility depends on total net bequest aggregated
    over all heirs; we believe that what really matters when the number of children is
    given exogenously is rather the amount of net bequest made per child.
5. This exercise is close to Pryor's (1973).
6. Considering another distribution did not affect the qualitative results.

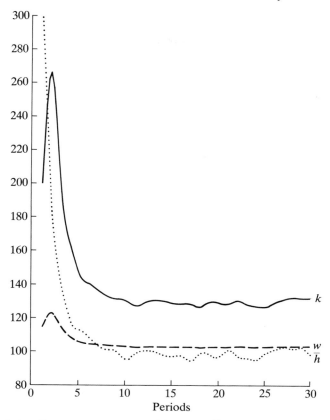

FIG. 7.4.   Convergence process of k, w, and $\bar{h}$ with uncertain lifetime.

7. One should however keep in mind that we are taking about at least 5 generations, that is, quite over 100 years. See Atkinson and Jenkins (1984).

References

Aaron, H., 'Demographic Effects on the Equity of Social Security Benefits', In M. Feldstein and R. Inman, (eds.), *The Economics of Public Service* (MacMillan, London, 1977).

Atkinson, A. B. and S. P. Jenkins, 'The Steady State Assumption and the Estimation of Distributional and Related Models', *Journal of Human Resources* **19** (1984), 358–76.

Barro, R. J., 'Are Government Bonds Net Wealth?', *Journal of Political Economy* **82** (1974), 358–76.

—— 'Public Debt and Taxes', in *Money, Expectations and the Business Cycles,*

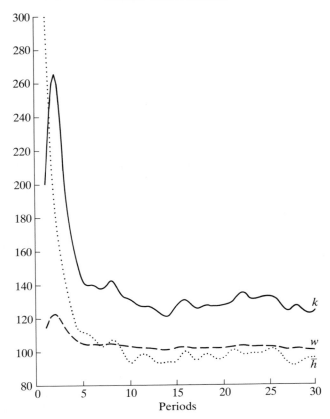

FIG. 7.5.   Convergence process of k, w, and $\bar{h}$ with variable fertility and lifetime.

Essays in Macroeconomics (Academic Press, New York, 1981), 227–41.

Becker G.S., *A Treatise on the Family* (Harvard University Press, Cambridge, Ma., 1981).

Carmichael, J., 'On Barro's Theorem of Debt Neutrality: the Irrelevance of Net Wealth', *American Economic Review* **72** (1982), 202–13.

Crama, Y. and P. Pestieau, 'Transmission and Distribution of Wealth with a Variable Number of Children', *Economic Letters* **10** (1982), 193–6.

Cremer, H., D. Kessler, and P. Pestieau, 'Fertility Differentials and the Regressive Effects of Public Debt', *Economica* **54** (1987), 79–87.

Danziger, S., R. Haveman, and R. Plotnick, 'How Income Transfers Affect Work, Saving and the Income Distribution', *Journal of Economic Literature* **19** (1981), 975–1028.

Diamond P., 'National Debt in a Neo-Classical Growth Model', *American Economic Review* **55** (1965), 1126–50.

Festy, P., *La fécondité des pays occidentaux de 1870 à 1979* (Presses Universitaires de France, Paris, 1979).

Kotlikoff, L. J., 'The Distributional Impact of Social Security: a Framework for Analysis', in *Florence International Population Conference* 2 (IUSSP, Liège, 1985), 485–99.

Pestieau, P., 'The Effects of Varying Family Size on the Transmission and Distribution of Wealth', *Oxford Economic Papers* **36** (1984), 400–17.

Pryor, F., 'Simulation of the Impact of Social and Economic Institutions on the Size Distribution of Income and Wealth', *American Economic Review* **63** (1973), 50–73.

Sheshinski, E. and Y. Weiss, 'Uncertainty and Optimal Social Security Systems', *Quarterly Journal of Economics* **96** (1981), 189–206.

Tobin, J., *Asset Accumulation and Economic Activity* (Basil Blackwell, Oxford, 1980).

Comments on Chapter 7

STEPHEN JENKINS

University of Bath

The specification of dynamic wealth distribution models is always a balancing act between, on the one hand, realism, and on the other, tractability. Within these constraints different authors have emphasized different influences, but because the precise contribution of one particular factor is usually conditional on what other factors are included, this creates difficulties in the interpretation of results across papers. It also means that 'one should be cautious in drawing conclusions about the impact of policy instruments without a complete model of the distribution' (Atkinson (1980) 63). By way of illustration note that the currently fashionable models emphasising the role of 'optimizing responses of parents to their own or to their childrens' circumstances' (Becker and Tomes (1979) 1165) employ very simple 'transmission' and 'demographic' assumptions, and yet there is a long tradition of so-called 'mechanical' or reduced-form models which has demonstrated that variations in these can have significant effects. (See, e.g. Atkinson and Harrison (1978); Meade (1976)).

Given these sentiments I therefore very much enjoyed the current paper, for it is in effect a sensitivity analysis of the effect of incorporating fertility differences between families into the well-known Barro (1974) framework. In the first part of the paper the authors argue that although pay-as-you-go (PAYG) social security remains neutral in aggregate, it will have a disequalizing effect on the distribution of inherited wealth. In the second part, simulations are used to illustrate this numerically and, additionally, to examine the effects of also including length-of-life uncertainty. In my remarks below I shall make some comments first on the model specifications used, and secondly on the interpretation of results.

Model specification

In the analytical model of Section II, individuals maximize a Cobb–Douglas utility function that depends on the net bequest per child, and the number of children *per se* has no effect on utility. The authors could have pointed out that their non-neutrality result is not completely robust to variations in this assumption; if, e.g., $u_t^i = \alpha \log c_{1t}^i + \beta \log c_{2t}^i + \gamma n_t^i \log h_{t+1}^i$, a specification related to that used by Sheshinski and Weiss (1981), then equation (9) becomes $\text{var}(h_{t+1}^i) = (\gamma r_{t+1})^2 \text{var}(h_{t+1}^i)$, and so in this case, the bequest

186

variance is independent of n^i_{t+1}. The authors say they believe that 'what really matters when the number of children is given exogenously is rather the amount of net bequest made per child' (note 4), but it is not clear that should necessarily be so. In essence they are arguing that children would be treated as if they were investment goods only (bequests by this generation leading to increases in future consumption), but there seems no reason to rule out consumption-type benefits entirely.

My second set of comments concerns the (re-)specification of the model for the simulations, but before turning to these I think it is worthwhile pointing out explicitly that the simulations do not simply provide numerical illustrations of known analytical results; as far as I am aware there is no theoretical paper to date that has jointly considered fertility differentials, length-of-life uncertainty, and social security in a model including bequest motives. With this observation in mind, and remembering how Atkinson and Harrison (1978, chapter 8) demonstrated that most of Pryor's (1973) simulation results could be derived analytically, I was motivated to consider what sort of progress one could make with such a theoretical model. However, things appear to get very complicated very quickly, and so the authors are indeed doing us a service with their simulations. To see this, consider the following simple model with a specification close in spirit to the paper. Taking the scenario set out in Section II but then grafting on length-of-life uncertainty as in Section IV, I assumed the optimization problem for each individual was to maximize with respect to s^i_t, c^i_{2t}: $\log(x^i_t - s^i_t) + \pi \log c^i_{2t} + \pi \log h^i_\pi + (1 - \pi) \log h^i_{1-\pi}$

where $\quad h^i_\pi = [rs^i_t - c^i_{2t} + a_{t+1}(\bar{n}\pi - 1)]/n^i_t$, using $p_t = \pi \bar{n} a_{t+1}$

$$h^i_{1-\pi} = [rs^i_t - n^i_t a_{t+1}]$$

$$c^i_{1t} = x^i_t - s^i_t$$

$$x^i_t = w + b^i_t - a_{t+1}$$

and w, r are exogenously given and constant. Disregarding non-negativity constraints, the first order conditions imply

$$x^i_t - s^i_t = (n^i_t/r)[h^i_\pi h^i_{1-\pi}/(\pi h^i_{1-\pi} + (1 - \pi)h^i_{1-\pi})]$$

$$c^i_{2t} = n^i_t h^i_\pi$$

and hence

$$c^i_{2t} = (rs^i_t + a_{t+1} g_t)/2, \text{ and}$$

$$A(s^i_t)^2 + Bs^i_t + C = 0$$

where $g_t \equiv (n\pi - 1)$

$A \equiv r^2(2 + \pi)$

$B \equiv a_{t+1}(g_t - n_t^i) - rx_t^i(1 + \pi)$

$C \equiv (a_{t+1})^2 n_t^i g_t - a_{t+1}rx_t^i [(1 - \pi)g_t - 2\pi n_t^i].$

However, these complicated expressions are not very informative, and I have been unable to make much further progress to date investigating the potential non-uniqueness of the optimal plan, let alone the aggregate and distributional implications.

This brings us back to the simulations and their specification. In my original comments, I wondered why marriage was introduced here but now note that it is to allow a constant population without too many childless families. Nevertheless I would have liked this point to have been elaborated further, for the authors' declared aim is to compare the opposing effects of fertility differences and length-of-life uncertainty, and it is harder to discern these when something else is altered. It also raises questions about the sensitivity of results to alternative assumptions about the pattern of mating and the authors' comment that 'other mating rules were also tried but deleted as they did not add anything relevant to the analysis' is not very clear. For example, results appear relatively robust to different values of the elasticity of substitution; do they mean variations in mating patterns had even less effect? I would also have liked the concept of 'lifetime income' (according to which marriage matching was done) to have been explained more; it is relatively ambiguous in a context of length-of-life uncertainty.

Interpretation of results

I have little to say about the interpretation of the theoretical results in Section II, except that I think the authors could have highlighted more the presence of terms related to fertility differences in the expressions for the variance of bequests (equations 12 and 16): after all, these are the basis of one of the key messages of the paper! And on a technical note: while the expression $E(1/n_t) - 1/E(n_t)$ is related to the variance of n_t ($= \text{var}(n_t)/E^3(n_t) + R$), it is not a very good 'approximation' as the underlying Taylor series is not convergent and its terms alternate in sign.

The results of the simulations are summarized in Tables 7.1 and 7.2 and associated Figures. Given my remarks above about the problems of incorporating both fertility difference and length-of-life uncertainty into models, Figure 7.1 is very interesting for it indicates very clearly that the joint effect of the two influences is not a simple linear combination of their separate effects; an illustration of the interdependency mentioned in my opening paragraph (though remember my caveat about marriage).

A second striking feature of the tables is that average utility is virtually unchanged as one goes down the columns of each panel. One might draw the conclusion that social welfare is remaining much the same, for given the constant population, $\bar{u}$ is simply a constant multiple of the Utilitarian unweighted-sum-of-individual-utilities SWF. However this view is open to the criticism that it is making unwarranted cardinal comparisons between situations, and in any case, it is not clear that the Utilitarian SWF is an appropriate one. One's position on this matters, because it bears directly on how one evaluates the outcomes of the different policy scenarios; it is my impression that the literature to date has tended to look at outcomes in terms of the effects on the distributions *per se* of consumption, saving, bequests, etc and not in terms of overall social welfare.

Although the authors do not discuss the status of their index, there are nevertheless some remarks about equity in the paper's final paragraph. I shall finish with some brief comments stimulated by the authors' observation that it 'appears that through unfunded social security and debt financing, public authorities discriminate against large families'. Is it appropriate to talk of discrimination? To be sure, the proportion of total tax revenues provided by a given *family* (i.e. the sum over all children from i at $t+1$) is larger for large families relative to smaller ones, but on the other hand, each *individual* at $t+1$ makes the same contribution (each pays the same a_{t+1} and receives the same pension at $t+2$). PAYG social security is being interpreted by the authors as a mechanism for implementing redistribution between generations of the same family (an 'annuity' perspective), in which case the redistribution between families may well be inequitable. A different view is that PAYG social security is a mechanism whereby one generation collectively makes provision for another (a 'tax-transfer' perspective), so that contributions and receipts should be assessed on rather a different basis and the paper's results are not necessarily inequitable. (See also Thompson (1983, section IC). Real-life social security systems have features reflecting both perspectives.) Note that if one were to emphasize the authors' interpretation, this would provide another rationale for making family size endogenous, for the institutional structure set up provides an incentive to avoid 'discrimination' by reducing family size.

References

Atkinson, A.B., 'Inheritance and the Redistribution of Wealth', in G.M. Heal and G.A. Hughes (eds.), *Public Policy and the Tax System* (Allen and Unwin, London, 1980).

—— and A.J. Harrison, *Distribution of Personal Wealth in Britain* (Cambridge University Press, Cambridge, 1978).

Barro, R. J., 'Are Government Bonds Net Wealth?', *Journal of Political Economy* **82** (1974), 1095–117.

Becker, G. S. and N. Tomes, 'An Equilibrium Theory of the Distribution of Income and Intergenerational Mobility', *Journal of Political Economy* **87** (1979), 1153–89.

Meade, J. E., *The Just Economy* (Allen and Unwin, London, 1976).

Pryor, F., 'Simulation of the Impact of Social and Economic Institutions on the Size Distribution of Income and Wealth', *American Economic Review* **63** (1973), 50–73.

Sheshinski, E. and Y. Weiss, 'Uncertainty and Optimal Social Security Systems', *Quarterly Journal of Economics* **96** (1981), 189–206.

Thomson, L. H., 'The Social Security Reform Debate', *Journal of Economic Literature* **11** (1983), 1425–67.

Uncertainty, Risk, and the Distribution of Wealth

8 Distributional Aspects of the Life Cycle Theory of Saving

RICHARD VAUGHAN*

University College, London

In the present paper it is proposed to investigate the formal relationship that exists between the life cycle model of saving and the nature of the equilibrium distribution of wealth which results from such behaviour. The analysis follows the distributional approach initiated in the context of wealth distribution by Sargan (1957) and Wold and Whittle (1957). The term 'distributional' in this paper will be used in the narrow sense to refer to a model which includes an equation determining the evolution of a size distribution function, where the equation itself is expressed in terms of that distribution function, e.g. $\partial f(x,t)/\partial t = \phi(.)$, where $f(x,t)$ refers to the number of agents having characteristic x at time t; and where $\phi(.)$ is some function to be specified, usually including terms in $f(x,t)$.

The problem posed in the title has indeed a history almost as long as the life cycle theory itself. The development of the 'new' theories of the consumption function, in particular the analyses of Modigliani and Brumberg (1954) and Friedman (1957), focused attention on the relationship between consumption and a wider definition of resources available to the individual than current income; thus the part that wealth, human and material, plays in such decisions was brought into greater prominence. Interest in these early studies remained largely centred on the determinants of current aggregate consumption, rather than on the implications for the distribution of wealth; however it may be noted that Friedman (1957) does consider briefly the implications of his consumption hypothesis as regards the distribution of wealth, and indeed that the study of wealth distributions can provide additional evidence in support (or refutation) of any consumption hypothesis.

In the most recent literature on wealth distribution, the life cycle theory of saving, with extension to cover interpersonal transfers, appears to be the cornerstone on which most analyses are founded. The papers split broadly into two classes, concerned respectively with intra- and intergenerational accumulation and transmission.[1] The present paper follows a somewhat different path to these analyses, however with the common factor of the life

* I am indebted to Professor E. Malinvaud and an anonymous referee for their comments on the analysis, particularly in reference to optimal savings behaviour and the problems associated with the lower boundary conditions for the solution of the distributional equations. The comments received by other participants at the seminar were also most useful in preparing the paper for publication. The usual disclaimer applies.

cycle hypothesis. In brief, the model assumes a changing population of individual agents, which are born, die, and pass wealth on to their heirs. The behaviour of individuals is determined by the life cycle hypothesis within an uncertain environment. In the simplest version of the model, individuals face identical expectations of return on their human and non-human capital, however since such returns are uncertain, they may each face a different realization of the stochastic process which generate such returns. As a result of their decisions to save and consume, and the uncertain outcome of events (including the possibility of death), the wealth of the individuals will change over time, which will therefore result in the evolution of the size distribution of wealth. The basic problem faced in the present paper is then to determine the equilibrium distribution of wealth (if any) which results, and to relate the properties of the equilibrium to the underlying behaviour of the individuals which comprise the distribution. In particular, it is hoped to relate statistical measures of the degree of economic inequality in income and wealth to such parameters as the degrees of risk aversion and time preference held by the population, and the level of uncertainty in income receipts faced by the population. In addition, the impact of taxation on such behaviour is explored, and its consequent ability to influence the degree of inequality in the equilibrium distribution of wealth.

The outline of the paper is as follows. In Section I we discuss the basic distributional methodology necessary for the subsequent analysis. Sections II and III outline the required model of life cycle behaviour and the implied cross-sectional savings function, which in Section IV is used to specify a complete distributional model. Section V is concerned with the generation of the resulting equilibrium distribution of wealth, whilst Section VI considers some comparative static exercises in relation to inequality measures defined on the equilibrium. In Section VII the impact of a linear tax/benefit system, including properties of the optimal tax, is studied; whilst Section VIII notes the implications of the model for aggregate savings behaviour. In the concluding section major structural differences between distributional and other models are discussed, including the role and definition of equilibrium; together with remarks concerning the robustness of the present specification.

I   Distributional framework

In this section we discuss the basic distributional methodology and outline four principal aspects of the problem which are incorporated in the formal model below.

The problem which confronts us is the explanation of changes which occur in the distribution of a large number of individual agents defined on some variate. The 'individual' referred to may be, e.g. an individual person or family group (or indeed in a wider context a corporate entity or other legal construct); the variate may be, e.g. income, wealth, or market capitalization, or it may be a multidimensional variate, e.g. the distribution of families according to income and wealth. The distribution itself is just one component of the wider economy, and the individuals which comprise the distribution are presumed to take independent economic action given the conditions prevailing in this wider context; e.g. the individual may decide to save and consume given the wage profile and the spectrum of interest rates prevailing in the market. The individuals who comprise the distribution may change, and the size of the total population may also change; in the case of individual persons there are biological births and deaths, and immigration/emigration with respect to the economy concerned; in the case of family units we have the biological reasons, in addition we have the birth of families when individuals split from existing families, and the deaths of families when individuals 'merge' through marriage. Naturally, alternative criteria for births and deaths may be specified other than in biological terms; e.g. it may be advantageous to define 'birth' in terms of some value of the state variable, e.g. an individual is 'born' when net wealth exceeds some prescribed value, conversely for 'deaths'.

From the above brief description of the environment and the individuals which comprise a distribution we propose to delimit four aspects of the problem which merit special attention:

(i)   the problem of the behaviour of the individuals which comprise the distribution function under study.

(ii) the problem of the determination of the macro-parameters which influence the individuals' behaviour, and the interaction between the mass of individual actions and the values of the macroparameters.

(iii) the influence of 'demographic' effects, or 'exit' and 'entry' on the distribution.

(iv) although to some extent implied by (i), (ii), and (iii), the equation which governs the size distribution function, with its attendant initial and boundary conditions.

The equation governing the evolution of the distribution function may be set up on 'accounting lines', and refers to the equality of certain flows of individuals on the state space. The distribution equation may in fact be viewed as an 'identity' or balancing equation for the net movement of individuals across any given wealth range; it cannot be falsified if correct cognizance is taken of the fact that individuals may move continuously over the state space, and also by discrete jumps at discrete moments of time. When specific forms for the coefficients of this equation are given, determined by the models of individual behaviour, the macroparameters, and possibly the demographic assumptions, then the equation is open to refutation.

As well as formulating the equation governing the 'main body' of individuals on the state space, we also have to take account of the conditions at the 'boundaries' of this space. Here the equations of individual accumulation need not apply. An example would be the case where we have an upper limit on the amount the individual might borrow. In such cases we have to specify the discontinuities in behaviour as regards individual accumulation, into constraints on the solution of the distributional equation.

Besides the specification of boundary conditions, we also have to state the initial conditions; in this case the initial distribution of individuals on the state space at the commencement of the working of the model, from which all subsequent distributions evolve.

The above elements, (i)–(iv), we believe constitute an adequate framework for the analysis of most size distribution problems in economics. Although we regard it necessary that an element from each of these 'boxes' be present in the model we consider, these elements may be as elaborate or as vestigial as we please. Thus if we wish to focus attention on the effects of saving and consumption on the distribution of wealth we may construct an elaborate theory of consumer behaviour, whilst incorporating the simplest of assumptions as regards births, deaths, and inheritances, and the determination of the macroparameters; conversely, we might wish to discuss complicated inheritance procedures, or a complex theory regarding determination of factor payments, whilst simplifying other aspects of the model. In the next section we specify the behaviour of the representative individual, i.e. item (i) of the above agenda, whilst in Section IV we complete the model by adding items (ii)–(iv) and generate the consequent equilibrium distribution of wealth.

II   The individual and the accumulation of wealth

In this section we shall be concerned with the formulation of individual savings behaviour. The procedure adopted is to specify the behaviour of the representative individual, and thence derive the implications for the cross-sectional savings function. The behaviour considered is based on assumptions that are traditional to the life cycle hypothesis. The individual faces a world in which both receipts of labour income and interest earned on wealth (represented by the sole financial asset) are not known with certainty; the individual however does know the stochastic dynamics of the income generating process. The price of the consumption good relative to the financial asset is assumed fixed. The individual plans consumption over an uncertain lifetime to maximize expected welfare, which is dependent on the consumption stream and on the amount of the financial asset left at death.

We adopt the following notation: $c(t)$, consumption level enjoyed at time t; w, the expected wage per unit period; r, the expected interest rate received on net wealth, $k(t)$; τ, the length of the individual's uncertain lifetime. Formally, we have

Assumptions 1

(i) The budget constraint of the representative individual is,

$$dk = (w + rk(t) - c(t))dt + \sigma(w + rk(t))dz \tag{1}$$

where dz stands for a Wiener process, and $w + rk(t) - c(t)$ and $\sigma^2(w + rk(t))^2$ are the instantaneous expected change in wealth and variance per unit time respectively.

(ii) The individual plans consumption over an uncertain lifetime τ, so as to maximize,

$$E_0 \int_0^\tau e^{-\xi t} U(c(t))dt + e^{-\xi \tau} V(k(\tau)) \tag{2}$$

where the expectation operator is conditional on the known value, $k(0)$, owned by the individual in the initial period of that individual's life (the inheritance), and is taken over all possible values of the random variables. $U(c(t))$ is the utility associated with the rate of consumption at each moment of time; $V(k(\tau))$ the utility associated with the terminal stock of wealth (the bequest motive); both being discounted at the rate $\xi > 0$.

(iii) The utility functions are both of constant elasticity type and defined by,

$$U(c(t)) = \frac{c(t)^{1-\epsilon}}{1 - \epsilon}; \tag{3}$$

$$V(k(\tau)) = \frac{B(w + rk(\tau))^{1-\epsilon}}{1 - \epsilon}, \tag{4}$$

$\epsilon \geq 0$, $B \geq 0$; i.e. ϵ is the elasticity of marginal utility with respect to consumption. If $B = 0$, no weight is attached to terminal transfers.

(iv) The individual is assumed to have a probability of dying in the interval δt of $\lambda \delta t + o(\delta t)$, $\lambda > 0$.

The above are pretty standard assumptions for such lifecycle models; however, two assumptions differ slightly from the usual formulations, and are perhaps therefore worthy of further comment.

Firstly, with respect to the budget constraint, we have assumed the instantaneous variance to depend on total income, inclusive of wage receipts, rather than simply on the level of wealth or interest payments; i.e. to embody the above mentioned assumption that uncertainty attaches to all income streams. If such is the case, it may be argued, then should not different uncertainties apply dependent on the income source? A possible justification for the use of the all-inclusive form (1) is to view the income stream as generated by the uncertain yield of a composite asset composed of both human and non-human capital. It is known that for iso-elastic marginal utility (e.g.

Merton (1969)) the portfolio selection decision is independent of the consumption decision; hence r and σ^2 may be viewed as composite parameters resulting from the prior determination of the optimal portfolio selection rule.

Secondly, we have assumed that the individual attaches utility to the (expected) income that is received by the heirs, rather than simply the non-human wealth that is transferred; also that the marginal utility of the bequest function is identical to that from consumption. We may attempt a justification of these assumptions along the lines suggested by Blinder (1974); suppose that each generation views its descendents as an infinite-lived family with the same tastes as its own. The total resources which the heirs will have are therefore given by the sum of its human capital plus the amount of its inheritance, i.e.,

$$\text{Total resources} = (w/r) + k(\tau) \tag{5}$$

at time τ. These resources may be used to purchase an infinite consumption stream, growing at rate g; and so discounting this stream at interest rate r, we have,

$$(w/r) + k(\tau) = \int_{t=\tau}^{\infty} C_\tau \, e^{g(t-\tau)} \, e^{-r(t-\tau)} \, dt$$

$$= C_\tau/(r-g) \tag{6}$$

i.e. $C_\tau = (r-g) \left(\dfrac{w}{r} + k(\tau) \right)$; where we have assumed that $r > g$. The utility which the individual expects the heirs to derive from this consumption is given by,

$$W_h = \int_{t=\tau}^{\infty} \frac{c(t)^{1-\epsilon}}{(1-\epsilon)} \, e^{-\xi(t-\tau)} \, dt$$

$$= \frac{C_\tau^{1-\epsilon}}{(1-\epsilon)(\xi - g(1-\epsilon))} \tag{7}$$

and hence, using (6), gives,

$$W_h = \frac{B(w + rk(\tau))^{1-\epsilon}}{(1-\epsilon)} \quad \text{with } B = \frac{(1-(g/r))^{1-\epsilon}}{(\xi - g(1-\epsilon))} \tag{8}$$

which may be recognised as the form (4). Note that under this interpretation B cannot be viewed as a constant (which for simplicity, we assume for the remainder of the paper), but as a function of the expected growth rate of consumption, discount rate and interest rate which the individual expects his heirs to face. The above argument follows Blinder (1974), except that Blinder does not consider any other resources which the heirs may have in planning consumption other than the inheritance.

The cumulative probability distribution of the individual dying before reaching the age τ is $(1 - e^{-\lambda \tau})$, thus (2) may be written as,

$$E_0^* \int_0^\infty e^{-\lambda \tau} \left[\int_0^\tau e^{-\xi t} U(c(t)) dt + e^{-\xi \tau} V(k(\tau)) \right] d\tau \tag{9}$$

Integrating (5) by parts, we have,

$$E_0^* \int_0^\infty [e^{-(\xi+\lambda)t} U(c(t)) + \lambda e^{-(\xi+\lambda)t} V(k(t))] dt \tag{10}$$

Thus the problem of choice of a consumption stream over an uncertain lifetime is transformed into an equivalent problem of choice over an infinite lifetime. Note that the term denoting the utility derived from the terminal capital stock has now become a component of the 'instantaneous' utility function, and E_0^* is the expectations operator over all random variables, except τ.

The formal problem is therefore to maximise (10) subject to the budget constraint (1). In addition, it is desired that certain initial and boundary conditions have to be satisfied. The initial condition is that the individual's wealth is $k(0)$; for the terminal condition we require that any solution path for the $c(t)$ must imply a finite value for the functional (10). In addition we desire that $c(t) > 0, 0 < t < \infty$, and that $k(t) \geqslant k_L$, both with probability unity. We shall consider the unrestricted solution, and then note the particular subsets of this solution (if any) which do not violate the initial and boundary conditions.

Maximising (10) subject to (1), we have the standard result,

Proposition 1

The optimal choice of consumption stream for the model satisfying Assumptions 1 is,[2]

$$c(t) = (1-s)(w + rk(t)) \tag{11}$$

where $(1-s) = (\delta - (1-\epsilon)r - \lambda D + \frac{1}{2}\sigma^2 r^2 \epsilon(1-\epsilon))/r\epsilon$; and where D is implicitly defined by $B = D(1-s)^{-\epsilon}/r$ and with $\delta = \xi + \lambda$.

Proof: Appendix 1

Thus we have the well known result that consumption is always a constant proportion of current income over time; this proportion being independent of the current age, income, or wealth of the individual. For (10) to constitute a feasible solution we require $c(t) > 0$ which provided $k(t) > -(w/r)$ is guaranteed if $(1-s) > 0$. The condition $k(t) \geqslant k_L$ is not met unless we assume that the individual can dissave up to the capitalized value of the 'certain' earned income stream, i.e. unless $k_L = -(w/r)$. However, given the assumption that the individual might die at any time, it may be unreasonable to suppose that any agent would be prepared to lend solely on the security of possible future wage receipts. Of course, if the lender can enforce payment of interest on the individual's heirs, then negative wealth holdings need not appear so unreasonable. The problem of the lower boundary will be considered further in the next section. The conditions under which (10) converges is considered in the Appendix; convergence is guaranteed if $s > 0$ and $\epsilon > 1$, but may also hold if $\epsilon < 1$.

Concerning comparative statics on the savings propensity, remembering that $\delta = \xi + \lambda$, we have,[3]

$$s = (r - \xi - \lambda(1-D) - \tfrac{1}{2}\sigma^2 r^2 \epsilon (1-\epsilon))/r\epsilon \tag{12}$$

The effect of changes in the probability of death, λ, on the savings propensity depends on whether $D \gtreqless 1$. λ may be seen as a factor which firstly increases the *de facto* discount rate δ, thus if there were no bequest motive for saving, an increase in λ would reduce s. On the other hand, λ is a factor which weights the utility of terminal wealth, and an increase in λ here strengthens the individual's desire to save. Which of these two influences predominates therefore depends on the magnitude of the constant D; note that if $D = 1$, then changes in the probability of death have no effect on s. The parameter σ/s may be recognised as the coefficient of variation of the change in wealth at each wealth level; an increase in σ will increase s if $\epsilon > 1$, and reduce s if $\epsilon < 1$. If $\epsilon = 1$, then s is invariant to changes in σ. If $\epsilon > 1$ and $D > 1$, then an increase in r increases s, otherwise the change in the savings propensity is ambiguous. Concerning the elasticity parameter ϵ, $\partial s/\partial \epsilon < 0$ if $s > 0$ and $\epsilon \leq \tfrac{1}{2}$; whilst $\partial s/\partial \epsilon > 0$ if $s < 0$ and $\epsilon \geq \tfrac{1}{2}$; otherwise the sign is ambiguous.

The model may also be interpreted in terms which relate rather more closely to existing theories of consumer behaviour under uncertainty. Let

$$k^*(t) = (w/r) + k(t) \tag{13}$$

be interpreted as the sum of human and non-human capital available to the individual at time t; as noted above, r may be seen as the return on this total capital, and income as $rk^*(t)$. The budget equation (1) may then be written as,

$$dk = (rk^*(t) - c(t))dt + \sigma^* k^*(t)dz \tag{14}$$

where we let $\sigma^* = \sigma r$, and henceforth treat as an independent parameter. For purposes of comparison with the existing literature we assume no bequest motive, i.e. $B = D = 0$; the optimal choice of consumption stream may then be written as,

$$c(t) = c^* k^*(t) \tag{15}$$

where c^* is the marginal propensity to consume from total capital, and,

$$c^* = (\delta - (1-\epsilon)r + \tfrac{1}{2}\sigma^{*2}\epsilon(1-\epsilon)\,)/\epsilon \qquad \epsilon \neq 1$$
$$= \delta \qquad\qquad\qquad\qquad\qquad\qquad\quad \epsilon = 1. \tag{16}$$

The above may be shown to be equivalent to those of Merton (1969) for the case of the composite asset.

Comparative static properties of consumption associated with changes in the mean return r, and variance σ^{*2}, are now relatively easy to calculate, and also bring rather more clearly into perspective the role of the parameter ϵ.

In Appendix 1 we have defined,

$$S(k,0) = \operatorname*{Max}_{c(t)} E_0 \int_{t=0}^{\infty} e^{-\delta t} U(c(t)\,)\,dt \tag{17}$$

subject to the budget constraint, as the expected total utility which the individual will enjoy, as viewed from time period 0. Partial derivatives of the consumption stream with respect to r or σ^{*2}, holding $S(k,0)$ constant, may therefore be viewed as intertemporal generalizations of the 'substitution effect'; e.g. $\partial c/\partial r$, may be broken down into corresponding 'substitution', $[\partial c/\partial r]_{\overline{S}}$ and 'income', $\partial c/\partial r - [\partial c/\partial r]_{\overline{S}}$, effects. Table 8.1 summarizes these effects for r and σ^{*2}.

The parameter ϵ is Pratt's (1964) measure of relative risk aversion. Considering the effects of changes in r, for individuals with low relative risk aversion, $\epsilon < 1$, the substitution effect can be seen to outweigh the income effect, and an increase in the rate of interest leads to a reduction in consumption; conversely for individuals with high relative risk aversion, $\epsilon > 1$. If $\epsilon = 1$, the Bernoulli case, then the income effect is exactly counterbalanced by the substitution effect, and hence changes in r have no effect on consumption. Concerning the effects of changes in σ^{*2}, for individuals with low relative risk aversion, $\epsilon < 1$, the substitution effect outweighs the income effect, and an increase in uncertainty increases consumption; conversely if $\epsilon > 1$. Again, for the Bernoulli case $\epsilon = 1$, the income and substitution effects are exactly counterbalanced.

It may therefore be seen that ϵ has a dual role; both in respect of the timing of consumption, which would apply in the absence of the risk factor σ^{*2}; and

TABLE 8.1. Income and Substitution Effects on $c(t)$ of r and σ^{*2}.

Parameter	Income Effect	Substitution Effect	Total Effect
r	k^*	$-k^*/\epsilon$	$\left(\dfrac{\epsilon-1}{\epsilon}\right)k^*$
σ^{*2}	$-\tfrac{1}{2}\epsilon k^*$	$\tfrac{1}{2}k^*$	$\tfrac{1}{2}(1-\epsilon)k^*$

in determining the response of the individual to risk. Such effects may be summarized in the consumption elasticies with respect to r and $\sigma*^2$,

$$e_{cr} = \frac{r(\epsilon - 1)}{c^*}; \tag{18}$$

$$e_{c\sigma*^2} = -\frac{1}{2}\frac{\sigma*^2(\epsilon - 1)}{c^*}. \tag{19}$$

For equiproportionate changes in r and $\sigma*^2$, then,

$$\begin{array}{l}\text{Proportionate Change}\\ \text{in Consumption}\end{array} = \frac{r(\epsilon - 1)}{c^*}\left[\frac{1}{\epsilon} - \frac{\sigma*^2}{2r}\right]\begin{array}{l}\text{Proportionate Change}\\ \text{in } r \text{ and } \sigma*^2.\end{array}$$

$$\tag{20}$$

For high risk averters 'the timing of consumption' factor predominates, and consumption increases if $\frac{1}{2}\sigma*^2/r < 1/\epsilon$; conversely if $\epsilon < 1$.

The above comparative static results are quite well known in the literature; however, their influence on economic inequality has not been studied to any great extent, and therefore the above results will be particularly useful in considering the comparative static exercises on the inequality coefficients in Section VI.

III The cross-sectional savings function

In the above discussion we have been concerned with the wealth accumulation of a single individual. However it is the cross-sectional savings function which is required in the next section to generate the wealth distribution. In considering the relation between individual savings behaviour we are faced, of course, with an aggregation problem. In order to facilitate a solution we therefore make the following assumptions:

Assumptions 2

(i) Each individual follows an identical optimization procedure which results in wealth being determined by equation (1), with consumption determined as in Proposition 1.

(ii) The only difference as between individuals at a given date is in their values of the state variables, i.e. wealth, and in the particular realization of the stochastic term which enters equation (1). Each individual's realization of the stochastic term is independent from the realization of every other individual.

The probability distribution of a single individual's *change* in wealth at a given moment t is normal with mean and variance given respectively by,

$$u_s = s(w + rk); \tag{21}$$

$$u_{ss} = \sigma^2(w + rk)^2 \tag{22}$$

which is simply a restatement of the meaning of (1) when (11) holds.

Now consider a population of N individuals, all of whom have identical wealth k at time t; we require the distribution of these individuals over changes in wealth. It follows that we cannot determine exactly a cross-sectional savings function, but only the *most probable* configuration of individuals over values of $v = dk$ which may arise; i.e. there is a finite probability, for example, that individuals with exactly the same wealth will all have the same value of v at the same time, since it is assumed that each individual's change in wealth is generated by an independent stochastic process. However, the following may be demonstrated,

Proposition 2

If Assumptions 2 hold, then the most likely cross-sectional distribution of wealth changes that are observed at each wealth level k will be that of a normal distribution with mean and variance defined by (21) and (22).

Proof: Appendix 2.

The assumption of a Poisson process generating death ensures that the probability of death is not dependent on the age of the individual. In the case where such a probability is age dependent, or a known life span is postulated, then the age of the individual will enter as a determinant of current savings. Such complications may be considered within the present model if it is remembered that we are dealing with cross-sectional savings relationships. If an equilibrium distribution exists then we may consider the joint distribution of individuals over wealth, age, or any other variables which may be thought to influence current savings.

As an example, consider m groups of individuals with identical wealth k at time t; within each group, mean and variance of the change in wealth are given by $s_i(w + rk)$, $\sigma_i^2(w + rk)^2$ and the number within each group is n_i, such that $\sum_i n_i = N$. The complete distribution of individuals over changes in wealth at wealth k is then given by the statistical mixture of the m group distributions. In the present case, we simply require the mean and variance of this mixture:

$$E(v) = \frac{1}{N} \sum_i u_s^i n_i = s(w + rk) \tag{23}$$

where $s = \sum_i s_i n_i / N$.

$$\text{Var}(v) = \frac{1}{N} \sum_i \sum_j (v_{ij} - s)^2 \tag{24}$$

which may be written as,

$$\text{Var}(v) = \sigma^2 (w + rk)^2 \tag{25}$$

with,

$$\sigma^2 = \frac{1}{N} \sum_i n_i \sigma_i^2 + \frac{1}{N} \sum_i (s_i - s)^2 n_i \tag{26}$$

i.e. the well-known weighted average of within group and between group variance. The analysis to generate the equilibrium distribution of wealth then follows as below, with the interpretation of s and σ^2 as composite values defined by (23) and (25). In more complicated cases s and σ^2 may themselves become functions of wealth; however without specification of the functional forms analytic solutions for the equilibrium distributions cannot be attempted.

IV   The individual and the distribution of wealth

The preceding sections were concerned with the behaviour of the individual, and the relationship between such behaviour and the cross-sectional savings function. In the present section we incorporate such behaviour within the framework of a distributional model. In addition, it is necessary to specify what happens to the individuals' wealth on death, i.e. the inheritance mechanism, and a statement of the appropriate boundary conditions, including that relating to possible negative wealth holdings.

The model can be outlined briefly as follows: in each time period we have a number of individuals distributed over certain wealth ranges, defined by the frequency distribution function of wealth, $h(k, t)$, denoting the number of individuals owning wealth k at time t. The change in wealth of each individual is governed by the life cycle hypothesis outlined in the previous sections, which as time passes generate changes in the initial distribution of wealth, $h(k, 0)$. The 'macroparameters' w and r are assumed fixed, exogenous to the behaviour of the individuals. In the simplest version of the model, wealth is passed on death to a single heir (the primogeniture assumption), previously assumed penniless; all individuals who do not inherit wealth at birth are presumed to enter the distribution penniless.

Formally, we may specify the mechanism generating the evolution of the distribution of wealth as follows:

Assumption 3

Within a given interval of time, δt, individuals may jump between wealth levels; the cumulative density function (c.d.f.) of these changes are defined by the continuous and differentiable function $G(k, k^*; \delta t)$, which gives the proportion of individuals having terminal wealth less than or equal to k conditional on initial wealth being k^*. The parameters of this distribution will be presumed to be dependent on the interval of time δt.

On the basis of the above assumption, the equation for the evolution of the c.d.f. of wealth, $H(k, t) = \int_{k_L}^{k} h(k, t)\, dk$ is therefore given by,

$$H(k, t + \delta t) = \int_{k_L}^{\infty} \frac{\partial H(k^*, t)}{\partial k^*}\, G(k, k^*; \delta t) dk^* \tag{27}$$

The equation may be interpreted as stating that the number of individuals having wealth less than or equal to k at time $(t + \delta t)$ equals the number of individuals in various wealth ranges at time t, weighted by the proportions in those ranges having a jump to a wealth range less than or equal to k, within the time period from t to $(t + \delta t)$.

As a consequence of the life cycle hypothesis, we have proposition 2 holding, i.e. the distribution $G(k, k^*; \delta t)$ is a normal distribution, with mean and variance defined respectively by (21) and (22). We may thus derive the result,

Proposition 3

The equation governing the evolution of $h(k, t)$, given A.1, A.2, A.3, is

$$\frac{\partial h(k, t)}{\partial t} = - \frac{\partial}{\partial k} (u_s(k) h(k, t)) + \frac{1}{2} \frac{\partial^2}{\partial k^2} (u_{ss}(k) h(k, t)) \tag{28}$$

Proof: Appendix 3.

Let us now turn to the specification of appropriate boundary conditions. It is useful to introduce the idea of the 'net flow' of individuals across a wealth range, in terms of which the boundary conditions can be expressed.

Definition 1

The 'net flow' of individuals across wealth range k is defined as,

$$\mathscr{F}(h(k, t)) = u_s h(k, t) - \frac{1}{2} \frac{\partial}{\partial k} (u_{ss} h(k, t)) \tag{29}$$

under the convention that net flow in the direction of higher wealth values is to be taken as a positive value.

The intuitive reason for this definition will now be seen. The number of individuals owning wealth greater than or equal to k is,

$$F(k,t) = \int_k^\infty h(k,t)dk = \left(\lim_{k \to \infty} H(k,t) \right) - H(k,t) \tag{30}$$

Now integrating equation (28) over the range $\left[k, \lim_{k \to \infty} \right]$, and using Definition 1, we arrive at the relationship,

$$\frac{\partial F(k,t)}{\partial t} = \mathscr{F}(h(k,t)) - \lim_{k \to \infty} \mathscr{F}(h(k,t)) \tag{31}$$

Equation (31) thus states that the change in the number of individuals owning wealth greater than or equal to k at time t, equals the net flow of individuals across wealth range k, less the net flow of individuals out of the distribution at very high wealth values.

In the present model we assume that no individual may leave the distribution except through death; in which case wealth is inherited by a single heir. The net flow across the upper boundary is therefore zero; a consideration we therefore formalise as,

Assumption 4

The upper boundary condition of the model is,

$$\lim_{k \to \infty} \mathscr{F}(h(k,t)) = 0 \tag{32}$$

Of course, combining (32) with (31), we have the immediate identification,

$$\frac{\partial F(k,t)}{\partial t} = \mathscr{F}(h(k,t)) \tag{33}$$

i.e. the change in the number of individuals owning wealth at or above k equals the net flow of individuals across that range.

Let us now turn to the lower boundary constraint. In most life cycle models of saving it is suggested that a lower limit be placed on the individual's wealth holding. The individual might wish to consume amounts permanently in excess of current income receipts, which can only be achieved by running down the wealth stock. To avoid the possibility of the individual enjoying large amounts of consumption throughout life with no supporting stream of receipts, a lower wealth bound, k_L, is usually imposed. The constraint may be recognised as institutional, it is imposed by prospective lenders; there may be nothing in the individual's inherent 'make-up' which would prevent the individual from forever borrowing, running further into debt, using the proceeds of this additional borrowing to service existing debt and consumption. In the context of the above life cycle model, setting k_L below $-(w/r)$ would be a redundant constraint, since at most, individuals dissave up to this value. It may be argued that k_L can never be positive if it is assumed that individuals are free to dispose of their wealth in whatever way they please. It is also important to distinguish clearly between the constraint that is imposed on the individual's accumulation and that which is imposed on the solution to the distributional equation (28). In what follows we shall consider the distribution for non-negative wealth values only, thus for the purposes of the solution of equation (28) the lower boundary is set at $k_L = 0$ (although for the sake of generality we retain an explicit statement of k_L in most of the following formulae). However, does not such a boundary constraint conflict with the solutions for optimal individual accumulation considered in Section II, in which no such restrictions were imposed on individual behaviour?

The apparent inconsistency may be resolved as follows. By considering a boundary of $k_L = 0$, for the distributional equation, we do not rule out the eventuality of individuals owning negative wealth, if such is implied by their optimizing behaviour; however, all that we require to specify a consistent model of wealth distribution over non-negative wealth values, are the flow conditions at the interface k_L. At this point we have,

$$\text{Net flow of individuals across } k_L \text{ as a result of accumulation/decumulation} = \mathcal{F}(\text{h}(k_L, t)_{acc} \tag{34}$$

where the subscript *acc* distinguishes this particular flow which may be either positive or negative; if positive we have a net flow *from* the negative wealth ranges, if negative a net flow *to* the negative wealth ranges. In equilibrium growth we shall impose the condition,[4]

$$\mathcal{F}(\text{h}(k_L, t))_{acc} = 0 \tag{35}$$

i.e. gross flows to and from the negative wealth ranges are exactly counterbalanced. If access to the negative wealth ranges can only be attained through k_L, then such a condition would imply absolute constancy in the numbers spread over the negative wealth ranges, i.e. between $k = -(w/r)$ and $k = 0$.

In addition, we have to consider the effects of the birth of new individuals. The distinguishing feature of primogeniture in our model is that we assume a continuing influx of penniless individuals, whilst the wealth holdings of individuals who die are immediately transferred to a single individual, previously assumed to have no wealth. It is not necessary to relate the individuals who die to the birth of new individuals; some individuals may die childless in the biological sense. The model thus only requires knowledge of the 'macro' flow of individuals into and out of the distribution. However, a more stylized version of the model in terms of the children associated with a single individual is also possible. In this case we assume that each individual has n children which are 'born' immediately prior to death; of these children, one receives all the parent's wealth, the other $(n-1)$ enter the distribution penniless. The 'stylized' version of the model may aid interpretation of parameters which relate to the macro flows of births and deaths.

Let us now formalize these assumptions in terms of the boundary conditions. We may note that the total population, $N(t)$, at any point in time is given by,

$$F(k_L, t) = N(t) \tag{36}$$

Of this population, constant proportions $\mu, \lambda > 0$ are assumed to be born and die in each period, thus we have,

Assumption 5

The rate of change of the population is,

$$\frac{dN(t)}{dt} = (\mu - \lambda)N(t) = gN(t) \tag{37}$$

$\mu/\lambda = n > 1$; i.e. $g = \lambda(n-1)$. n may be viewed as the number of children which are 'born' to every person immediately prior to death.

Now consider the number of individuals who enter the distribution penniless. In each period $\lambda N(t)$ individuals receive their 'parents'' wealth; since there is no tax on transference, these individuals immediately step into their 'parents'' shoes, and we may view the 'parent' as never really dying, at least in relation to the evolution of the wealth distribution. The number of individuals who enter the distribution penniless are thus equal to the number of births less the number who inherit their 'parents'' wealth, which is thus the rate of change of the population defined by (37). So combining (35) and (37), we have the lower boundary condition,

Assumption 6

The net flow of individuals across $k_L = 0$, defining the lower boundary condition of the model, is given by,

$$\mathscr{F}(h(k_L, t)) = \mathscr{F}(h(k_L, t))_{acc} + \mathscr{F}(h(k_L, t))_{births} \tag{38}$$

which in equilibrium growth, with $\mathscr{F}(h(k_L, t))_{acc} = 0$, gives

$$\mathscr{F}(h(k_L, t)) = gF(k_L, t) \tag{39}$$

Finally, to complete the specification of the model we note the distribution of wealth which exists at the start-up point.

Assumption 7

In the initial period, $t = 0$, the distribution of wealth is defined by,

$$h(k,0) = h^0(k) \quad k_L \le k < \infty \tag{40}$$

where $h^0(k)$ is continuous and differentiable up to the required order.

As we see in the next section, this last assumption is not required for the specification of the equilibrium distribution, and is mentioned here only for the sake of completeness.

It was assumed above that the rule of primogeniture in inheritance was applicable, and that on death wealth was transferred to a penniless individual. Here we shall briefly note a general equation which may be utilized for the analysis of alternative inheritance rules, and which gives an alternative perspective on the distributional equation (28).

In addition to the kernel $G(k, k^*; \delta t)$ in (27) defining the movement of individuals across wealth ranges as a result of saving, we may also conceive of a separate, independent kernel $G^1(k, k^*)$ which defines movement across wealth ranges as a result of interpersonal transfers of wealth (including gifts and inheritance). The equation corresponding to (28) would then be given by,

$$\frac{\partial h(k,t)}{\partial t} = -\frac{\partial}{\partial k}(u_s h(k,t)) + \frac{1}{2}\frac{\partial^2}{\partial k^2}(u_{ss} h(k,t)) - \lambda h(k,t)$$

$$+ \int_{k_L}^{\infty} h(k^*,t) g^1(k, k^*) dk^* \tag{41}$$

where $g^1(k, k^*) = \partial G^1(k, k^*)/\partial k$. Equation (41) may be seen as the formal demographic accounting identity,

$$\frac{\partial h(k,t)}{\partial t} = \begin{array}{c}\text{Net change in}\\\text{numbers as a}\\\text{result of saving}\end{array} - \begin{array}{c}\text{Number of}\\\text{individuals}\\\text{who die in}\\\text{wealth range } k\end{array} + \begin{array}{c}\text{Net change in}\\\text{numbers as a}\\\text{result of}\\\text{transfers.}\end{array}$$

If the transfer kernel induces a constant flow across wealth ranges then it may be shown that an equivalent form to the primogeniture solution results; if the net effect of the transfer flow plus deaths is not significant then of course we arrive back with (28). In this formulation, no assumption has to be made concerning the passing of wealth at death to a person with zero wealth; wealth may be transferred during life, and the recipient may already own existing wealth.

V   The equilibrium distribution of wealth

The problem of determining the evolution of the distribution of wealth can be succinctly stated as that of finding a $h(k,t) \geq 0$, for all k, $k_L \leq k < \infty$; $t \geq 0$, which satisfies (28), the boundary conditions (32) and (39), and the initial condition (40). As can be seen, the four elements stated in Section II are present in the formulation; the only vestigial element being the role of the 'macroparameters', w and r, which are presumed exogenous.[5]

In the present paper we shall not be concerned with the problem of distributional dynamics, but only with the equilibrium solution. Accordingly we find it appropriate to define the equilibrium concept, and thence derive the flow condition which must hold in such circumstances.

Definition 2

The equilibrium distribution $h(k,t) \geq 0$, $k_L \leq k < \infty$, is that which satisfies (28), (32), (39) and the condition,

$$\frac{\partial}{\partial t} \left(F(k,t)/F(k_L,t) \right) = 0 \tag{43}$$

i.e. the distribution in which the relative numbers of individuals in each of the wealth ranges remains constant over time.

The following is an immediate implication.

Proposition 4

Given a constant growth rate of the population, g, then the equilibrium distribution must satisfy the flow condition,

$$\mathscr{F}(h(k,t)) = gF(k,t), k_L \leq k < \infty \tag{44}$$

Proof:
Equation (43) states,

$$\frac{\partial F(k,t)}{\partial t} - \frac{F(k,t)}{F(k_L,t)} \frac{\partial F(k_L,t)}{\partial t} = 0 \tag{45}$$

given that $F(k_L,t) > 0$. A constant growth rate of the population however implies,

$$\frac{\partial F(k_L,t)}{\partial t} = gF(k_L,t) \tag{46}$$

and so (45) becomes, using (33),

$$\frac{\partial F(k,t)}{\partial t} = \mathscr{F}(h(k,t)) = gF(k,t) \tag{47}$$

Thus for an equilibrium distribution the net flow of individuals across any wealth range, k, must be proportional to the number of individuals who have wealth greater than or equal to k. This somewhat self evident proposition may be recognised as an extension to *all* wealth ranges of the lower boundary condition (39).

We may now proceed to the derivation of the equilibrium distribution of wealth, embodied in the following proposition.[6]

Proposition 5

The equilibrium distribution of wealth consequent on individual savings behaviour defined by (21), (22) and satisfying the flow condition (44), and boundary conditions (32) and (39), is,

$$F(k,t) = N(0)e^{gt}\left[\frac{w+rk}{w+rk_L}\right]^{-\alpha} \tag{48}$$

where the coefficient α is defined by,

$$\alpha = \frac{1}{2} - \frac{s}{\sigma^2 r} + \left[\left(\frac{s}{\sigma^2 r} - \frac{1}{2}\right)^2 + \frac{2g}{\sigma^2 r^2}\right]^{\frac{1}{2}} \tag{49}$$

Proof:
As a trial solution let,

$$h(k,t) = N(0)e^{gt}h(k) \tag{50}$$

hence, with u_s and u_{ss} defined by (21) and (22), $h(k)$ must satisfy,

$$-\frac{1}{2}\frac{\partial^2}{\partial k^2}\left(\sigma^2(w+rk)^2 h(k)\right) + \frac{\partial}{\partial k}\left(s(w+rk)h(k)\right) - gh(k) = 0 \tag{51}$$

As a further trial let,

$$h(k) = (w+rq)^q \tag{52}$$

and so substituting (52) in (51), and noting that $(w+rk) \neq 0$, $k \geqslant k_L$, we require to find q satisfying,

$$\sigma^2 r^2 q^2 + (3\sigma^2 r^2 - 2sr)q - 2(sr - \sigma^2 r^2 - g) = 0 \tag{53}$$

The two roots are,

$$q_{1(-),2(+)} = \left(\frac{sr}{\sigma^2 r^2} - \frac{3}{2}\right) \pm \left[\left(\frac{sr}{\sigma^2 r^2} - \frac{1}{2}\right)^2 + \frac{2g}{\sigma^2 r^2}\right]^{\frac{1}{2}} \tag{54}$$

Since the trial solution may be multiplied by any constant and still satisfy (53), we therefore have as a possible solution,

$$h(k) = C_1(w+rk)^{q_1} + C_2(w+rk)^{q_2} \tag{55}$$

where C_1 and C_2 are arbitrary constants.

In addition however, any solution must satisfy the normalization condition,

$$\int_{k_L}^{\infty} h(k,t)dk = N(0)e^{gt} \text{ or } \int_{k_L}^{\infty} h(k)dk = 1 \tag{56}$$

Thus substituting (55) in (56) we require,

$$C_1 \left[\frac{(w+rk)^{q_1+1}}{(q_1+1)r}\right]_{k_L}^{\infty} + C_2 \left[\frac{(w+rk)^{q_2+1}}{(q_2+1)r}\right]_{k_L}^{\infty} = 1 \tag{57}$$

Since $g > 0$, $q_1 + 1 < 0$ whilst $q_2 + 1 > 0$, and so for (57) to be satisfied we must have $C_2 = 0$. With C_1 then determined from (57) the solution for $h(k)$ is,

$$h(k) = \frac{-(q_1+1)r}{(w+rk_L)} \left[\frac{(w+rk)}{(w+rk_L)}\right]^{q_1} \tag{58}$$

and with $F(k,t) = N(0)e^{gt} \int_{k_L}^{\infty} h(k)dk$, we arrive at (48). Note that the boundary conditions (32) and (39) are satisfied.

The normalised distribution of (48) may be recognised as an exact Paretian Type in income, $y = w + rk$, and asymptotically Paretian in wealth.[7]

The Paretian coefficient (49) may be greater or less than unity, and is always positive. The fact that α may be less than unity would imply that mean wealth is infinite; in the present model such would result from a disjunction between the rate of population growth, and the parameters which determine the growth rate of aggregate capital, s and r; the rate of growth of capital being permanently in excess of that of the population.[8]

At this point we may inquire as to whether the theory generates 'realistic' values for the Pareto coefficient. All the parameters entering (49) are reasonably familiar, except perhaps for σ, the coefficient of variation of savings. Taking rule of thumb values, $s = 0.20$, $g = 0.01$, $r = 0.03$, and $\sigma = 0.20$ gives a value of $\alpha = 1.66$. The value of $\sigma = 0.20$ lies close to the Klein and Morgan (1951) estimates of the standard deviation of saving as a proportion of mean income; which for higher income ranges was close to 0.19. For the lowest income range the estimate of σ was closer to 0.5; using this estimate for σ, retaining the other parameter values gives an $\alpha = 1.64$. Both of these values lie close to the range of commonly observed values of α, at least for the UK and a number of Scandinavian countries.

VI Economic inequality

One of the advantages of working with models which generate the functional form of the equilibrium distribution, is that one is free to define any particular inequality index on the distribution, without initially having to frame the model in terms of that index. Thus working with the distribution of income, $y = w + rk$, $k \geq k_L$, which is exactly Paretian Type I, we may note the relationship between certain inequality indices and α. Thus for the Atkinson index, where ρ is the inequality aversion parameter ($\rho \neq 1$), we have,

$$A = 1 - \frac{(\alpha - 1)}{\alpha} \left[\frac{\alpha}{\alpha + \rho - 1} \right]^{1/(1-\rho)} \tag{59}$$

and other simple relationships in terms of α may be established for many of the popular inequality measures, e.g. the Coefficient of Variation, Gini Coefficient, and Variance of Logarithms.[9] It may be established, both for the Atkinson index and the others mentioned that $\partial \text{Index}/\partial \alpha < 0$ (when such measures exist). An increase in the value of α, i.e. the Pareto line becoming steeper, has usually been thought of as a reduction in inequality, and this appears to be confirmed for the Type I distribution in terms of the above mentioned measures; although there has been a continuing debate as to the meaning of the Pareto coefficient and an independent definition of 'inequality' (e.g. Samuelson (1965), in relation to the class of Pareto-Levy distributions).

Comparative statics performed on α can hence be immediately transformed into their impact on the above measures (and indeed many others). It is simpler to work with a relationship implicitly defining α, which on squaring (49) and rearranging, gives,

$$\alpha rs - g + \tfrac{1}{2}\sigma^2 r^2 \alpha (\alpha - 1) = 0 \tag{60}$$

Following from the discussion at the end of the last section it will be assumed that parameter values are restricted to the case where a value of $\alpha > 1$ is generated; further that s is positive, or more strictly $s > -\tfrac{1}{2}\sigma^2 r(2\alpha - 1)$. The case where s does not satisfy this restriction is noted briefly below.

6.1 Changes in savings propensity, s

$$\frac{\partial \alpha}{\partial s} = -\alpha (s + \tfrac{1}{2}\sigma^2 r(2\alpha - 1))^{-1} < 0 \tag{61}$$

i.e. an increase in s unambiguously leads to an increase in inequality. The result appears to be an inevitable consequence of increasing the average rate of growth for everybody, which ensures a greater proportion of individuals above any point on the income scale (apart from the lower boundary) and thus a lowering of α.

6.2   Changes in the interest rate, *r*

$$\frac{\partial \alpha}{\partial r} = - \left(\alpha s + \sigma^2 \alpha (\alpha - 1) + \alpha \frac{\partial s}{\partial r}\right) (s + \tfrac{1}{2}\sigma^2 r(2\alpha - 1))^{-1} \tag{62}$$

As noted in Section II, the sign of $\partial s / \partial r$ is ambiguous; if $\epsilon > 1$ and $D > 1$, then $\partial s / \partial r > 0$ and so $\partial \alpha / \partial r < 0$; i.e. an increase in inequality; otherwise $\partial s / \partial r \gtrless 0$ and so $\partial \alpha / \partial r \gtrless 0$. It can however be seen that unless the effect of *r* is strong enough to reduce the savings propensity by a sufficient degree, the effect of increasing *r* will always be to increase inequality. Again the main avenue through which this result is reached is by the effect on the average growth rate of wealth, *sr*, as noted in (i) above.

6.3   Changes in growth rate of population, *g* (λ fixed, *n* varies)

By holding λ fixed and allowing changes in *g* to occur via *n* we are able to note the 'pure' effect of population growth with no corresponding changes in *s* (via λ).

$$\frac{\partial \alpha}{\partial g} = (sr + \tfrac{1}{2}\sigma^2 r^2 (2\alpha - 1))^{-1} > 0 \tag{63}$$

i.e. an increase in *g* leads to a reduction in inequality. An apparent consequence of raising the growth rate of the population relative to the average growth rate of wealth, is a smaller proportion of individuals above any point on the income scale (apart from the lower boundary) and thus a raising of α.

6.4   Changes in coefficient of variation, σ

$$\frac{\partial \alpha}{\partial \sigma^2} = - \left(\alpha \frac{\partial s}{\partial \sigma^2} + \tfrac{1}{2} r(\alpha - 1)\alpha\right) (s + \tfrac{1}{2}\sigma^2 r(2\alpha - 1))^{-1} \tag{64}$$

If $\epsilon < 1$, then $\partial s / \partial \sigma^2 < 0$, and if this change is sufficiently strong this could lead to $\partial \alpha / \partial \sigma^2 > 0$, i.e. a reduction in inequality. However, this mechanism essentially works through changes in *s*, as noted in (i). If $\partial s / \partial \sigma^2 = 0$ (reinforced if $\partial s / \partial \sigma^2 > 0$) then we have the 'pure' effect of changes in σ^2 on inequality, leading to a reduction in α, and hence an increase in inequality. Given the apparent symmetry of the distribution of changes in wealth, it might appear that no intuitive explanation for the effect of σ^2 could be offered. It is however suggested that it is the impact of the lower boundary which is causing this effect, by truncating the high negative wealth changes of their impact on the distribution. A raising of σ^2 increases the relative importance of such ignored wealth changes, the larger proportion of high positive wealth changes of course receiving their full weight.

6.5   Changes in ξ, *D* and ε

The remaining parameters influence on inequality is through their influence on *s*. Following the discussion at the end of Section II, we may simply note that since $\partial\alpha/\partial s < 0$, and that $\partial s/\partial\xi < 0$ and $\partial s/\partial D > 0$, then an increase in the discount rate reduces inequality; whilst a strengthening of the inheritance motive for saving increases inequality. If $s > 0$ and $\epsilon \leq \frac{1}{2}$ then $\partial s/\partial\epsilon < 0$, and so an increase in ϵ reduces inequality.

We have in the above assumed $s > -\frac{1}{2}\sigma^2 r(2\alpha - 1)$; reversing this inequality gives a mirror image of the above results.

Comparative statics may also be performed on the 'total capital' version of the model. The marginal propensity to consume out of total capital is given by,

$$c^* = r(1 - s) \tag{65}$$

and so substituting for c^* and σ^{*2} in (60), we have,

$$\alpha(r - c^*) - g + \tfrac{1}{2}\sigma^{*2}\alpha(\alpha - 1) = 0 \tag{66}$$

and so we may derive,

$$\frac{\partial\alpha}{\partial c^*} = \frac{\alpha}{(r - c^*) + \tfrac{1}{2}\sigma^{*2}(2\alpha - 1)} \tag{67}$$

Considering only the case of $s > 0$, then $(r - c^*) > 0$, and so with $\alpha > 1$, $\partial\alpha/\partial c^* > 0$, an increase in the propensity to consume out of total capital leads to a reduction in inequality. In the absence of a bequest motive, we have seen that,

$$\frac{\partial c^*}{\partial r} = \frac{\epsilon - 1}{\epsilon}; \quad \frac{\partial c^*}{\partial\sigma^{*2}} = \tfrac{1}{2}(1 - \epsilon) \tag{68), (69}$$

hence the impact of such parameter changes on inequality depends on the degree of relative risk aversion which is prevalent within the community; the effects are summarized in Table 8.2.

The above qualitative effects apply if inequality is measured by the Pareto coefficient, or certain transforms thereof, e.g. the Atkinson (A) or Gini (G) measures. The complete switch in the effects of r and σ^{*2} on inequality, dependent on the prevalence of a particular response to risk within the community, is quite striking; as such this emphasizes the importance of an appropriate model of individual behaviour within any distributional framework, prior to any reasoned assessment of the effects of such parameters on

TABLE 8.2.   Effects on Inequality (α, A and G) of changes in r and σ^{*2}.

Increase in:	Relative Risk Aversion		
	$\epsilon < 1$	$\epsilon = 1$	$\epsilon > 1$
r	Inequality increases	No effect	Inequality decreases
σ^{*2}	Inequality decreases	No effect	Inequality increases

any measure of inequality. Such an argument may, of course, be made irrespective of the merits of the life cycle model used in the present framework.

VII   Taxation and welfare

In the present section we consider the impact of a linear tax/benefit system on the distribution of income and wealth generated, and thus consequently on the level of economic welfare. Some consideration is then given to the derivation of an optimal choice of tax rate within the linear tax system. We first derive the implications for individual behaviour, and then the consequences for the distribution.

Assumption 8

Individuals are each given a tax free payment of y_0; all other income is taxed at the same proportionate rate, T. The individual's disposable income, y_d, is given by,

$$y_d = y_0 + (1 - T)(w + rk) \tag{70}$$

for $y_0 \geq 0$, $0 \leq T \leq 1$, $k_L \leq k < \infty$.

The relationship between y_0 and the tax rate T will be considered below dependent on whether the system is self-financing.

The individual is assumed to plan consumption according to the life cycle model of Section II, except that replacing A.1(i) we have:

Assumption 9

The budget constraint of the representative individual is,

$$dk = (y_0 + (1 - T)(w + rk(t)) - c(t))dt + \sigma y_d dz \tag{71}$$

We have therefore assumed that uncertainty with respect to changes in wealth is now related to disposable income. Of course, σ may have quite a different value to the corresponding parameter in (1), reflecting possible uncertainties with respect to welfare receipts or tax payments.

As may be seen, by defining $w^* = y_0 + (1 - T)w$, and $r^* = (1 - T)r$, exactly the same analysis as in Sections II and III may be carried out; resulting in the corresponding propositions:

Proposition 6

The optimal choice of consumption stream for the model satisfying A.8, A.9, A.1(ii)–(iv) is,

$$c(t) = (1-s^*)y_d \tag{72}$$

where $(1-s^*) = (\delta - (1-\epsilon)r(1-T) - \lambda D + \sigma^2 r^2(1-T)\epsilon(\epsilon-1))/r\epsilon$; and where D is implicitly defined by $B = D(1-s^*)^{-\epsilon}/r(1-T)$.

Proof: As for Proposition 1 with w^* and r^* replacing w and r.
Equations (21) and (22) are replaced by,

$$u_s^* = s^* y_d; \quad u_{ss}^* = \sigma^2 y_d^2 \tag{73}, (74)$$

and replacing Proposition 5,

Proposition 7

The equilibrium distribution of wealth consequent on individual savings behaviour defined by (73) and (74) and satisfying the flow condition (44), and boundary conditions (32) and (39) is,

$$F(k,t) = N(0)e^{gt}(y_d/y_L)^{-\alpha} \tag{75}$$

where $y_L = y_0 + (1-T)(w+rk_L)$ and,

$$\alpha = \frac{1}{2} - \frac{s^*}{\sigma^2 r^*} + \left[\left(\frac{s^*}{\sigma^2 r^*} - \frac{1}{2}\right)^2 + \frac{2g}{\sigma r^{*2}}\right]^{\frac{1}{2}} \tag{76}$$

Proof: As for Proposition 5 with s^*, w^*, and r^* replacing s, w, r.

Before considering the effects of the tax system on economic welfare, let us note the impact on economic inequality. The principal effect is via the impact of the marginal tax rate T on the *de facto* rate of interest $r^* = r(1-T)$. A similar argument as in Section 6.2 should therefore be followed. Let us here particularly enquire as to whether any 'perverse' effects of changes in taxation can occur; by 'perverse' in this context we mean whether an increase in the marginal tax rate may increase inequality rather than reduce it. At this stage, since inequality in disposable income depends on α (using our afore-mentioned measures of inequality), which is independent of y_0, we do not need to enquire whether the tax system is self financing or not.

The equation, using (76), implicitly defining α is,

$$\alpha s^* r(1-T) - g - \tfrac{1}{2}\sigma^2 r^2(1-T)^2 \alpha(\alpha-1) = 0 \tag{77}$$

and we have,

$$\frac{\partial \alpha}{\partial T} = \frac{s^* r\alpha - \alpha(1-T)r\dfrac{\partial s^*}{\partial T} + \sigma^2 r^2 \alpha(\alpha-1)(1-T)}{s^* r(1-T) + \tfrac{1}{2}\sigma^2 r^2(1-T)^2(2\alpha-1)} \tag{78}$$

Assuming that $s^* > -\tfrac{1}{2}\sigma^2 r(1-T)(2\alpha-1)$, then if $\epsilon > 1$ and $D > 1$, we have $\partial s^*/\partial T < 0$ and so $\partial \alpha/\partial T > 0$; otherwise the sign of $\partial s^*/\partial T$ is ambiguous, and so is that of $\partial\alpha/\partial T$. It can however be seen that unless the effect of T is sufficiently strong so as to raise s^* to more than outweigh the positive components of the numerator of (78), then the 'perverse' effect of a higher T increasing inequality cannot arise and we will have the 'normal' result $\partial\alpha/\partial T > 0$.

Let us now consider the effects of such a tax/benefit system on aggregate economic welfare.

Assumption 10

The social welfare function is of the additive utilitarian form defined on disposable income:

$$W = \int_{y_L}^{\infty} W(y_d)\,h(y_d)\,dy_d \tag{79}$$

where $W(y_d) = y_d^{1-\rho}/(1-\rho)$ and $y_L = y_0 + (1-T)(w+rk_L)$.
We may immediately derive,

Proposition 8

The equilibrium level of economic welfare under Proposition given A.10 is,[10]

$$W = \frac{\alpha}{(\alpha+\rho-1)}\,(y_L^{1-\rho}/(1-\rho)) \tag{80}$$

Proof: Substituting normalized distribution $h(y_d)$ implied by (75) in (79).

In order to progress further we require knowledge as to whether the tax/benefit system is self-financing. If the system is self-financed then total receipts must be counterbalanced by total payments, i.e.,

$$y_0 N(t) = T\int_{k_L}^{\infty} (w+rk)\,h^T(k,t)\,dk \tag{81}$$

where $h^T(k,t)$ denotes the post-tax/benefit frequency density function (f.d.f.) of wealth implied by Proposition 7.

Now,

$$\bar{y} = y_0 + (1-T)(w+r\bar{k}) \tag{82}$$

and since we have self-financing,

$$y_0 = T(w+r\bar{k}) = T\bar{y} \tag{83}$$

where, $\bar{k} = \dfrac{1}{N(t)} \displaystyle\int_{k_L}^{\infty} kh^T(k,t)\,dk$ (84)

In addition, as we see from Proposition 7, the distribution of disposable income is exactly Paretian, so,

$$\bar{y} = \frac{\alpha}{(\alpha - 1)}\, y_L \tag{85}$$

which on combining with (83) and remembering $y_L = y_0 + (1 - T)(w + rk_L)$ allows us to solve for y_L as,

$$y_L = \frac{(\alpha - 1)(1 - T)}{\alpha(1 - T) - 1}\,(w + rk_L) \tag{86}$$

Thus combining (86) with (80), we have for the self-financing linear tax/benefit system aggregate economic welfare defined by,

$$W = \left[\frac{(\alpha - 1)(1 - T)}{\alpha(1 - T) - 1}\right]^{1-\rho} \frac{\alpha}{(\alpha + \rho - 1)} \frac{(w + rk_L)^{1-\rho}}{(1 - \rho)} \tag{87}$$

Welfare is therefore a function of the sole tax parameter T, and the optimal tax rate may be determined where W attains a maximum on the interval $0 \le T \le 1$.

As a first consideration, let us choose between the cases $T = 0$, and $T = 1$. The case $T = 0$ needs little explanation; it is the welfare which results when no tax/benefit system is in operation. From (87) we have,

$$W(0) = \frac{\alpha(0)}{(\alpha(0) + \rho - 1)} \frac{w^{1-\rho}}{(1 - \rho)} \tag{88}$$

where we have included our assumption $k_L = 0$, and written W and α, as explicit functions of T.

The case $T = 1$ requires a little explanation; letting $T = 1$ in (87) and using the appropriate limit procedures (since $\displaystyle\lim_{T \to 1} \alpha(T) = \infty$, as may be seen from (76)), we arrive at,

$$W(1) = \frac{w^{1-\rho}}{(1 - \rho)} \tag{89}$$

Under our assumption of exogeneity of factor prices, this solution indeed makes intuitive sense. If all income is confiscated except for the state benefit y_0, individuals under the life cycle hypothesis have no incentive to save (assuming that the wealth asset itself cannot be consumed, and any sales are treated as income). With population growing at rate g, then in long run equilibrium growth, mean interest payments taxed and available for redistribution approach zero — hence the only substantive income taxed is the common wage payment w, which given the self-financing nature of the system, is immediately distributed back to the population. Every individual therefore receives benefit w, which generates welfare given by (89).

We thus immediately note that,

$$W(0) = \frac{\alpha(0)}{(\alpha(0) + \rho - 1)} \, W(1) \tag{90}$$

i.e. under the above assumptions welfare under a no tax system will always be higher than under a confiscatory tax system. (Remembering that when $\rho > 1$, welfare is measured along the negative axis).

Now let us consider whether a positive marginal tax rate will ever be levied, or will a zero tax always be the optimum.

Standardizing welfare on $W(1)$ and taking logarithms of (87) we may show,

$$\frac{\partial \log(W(T)/W(1))}{\partial T} = \frac{(1-\rho)}{\alpha(T)(1-T)-1} \left[\frac{1}{(1-T)} - \frac{\alpha(T)T\rho + (\alpha(T)-1)^2}{(\alpha(T)-1)(\alpha(T)+\rho-1)\alpha(T)} \frac{\partial\alpha(T)}{\partial T} \right] \tag{91}$$

The first order condition for a maximum is therefore,

$$\frac{\alpha(T)T\rho + (\alpha(T)-1)^2}{(\alpha(T)-1)(\alpha(T)+\rho-1)\alpha(T)} \frac{\partial\alpha(T)}{\partial T} = \frac{1}{(1-T)} \tag{92}$$

Now, for an interior maximum $(1-T) > 0$, $\alpha(T) > 1$, $\rho > 0$, by assumption, and so the coefficient of $\partial\alpha(T)/\partial T$ in (92) is always positive. Hence, for (92) to hold we must have $\partial\alpha(T)/\partial T > 0$, i.e. the 'normal' relation not the 'perverse' relation of Section VI. If $\partial\alpha(T)/\partial T < 0$, then we must have a corner solution, and since as we have seen above $T = 1$ will never be chosen, a tax rate $T = 0$ must be implied.

The fact that a first order condition might be satisfied still does not rule out the superiority of $T = 0$; can we ever state the contrary without solving for T which satisfies (92), and thence ascertaining $\partial^2 W(T)/\partial T^2$. The possibility of certain parameters allowing an interior solution can be seen by considering the sign of (91) at $T = 0$. If this turns out to be positive (which certainly cannot be ruled out *a priori*), then we know that $\log(W(T)/W(1))$ has to fall later to 0, as $\lim_{T \to 1} (W(T)/W(1)) = 1$, thus ensuring the existence of an optimal tax rate $T \neq 0$.

A check on the validity of the above results can be made by approaching the problem from a different angle. Let us assume that the welfare criterion is to maximize the welfare of the worst-off person in society, i.e. the Rawlsian Maximin Principle. We then wish to use the tax/benefit system to maximize the value of y_L.

Now from (86) (with $k_L = 0$),

$$y_L = \frac{(\alpha(T) - 1)(1 - T)}{\alpha(T)(1 - T) - 1} w \tag{93}$$

and so,

$$\frac{\partial y_L}{\partial T} = \frac{(\alpha(T) - 1) - T(1 - T)\dfrac{\partial \alpha(T)}{\partial T}}{(\alpha(T)(1 - T) - 1)^2} w \tag{94}$$

and hence the first order condition for a maximum is,

$$\alpha(T) - 1 = T(1 - T)\frac{\partial \alpha(T)}{\partial T} \tag{95}$$

Letting $\rho \to \infty$ is the social welfare function (S.W.F.) (79) is known to replicate such Rawlsian principles, so letting $\rho \to \infty$ in (92) we again arrive at the first order condition (95). Since, from (86),

$$y_L = \left(1 + \frac{T}{\alpha(T)(1 - T) + 1}\right) w > w \tag{96}$$

we can see that the corner solution $T = 0$ is ruled out in this case. Thus we have one firm example of an optimal tax rate $T \neq 0$.

An alternative perspective on the determinants of the optimal tax rate, and the trade-off between growth and equity, may be seen by differentiating (80) with respect to T; we note that

$$\frac{\partial W}{\partial T} = \frac{\partial W}{\partial \alpha} \frac{\partial \alpha}{\partial T} + \frac{\partial W}{\partial y_L} \frac{\partial y_L}{\partial T} \tag{97}$$
$$\quad\quad (-) \;\; (+) \quad\;\; (+) \;\; (+/-)$$

We have,

$$\frac{\partial W}{\partial \alpha} = -\frac{\alpha}{(\alpha + \rho - 1)} y_L^{-\rho} \frac{(1 - T)T}{(\alpha(1 - T) - 1)^2} - \frac{1}{(\alpha + \rho - 1)} y_L^{1-\rho} < 0 \tag{98}$$

$$\frac{\partial W}{\partial y_L} = \frac{\alpha}{(\alpha + \rho - 1)} y_L^{-\rho} > 0 \tag{99}$$

whilst $\partial \alpha / \partial T$ is given by equation (78), and for the 'normal' case is positive; the sign of $\partial y_L / \partial T$ is shown by equation (94) to be ambiguous. The qualitative impact of changes in T on welfare can now be assessed from (97).

An increase in the tax rate, leading to a lower α via the savings mechanism, implies a smaller proportion of individuals above any given income or welfare range, and hence a lower level of welfare — as seen by the qualitative impact of the first term in (97). Counterbalanced against this effect we have the impact of changes in y_L as a result of changes in the tax rate. If y_L is raised, so is the level of welfare. Hence the counterbalance depends on the ability of higher taxes to raise the incomes of the poor. If $\partial y_L / \partial T$ were negative, then no positive tax rate would ever be levied; $\partial W / \partial T$ is unambiguously negative, and a corner solution $T = 0$ would result. If however $\partial y_L / \partial T$ had a positive sign, at least over some range of permissible values of T, then the possibility of an interior maximum results. In such a case we then have a trade-off between lower welfare as a result of slower growth of individuals' wealth, as a result of higher taxes on savings (the first term of (97)), against the increase in welfare resulting from the higher incomes of the poor made possible by the higher transfer payments resulting from higher taxes (the second term of (97)).

VIII   Aggregate savings behaviour

In this section we note briefly the implications for aggregate savings behaviour of the distributional model. It may be expected that given the linearity of the individual savings function, that aggregate savings behaviour would follow the same functional form. However, due to the existence of a lower boundary on wealth holding, and the influx of new individuals, this is not the case.

In order to derive the aggregate savings equation, we consider the evolution of the partial first moment distribution function of wealth.

Let,

$$K(k,t) = \int_{k_L}^{k} k\mathrm{h}(k,t)\mathrm{d}k \tag{100}$$

denote the value of total wealth owned by individuals having wealth between k_L and k. Then by an argument analogous to that followed in deriving (28), the equation governing the evolution of this quantity can be shown to be,

$$\frac{\partial \mathrm{K}(k,t)}{\partial t} = \int_{k_L}^{k} k \left[\tfrac{1}{2} \frac{\partial^2}{\partial k^2} (\mathrm{h}(k,t)u_{ss}) - \frac{\partial}{\partial k} (\mathrm{h}(k,t)u_s) \right] \mathrm{d}k \tag{101}$$

Differentiating w.r.t. k letting $\mathrm{w}(k,t) = \partial \mathrm{K}(k,t)/\partial k$, and using the relation (29), we may show,

$$\frac{\partial \mathrm{w}(k,t)}{\partial t} = -k \frac{\partial}{\partial k} (\mathscr{F}(\mathrm{h}(k,t))) \tag{102}$$

holding for $k_L \leq k < \infty$. Integrating (102) over the wealth range (k_L, ∞), we may then derive the equation governing aggregate wealth as,

$$\frac{dK(t)}{dt} = \int_{k_L}^{\infty} u_s(k) h(k,t) dk - [k\mathscr{F}(h(k,t))]_{k_L}^{\infty} - [\tfrac{1}{2} u_{ss}(k) h(k,t)]_{k_L}^{\infty}$$

(103)

where $K(t) = \int_{k_L}^{\infty} k h(k,t) dk.$

If u_s and u_{ss} are defined by (21) and (22), (103) therefore becomes,

$$\frac{dK(t)}{dt} = s(wN(t) + rK(t)) + k_L \frac{dN(t)}{dt} - [\tfrac{1}{2} u_{ss}(k) h(k,t)]_{k_L}^{\infty} \quad (104)$$

where we have utilized the boundary conditions (32) and (39). The first term of the aggregate savings relation reflects our assumptions regarding the mean savings term $u_s(k)$, now seen as savings from total income of wage payments and interest receipts. The second term may be seen as the net addition to total wealth brought in by the flow of individuals through the lower boundary; in the present case we have assumed that $k_L = 0$, and hence so is this second term. The final term of the expression does not disappear when $k_L = 0$, and may be viewed as a consequence of the assumption of a normal distribution of savings at each income level, yet a truncation of these distributions at k_L; it may perhaps be best viewed as a component of average savings.

In terms of per capita wealth holdings, (104) becomes, letting $K(t)/N(t) = \bar{k}(t)$,

$$\frac{\partial \bar{k}(t)}{\partial t} = s(w + r\bar{k}(t)) + g(k_L - \bar{k}(t)) - \frac{1}{N(t)} [\tfrac{1}{2} u_{ss}(k) h(k,t)]_{k_L}^{\infty}$$

(105)

which of course may be recognized as the distributional counterpart of the equation for capital accumulation found in many macroeconomic models of economic growth. Equation (105) must of course generate results which are consistent with the analysis of preceding sections.

In order to show consistency, consider the case of equilibrium growth. Then $d\bar{k}(t)/dt = 0$, and the equilibrium distribution of wealth is given by (48).

Substituting (48) in (105), we therefore have,

$$s(w + r\bar{k}) - g\bar{k} + gk_L - \tfrac{1}{2} \sigma^2 r\alpha(w + rk_L) = 0 \quad (106)$$

Now from (85),

$$w + r\bar{k} = \frac{\alpha}{(\alpha - 1)} (w + rk_L) \quad (107)$$

and so substituting (107) in (106) we arrive at,

$$\alpha rs = g - \tfrac{1}{2}\sigma^2 r^2 \alpha(\alpha - 1) \tag{108}$$

which is exactly relationship (60).

The use of aggregate relations may be used to effect a closure of the model by making factor payments endogenous, for their utilization within the context of a distributional model see e.g. Vaughan (1979), (1981).

IX   Conclusion

In this paper we have constructed a model using a basic life cycle theory of saving as the principal determinant of the evolution of the distribution of wealth. The distributional approach followed is a development of that taken by Sargan (1957) and Wold and Whittle (1957), and contrasts to some degree with more recent approaches to the impact of savings and inheritance behaviour on the distribution of income and wealth. The differences in structure can be seen clearly in the treatment of the representative individual and the relation of such to the equilibrium distribution which might result. In the non-distributional approach the individual clearly occupies centre stage; typically, a model is constructed in which the wealth of the individual is recursively dependent on wealth in the preceding period, income received, and on decisions made with respect to savings, interpersonal transfers, and other portfolio behaviour. The individual proceeds through time, and the equilibrium value of wealth (if it exists) determined as a function of several exogenous parameters. A distribution function, or characteristic (e.g. variance), of one or more of the exogenous variables is then postulated, which via the appropriate transformation allows the distribution of wealth, or related characteristic, to be calculated. The same principles have been applied, irrespective of whether an inter- or intragenerational model is being constructed.

It would appear therefore that a *sine qua non* of this approach is that an equilibrium of the individual agent must exist, otherwise no equilibrium distribution of wealth can result. In other words, an equilibrium distribution of wealth results from each individual agent being in equilibrium, i.e. to use Hahn's term a 'macro-equilibrium' is a consequence of a multiplicity of individual 'micro-equilibria'.[11]

In contrast, in the distributional approach, no individual need ever be in equilibrium; taking the case of the representative individual as defined by average behaviour, we note that given $s > 0$ in the above model, the average individual continues to accumulate wealth throughout the lifetime, as does the individual's heirs. 'Macroequilibrium' of the distribution does not therefore result from any necessarily inherent tendency to a 'microequilibrium'. As well as embodying this additional concept of equilibrium, the distributional approach also incorporates certain elements which would be difficult, if not impossible, to incorporate in any other approach; we refer here to the inflow/outflow of individuals at any point on the wealth scale, and the specification of alternative boundary conditions, representing economic and/or demographic constraints, on the distribution. The individual thus no longer occupies centre stage, or rather more accurately, the isolated individual no longer occupies this role.

Finally, the questions may be asked; how robust are the findings of the present model, and to what extent may the framework presented be adapted to alternative specifications of individual behaviour? It should be apparent that as the life cycle hypothesis is changed, so would the equilibrium distribution of wealth that is generated, and likewise the comparative static implications regarding such factors as risk, uncertainty, and taxation on measures of economic inequality. If the model is not robust in this sense, at least in its favour it can be said that we have followed a standard technical formulation of the life cycle hypothesis, together with parametrization in terms of the iso-elastic utility function, and therefore the results from this restrictive, although popular, case should not be without some interest.[12] More importantly, perhaps, is the practical demonstration that the generation of distributions of income and wealth is acutely sensitive to the particular formulation of the behaviour of the individuals which comprise the distribution; such behaviour is not 'washed out' by the stochastic elements of the model which may appear to have been the implications of earlier stochastic models of income and wealth distributions. Even within the present framework we have seen the importance of the assessment of risk in influencing the effects of a number of parameters on inequality. Thus we re-emphasize the importance of the role of an appropriate model of individual behaviour within any distributional framework prior to any reasoned analysis of the determinants of economic inequality.

Notes

1. The literature relating the LCH to the distribution of wealth has expanded greatly in recent years. Models concerned primarily with the intergenerational distribution of wealth (in the widest sense) include the papers by Atkinson (1971*a*), (1980), Baranzini (1982), Becker and Tomes (1979), Bevan (1979), Laitner (1979*a, b, c*), Loury (1981), Pestieau and Possen (1979), Pestieau (1982), Russell (1982), and Shorrocks (1979); with the intragenerational distribution problem, papers include Atkinson (1971*b*), Davies and Shorrocks (1978), Flemming (1979), and Oulton (1976). In addition, a number of empirical tests of the inter-generational model have been undertaken, including the analyses of Adams (1980), Menchik (1979), and Menchik and David (1983). Studies which model the distribution of wealth but use a descriptive rather than optimizing framework for individual behaviour include Blinder (1973), Bourguignon (1981), Sargan (1957), Schlicht (1975), Shorrocks (1975), Stiglitz (1969), (1978), Wold

and Whittle (1957). Many of these latter papers, particularly those stemming from Stiglitz (1969) have clear antecedents in the theory of macroeconomic growth literature of the early 1960s. The present paper uses techniques developed in Vaughan (1979), which were there applied to the analysis of descriptive class savings behaviour. A survey of the L C H up to the start of the above literature is Modigliani (1975); whilst a survey of distributional and other aspects of wealth distribution modelling may be found in Atkinson and Harrison (1978).

2. For the case $\epsilon = 1$, $s = (r - \delta + \lambda Br)/(1 + \lambda B)r$.

3. The case $r = 0$ leads to problems with respect to the lower boundary. As $r \rightarrow 0$ so desired consumption exceeds current income for the 'representative' individual, i.e. the wealth stock is depleted and would tend to fall to the lower boundary. However, as $r \rightarrow 0$, the 'endogenous' lower boundary $-(w/r)$ itself falls; and hence the representative individual would continue to dissave and borrow to finance consumption without limit.

4. If this condition were imposed at all times, and not simply in equilibrium, then it may be recognised as a 'reflecting' boundary, widely used in stochastic dynamic theory. Thus an alternative interpretation is that when individuals come up against the boundary at k_L, they are simply thrown back into the distribution to take their subsequent chances. It would then have to be assumed that individuals were too myopic not to take such an occurrence into account in their optimization decisions as regards consumption and saving. A wide variety of other boundary conditions may be imposed at k_L, including an 'absorbing' boundary in which individuals who reach k_L are precluded from any subsequent accumulation or decumulation of wealth, and mixtures of 'reflecting' and 'absorbing' boundaries; each variant may have important implications for the equilibrium distribution of wealth that results.

5. The assumption of constant w and r can be justified under the assumption that the macroeconomy has attained equilibrium along with the distribution of wealth, e.g., via the neoclassical mechanism utilized in Stiglitz (1969). For an extension of the present framework in which w and r are endogenous to the model see Vaughan (1979), (1981).

6. Alternative forms for the savings coefficients u_s, and u_{ss} would of course generate different equilibrium solutions.

7. The Paretian result should be related to the model of Wold and Whittle (1957) and to earlier papers, and appears to be a common characteristic of an 'equiproportionate jump' Markov process with a lower 'reflecting' boundary, or its equivalent; see Atkinson and Harrison (1978) for further discussion of models of this type within the context of wealth distribution.

8. The extension to the case where it is presumed that average wages are growing at the rate m can be accomplished by the transformation $\tilde{k}(t) = k(t)e^{mt}$, leading to the budget equation,

$$d\tilde{k} = (w_0 + (r-m)\tilde{k}(t) - c(t))dt + \sigma(w_0 + (r-m)\tilde{k}(t))dz$$

The analysis then follows as in the above, except that the interest rate is to be interpreted as the excess over the rate of growth of earned income (restricting the model to the case $r > m$).

9. Relationships between α and a number of inequality measures are well known in the literature for the exact Pareto Type I distribution; e.g.,

Coefficient of Variation Squared $= 1/\alpha(\alpha - 2)$

Gini Coefficient $= 1/(2\alpha - 1)$

Variance of Logarithms $= 1/\alpha^2$

as well as the Atkinson index noted in the text.

10. For the case $\rho = 1$, $W(T) = \log(y_L) + (1/\alpha(T))$.

11. Hahn (1973). Note also the discussion in Section 8.3 of Atkinson and Harrison (1978).

12. The guidelines established in Section I, together with the distributional equations of Section IV, with alternative values for u_s and u_{ss}, should be of sufficient flexibility to incorporate a number of models of individual behaviour, including alternative inheritance schemes. Whilst in such cases it may be difficult to proceed to purely analytical solutions as attempted in the present paper, problems associated with the existence and uniqueness of distributional solutions may be reasonably attempted, along with the important questions associated with non-steady state solutions.

Appendix 1

Proposition 1

The optimal choice of consumption stream for the model satisfying Assumptions 1 is,

$$c(t) = (1 - s)(w + rk(t))$$ (1.1)

where $(1 - s) = (\delta - (1 - \epsilon)r - \lambda D + \frac{1}{2}\sigma^2 r^2 \epsilon(1 - \epsilon))/r\epsilon$; and where D is implicitly defined by $B = D(1 - s)^{-\epsilon}/r$.

Proof

The problem may be formally stated as,

$$\underset{\{c(t)\}}{\text{Max}} \; E_0 \int_0^\infty [e^{-(\lambda+\xi)t} U(c(t)) + \lambda e^{-(\lambda+\xi)t} V(k(t))] \, dt$$ (1.2)

subject to the budget constraint,

$$dk = (w + rk - c) \, dt + \sigma(w + rk) \, dz$$ (1.3)

and the initial condition $k(t) = k(0)$. Further, along the optimal path we require that the integral (1.2) converges, and that $c(t) > 0$, $k(t) \geqslant k_L$, with certainty; where k_L is some lower bound on wealth. E_0 is the conditional expectation operator, given $k(0)$, over all sample paths $c(t)$, $k(t)$.

Letting the optimal value function be,

$$S(k,t) = \underset{\{c(t)\}}{\text{Max}} \int_t^\infty [e^{-(\lambda+\xi)t} U(c(t)) + \lambda e^{(\lambda+\xi)t} V(k(t))] \, dt$$ (1.4)

then according to Bellman's Principle of Optimality, the fundamental partial differential equation which $S(k,t)$ must satisfy is,

$$0 = \underset{\{c(t)\}}{\text{Max}} \left[e^{-\delta t}(U(c(t)) + \lambda V(k(t))) + \frac{\partial S(k,t)}{\partial t} \right.$$

$$\left. + \frac{\partial S(k,t)}{\partial k}(w + rk - c) + \frac{1}{2} \frac{\partial^2 S(k,t)}{\partial k^2} \sigma^2(w + rk)^2 \right]$$ (1.5)

subject to the condition which ensures convergence of (1.2)

$$\lim_{t \to \infty} S(k,t) = 0$$ (1.6)

and where we have defined $\delta = \xi + \lambda$.

228

The first order condition for a maximum of (1.5) is,

$$e^{-\delta t} U_c(c(t)) - \frac{\partial S(k,t)}{\partial k} = 0 \tag{1.7}$$

and the second order condition,

$$e^{-\delta t} U_{cc}(c(t)) < 0 \tag{1.8}$$

In order to derive an analytic solution we require to specify explicit functional forms for the utility functions U(.) and V(.). We have assumed,

$$U(c(t)) = c^{1-\epsilon}/(1-\epsilon); \tag{1.9}$$

$$V(k(t)) = B(w+rk)^{1-\epsilon}/(1-\epsilon) \tag{1.10}$$

where $B \geqslant 0$, and $\epsilon > 0$, $\epsilon \neq 1$.

Substituting (1.9) and (1.10) in (1.5) and (1.7), we thus have the following two equations to solve for $S(k,t)$ and $c(t)$,

$$e^{-\delta t}\left(\frac{c^{1-\epsilon}}{1-\epsilon} + \frac{\lambda B}{1-\epsilon}(w+rk)^{1-\epsilon}\right) + \frac{\partial S(k,t)}{\partial t} + \frac{\partial S(k,t)}{\partial k}(w+rk-c)$$

$$+ \frac{1}{2}\frac{\partial^2 S(k,t)}{\partial k^2}\sigma^2(w+rk)^2 = 0 \tag{1.11}$$

$$c(t) = \left[e^{\delta t}\frac{\partial S(k,t)}{\partial k}\right]^{-1/\epsilon} \tag{1.12}$$

Substituting (1.12) in (1.11), we have the equation for $S(k,t)$ as,

$$e^{-\delta t}\frac{\lambda B}{1-\epsilon}(w+rk)^{1-\epsilon} + \frac{e^{-\delta t}}{(1-\epsilon)}\left[e^{\delta t}\frac{\partial S}{\partial k}\right]^{(\epsilon-1)/\epsilon} + \frac{\partial S}{\partial t} + \frac{\partial S}{\partial k}(w+rk)$$

$$+ \frac{1}{2}\frac{\partial^2 S}{\partial k^2}\sigma^2(w+rk)^2 - e^{-\delta t}\left[e^{\delta t}\frac{\partial S}{\partial k}\right]^{(\epsilon-1)/\epsilon} = 0. \tag{1.13}$$

An evident trial solution for (1.13) is,

$$S(k,t) = e^{-\delta t}A(w+rk)^{1-\epsilon} \tag{1.14}$$

where A is some constant. Substituting (1.14) in (1.13), we may show that,

$$A = \frac{1}{(1-\epsilon)r}\left[\frac{\delta - (1-\epsilon)r - \lambda D + \frac{1}{2}\sigma^2 r^2 \epsilon(1-\epsilon)}{r\epsilon}\right]^{-\epsilon} \tag{1.15}$$

where we have written the predefined constant B as $B = D(1-s)^{-\epsilon}/r$.

Thus we have the prospective solution for $S(k,t)$ as,

$$S(k,t) = e^{-\delta t} \frac{1}{(1-\epsilon)r} (w+rk)^{1-\epsilon} \left[\frac{\delta - (1-\epsilon)r - \lambda D + \frac{1}{2}\sigma^2 r^2 \epsilon (1-\epsilon)}{r\epsilon} \right]^{-\epsilon}$$

(1.16)

and hence from (1.12),

$$c(t) = \frac{\delta - (1-\epsilon)r - \lambda D + \frac{1}{2}\sigma^2 r^2 \epsilon (1-\epsilon)}{r\epsilon} (w+rk)$$

(1.17)

It may be shown that the second order condition for a maximum (1.8) is satisfied, but what of the boundary conditions (1.6), $k(t) \geqslant k_L$, and the feasibility condition $c(t) > 0$. The stochastic differential equation governing wealth, substituting (1.17) in (1.3) is,

$$dk = s(w+rk)dt + \sigma(w+rk)dz$$

(1.18)

If $s < 0$, then evidently the expected value of the individual's wealth will decline over time; but as k approaches $-(w/r)$ so both the deterministic and stochastic components of (1.18) approach zero, so the wealth of the individual cannot fall below $-(w/r)$; this result may be formally shown by generating the probability distribution of $k(t)$. Thus provided $(1-s) > 0$, so consumption can never become negative; this also ensures that $(1-s)^{-\epsilon} > 0$, and hence $D > 0$, given $B > 0$. The condition $k \geqslant k_L$ is however violated unless k_L is set at $-(w/r)$ or below.

The solution path for expected wealth, given $k(0)$, is

$$E(k(t)) = \left(k(0) + \frac{w}{r} \right) e^{srt} - \frac{w}{r}$$

(1.19)

and so,

$$S(k,t) = A(w + rk(0))^{1-\epsilon} e^{(sr(1-\epsilon)-\delta)t}$$

(1.20)

Thus (1.6) is satisfied provided $sr(1-\epsilon) - \delta < 0$; this condition is automatically satisfied if $s > 0$ and $\epsilon > 1$.

Appendix 2

Proposition 2

If Assumptions 2 hold then the most likely cross-sectional distribution of wealth changes that are observed at each wealth level k will be that of the normal distribution with mean and variance defined by (21) and (22).

Proof

We may split up the range of wealth changes, v, into a number of sections, i.e.,

$$h_0 = -\infty, v_0; \quad h_1 = v_0, v_1, \ldots; \quad h_m = v_{m-1}, \infty$$

Then the probability of any one individual having a value of v within any one of the ranges is given by,

$$p_i = \int_{v_{i-1}}^{v_i} f(v)\,dv \quad \text{for } i = 0, \ldots, m \tag{2.1}$$

where $f(v) = N(u_s^*, u_{ss}^*)$.

Given N individuals and m wealth ranges, the probability of any particular configuration $N_1, N_2, \ldots, N_m$ where $N = N_i$, is given by,

$$P_m^N = \frac{N!}{N_1!\, N_2! \ldots N_m!} p_1^{N_1} p_2^{N_2} \ldots p_m^{N_m} \tag{2.2}$$

where the p_i are the *a priori* probabilities of any particular individual being in range i, given by (2.1).

To derive the distribution with the maximum probability of being observed, we maximize P_m^N subject to the condition $\sum_i N_i = N$. Any monotonic increasing function of P_m^N can be used to give the same result, and so we use $\log(P_m^N)$.

We have the Lagrangian,

$$L = \log\left(N! \bigg/ \prod_i N_i!\right) + \sum_i N_i \log p_i + \lambda_1\left(\sum_i N_i - N\right) \tag{2.3}$$

Using Stirling's Approximation, $\log N! \simeq N \log N - N$, we have

$$L = N \log N - N - \sum_i (N_i \log N_i - N_i) + \sum_i N_i \log p_i$$

$$+ \lambda_1\left(\sum_i N_i - N\right) \tag{2.4}$$

The first order conditions for a maximum are,

$$\log N_i = \log p_i + \lambda_1 \quad i = 1, \ldots, m \tag{2.5}$$

and these m equations together with the constraint enable us to solve for the $(m+1)$ unknowns, the N_i and λ_1. We accordingly have,

$$\exp(\lambda_1) = N; \quad N_i/N = p_i \tag{2.6, 2.7}$$

the second order conditions for a maximum being satisfied. Thus as (2.7) shows, the most probable observed distribution of individuals over wealth changes is equal to the same distribution as each individual's probability distribution over such changes, in this case as $N(u_s, u_{ss})$.

Appendix 3

Proposition 3

The equation governing the evolution of $h(k,t)$, given A.1, A.2, A.3 is,

$$\frac{\partial h\,(k,t)}{\partial t} = -\frac{\partial}{\partial k}\,(u_s(k)h(k,t)) + \tfrac{1}{2}\,\frac{\partial^2}{\partial k^2}\,(u_{ss}(k)h(k,t)) \qquad (3.1)$$

Proof

Assumption 3 gives us the following equation for the evolution of the c.d.f. $H(k,t)$,

$$H(k,t+\delta t) = \int_{k^*} \frac{\partial H\,(k^*,t)}{\partial k^*}\,G(k,k^*;\delta t)\mathrm{d}k^* \qquad (3.2)$$

Expanding $H(k,t+\delta t)$ in a Taylor series about the point (k,t), then differentiating with respect to k, we arrive at,

$$\frac{\partial h\,(k,t)}{\partial t}\,\delta t = -h(k,t) + \int_{k^*} h(k^*,t)g(k,k^*;\delta t)\mathrm{d}k^* + o(\delta t) \qquad (3.3)$$

where $\partial H(k,t)/\partial k = h(k,t)$; $\partial G(k,k^*;\delta t)/\partial k = g(k,k^*;\delta t)$; and $o(\delta t)$ implies a series of terms in δt such that $\displaystyle\lim_{\delta t \to 0} o(\delta t)/\delta t = 0$. Equivalently, (3.3) may be written in terms of the size of the jump in wealth; letting $x = k - k^*$, we have,

$$\frac{\partial h\,(k,t)}{\partial t}\,\delta t = -h(k,t) + \int_{x} h(k-x,t)g^*(x,k-x;\delta t)\mathrm{d}x + o(\delta t) \quad (3.4)$$

where $g^*(x,k-x;\delta t)$ denotes the proportion of individuals with initial wealth $(k-x)$ who make a jump in wealth of size x, within the period δt.

Expanding $h(k-x,t)$ and $g^*(x,k-x;\delta t)$ in Taylor series about the points (k,t) and (x,k) respectively, and letting

$$\mu^j = \int_{x} x^j g^*(x,k;\delta t)\mathrm{d}x; \quad j = 1,2,\dots \qquad (3.5)$$

i.e. the jth moment of the jump function $g^*(x,k;\delta t)$, then we may show,

$$\int_{x} h(k-x,t)g^*(x,k-x;\delta t)\mathrm{d}x = h(k,t) + \sum_{j=1}^{\infty}\left[\frac{(-1)^j}{j!}\,\frac{\partial^j}{\partial k^j}\,(\mu^j h(k,t))\right]$$

$$(3.6)$$

Hence substituting (3.6) in (3.4) we have,

$$\frac{\partial h\,(k,t)}{\partial t}\,\delta t = \sum_{j=1}^{\infty} \left[\frac{(-1)^j}{j!}\,\frac{\partial^j}{\partial k^j}\,(\mu^j h(k,t)\,) \right] + o(\delta t) \qquad (3.7)$$

Now under A.1, A.2, $g^*(x,k;\delta t)$ is normal with mean and variance defined respectively by $u_s(k)\delta t$, and $u_{ss}(k)\delta t$. Given normality, all odd moments higher than the first are zero; whilst for the even moments we have,

$$\mu^{2j} = \frac{(2j)!}{j!\,2^j}\,(\mu^2)^j; \; j = 1,2,\ldots \qquad (3.8)$$

Hence all moments of $g^*(x,k;\delta t)$ higher than the second are either identically zero, or $o(\delta t)$. Thus (3.7) may be written,

$$\frac{\partial h\,(k,t)}{\partial t}\,\delta t = -\frac{\partial}{\partial k}\,\{u_s(k)\delta t\,h(k,t)\}$$

$$+\,\tfrac{1}{2}\,\frac{\partial^2}{\partial k^2}\,\{(u_{ss}(k)\delta t + (u_s(k)\delta t)^2)h(k,t)\} + o(\delta t) \;(3.9)$$

and so dividing through by δt and letting $\delta t \to 0$, we have the equation governing the evolution of the frequency distribution function of wealth as (3.1). Equation (3.1) may be recognized as the Fokker–Planck diffusion equation; for uses in the physical sciences see the papers in Wax (1954), and for derivation of similar equations in the field of wealth distribution and stochastic growth theory the papers by Sargan (1957), Wold and Whittle (1957), Bourguignon (1974) and Merton (1975). The above derivation is well known in the statistical field and was used in the paper by Vaughan (1979).

References

Adams, J.D., 'Personal Wealth Transfers', *Quarterly Journal of Economics* **95** (1980), 159–80.

Atkinson, A.B., 'Capital Taxes, the Redistribution of Wealth and Individual Savings', *Review of Economics Studies* **38** (1971a), 209–28.

—— 'The Distribution of Wealth and the Individual Life Cycle', *Oxford Economic Papers* **23** (1971b), 239–54.

—— 'Inheritance and the Redistribution of Wealth', in G. A. Hughes and G. M. Heal (eds.), *Public Policy and the Tax System* (Allen and Unwin, London, 1980).

—— and A.J. Harrison, *Distribution of Personal Wealth in Britain*, (Cambridge University Press, Cambridge, 1978).

Baranzini, M., 'Can the Life Cycle Help in Explaining Income Distribution and Capital Accumulation?', in M. Baranzini (ed.), *Advances in Economic Theory* (Basil Blackwell, Oxford, 1982).

Becker, G.S. and N. Tomes, 'An Equilibrium Theory of the Distribution of Income and Intergenerational Mobility', *Journal of Political Economy* **87** (1979), 1153–89.

Bevan, D.L., 'Inheritance and the Distribution of Wealth', *Economica* **46** (1979), 381–402.

Blinder, A.S., 'A Model of Inherited Wealth', *Quarterly Journal of Economics* **87** (1973), 608–26.

—— *Toward an Economic Theory of Income Distribution* (MIT Press, Cambridge, Ma., 1974).

Bourguignon, F., 'A Particular Class of Continuous-Time Stochastic Growth Models', *Journal of Economic Theory* **9** (1974), 141–68.

—— 'Pareto Superiority of Unegalitarian Equilibria in Stiglitz's Model of Wealth Distribution with Convex Saving Function', *Econometrica* **49** (1981), 1469–75.

Davies, J.B. and A.F. Shorrocks, 'Assessing the Quantitative Importance of Inheritance in the Distribution of Wealth', *Oxford Economic Papers* **30** (1978), 138–49.

Flemming, J.S., 'The Effects of Earnings Inequality, Imperfect Capital Markets and Dynastic Altruism on the Distribution of Wealth in Life Cycle Models', *Economica* **46** (1979), 363–80.

Friedman, M., *A Theory of the Consumption Function* (NBER, Princeton University Press, Princeton, 1957).

Hahn, F.H., *On the Notion of Equilibrium in Economics* (Cambridge University Press, Cambridge, 1973).

Klein L.R. and J.N. Morgan, 'Results of Alternative Statistical Tests of Sample Survey Data', *Journal of the American Statistical Association* **46** (1951), 442–60.

Laitner, J., 'Household Bequest Behavior and the National Distribution of Wealth', *Review of Economic Studies* **46** (1979*a*), 467–84.

—— 'Household Bequests, Perfect Expectations and the National Distribution of Wealth', *Econometrica* **47** (1979*b*), 1175–93.

—— 'Bequests, Golden-Age Capital Accumulation and Government Debt', *Economica* **46** (1979*c*), 403–14.

Loury, G.C., 'Intergenerational Transfers and the Distribution of Earnings', *Econometrica* **49** (1981), 843–67.

Menchik, P.L., 'Intergenerational Transmission of Inequality: an Empirical Study of Wealth Mobility', *Economica* **46** (1979), 349–62.

—— and M. David, 'Income Distribution, Lifetime Savings and Bequests', *American Economic Review* **73** (1983), 672–90.

Merton, R.C., 'Lifetime Portfolio Selection Under Uncertainty: the Continuous-Time Case', *Review of Economics and Statistics* **51** (1969), 247–67.

—— 'An Asymptotic Theory of Growth Under Uncertainty', *Review of Economic Studies* **42** (1975), 375–93.

Modigliani, F. 'The Life cycle Hypothesis of Saving Twenty Years Later', in M. Parkin and A.R. Nobay, (eds.), *Contemporary Issues in Economics* (Manchester University Press, Manchester, 1975).

—— and R.E. Brumberg, 'Utility Analysis and the Consumption Function: an Interpretation of Cross-Section Data', in K.K. Kurihara (ed.), *Post Keynesian Economics* (Allen and Unwin, London, 1954).

Oulton, N., 'Inheritance and the Distribution of Wealth', *Oxford Economic Papers* **28** (1976), 86–101.

Pestieau, P., 'Determining an Optimal Wealth Tax: a Difficult Question', in D. Kessler, A. Masson, and D. Strauss-Kahn (eds.), *Accumulation et Répartition du Patrimoine* (Economica-Editions du CNRS, Paris, 1982).

—— and U. M. Possen, 'A Model of Wealth Distribution', *Econometrica* 47 (1979), 761–72.

Pratt, J., 'Risk Aversion in the Small and in the Large', *Econometrica* 32 (1964), 122–36.

Russell, T., 'The Share of Top Wealth Holders: the Life Cycle, Inheritance and Efficient Markets', in D. Kessler, A. Masson, and D. Strauss-Kahn, (eds.), *Accumulation et Répartition du Patrimoine* (Economica-Editions du CNRS, Paris, 1982).

Samuelson, P. A. 'A Fallacy in the Interpretation of Pareto's Law of Alleged Constancy of Income Distribution', *Rivista Internazionale di Scienze Economiche e Commerciali* 12 (1965), 246–53.

Sargan, J. D., 'The Distribution of Wealth', *Econometrica* 25 (1957), 568–90.

Schlicht, E. 'A Neoclassical Theory of Wealth Distribution', *Jahrbücher für Nationalökonomie und Statistik* 189 (1975), 78–96.

Shorrocks, A. F., 'On Stochastic Models of Size Distributions', *Review of Economic Studies* 42 (1975), 631–41.

—— 'On the Structure of Inter-generational Transfers between Families', *Economica* 46 (1979), 415–25.

Stiglitz, J. E., 'Distribution of Income and Wealth Among Individuals', *Econometrica* 37 (1969), 382–97.

—— 'Equality, Taxation and Inheritance', in W. Krelle and A. F. Shorrocks (eds.), *Personal Income Distribution* (North–Holland, Amsterdam, 1978).

Vaughan, R. N., 'Class Behaviour and the Distribution of Wealth', *Review of Economic Studies* 46 (1979), 447–65.

—— 'Growth, Inequality and the Distribution of Wealth', Paper presented to the European Meeting of the Econometric Society, mimeo, (1981).

Wax, N. (ed.), *Selected Papers on Noise and Stochastic Processes*, (Dover, New York, 1954).

Wold, H. O. A. and P. Whittle, 'A Model Explaining the Pareto Distribution of Wealth', *Econometrica* 25 (1957), 591–95.

Comments on Chapter 8

EDMOND MALINVAUD

Institut National de la Statistique et des Etudes Economiques

You must realize that the paper we are discussing is an impressive piece of analytical work. Considering a population of people whose incomes are subject to uncertainty, it determines the optimal saving behaviour of individuals and the resulting equilibrium stationary distribution function of wealth in this population. The determination is (almost) complete so that a number of conclusions can be drawn, for instance as to how the equilibrium wealth inequality varies as a function of various parameters:

the degree of time preference,
the degree of risk aversion,
the speed of renewal of one generation by the next,
the degree of uncertainty of incomes,
the rate of increase of the population,
the rate of taxation of incomes.

This is achieved by the use of powerful mathematical tools and fierceful analytical derivations. You cannot expect a discussant to have checked all this mathematics and, to be frank, I find some of it unfamiliar and difficult to deal with. But, whenever I checked, I found the result to be correct, except in one special instance, about which I may very well be mistaken. Therefore I have confidence in the results presented in this paper.

The price paid by the author for dealing so completely with his subject is to introduce a specification that makes explicit derivations possible. While the approach and methodology are generally valid, they do not permit the solution of other specifications, which we may consider to be as interesting as, or even more interesting than, the present one.

I have no fundamental objection to an approach using a convenient particular specification. Indeed, in some of my work, I have used such an approach. Working out a complete solution in a particular case, one explores how a theory operates, one is forced to deal with points that one would tend to neglect within a heuristic frame of thought but that may turn out to be important. The results that are found may suggest properties with a more general validity or new problems to be explored.

The question, however, remains as to whether the results derived from a particular specification apply to other specifications. Answering this question is always important, but particularly difficult when the specification has been chosen for analytical convenience. In a few places the author tries to answer queries about what would happen in other cases, but he cannot go very far and I found the statements particularly uninformative; for instance, when the possible influence of age on the saving rate is discussed, it is recognized that the saving rate might then also depend on wealth, which would make derivation of the equilibrium wealth distribution untractable; but conditions for the saving rate to be independent of wealth are not given.

This being the situation, I believe my role as a discussant is to stress what is special in the assumptions of the paper. I shall do so considering successively the specification of the individual consumer, the uncertainty of incomes, the assumption about the population and its evolution.

The most specific hypothesis about the individual is what I call 'the no-aging assumption'. The individual works as long as he lives, always earning the same exogenous labour income. The probability of his death does not change with age either. Whether we can then still speak of a life cycle, as is stated in the title of the paper, appears doubtful to me. Another special assumption is to assume a constant relative risk aversion, whereas K. Arrow for instance has argued that relative risk aversion should be decreasing as a function of wealth. These two assumptions play an important role in explaining why optimal behaviour implies a constant saving rate, which of course helps the analyst.

Assumptions about uncertainty imply that randomness directly concerns the full income of the individual and does not depend on the composition of this income; in other words, different uncertainties do not apply to labour and capital incomes. This also explains why the saving rate on labour income is the same as the saving rate on capital income, in contradiction to what was assumed in the article published by Vaughan in 1979.

Needless to say, the assumption that individual incomes are stochastically independent is also special in comparison with what happens in the real world. Similarly, assuming a Wiener process rules out the fact that favourable or unfavourable current random shocks may long affect future incomes. All this means that not all dimensions of uncertainty are taken into account.

But perhaps the discussion should concentrate on the treatment of the population, about which I find, unless I am mistaken, that the paper is not clear.

First, there is the strange assumption that, when an individual dies, he transmits his wealth to one and only one individual who previously did not exist and begins working only at this time. How to make this realistic, I do not know. But I should like to point out a reasonable consequence of the assumption. As the author says, these individuals, who so enter the wealth distribution, 'immediately step into their parent's shoes' and 'we may view the parent as never really dying'. Then why should we not directly deal with infinitely longlived consumers and take $\lambda = 0$ in the individual objective function (10)? This would make more sense, in this context, than keeping a positive λ and a utility function $V(k)$ of terminal wealth, whose rationale may be difficult to elucidate. It would also definitely simplify the comparative statics discussion of the determinants of the saving propensity.

The second difficulty concerning the assumptions about the population results from the presence of the lower boundary k_L for k. Reading the paper, one sees that the author was indeed bothered all along with this boundary problem. But I do not find him clear enough on what the solution means with respect to the assumptions to be made.

In the equilibrium process a number of pre-existing consumers find that at some time their wealth tends to fall below k_L. What then happens to them? Different stories can probably be told that are consistent with the equations of the paper. One, however, cannot be told, namely that consumption is then constrained, so that wealth no longer decreases; indeed, the risk of confronting such a constraint would then have to be explicitly taken into account from the beginning in the consumer decision problem. I propose the following story.

These unfortunate individuals who find their wealth falling below k_L enter into a pool of assisted consumers who keep working, consuming, receiving incomes, and recording their wealth, which is now smaller than k_L; but they are no longer counted as members of the normal population, as long as their wealth does not increase again above k_L. The number of members of the population however does not decrease; on the contrary it increases at rate g. Indeed, some old assisted consumers and some consumers born from heaven enter again from below into the normal population. As a *net result* of these movements downward and upward across the boundary, the normal population is assumed to increase at the rate g.

Again, I do not want to discuss the realism of this story. In particular, so far as I can see, nothing guarantees that, in the equilibrium regime, the population of assisted consumers does not indefinitely increase. I would rather like to stress that the same rate of increase g does not mean the same gross flows across the boundary, when such parameters as time preference, the degree of risk aversion or the importance of uncertainty vary. This remark should have some bearing on the interpretation to be given to the comparative static results on the distribution of wealth.

Now, after pointing out what I find to be a serious difficulty, I must hasten to add that the same difficulty concerning the lower bound or left part of the distribution was faced by all previous attempts at deriving the Pareto distribution as the equilibrium distribution resulting from a population model; it seems to me that these previous attempts did not deal so well with the difficulty. This may be one reason why some people favored models leading to the log-normal distribution as an equilibrium distribution.

In these comments I have tried to be critical, because this is the normal role of a discussant. But, at least for those who did not carefully study the paper and who want to decide from my comments whether they should study it, I must praise at the end the great virtue of a treatment, dealing in a fully integrated and rigorous way with all aspects of the accumulation of wealth. From such a treatment we learn two things:

(1) how to think about the links between assumptions concerning individual behaviour, uncertainties, evolution of the population, and the resulting income and wealth distribution;

(2) how such things as aggregate wealth or wealth inequality finally change when parameters are changed within a particular specification. Some of these changes may look surprising; if so, we have to understand why and our understanding of the whole problem then improves.

9 Wealth Holdings and Entrepreneurial Activity

ANTHONY F. SHORROCKS*

University of Essex

Casual empiricism suggests that most large wealth holdings can be traced either directly or indirectly, via inheritance, to some combination of events that created an original fortune. In recent times these events have typically been related to the successful identification and exploitation of market opportunities. Yet the behaviour of individuals seeking favourable market opportunities has played little part in the formal analysis of wealth holdings. Instead the usual focus of attention is either on the accumulation of savings for lifecycle, bequest or other motives, which does not provide a credible explanation of the formation of large fortunes; or else on inheritance, which can help account for the preservation of large asset holdings over several generations, but does not explain how those fortunes were originally established.

This paper examines the actions of individuals who can devote their time to risky activities which offer the possibility of large rewards. Those who engage in such activities are called 'entrepreneurs', reflecting the fact that the expenditure of time and the adoption of risks are central features of what are usually regarded as entrepreneurial activities. However other typical aspects of entrepreneurial behaviour, such as the employment of factors of production, are omitted from consideration.

Two kinds of entrepreneurial activity are considered. One requires only the expenditure of time and may be undertaken by anyone. It involves searching for a limited number of opportunities associated with a large reward. The second type of entrepreneurial activity also involves a search for large prizes, but requires inputs of both time and money, and is only accessible to those who have already been successful entrepreneurs. Individuals can also choose not to be an entrepreneur, and instead work for a fixed wage. To add extra complications, each person is free to combine with any number of other individuals engaged in the same activity, to pool the risk and rewards. Furthermore, the probability of success corresponding to each kind of risk is not given exogenously, but determined by the total number of persons engaged in that activity.

The issues examined in this paper concern primarily the optimal behaviour of individuals in the context of the options described: the decision whether or

* I have benefitted from discussions with Ravi Kanbur and, most especially, John Hartwick whose joint paper (Buckholtz *et al.*) provided a major stimulus for this study.

241

not to become an entrepreneur; and whether or not to diversify by sharing risks with others. The equilibrium structure of returns in each kind of risk activity, determined by competition amongst the participants, is also considered. One interesting conclusion is the tendency for individuals to bid down the prospects in the freely available entrepreneurial activity below the point at which the risk would normally be rejected. Even more interesting is the tendency for individuals to specialize in a single risk when engaged in the freely available entrepreneurial activity, and to diversify as much as possible once access to the other kind of risk has been achieved. While it may be an exaggeration to describe this phenomenon as an established feature of the real world, it is not difficult to think of particular individuals who became rich specializing in one narrow activity, and then diversified their wealth holdings once successful.

Although the model developed in this paper bears little resemblance to any previous study of wealth holdings, particular aspects are evident in a number of earlier studies. The central notion that individual wealth levels influence the types of investment opportunities open to individuals echoes recent interest and research into imperfect capital markets. However, the impact of capital market imperfections on wealth holdings have rarely been considered, and have never been formally examined in the context of entrepreneurial activity. There are also similarities with the work on stochastic models of wealth distribution (see, for example, Shorrocks (1975)), which emphasize the stochastic structure of the process of wealth generation. But these models tend to neglect the systematic influences on wealth holdings, and the consequences of rational individual behaviour, both of which feature strongly in the model outlined here. Finally there is a growing literature on risk taking behaviour that is relevant to the choice of entrepreneurial occupations and subsequent entrepreneurial activity. The studies by Kihlstrom and Laffont (1979) and Kanbur (1979, 1982) have some similarities with the present paper, since they are concerned with the choice between entrepreneurial and labouring activities in a general equilibrium environment which allows the rewards to entrepreneurship to be determined by competition. However they are single period models in which occupational choice is decided by risk aversion. All individuals face the same set of entrepreneurial options and do not have an opportunity to share risks. So the types of questions concerning wealth holdings, and wealth determining behaviour, considered in this paper are not addressed.

I   The model

Individuals are assumed to live for T periods. During each period they engage in one of three possible activities. They may work for a wage w (the working or w-strategy), or become 'entrepreneurs' undertaking either 'low-budget' or 'high-budget' risks. Low-budget risks require only the input of time (or the monetary equivalent of that time), while high-budget risks need a substantial monetary investment[1] in addition to time and are only accessible to those who have already demonstrated their success as a low-budget entrepreneur. The letters ℓ and h will denote 'low-budget' and 'high-budget', respectively, when reference is made to ℓ-entrepreneurs, ℓ-risks, the h-strategy, and so on.

The rewards to ℓ-risks are characterised by f_ℓ 'fortunes' or 'prizes', each of value F_ℓ, which await discovery each period by the participants in this activity. All ℓ-entrepreneurs have the same probability $p\epsilon(0, 1)$ of acquiring the prize F_ℓ (and zero probability of acquiring more than one prize). Although treated as a parameter by individuals, p is endogenously determined and given by

$$p = \frac{f_\ell}{N_\ell},$$ (1)

where N_ℓ is the total number of ℓ-entrepreneurs. Therefore, taking account of the wage foregone in entrepreneurial activities, the expected net return per person to an ℓ-risk is

$$R_\ell := pF_\ell - w = \frac{f_\ell F_\ell}{N_\ell} - w$$ (2)

Low-budget entrepreneurs have the option of diversifying their risk, by agreeing with others to an equal division of their joint proceeds. If k individuals pool their efforts in this way, they each have a probability p_{kj} of a $1/k$th share in j fortunes, where, for small k, p_{kj} can be approximated by the binomial expression

$$^kC_j(1-p)^{k-j}p^j.$$ (3)

In the extreme case, if all ℓ-investors agree to an equal division of the aggregate reward, each will receive $f_\ell F_\ell/N_\ell$ with probability one, and the net return per person is R_ℓ.

High-budget risks require an asset input of F_ℓ as well as the time input. Each period there are f_h prizes of value F_h, which the h-entrepreneurs compete to discover. All h-risks are associated with the probability π of obtaining a single fortune given by

$$\pi = \frac{f_h}{N_h},$$ (4)

where N_h is the total number of h-entrepreneurs.[2] So the expected net return to an h-risk is

$$R_h := \pi F_h - F_\ell - w = \frac{f_h F_h}{N_h} - F_\ell - w.$$ (5)

As with ℓ-risks, h-entrepreneurs are allowed to pool risks with other h-entrepreneurs. In a consortium of k persons, each will obtain jF_h/k with a probability approximated by the binomial term

$$\pi_{kj} = {}^kC_j(1 - \pi)^{k-j}\pi^j. \tag{6}$$

In the extreme case of complete diversification, each h-entrepreneur obtains f_hF_h/N_h with probability one, and the return per person is given by R_h.

The asset prerequisite of F_ℓ means that h-risks are accessible to successful ℓ-entrepreneurs. However it is also conceivable that other individuals, via accumulated earnings, borrowing, or pooling assets, could acquire the minimum asset stake. To prevent this happening, it is assumed that h-entrepreneurs must have a successful entrepreneurial track record. This may be achieved by a single (undiversified) success, half shares in two successful risks, third shares in three successful risks, and so on. More precisely, any individual who in period θ belongs to a consortium of k_θ ℓ-entrepreneurs which has j_θ successes, will be assigned the 'success index'

$$S_t = \sum_{\theta=1}^{t} j_\theta/k_\theta \tag{7}$$

after t periods, and has subsequent access to h-risks only if $S_t \geq 1$. S_t may be regarded as an indicator of entrepreneurial credibility.[3] It is not unreasonable to suppose that a minimum level of credibility would be needed if h-risks require financial guarantees, insurance, or private market information.

An increase in the total reward to h-risks, f_hF_h, makes these risks more attractive. It encourages individuals to take h-risks and to wish to become h-entrepreneurs. To avoid a degenerate situation in which no h-risk activities are performed, we will assume that f_hF_h is large enough to ensure

Assumption 1 Some individuals are h-entrepreneurs.

Since prior ℓ-risk success is necessary for access to h-risks, this assumption also ensures that some individuals are ℓ-entrepreneurs. At the opposite extreme, all individuals in the economy will be entrepreneurs and none will be employees. To prevent this occurring, we shall suppose

Assumption 2 Some individuals (strictly) prefer to be workers.

One example of a low-budget risk activity might be prospecting for minerals above ground, where the major input is time and the reward corresponds to a discovery of rich deposits. Increased competition amongst prospectors results in duplication of effort (examining ground already covered) and drives down the probability of success. Alternatively one might think of individuals spending time inventing a new product (such as the Polaroid camera) or locating major gaps in the market for goods and services (with the reward corresponding to the capitalized value of that information). High-budget activities might include prospecting below ground (say, off-shore oil drilling), risky real-estate purchases or, perhaps more usually, developing an interesting but speculative idea for a new good or service into a marketable proposition.

Since the focus of attention in this paper is the entrepreneurial decisions of individuals in the context of the options described, the remaining aspects of the model are specified as simply as possible. We assume that the n identical persons born into any age cohort receive no inheritances, nor make bequests. They aim to maximize the expected value of (undiscounted) utility

$$U = \sum_{t=1}^{T} u(c_t) \tag{8}$$

where c_t denotes consumption at age t and occurs after the outcome of the age t activity is known. There is a safe asset in which individuals can invest surplus wealth at the certain rate of interest $r = 0$. Individuals can also borrow to finance consumption (but not h-risks) at the same rate of interest, as long as they remain within their lifetime budget constraint.

Finally we assume that individuals are risk neutral and therefore, without loss of generality, choose $u(c) = c$. This assumption may seem strange in a model directed towards risk-taking behaviour. But, as we shall see, the implications are non trivial and point towards general conclusions that are likely to hold for strictly concave utility functions. Furthermore, the risk-neutral assumption simplifies the problem to the point where it becomes tractable. Given the complex nature of the potential strategies facing the individuals, it may be the only means of obtaining an explicit solution.

II Formulating the activity decision problem

One immediate advantage of the risk-neutrality assumption is that the value of U in (8) is independent of the intertemporal distribution of consumption. Thus we may suppose that all consumption takes place at the end of the life-time, and reformulate the problem as one of attempting to maximize the expected value of terminal wealth W_T by a suitable choice of activity and diversification strategies in each period. Given the wealth level W_t and success index S_t at the end of period t, this maximum expected value of terminal wealth will be denoted by

$$V_t(W_t, S_t)$$

where

$$V_T(W, S) = W. \tag{9}$$

Progress towards a solution can be achieved by using the methods of

Dynamic Programming to link $V_t(.)$ to $V_{t+1}(.)$. However it will be useful first to employ some intuitive arguments which reduce the number of strategies under consideration. The substantive consequences of these arguments are contained in a sequence of propositions which will be justified in a more rigorous manner later on.

We begin by noting that h-entrepreneurs choose not to work or to undertake ℓ-risks. Given that some h-entrepreneurs exist (Assumption 1), and given that risk-neutral individuals select the option offering the highest expected return, it follows that:

Proposition 1 $R_h \geqq \max \{0, R_\ell\}$.

By the same token, since some individuals prefer to be workers (Assumption 2) and could at least have chosen ℓ-risks, it must be the case that:

Proposition 2 $R_\ell < 0$.

This raises the question why *any* risk neutral individuals should voluntarily undertake the actuarially unfair ℓ-risks. The answer is to be found in the potential access to h-risks. However, unless $R_h > 0$ there is no advantage to be gained from this access, and no reason to accept the unfavourable ℓ-risks. It therefore follows that:

Proposition 3 $R_h > 0 > R_\ell$.

Now consider the view of h-entrepreneurs towards diversification. Although diversification does not alter their expected return, it reduces the probability of a substantial loss of assets that would reduce their wealth below the threshold value F_t and deny them access to future h-risks. This particularly undesirable prospect can be eliminated entirely if and only if all h-entrepreneurs pool their resources and accept the certain return R_h. Therefore:

Proposition 4   It is optimal for h-entrepreneurs to diversify completely and ensure the certain return R_h.

In contrast, ℓ-entrepreneurs have no incentive to diversify if $R_\ell < 0$. For the expected immediate return from ℓ-risks remains the same, and is less than the individuals would obtain in employment; and the possibility of accumulating a sufficiently large share in enough successful ℓ-risks to become an h-entrepreneur (which is the only compensation for the negative value of R_ℓ) is postponed. Hence:

Proposition 5   It is optimal for ℓ-entrepreneurs to specialize completely in a single ℓ-risk.

These proposition enable the consequences of the options facing any individuals to be easily calculated. Given wealth W and success index S after t

periods, an individual who works in period $t+1$ will value his stock variables (wealth and success index) at the end of that period as

$$V_{t+1}(W+w,S).$$

Alternatively, if the ℓ-strategy is adopted, a single undiversified risk will be undertaken by Proposition 5. There is therefore a probability p that wealth will increase by F_ℓ and the success index by 1, and a probability $1-p$ that both will remain unchanged, producing the expected valuation

$$pV_{t+1}(W+F_\ell,S+1) + (1-p)V_{t+1}(W,S).$$

Those who are eligible for, and choose to take, h-risks will, by Proposition 4, diversify completely, and wealth will increase by $\pi F_h - F_\ell$. The stock valuation after $t+1$ periods is then

$$V_{t+1}(W+\pi F_h-F_\ell,S).$$

By the fundamental theorem of Dynamic Programming we can now infer:

$$V_t(W,S) = \max \begin{cases} \text{(w)} & : V_{t+1}(W+w,S) \\ (\ell) & : pV_{t+1}(W+F_\ell,S+1) + (1-p)V_{t+1}(W,S) \\ \text{(h)} & : V_{t+1}(W+\pi F_h-F_\ell,S) \text{ if } W \geq F_\ell \text{ and } S \geq 1 \end{cases}$$

(10a)

where

$$V_T(W,S) = W. \tag{10b}$$

Option (h) is not available if $W < F_\ell$ and/or $S < 1$. Given the terminal condition (10b), the recursive relationship (10a) can be solved for all t and this determines the optimal strategy in each period, conditional on the current values of W and S.

III Optimal entrepreneurial decisions

Consider the solution of (10) when $W \geq F_\ell$ and $S \geq 1$. By induction, the solution takes the form

$$V_t(W,S) = W+(T-t)w+(T-t)R^* \quad \forall t \leq T, \tag{11}$$

where $R^* = \max\{0,R_\ell,R_h\}$. For this holds trivially when $t = T$; and when $t < T$

$$V_t(W,S) = \max \begin{cases} \begin{aligned} \text{(w)} \;&: \; V_{t+1}(W+w,S) \\ &= W + (T-t)w + (T-t-1)R^* \\ \text{(ℓ)} \;&: \; pV_{t+1}(W+F_\ell,S+1) + (1-p)V_{t+1}(W,S) \\ &= p\{W + F_\ell + (T-t-1)(w+R^*)\} \\ &\quad + (1-p)\{W+(T-t-1)(w+R^*)\} \\ &= W + (T-t)w + (T-t-1)R^* + R_\ell \\ \text{(h)} \;&: \; V_{t+1}(W+\pi F_h - F_\ell, S) \\ &= W + \pi F_h - F_\ell + (T-t-1)(w+R^*) \\ &= W + (T-t)w + (T-t-1)R^* + R_h \end{aligned} \end{cases}$$

$$= W + (T-t)w + (T-t-1)R^* + \max\{0,R_\ell,R_h\}$$

$$= W + (T-t)w + (T-t)R^*.$$

No h-risks are undertaken if $R^* > R_h$. Since this contradicts Assumption 1, it follows that $R_h = R^* \geqq \max\{0,R_\ell\}$. So Proposition 1 is true, and (11) may be rewritten as

$$V_t(W,S) = W + (T-t)w + (T-t)R_h \quad \forall t \leq T, \tag{12}$$

whenever $W \geqq F_\ell$ and $S \geqq 1$. Note that the h-risk activity is strictly preferred to the other options if $R_h > \max\{0,R_\ell\}$. In these circumstances, therefore, those eligible for h-risks will always adopt the h-strategy and, since complete diversification ensures that wealth remains above F_ℓ, will continue to do so for the remainder of their lives.

Now consider the solution of (10) when $W < F_\ell$ and/or $S < 1$. By induction the solution can be written in the form

$$V_t(W,S) = W + (T-t)w + B_t \quad \forall t \leq T \tag{13}$$

where

$$B_T = 0 \tag{14a}$$

$$B_t := B_{t+1} + \max\{0,b_{t+1}\} = p \sum_{\tau=t+1}^{T} \max\{0,b_\tau\} \quad \forall t < T \tag{14b}$$

$$b_t := R_{\ell t} - pB_t = R_{\ell t} - p \sum_{\tau=t+1}^{T} \max\{0,b_\tau\} \tag{15}$$

$$R_{\ell t} := R_\ell + p(T-t)R_h. \tag{16}$$

For this clearly holds if $t = T$; and if $t < T$ we obtain, using (12),

$$V_t(W,S) = \max \begin{cases} \begin{aligned} \text{(w)} \;&: \; V_{t+1}(W+w,S) = W+(T-t)w + B_{t+1} \\ \text{(ℓ)} \;&: \; pV_{t+1}(W+F_\ell,S+1) + (1-p)V_{t+1}(W,S) \\ &= p\{W+F_\ell + (T-t-1)(w+R_h)\} \\ &\quad + (1-p)\{W+(T-t-1)w + B_{t+1}\} \\ &= W + (T-t)w + R_\ell + p(T-t-1)R_h \\ &\quad + (1-p)B_{t+1} \end{aligned} \end{cases}$$

$$= W + (T-t)w + B_{t+1} + \max\{0, R_\ell + p(T-t-1)R_h - pB_{t+1}\}$$
$$= W + (T-t)w + B_{t+1} + \max\{0, b_{t+1}\}$$
$$= W + (T-t)w + B_t.$$

In this formulation of the solution, R_{tt} may be interpreted as the overall return to an ℓ-risk in period t, which comprises the immediate net expected return, R_ℓ, plus the valuation attached to the probability p of gaining access to h-risks (which would give R_h more than the employment strategy in each of the remaining $T-t$ periods). B_t represents the total net advantage imputed to access to entrepreneurial activities in all periods subsequent to t, while b_t indicates the desirability of undertaking an ℓ-risk in period t, since the ℓ-risk is accepted if $b_t > 0$ and rejected if $b_t < 0$.

From (16) and Proposition 1, we deduce

$$R_{tt} = R_{\ell,t+1} + pR_h \geqq R_{\ell,t+1} \quad \forall t < T. \tag{17}$$

If $R_{tt} \leqq 0$, it follows that $R_{tr} \leqq 0 \; \forall r \geqq t$, and successive substitution into (15) yields

$$R_{tt} \leqq 0 \quad \text{implies} \quad b_r = R_{tr} \quad \forall r \geqq t. \tag{18}$$

From (14) and (15) we also have

$$\begin{aligned} b_t &= R_{tt} - pB_t \\ &= R_{\ell,t+1} + pR_h - p(B_{t+1} + \max\{0, b_{t+1}\}) \\ &= b_{t+1} - p\max\{0, b_{t+1}\} + pR_h \end{aligned} \tag{19}$$

and, in particular,

$$b_t > 0 \quad \text{if} \quad b_{t+1} > 0. \tag{20}$$

Thus if the ℓ-strategy is (strictly) preferred at age t, it must be preferred at all ages $\tau < t$. Similarly,

$$b_t \geqq 0 \quad \text{if} \quad b_{t+1} \geqq 0, \tag{21}$$

so if the w-strategy is not preferred at age t, then it cannot be preferred at any age $\tau < t$.

We now distinguish the three cases:

(I) $R_h \geqq R_\ell \geqq 0$
(II) $R_h = 0 > R_\ell$
(III) $R_h > 0 > R_\ell$

which, given Proposition 1, exhaust all the possibilities. In case (I),

$$b_T = R_{tT} = R_\ell \geqq 0$$

and it follows from (21) that $b_t \geqq 0 \; \forall t$. Then no individual in any age group prefers the w-strategy to either the ℓ-risk or, since $R_h \geqq 0$, to the h-risk. This contradicts Assumption 2. Case (I) cannot therefore apply, and Proposition 2 must hold.

In case (II) we obtain $R_{\ell t} = R_\ell < 0 \ \forall t$. It follows from (18) that $b_t = R_{\ell t} < 0 \ \forall t$. Thus the ℓ-risk is never accepted and, as a consequence, there are no h-entrepreneurs. Since this contradicts Assumption 1, case (II) is not feasible and we are left with case (III), as stated in Proposition 3.

Case (III) is not, in fact, sufficient to ensure a solution. For if the additional constraint

$$R_\ell + p(T-1)R_h \geqq 0 \tag{22}$$

is violated, we have $R_{\ell t} < 0 \ \forall t$. Then, by (18), $b_t < 0 \ \forall t$ and there are no entrepreneurs of either type. However if (22) holds, we may define

$$T^* = \max \{t \mid R_{\ell t} \geqq 0\}$$

noting that $T^* \geqq 1$, by (22); and $T^* < T$, since $R_{\ell T} = R_\ell < 0$. By construction, $R_{\ell t} < 0 \ \forall t > T^*$ and hence, by (18), $b_t < 0 \ \forall t > T^*$. Thus the ℓ-strategy is rejected at all ages $t > T^*$. Furthermore either $R_{\ell T^*} > 0$, in which case $b_{T^*} > 0$ and, by (20), $b_t > 0 \ \forall t \leq T^*$; or else $R_{\ell T^*} = 0$, in which case $b_{T^*} = 0$ and, by.(19) given $R_h > 0$, $b_t > 0 \ \forall t < T^*$. So the ℓ-risk is accepted at all ages $t < T^*$; and the ℓ-strategy is either strictly preferred or indifferent to the w-strategy at age T^*, depending on whether $R_{\ell T^*}$ is greater than or equal to zero.

The optimal entrepreneurial behaviour can therefore be summarized as follows: A feasible solution is possible if Proposition 3 and condition (22) hold, so that

$$p(T-1)R_h \geqq -R_\ell > 0.$$

Individuals begin taking ℓ-risks at age 1 and, if unsuccessful, continue taking ℓ-risks up to, and possible including, age T^*, after which the w-strategy is adopted. Successful ℓ-entrepreneurs take h-risks for the remainder of their lives.

IV   Attitudes towards diversification

We now turn to the question of whether ℓ- and h-entrepreneurs will choose to pool risks, considering first the behaviour of those whose wealth and success index at age $t-1$ make them eligible to take h-risks. For such individuals, the valuation of wealth at the end of the next period is given by

$$V_t(W,S) = W + (T-t)w + (T-t)R_h \quad \text{if } W \geqq F_\ell$$

$$V_t(W,S) = W + (T-t)w + B_t \quad\quad\ \text{if } W < F_\ell \tag{23}$$

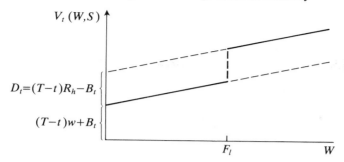

FIG. 9.1. The valuation of wealth schedule.

using (12) and (13). This schedule, illustrated in Fig. 9.1, consists of two linear segments with a discontinuity at F_t, which makes the function non-concave.

Notice that

$$D_t := (T-t)R_h - B_t > 0 \quad \forall t < T. \tag{24}$$

For if $b_t \leq 0$, it follows from (20) that $b_\tau \leq 0 \ \forall \tau \geq t$. Hence (14) and Proposition 3 imply $B_t = 0$ and $D_t = (T-t)R_h > 0$. Alternatively, if $b_t > 0$ we have

$$pD_t = p(T-t)R_h - pB_t > R_t + p(T-t)R_h - pB_t$$
$$= R_{tt} - pB_t = b_t > 0,$$

using (15), (16), and Proposition 3. D_t can be regarded as the lump sum loss resulting from exclusion from future h-risks if wealth falls below F_t. The fact that it is postive for all $t < T$ ensures the discontinuity in the graph of $V_t(W,S)$.

An h-entrepreneur who agrees to belong to a risk-sharing consortium of k persons can expect an equal share of $X^{(k)}$ successful risks, where $X^{(k)}$ is a (discrete) random variable whose density and distribution functions will be denoted by

$$g^{(k)}(j) = \text{Prob}(X^{(k)} = j) \quad j = 0, 1, \ldots, k.$$
$$G^{(k)}(j) = \text{Prob}(X^{(k)} < j).$$

We note that the expected number of consortium successes is given by

$$E\{X^{(k)}\} = \sum_{j=0}^{k} jg^{(k)}(j) = k\pi, \tag{25}$$

and that

$$G^{(N_h)}(j) = \begin{cases} 0 & j \leq f_h \\ 1 & j > f_h, \end{cases} \tag{26}$$

since the consortium of all h-entrepreneurs is guaranteed to gain the f_h available rewards. For low values of k, $g^{(k)}(j)$ can be approximated by the binomial probability π_{kj} of (6). However the fixed number of rewards means that the correspondence between $g^k(j)$ and π_{kj} is not exact, and would clearly be inappropriate for values of j greater than f_h.

Given that an h-entrepreneur needs to invest wealth F_ℓ in h-risks, a member of a k-person consortium with wealth W at time $t-1$ can expect to have wealth

$$W - F_\ell + \frac{j}{k} F_h$$

at the end of period t with probability $g^{(k)}(j)$. Using (23) and (24), the value of current wealth is given by

$$V^{(k)}_{t-1}(W,S) = \sum_{j=0}^{k} g^{(k)}(j) \, V_t \left(W - F_\ell + \frac{j}{k} F_h, S \right)$$

$$= W - F_\ell + (T-t)(w + R_h)$$

$$+ \sum_{j=0}^{k} g^{(k)}(j) \frac{j}{k} F_h - D_t G^{(k)}(k\theta) \tag{27}$$

where

$$\theta := \frac{2F_\ell - W}{F_h}$$

represents the proportion of successful risks (i.e. $X^{(k)}/k$) required to keep the individual above the threshold value F_ℓ, given current wealth W. Substituting (25) we obtain

$$V^{(k)}_{t-1}(W,S) = W + (T-t+1)(w + R_h) - D_t G^{(k)}(k\theta),$$

and the optimal risk sharing strategy of the individual is determined by the value of k which maximizes $V^k_{t-1}(W,S)$ or, equivalently, that which minimizes $G^{(k)}(k\theta)$, since $D_t > 0$ for $t < T$. This is accomplished by choosing $k = N_h$. For $\theta \leq F_\ell/F_h$ whenever $W \geq F_\ell$, and $R_h > 0$ ensures $f_h F_h > F_\ell N_h$ by (5). So

$$N_h \theta \leq \frac{N_h F_\ell}{F_h} < f_h,$$

and using (26)

$$G^{(N_h)}(N_h \theta) \leq G^{(N_h)}(f_h) = 0.$$

Thus the complete diversification strategy ensures $G^{(k)}(k\theta) = 0$, and guarantees that $V_{t-1}^{(k)}(W, S)$ achieves its maximum value. This confirms Proposition 4.

To support the claim that ℓ-entrepreneurs specialize in a single risk, as stated in Proportion 5, we will consider an alternative strategy in which individuals are members of a risk-sharing consortium of k persons in every period, departing from this strategy only when access to h-risks has been achieved. In t periods, therefore, individuals share in kt risks, perceived to be independent with success probability p. Since the success index S of a consortium member increases by $1/k$ (and wealth by F_t/k) following each success, an individual will leave the consortium and become an h-entrepreneur as soon as a minimum of k successes have been recorded.

It will be helpful to regard the consortium risks as taking place sequentially, so that we can refer to the Kth trial of the consortium, where K can take any positive integral value. Let $z^{(k)}$ represent the number of the trial at which k successes are first recorded (and hence access to h-risks are achieved). Then

$$q_K^{(k)} = \text{Prob } \{z^{(k)} = K\}$$

$$= \text{Prob } \{k-1 \text{ successes in } K-1 \text{ trials}\} \times \text{Prob } \{\text{success at } K\text{th trial}\}$$

$$= {}^{K-1}C_{k-1} p^{k-1}(1-p)^{K-k} \times p.$$

In addition, the probability generating function for $z^{(k)}$ may be written

$$Q^{(k)}(x) := \sum_{K=1}^{\infty} q_K^{(k)} x^K = \left(\frac{px}{1-(1-p)x}\right)^k, \tag{28}$$

and the expected value of $z^{(k)}$ is computed as

$$E\{Z^{(k)}\} = \sum_{K=1}^{\infty} K q_K^{(k)} = \left.\frac{dQ^{(k)}(x)}{dx}\right|_{x=1} = kp. \tag{29}$$

Now consider an individual evaluating the options at the beginning of his life. The decision to join a consortium depends on only two factors: whether membership will increase the expected immediate return; and whether membership will affect the expected number of periods in which the individual has access to h-risks. The first of these factors is of no significance, since the expected immediate return is the same for all values of k (including $k = 1$). This can be seen by comparing the expected return per period $R_t = pF_t - w$ associated with a single specialized risk (corresponding to $k = 1$), with the expected return per period from a k-consortium given by

$$\frac{F_\ell}{k} \sum_{j=1}^{k} {}^{j}C_k j \, p^j (1-p)^{k-j} - w = \frac{F_\ell}{k} kp - w = R_\ell.$$

However the number of periods in which the individual expects to remain below the threshold success level, and hence does not achieve access to h-risks, does depend on the consortium size. This expected number of periods is given by

$$\mu^{(k)} = \sum_{t=1}^{\infty} t \sum_{s=1}^{k} q^{(k)}_{k(t-1)+s} \tag{30}$$

since

$$\sum_{s=1}^{k} q^{(k)}_{k(t-1)+s}$$

indicates the probability that the kth consortium success will occur after trial $k(t-1)$ but no later than trial kt: in other words in period t. From (30) we then obtain

$$\mu^{(k)} > \frac{1}{k} \sum_{K=1}^{\infty} K q^{(k)}_K \quad \forall k > 1$$

and using (29) it follows that

$$\mu^{(k)} > \frac{1}{k} kp = p = \mu^{(1)} \quad \forall k > 1.$$

Joining a consortium of $k > 1$ individuals therefore tends to increase the number of periods the individual remains as an ℓ-entrepreneur, and postpones the date of access to h-risks. This suggests that the individual has no incentive to join a consortium, and will instead specialize in a single ℓ-risk in each period.

V Concluding remarks

This paper has attempted to model some of the central aspects concerned with the original creation of large fortunes via entrepreneurial activity. In the framework proposed, individuals engage in 'low-budget' risks in order to acquire the wealth and credibility necessary to gain access to the desirable 'high-budget' risks. It has been argued that competition for access to h-risks is likely to be so strong that the immediate return to low budget risks becomes negative. Thus one implication of the model is that we may observe large numbers of individuals accepting risks that appear to be actuarially unfair. Since it would be quite consistent for individuals to take these unfair gambles at the same time as insuring against losses, the model suggests a somewhat different explanation of the gambling–insurance paradox to that offered by Friedman and Savage (1948).

A second implication on which attention has been focused concerns the likelihood that the attitude of individuals towards risk-diversification will be qualitatively different depending on whether individuals have small or large wealth holdings, with the wealthy tending to diversify as much as possible, while those less well off adopt the opposite extreme of complete specialization. This contrasting behaviour has nothing to do with changes in the degree of risk aversion at different wealth levels. Instead the diversification ambition of the wealthy reflects the desire to protect their privileged access to a class of desirable risks; while the specialization strategy of the less wealthy gives the best chance of joining the privileged group in the minimum possible time. This significant change in the attitude towards diversification at different wealth levels has not been emphasized in earlier studies, although it appears to be a widespread phenomenon.

There are several obvious ways in which the framework proposed here could be extended and improved. For example, the assumption that individuals are risk-neutral could be replaced by one allowing individuals to have different degrees of risk aversion.[4] One consequence of this change would be variations in the date at which unsuccessful ℓ-entrepreneurs terminate their efforts. Indeed, a substantial number of risk-averse individuals may never engage in entrepreneurial activities, choosing instead to work in paid employment throughout their lives. This would, of course, be a more accurate portrayal of behaviour observed in the real world. However, the principal conclusions of the model, particularly those captured in Propositions 1–5, would seem to be fairly robust to this modification.

Another obvious way of extending the model would be to incorporate inheritances, bequests, and other factors influencing the intergenerational transmission of wealth holdings, like family size and patterns of marriage between wealth groups. Such an extension would allow the new fortunes created by one generation to be traced through successive generations, and hence provide a more complete picture of the process of wealth creation and preservation. The kind of model proposed may also help explain any tendency for large fortunes to be passed on substantially intact, rather than divided evenly between heirs in such a way that the special advantages of large wealth holdings are lost.

Finally it would be interesting to examine in more detail the equilibrium returns to each type of risk activity, and to consider how these interact with the optimal behaviour of individuals. In particular, it would be worth performing a comparative static exercise on the number and value of rewards in each risk activity, since these are the exogenous variables which ultimately influence individual responses and determine the distribution of wealth holdings.

Notes

1. The suggestion that small scale and large scale entrepreneurs differ not in their personal qualities, but only in their access to capital, is evident in the writings of Adam Smith. In Smith's illustration, the sea-port grocer 'must be able to read, write, and account, and must be a tolerable judge too of, perhaps, fifty or sixty different sorts of goods, their prices, qualities, and the markets where they are to be had cheapest. He must have all the knowledge, in short, that is necessary for a great merchant, which nothing hinders him from becoming but the want of a sufficient capital.' (1937, 112).
2. Note that N_ℓ and N_h are assumed to be sufficiently large that p and π are both less than one.
3. Note that S_t is not affected by unsuccessful investments, and hence treats previous success and failure asymmetrically.
4. This line of development would establish a closer link with the analysis of entrepreneurship provided by Kihlstrom and Laffont (1979) and Kanbur (1979, 1982).

References

Buckholtz, P., J. M. Hartwick, B. Madill, and M. T. Wasan, 'An Economy Driven by Individuals Accumulating Wealth in Uncertain Environments', Queens University, Ontario, Canada, mimeo, (1982).

Friedman M. and L. J. Savage, 'The Utility Analysis of Choices Involving Risk', *Journal of Political Economy* **56** (1948), 279–304.

Kanbur, S. M. R., 'Of Risk Taking and the Personal Distribution of Income', *Journal of Political Economy* **87** (1979), 769–97.

—— , 'Entrepreneurial Risk Taking, Inequality and Public Policy: An Application of Inequality Decomposition Analysis to the General Equilibrium Effects of Progressive Taxation', *Journal of Political Economy* **90** (1982), 1–21.

Kihlstrom, R. E. and J. J. Laffont, 'A General Equilibrium Entrepreneurial Theory of Firm Formation Based on Risk Aversion', *Journal of Political Economy* **87** (1979), 719–48.

Shorrocks, A. F., 'On Stochastic Models of Size Distribution', *Review of Economic Studies* **42** (1975), 631–41.

Smith A., *An Inquiry into the Nature and Causes of the Wealth of Nations*, (The Modern Library, New York, 1937).

Comments on Chapter 9

FRANÇOIS BOURGUIGNON
École des Hautes Études en Sciences Sociales

Anthony Shorrocks's paper is an original piece of work in the field of wealth distribution. All individuals are alike, they are perfectly risk-neutral, they do not inherit large or small fortunes. Yet, some of them become permanently rich while others stop trying to be so after a few unsuccessful attempts. Of course, there is something exogenous in the model in order to generate such results. It consists of a fixed number of 'prizes' which randomly reward those who have been seeking for them. However, the nice part of the model is that there also is a kind of 'indivisibility' or non-convexity which prevents agents from sharing the risks and the benefits associated with the search for prizes. The fact that individuals engaging in 'high budget' risks must previously have been successful as 'low-budget' entrepreneurs introduces a non-convexity in the budget constraint of each agent which makes risk-sharing non-optimal at the first stage of fortune-seeking and optimal at the second stage. This representation of fortune-making is both convincing in relation with the real world and attractive from a purely technical point of view.

Yet, there is a bit of disappointment when one has finished reading the paper, in the sense that the model is not really closed. It is natural that the number of 'prizes' be exogenous, but the number of people chosing them, and, thus, the probability of winning, certainly are not. As it stands, the model would permit the prediction of the distribution of wealth as a function of those probabilities, whereas we would be more interested in explaining that distribution as a function of truely exogenous business opportunities offered to a given population. So, a general equilibrium framework which would explain the number of people engaging in fortune-seeking seems necessary.

Exploring that direction should also make the model closer to the real world. In particular, it would become possible to introduce commonly heard justifications for not engaging in entrepreneurial activity of the type: 'It is not worth my efforts because too many people are already looking for all possible business opportunities'. Basically, what is missing in the present state of the model to account for that type of behaviour is a third basic assumption or rather a modification of Assumption 2. It should be the case, not only that some individuals prefer not to engage in entrepreneurial activity *at some time* during their active life, what is actually implied by the optimal strategy which consists of stopping prize-search at some time $T^* > 1$, but *at all times*. In other words, some individuals already consider it not advantageous to search

257

for business opportunities during the first period. All individuals being alike, this would imply that the total direct and indirect — e.g. through access to 'high-budget' business — return to 'low-budget' entrepreneurial activity should be zero in each period, that is $R_{\ell t} = 0$ for all t. Competitively, this could be achieved by some additional individuals becoming low-budget entrepreneurs as long as the total return $R_{\ell t}$ is strictly positive, but driving the rate of return down by diminishing the probability of success. The same could be done at the upper level, by equalizing to zero the differential rate of return of becoming a high budget entrepreneur in case of success in low budget activities.

Of course such a setting raises the usual question of which individuals will undertake risks if they are all identical and if the expected return is zero. It is the same problem as that of which firms will leave a market in a competitive long-run equilibrium if demand falls. In the present case some dispersion in risk aversion would have to be reintroduced to solve that problem.

What then are the lessons to be learned from such a model? Leaving aside differences in risk-aversion, the competitive general equilibrium analysis as well as the basic model developed by Shorrocks makes wealth distribution the result of a pure random process. *Ex ante*, all individuals are alike and, under the competitive equilibrium assumption, their expected lifetime income is the same whatever the strategy they choose with respect to entrepreneurial activity. *Ex post* some of those who decided to gamble have been successful and are well off, whereas those who have been unlucky are worse off. Thus, wealth distribution essentially is the result of an actuarially fair lottery. As such, this is not a very new or interesting result. But it might also be possible to use Shorrocks' ingenious model in a different way to study the innovative efficiency of a society. A property of the model is that, in general, business opportunities are not all discovered because individuals stop searching for them when the discounted expected return becomes too low. If we suppose that growth performances, and thus, the wage rate, is affected by the number of technical or market innovations discovered by entrepreneurs, then the model should permit the analysis of the effect of redistribution policies upon the innovation rate. Clearly, if the *ex-post* distribution of wealth generated by the business lottery is considered as too unequal and, consequently, corrected by taxes which discriminate against successful entrepreneurs, entrepreneurial activity will diminish and less of the possible innovations will be undertaken. The present model offers a convenient framework to study this common neo-liberal argument against progressive taxation.

Accumulation Behaviour and the Distribution of Wealth

10 Life-Cycle Savings and the Individual Distribution of Wealth by Class

EDWARD N. WOLFF*

New York University

In this paper, I develop a two-class model of wealth distribution among individuals. As in Stiglitz (1969), Vaughan (1979) and others, it is assumed that there are two distinct economic classes: the 'capitalists' and the 'workers'. However, this model differs from previous such attempts in that it is assumed that the savings behaviour of workers follows a life-cycle model of consumption. As a result, there are two subclasses of workers: active and retired. Capitalists, on the other hand, are assumed to save a fixed proportion of their income. Moreover, production is assumed to follow a Cobb–Douglas production function with neutral technical change.

Two major theoretical results emerge from the model. First, in steady-state equilibrium the rate of interest and growth are related according to the so-called Pasinetti theorem. Second, in steady-state equilibrium, the relative inequality of wealth among individuals remains constant over time. Such a result differs from that which emerges from most variants of Stiglitz' model, where wealth inequality in steady-state equilibrium declines over time and approaches perfect equality in the limit.[1]

The model of worker savings will generally follow that of Summers (1981). Such a model seems better than the typical assumption of worker savings as proportional to or a linear function of income, since most studies do suggest that retirement is a very strong motive for worker savings (see, for example, Atkinson (1971), Wolff (1981), King and Dicks-Mireaux (1982), or Söderström (1982)). On the other hand, a model which assumed that all savings was generated by the life cycle model would appear inadequate to account for total savings or capital stock, as numerous studies have recently shown (see, for example, White (1978), Wolff (1981), or Kotlikoff and Summers (1981)). It thus appears reasonable to assume that there is a class of individuals in society who accumulate wealth largely for its own sake.

In a sense, the prediction of constant wealth inequality in the steady-state is somewhat unfortunate, since recent evidence indicates that there has been a sharp decline in personal wealth inequality in several industrialized countries. Smith (1987) found for the US that the share of net worth held by the top $\frac{1}{2}\%$ of wealth holders was 21.4% in 1958 and 21.9% in 1972 and then fell to

* I would like to thank Dominique Strauss-Kahn, those present at the seminar and, in particular, an anonymous referee for their valuable suggestions.

261

14.4% in 1976; likewise the share of the top 1% was 26.6% in 1958 and 27.7% in 1972 and then declined to 19.2% in 1976. Between 1972 and 1976, the share of every asset type, including stocks and bonds, held by the top percentiles declined sharply. Additional evidence does suggest that wealth inequality did increase between 1976 and 1981, with the share of the richest 0.8% accounting for 20% of total net worth. However, Whiteman (1984) reported that the share of net worth of the top quartile fell from 80.0% in 1962 to 70.9% in 1979.

For the United Kingdom the evidence is even more dramatic. Shorrocks (1987) reported that the share of the top 1% of wealth holders declined fairly continuously from 60.9% in 1923 to 23% in 1980, while the share of the top 5% fell from 82.0% to 43%. Moreover, when pension rights are included as part of personal wealth, the share of the top 1% fell from 27% in 1971 to 19% in 1981 with one calculation of pension wealth and from 21% to 12% using a different calculation.

For Sweden, Spant (1987) found that the share of net worth held by the richest 1% fell almost continuously from 50% in 1920 to 21% in 1975, while that of the top 5% fell from 60% to 28%. However, between 1975 and 1983, there was a slight increase in wealth inequality, with the share of the top 1% rising from 17% to 19.5% (based on market prices) and that of the top 2% from 24% to 26%.

For reasons that will become apparent in the development of the model, it is very difficult to ascertain the direction of movement of wealth inequality as the economy moves toward steady-state equilibrium. (Indeed, it is not possible to determine that the economy will move toward steady-state equilibrium or even that the steady-state equilibrium is stable). However, it is possible to determine the change in steady-state wealth inequality from change in the basic parameters of the system. We shall consider six such factors in the analysis: (i) change in productivity growth; (ii) change in the capitalist propensity to save; (iii) changes in the life span and retirement age; (iv) changes in the relative size of the capitalist class; (v) change in the covariance of earnings with age; and (vi) the effect of the growth of the social security system. As will be evident from the analysis, some of these factors may have played an important role in explaining the historical decline in wealth inequality.

The paper is divided into five parts. In Section I, the long-period growth model is developed. In Section II, the savings model for workers and capitalists is presented. Section III derives the steady-state equilibrium for the model. Section 4 considers the six factors discussed in the previous paragraph, and some simulation results are presented of their potential impact on wealth inequality movements over time. Conclusions are presented in the last section.

I The long-period growth model

For simplicity, I will assume a one-commodity economy, whose output is a Cobb–Douglas production function of its inputs. In addition, it will be assumed that neutral technical change occurs at a constant rate over time. Then,

$$X_t = a_0 e^{\gamma t} L_t^\alpha K_t^{(1-\alpha)} \tag{1}$$

where X_t is output at time t; L_t is employment at t; K_t is the capital stock at t; a_0, γ, and α are all constants; and $0 < \alpha < 1$. If we use a superscript dot ($\cdot$) to indicate time rate of change (e.g. $\dot{X}_t = dX_t/dt$) then (1) can be rewritten as:

$$\frac{\dot{X}_t}{X_t} = \gamma + \frac{\alpha \dot{L}_t}{L_t} + (1 - \alpha) \frac{\dot{K}_t}{K_t} \tag{1'}$$

It will be assumed that labour and capital are fully employed at each point in time and that the labour force increases at a constant rate n over time. Thence, (1') can be rewritten as

$$\frac{\dot{X}_t}{X_t} = \gamma + \alpha n + (1 - \alpha) \frac{\dot{K}_t}{K_t} \tag{1''}$$

The steady-state equilibrium condition (designated by a superscript, e) is given by a constant rate of growth of the capital stock:

$$\text{steady-state condition:} \quad \left(\frac{\dot{K}_t}{K_t} \right)^e = k^* \tag{2}$$

where k^* is a constant. It can be shown that this steady-state condition is stable in the sense that the economy will return to this state from any deviation from this position. Let us assume for the moment, following Solow (1956) and others, that savings is a constant proportion of income, where the savings rate is given by s. (In Section III, it will be proved that this is the case.) Then, the rate of growth of savings over time equals $\dot{X}_t/X_t$. In steady-state equilibrium, the rate of growth of savings must exactly keep pace with the rate of growth of the capital stock. Hence,

$$\left(\frac{\dot{X}}{X} \right)^e = \gamma + \alpha n + (1 - \alpha) \left(\frac{\dot{K}}{K} \right)^e = k^*$$

or

$$\left(\frac{\dot{X}}{X} \right)^e = k^* = n + \gamma/\alpha \tag{3}$$

and, in steady-state, total savings, S, is given by:

$$S = (n + g)K \tag{4}$$

where $g = \gamma/\alpha$.

The parameter g is also the rate of labour productivity growth in steady-state, since

$$\left(\frac{\dot{X}}{X}\right)^e - n = \gamma/\alpha = g \tag{5}$$

II The life-cycle savings model and the capitalist savings model

It shall be assumed that $p\%$ of the population consists of workers whose savings behaviour follows the life cycle model of household savings (LCM). The version presented here basically follows Summers (1981) (see Modigliani and Brumberg (1954) for the original version of the LCM). I shall assume that there is a one-to-one correspondence between workers and working class households. For the moment, it shall be assumed that each worker earns the same annual wage at time t, w_t.

Workers are assumed to choose a consumption plan to maximize lifetime utility subject to a lifetime budget constraint:

$$\max \int_0^T U(c_t)e^{-\delta t}\,dt \tag{6}$$

subject to

$$\int_0^T c_t\,e^{-rt}\,dt = \int_0^{T'} w_t\,e^{-rt}\,dt$$

where T represents the (certain) date of death and workers are assumed to exhaust their wealth at time of death; U is the utility function and c_t is annual consumption; δ is a personal discount factor, which is assumed to be constant over time and over c; and T' is the age of retirement.[2] The variable r here is the rate of interest, which is identical with the rate of profit, since there is only one asset in the model, capital K. Moreover, r is assumed to be constant in this model. It will be shown in the next section that r is constant only in steady-state equilibrium, so that the life-cycle maximization problem can be solved only in the steady-state. (This is not explicitly indicated in Summers' paper). Moreover, it will be assumed that wages grow at a constant rate over time. In the next section, it will be shown that this is the case only in steady-state equilibrium. (This point also is not explicitly mentioned by Summers).

As with Summers, we shall assume that all workers have a constant elasticity utility function, with a common value of ϵ, the elasticity of the marginal utility function. The solution to (6) then becomes

$$c_t = c_0 e^{[(r-\delta)/(1-\epsilon)]t} \tag{7a}$$

$$c_0 = \frac{w_0(e^{(h-r)T'} - 1)\left[\left(\dfrac{r-\delta}{1-\epsilon}\right) - r\right]}{(e^{((r-\delta)/(1-\epsilon)-r)T} - 1)(h-r)} \tag{7b}$$

where w_0 is the initial annual wage. We shall now assume that $\delta = r$ in order to make our problem tractable. There are various justifications for this. First, one can argue that δ is not really constant, but rather that individuals will borrow or lend until the marginal $\delta = r$. Second, we are interested here in aggregate consumption and therefore in the behaviour of the average individual. On average, δ must equal r for the financial market to be in equilibrium. The solution to the maximization problem (6) then becomes substantially simplified:

$$c_t = c_0 = \frac{rw_0(1 - e^{(h-r)T'})}{(e^{-rT} - 1)(h-r)} \tag{8}$$

Consumption is thus constant over the lifetime.

The aggregate consumption of the working class, C_w, depends on the age distribution, since initial consumption and earnings depend on time of entry into the labour force. Since the work force is assumed to grow at an annual rate n,

$$C_{w_t} = \int_0^T N_{0_t} c_{\theta_t} e^{-(h+n)t}\, dt = \frac{N_{0_t} c_{0_t}(e^{-(h+n)T} - 1)}{-(h+n)} \tag{9}$$

where N_{0_t} is the number of workers entering the labour force at time t and c_{0_t} is their consumption. The total size of the active labour force is given by:

$$L_t = \int_0^{T'} N_{0_t} e^{-nt} = \frac{N_{0_t}[e^{-nT'} - 1]}{-n} \tag{10}$$

Capitalist Savings. The remaining $(1 - p)\%$ of the population consists of capitalists. Capitalists are defined as those who inherited their wealth, never worked, and live exclusively off income from their capital. Since both workers and retirees also receive income from their capital, the income of capitalists at time t, Y_{c_t}, is given by:

$$Y_{c_t} = \beta_t r_t K_t \tag{11}$$

where β_t is the fraction of the capital stock owned by capitalists. (It is not necessary to assume that the rate of profit is constant). I shall assume that capitalists save a constant fraction of their income, m, so that:

$$S_{c_t} = m\beta_t r_t K_t \tag{12}$$

For the moment, I shall assume that the capitalist class also grows at the rate n over time and wealth is equally distributed among capitalists.

Wealth Holdings. We can now derive both the aggregate wealth holdings of each class, as well as individual wealth holdings. In terms of the current wage, w_t, a worker of age a holds net worth nw_{a_t} at time t given by:

$$nw_{a_t} = \int_0^a (w_t e^{-h(a-x)} - c_{0a}) e^{r(a-x)} \, dx, \quad a \le T'$$

$$nw_{a_t} = \frac{w_t}{(h-r)} (1 - e^{a(r-h)}) + \frac{c_{0a}}{r}(1 - e^{ra}), \quad a \le T' \tag{13}$$

where $w_{0a} = w_t e^{-ha}$ (and it is implicitly assumed that the profit rate and wage rate growth are constant). For a retired worker of age $a > T'$, his (her) wealth accumulated up to the time of retirement is given by $nw_{T'_t}$ and his (her) wage at time of retirement was $w_{t'} = w_t e^{-h(a-T')}$. Therefore, the net worth of a retiree of age a is given by

$$nw_{a_t} = \left[\frac{w_t e^{-h(a-T')}}{(h-r)} (1 - e^{T'(r-h)}) + \frac{c_{0a}}{r}(1 - e^{rT'}) \right] e^{r(a-T')}$$

$$- \int_{T'}^a c_{0a} e^{r(a-x)} \, dx, \quad a > T'$$

$$nw_{a_t} = \frac{w_t}{(h-r)} (e^{(r-h)(a-T')} - e^{(r-h)a}) + \frac{c_{0a}}{r}(1 - e^{ra}), \quad a > T' \tag{14}$$

The aggregate wealth of workers at time t, NW_{w_t}, is given by:

$$NW_{w_t} = \int_0^{T'} nw_{a_t} \cdot N_{0_t} e^{-na} \, da$$

$$NW_{w_t} = \frac{N_{0_t} w_t}{(h-r)} \left[\frac{1 - e^{-nT'}}{n} + \frac{1 - e^{(r-h-n)T'}}{r-h-n} + \frac{(1 - e^{(h-r)T'})}{(e^{-rT} - 1)} \right.$$

$$\left. \cdot \left(\frac{1 - e^{-(h+n)T'}}{h+n} + \frac{1 - e^{(r-h-n)T'}}{r-h-n} \right) \right] \tag{15}$$

In like fashion, the aggregate wealth of retirees, NW_{r_t}, can be derived:

$$NW_{r_t} = \frac{N_{0_t} w_t}{(h-r)} \left[(-1 + e^{-(r-h)T'}) \cdot \frac{e^{(r-h-n)T} - e^{(r-h-n)T'}}{r-h-n} + \frac{(1 - e^{(h-r)T'})}{(e^{-rT} - 1)} \right.$$

$$\left. \cdot \left(\frac{e^{-(h+n)T'} - e^{-(h+n)T}}{h+n} + \frac{e^{(r-h-n)T'} - e^{(r-h-n)T}}{r-h-n} \right) \right]. \tag{16}$$

Finally, the aggregate wealth of the capitalist class is given as a residual:

$$NW_{c_t} = K_t - NW_{w_t} - NW_{r_t} \tag{17}$$

III   Steady-state equilibrium

In order to prove that a steady-state equilibrium exists, it is necessary to show three results (that were treated as assumptions in Section I). First, there exists an aggregate savings rate S^e that is constant in the steady state. Second, the rate of profit r_t is constant in the steady state. Third, the rate of growth of real wages h is constant in the steady state.
  The proof is as follows: From (12)

$$S_{c_t} = \dot{K}_{c_t} = m\beta_t r_t K_t \tag{18}$$

where $K_{c_t} \equiv NW_{c_t}$. By definition,

$$\beta_t = K_{c_t}/K_t \tag{19}$$

Hence, from (18) and (19)

$$\dot{K}_{c_t}/K_{c_t} = mr_t \tag{20}$$

Define $k_{c_t} \equiv K_{c_t}/N_{c_t}$ to be the average wealth holdings of the capitalist class. By assumption,

$$\dot{N}_{c_t}/N_{c_t} = n \tag{21}$$

Hence,

$$\dot{k}_{c_t}/k_{c_t} = \dot{K}_{c_t}/K_{c_t} - n \tag{22}$$

From (20) and (22), it follows that

$$\dot{k}_{c_t} = k_{c_t}(mr_t - n) \tag{23}$$

The steady-state equilibrium condition (4) can be re-written as:

$$\dot{K}_t = (n+g)K_t \tag{24}$$

Assume that $\beta_t = \beta$ is constant in the steady-state. (This will be proved directly below). Then

$$\dot{K}_{c_t} = (n+g)K_{c_t} \tag{25}$$

From (22), then,

$$\frac{\dot{k}_{c_t}}{k_{c_t}} = g$$

or

$$\dot{k}_{c_t} = g\,k_{c_t} \tag{26}$$

Thence, from (23), the so-called Pasinetti theorem is obtained that:[3]

$$r_t = r^e = (n+g)/m \tag{27}$$

This result indicates that the rate of profit is constant in the steady state and, indeed, is given solely by n, g, and m. In particular, r^e is independent of the savings behaviour of the workers or of the class distribution of income.

Since the rate of profit is constant in the steady-state and, from (2) and (3), the capital stock and total output grow at the same rate, k^*, it directly follows that total profits also grow at k^*. Hence, total wages must also grow at k^* and from (5),

$$(\dot{w}_t/w_t)^e = g \tag{28}$$

that is, the wage rate also grows at a constant rate $g\,(=h)$ in the steady state.

In order to complete the proof, it remains to show that the worker's savings rate is constant in the steady state and that $\beta_t = \beta$, a constant in the steady state. This can be shown as follows:

From (4), steady-state growth implies:

$$(n + g)K = wL + rK - C$$

where $C = C_w + C_c$, and C_c is the total consumption of the capitalist class. Solving, we obtain:

$$\frac{S}{wL} = \frac{n+g}{n+g-r}\,(1 - C/wL) \tag{29}$$

From (8), (9), and (10),

$$\frac{C_w}{wL} = \frac{rn(1 - e^{(g-r)T})\,(e^{-(g+n)T} - 1)}{(g-r)\,(g+n)\,(e^{-rT} - 1)\,(e^{-nT'} - 1)} \tag{30}$$

In the steady state, then, C_w/wL is constant. Moreover, from (12),

$$\frac{C_c}{rK} = (1 - m)\beta_t$$

Since it has already been shown that factor shares are fixed in the steady state, then

$$\frac{C_c}{wL} = \frac{(1 - \alpha)(1 - m)\beta_t}{\alpha} \tag{31}$$

Then, from (29), (30), and (31), the savings rate in steady-state equilibrium is given by:

$$s = \frac{S}{Y} = \frac{\alpha(n+g)}{n + g - r}\left[1 - \frac{rn(1 - e^{(g-r)T'})(e^{-(g+n)T} - 1)}{(g - r)(g + n)(e^{-rT} - 1)(e^{-nT'} - 1)}\right.$$
$$\left. - \frac{(1 - \alpha)(1 - m)}{\alpha}\beta_t\right] \tag{32}$$

An inspection of the RHS of (32) indicates that all the variables are constant in the steady state, with the possible exception of β_t. We can now show that $\beta_t = \beta$, a constant in the steady state. From (10) and (15),

$$\frac{NW_w}{wL} = \frac{n}{(g - r)(1 - e^{-nT'})}\left[\frac{1 - e^{-nT'}}{n} + \ldots\right] = b_0$$

where the term in brackets is constant, as is b_0. Likewise, $NW_r/wL = b_1$, a constant in the steady state. Therefore,

$$\frac{NW_c}{K} = 1 - \frac{NW_w + NW_r}{K} = 1 - \frac{\alpha}{1 - \alpha}(b_0 + b_1)r$$

Finally, since r is constant in the steady state, so must $\beta = NW_c/K$.

Thus, we have shown that there does exist a constant savings rate that is consistent with the steady-state equilibrium.[4] Moreover, it should now be apparent that in the steady state, relative wealth inequality will also remain unchanged over time. The relative number of each of the three classes of individuals is fixed over time. The ratio of the number of active workers at time t, L_t, to the number of retirees, R_t, is given by:

$$\frac{L_t}{R_t} = \frac{e^{-nT'} - 1}{e^{-nT} - e^{-nT'}}$$

Since both the working class and capitalist class grow at $n\%$ per year (by assumption), their relative numbers remain fixed over time. The relative number of workers at each age level is also fixed over time, since the labour force grows at a fixed rate. From (8) and (13) the net worth of a worker aged a is given by:

$$nw_{a_t} = \frac{w_t}{(g - r)}\left[(1 - e^{a(r-g)}) + \frac{(1 - e^{(g-r)T'})(e^{-ga} - e^{a(r-g)})}{(e^{-rT} - 1)}\right],$$
$$a \le T' \tag{33}$$

Thus, the net worth of an individual aged a remains a constant ratio to w_t over time (since all the other variables are fixed over time). The same is true for retirees, since from (8) and (14),

$$nw_{a_t} = \frac{w_t}{(g - r)} \left[(e^{(r-g)(a - T')} - e^{a(r-g)}) \right.$$

$$\left. + \frac{(1 - e^{(g-r)T'})(e^{-ga} - e^{a(r-g)})}{(e^{-rT} - 1)} \right], \quad a > T' \tag{34}$$

Thus, the size distribution of wealth relative to w_t remains constant over time among workers and retirees in the steady state. Finally, the net worth of capitalists (recall that, by assumption, each capitalist has the same wealth holding) remains a fixed ratio of w_t over time. This follows from the fact that the total net worth of the capitalist class, NW_c remains a fixed proportion of $NW_{w_t} + NW_{r_t}$, and, from (15) and (16), NW_{w_t} and NW_{r_t} both move in proportion to w_t and n (through N_{0_t}) over time. Thus, relative wealth inequality in steady-state equilibrium remains fixed over time.[5]

IV   Simulation experiments

In this section, I consider the effect of shifts in selected parameter values on steady-state wealth inequality. Parameter shifts are chosen which appear to be historically relevant to the US in the twentieth century. Some assessment can then be made whether such parameter changes have contributed to the observed historical decline in wealth inequality in the US.

I shall continue to assume that wealth is equally distributed within the capitalist class and also among workers and retirees of the same age. The Gini coefficient will be used as the measure of wealth inequality, and it will be computed for four groups: (i) the (current) labour force; (ii) retirees; (iii) the total working class, consisting of current workers and retirees; and (iv) the total population. Solutions are shown for the steady state only, since the model is soluble in this state only.[6,7]

4.1   Productivity growth and the capitalist propensity to save

In the first set of simulations, steady-state solutions are shown for various values of labour productivity growth (g) and the capitalist propensity to save (m). In these simulations, the wage rate w_t has been set to unity (without loss of generality) and average wealth holdings are computed in terms of wage units. This follows from the fact that in the steady state both wages and the per capita capital stock increase at the (same) rate g, so that their ratio remains constant in the steady state. Other parameters are fixed as follows: (i) population growth (n) is set to 0.01, (ii) the retirement age (T') is set to 45 years; (iii) life expectancy (T) is set to 55 years; (iv) the proportion of the working class in the total population (p) is set to 0.9; and (v) the production function parameter α is set to 0.5. In addition, it is possible to compute the rate of interest (r) from equation (27).

Results are shown in Table 10.1. Some general observations are possible. First, the degree of wealth inequality among both current workers and the whole working class (current workers and retirees) is very high. The reason is that many current workers have negative net worth. Indeed, for most values of g and m the *average* wealth holdings of current workers is negative.[8] In this model, workers typically dissave from the start of their work life to around age 20 and then save from age 20 to retirement. However, positive net worth is attained only at about age 40, quite close to retirement. This result may appear somewhat odd on the surface but it should be remembered that the only wealth in this model is productive capital stock. In particular, housing and durables are not considered assets but rather part of consumption, though consumer debt and home mortgages would implicitly constitute part of financial debt. Indeed, at productivity growth rates of 2% or better, which has characterized the US economy since 1900, the working class as a whole has been a net debtor. In other words, the working class has tended to drain capital away from the business sector, rather than to provide capital to the business sector. This result of negative savings on the part of workers contrasts sharply with most two-class models, where workers are restricted to have zero or positive savings.

Second, retirees always have positive net worth. This is true in total and for each cohort. This is the case, since interest is their only source of income. Moreover, the Gini coefficient among retirees as a group is quite low, both relative to current workers and by historical standards.

Third, overall wealth inequality is quite high as measured by the Gini coefficient, though in many cases it is actually lower than wealth inequality within the working class. The reason for the high level of overall wealth inequality is that the average wealth holdings of the capitalists are substantially higher than that of the working class. In the case where workers have positive net worth on average, the average wealth holdings of the capitalist are typically 200 times greater than those of the worker. The overall Gini coefficient is almost completely determined by the between-class average wealth holdings, and the degree of wealth inequality within the working class has little effect on overall wealth inequality.

Fourth, with the capitalist propensity to save fixed, overall wealth inequality increases as productivity growth rises. The reason for this is that current workers save less (dissave more) at higher productivity growth rates, since they can repay their debts in cheaper (real) dollars. As a result, their average net worth becomes even more negative as productivity growth rises. Moreover, it also holds that if the interest rate r is fixed (and the parameter m is free to vary), overall wealth inequality moves inversely with the productivity growth rate.

TABLE 10.1. Wealth Inequality and Average Wealth Holdings for Selected Values of Productivity Growth (g) and the Capitalist Propensity to Save (m)[a]

Parameters			Gini Coefficients				Average Wealth Holdings[b]				
m	g	r	Current Workers	Retirees	Working Class	All	Current Workers	Retirees	Working Class	Capitalists	All
0.5	0.01	0.04	1.353	0.351	1.057	0.898	0.65	2.76	0.95	184.9	19.0
	0.02	0.06	—	0.352	—	1.035	-1.41	1.87	-0.95	137.5	12.0
	0.03	0.08	—	0.353	—	1.226	-2.91	1.21	-2.33	117.7	9.7
	0.04	0.10	—	0.355	—	1.430	-3.91	0.76	-3.25	106.6	7.7
0.6	0.01	0.033	1.159	0.353	0.955	0.894	0.78	2.80	1.06	211.5	22.1
	0.02	0.05	—	0.356	—	1.007	-1.28	1.96	-0.83	162.2	15.5
	0.03	0.067	—	0.357	—	1.192	-2.96	1.28	-2.36	131.8	11.1
	0.04	0.083	—	0.363	—	1.367	-4.27	0.87	-3.55	128.7	9.7
0.75	0.01	0.027	0.897	0.358	0.792	0.889	1.08	2.85	1.32	297.6	31.0
	0.02	0.04	—	0.361	—	0.980	-1.11	2.04	-0.67	199.5	19.3
	0.03	0.053	—	0.366	—	1.112	-2.95	1.45	-2.33	175.7	15.5
	0.04	0.067	—	0.367	—	1.325	-4.43	0.94	-3.68	143.7	11.0
0.9	0.01	0.022	0.805	0.360	0.728	0.888	1.23	2.87	1.46	373.7	38.7
	0.02	0.033	—	0.363	—	0.966	-1.01	2.08	-0.58	226.3	22.1
	0.03	0.044	—	0.366	—	1.023	-1.98	1.77	-1.46	206.6	19.3
	0.04	0.056	—	0.371	—	1.277	-4.56	1.01	-3.78	163.1	12.9

[a] Other parameter values are as follows: (i) $w_t = 1.0$; (ii) $n = 0.01$; (iii) $T' = 45$; (iv) $T = 55$; (v) $p = 0.9$; and (vi) $\alpha = 0.5$. The interest rate r is computed from equation (27)
[b] Values are in wage units

Fifth, with the productivity growth rate fixed, wealth inequality declines as the capitalist propensity to save increases or, equivalently, as the interest rate declines. The apparent reason is as follows: it was proved in Section III that the functional distribution of income is fixed in the steady state. As a result, all the neoclassical properties of the Cobb–Douglas production function hold in the steady state. In particular, the overall capital–labour ratio and, since p is fixed, the amount of capital per capita, is completely determined by the interest rate r and moves inversely with r. Hence, as r rises, average wealth holdings per capita fall, and the average wealth holdings of both the working class and the capitalist class decline to about the same degree. However, an increase in the interest rate will cause workers to dissave more in their early years, thus increasing wealth inequality within the working class. It is the last effect that appears to dominate and to cause the Gini coefficient to move in the same direction as the interest rate.

4.2   Changes in life span and retirement age

In the LCM, wealth accumulation patterns are quite sensitive to both life expectancy (T) and the age of retirement (T'). Simulations were tried varying these parameters, with results shown in Table 10.2. An increase in the life span from 55 to 58 years (cf. Tables 10.1 and 10.2) is associated with a modest decline in overall wealth inequality. The reason is that current workers, retirees, and the two groups together will hold greater net worth with increased life span, and the capitalist class will hold correspondingly less wealth. A further increase in the life span from 58 to 62 years is associated with a further decline in overall wealth inequality, also due to increased wealth holdings of the working class relative to the capitalist class. Finally, a decrease in the working life from 45 to 42 years also causes reduced wealth inequality and, again, due to the increasing relative wealth holdings of the working class.

Most industrialized countries have witnessed both increasing life spans as well as falling retirement ages over the last 50 years. An increasing number of years of retirement will induce workers to save more during their working years, and their average net worth during both working years and retirement years will consequently be higher. Both effects have likely led to the reduced overall wealth inequality observed in industrialized countries.

4.3   Size of the capitalist class

Another factor that might play a role in reduced wealth inequality is the changing relative size of the capitalist class. Simulation results were obtained from varying the value p, the percentage of the population in the working class (current workers plus retirees). For $r = 0.04$, $g = 0.02$, and other parameter values as shown in note a of Table 10.1, the overall Gini coefficient fell

TABLE 10.2. Wealth Inequality and Average Wealth Holdings for Selected Values of Productivity Growth (g), the Interest Rate (r), Lifespan (T), and Retirement Age (T')[a]

Parameters				Average Wealth Holdings					Overall Gini Coefficient
T	T'	g	r	Labour force	Retirees	Working Class	Capitalists	All	
58	45	0.02	0.04	−0.70	2.55	−0.14	187.4	18.6	1.052
			0.05	−0.95	2.43	−0.37	152.2	14.9	0.990
			0.06	−1.14	2.31	−0.55	129.0	12.4	1.019
		0.03	0.05	−2.65	1.78	−1.89	165.9	14.9	1.098
			0.06	−2.74	1.67	−1.98	141.9	12.4	1.141
			0.07	−2.78	1.56	−2.03	124.6	10.6	1.181
62	45	0.02	0.04	−0.24	3.12	0.47	173.3	17.8	0.941
			0.05	−0.58	2.96	0.16	140.5	14.2	0.969
			0.06	−0.86	2.80	−0.09	119.1	11.8	0.999
		0.03	0.05	−2.33	2.14	−1.38	154.4	14.2	1.081
			0.06	−2.50	1.99	−1.55	132.3	11.8	1.126
			0.07	−2.59	1.85	−1.66	116.3	10.1	1.168
55	42	0.02	0.04	−0.23	2.63	0.30	180.7	18.3	0.939
			0.05	−0.49	2.52	0.07	146.1	14.7	0.962
			0.06	−0.71	2.41	−0.13	123.4	12.2	0.986
		0.03	0.05	−2.01	1.88	−1.29	158.3	14.7	1.057
			0.06	−2.15	1.78	−1.42	135.0	12.2	1.096
			0.07	−2.32	1.67	−1.51	118.4	10.5	1.133

[a] Other parameter values are as follows: (i) $w = 1.0$; (ii) $n = 0.01$; (iii) $p = 0.09$; and (iv) $\alpha = 0.5$.

from 0.980 for $p = 0.9$ to 0.873 for $p = 0.8$ to 0.771 for $p = 0.7$. Thus, overall wealth inequality is quite sensitive to the percentage of the population in the capitalist class. However, it is difficult to say whether this has been historically relevant to the observed decline in wealth inequality.

4.4 The covariance of age and the wage

It has been assumed that the wage is equal for all workers. In actuality, wages vary considerably among workers and tend to increase with age. Suppose the wage structure (by age cohort) shifts upward at rate g' over time — i.e.,

$$w_{a,t+1} = w_{a_t} e^g$$

and at time t,

$$w_{a+1,t} = w_{a_t} e^{g'}$$

In addition, let us impose the constraint that the average wage, $\overline{w}_t$, is unity:

$$\overline{w}_t = w_{0_t} \cdot \frac{e^{(g'-n)T'} - 1}{g' - n} \cdot \frac{n}{1 - e^{-nT'}} = 1$$

where w_{0_t} is the entry wage at time t. Then, for an individual of age a,

$$w_{a+1,t+1} = w_{a_t} e^{(g+g')}$$

The solution is identical to that in section II, except that g is replaced by $g + g'$ and w_0 is now interpreted as the entry wage of the cohort adjusted for differences in wages between age cohorts.

The simulation results are identical to those obtained in Table 10.1, except that the productivity growth rate parameter g is now interpreted as the sum $g + g'$. In particular, with r and g (and hence m) fixed, the greater the effect of age on relative wages (g'), the greater wealth inequality is. Thus, a fall in the 'rate of return' to age (or experience) could have caused a reduction in wealth inequality.

4.5 Social security

The final factor to be considered in this analysis is the effect of the social security system on (fungible) wealth inequality. To model the social security system, let us assume: (a) that the social security tax rate s on earnings is fixed over time[9]; (b) social security is a pay-as-you-go system and hence the total social security taxes or contributions at time t, $TSST_t$, are fully paid out as benefits to retirees, $TSSB_t$:

$$TSST_t = TSSB_t;$$

and (c) each retiree is paid SSB in proportion to his total *undiscounted* lifetime earnings, ULE,[10] where

$$ULE_{a_t} = \int_0^{T'} w_0 e^{gx} dx = \frac{w_t e^{-ga}}{g}(e^{gT'} - 1)$$

Total undiscounted lifetime earnings for retirees, $TULE_t$, is then given by:

$$TULE_{r_t} = \int_{T'}^{T} ULE_{a_t} N_{0_t} e^{-na} da$$

$$= \frac{N_{0_t w_t}}{g}(e^{gT'} - 1)\frac{e^{-(g+n)T'} - e^{(g+n)T}}{g+n}$$

Moreover,

$$TSST_t = sw_t L_t = sw_t N_{0_t}\frac{(1 - e^{-nT'})}{n}$$

Hence, the social security benefit received by a retiree of age a is given by

$$SSB_{a_t} = \frac{TSST_t}{TULE_{r_t}} \cdot ULE_{a_t} \qquad , a > T'$$

$$= \frac{sw_t(g+n)(1-e^{-nT'})e^{-ga}}{n[e^{-(g+n)T'}-e^{-(g+n)T}]} \qquad , a > T'$$

The total lifetime income of a person aged a, TLI, is then given by

$$TLI_{a_t} = \int_0^{T'} (1-s)w_0 e^{(g-r)x}dx + \int_{T'}^{T} SSB_{a_t} e^{(g-r)x}dx$$

Annual consumption c is then given by:

$$c_{a_t} = c_{0_a} = \frac{TLI_{a_t} \cdot r}{(e^{-rt}-1)}$$

The solution for nw_a then follows (13) and (14).

Simulation results are given in Table 10.3 from varying the social security tax rate s. The principal result is that an increase in the social security tax rate leads uniformly to an increase in both overall wealth inequality and wealth inequality among retirees. As the social security tax rate increases, both current workers and retirees save less (dissave more), the capitalists accumulate more wealth, and their wealth holdings relative to the working class increases. Indeed, for certain parameter values and with the social security tax rate sufficiently high, retirees hold negative wealth on average and for each age cohort. Only at death do they repay their debts. Thus, the increasing tax rates observed for the social security system in the US since 1935 may have contributed to increasing (fungible) wealth inequality.[11]

V   Conclusion

Two principal theoretical results emerge from the model developed in this paper. First, the specification of a life cycle savings model for workers in a two-class model is found to be consistent with the Pasinetti results regarding the rate of interest and productivity growth in steady-state equilibrium. Second, in steady-state equilibrium, wealth inequality among individuals is found to remain constant over time.

There are several limitations and provisos to the model that should be mentioned. First, the capitalist class is modelled passively in terms of a constant savings rate, equal wealth among members, and a constant growth rate in numbers. It might prove more fruitful to model their behaviour in terms of bequest motives and to assume a variety of estate-splitting patterns. Second, I have assumed that the working class and capitalist class are distinct and that

TABLE 10.3. Wealth Inequality and Average Wealth Holdings for Selected Values of the Social Security Tax Rate (s), Interest Rate (r), and Productivity Growth (g)[a]

Parameters			Gini Coefficients		Average Wealth Holdings				
r	g	s	Retirees	All	Labour Force	Retirees	Working Class	Capitalists	All
0.04	0.02	0	0.361	0.980	−1.1	2.0	−0.7	199	19.3
		0.02	1.217	1.007	−1.7	0.4	−1.4	206	19.3
		0.03	—	1.021	−2.0	0.4	−1.8	209	19.3
		0.04	—	1.036	−2.3	−1.2	−2.1	213	19.3
		0.05	—	1.052	−2.6	−2.0	−2.5	216	19.3
		0.07	—	1.087	−3.2	−3.6	−3.2	223	19.3
0.05	0.02	0	0.356	1.007	−1.3	2.0	−0.8	162	15.5
		0.02	0.818	1.026	−1.6	0.9	−1.3	166	15.5
		0.03	1.283	1.036	−1.8	0.4	−1.5	168	15.5
		0.04	—	1.046	−1.9	−0.1	−1.7	170	15.5
		0.05	—	1.056	−2.1	−0.6	−1.9	172	15.5
		0.07	—	1.079	−2.4	−1.7	−2.3	176	15.5
0.05	0.03	0	0.366	1.112	−2.9	1.4	−2.3	176	15.5
		0.02	—	1.201	−4.4	−2.2	−4.1	192	15.5
		0.03	—	1.251	−5.1	−4.1	−5.0	199	15.5
		0.04	—	1.304	−5.8	−5.9	−5.8	207	15.5
		0.05	—	1.361	−6.6	−7.8	−6.7	215	15.5
		0.07	—	1.484	−8.0	−11.5	−8.5	231	15.5
0.06	0.03	0	0.362	1.154	−3.0	1.4	−2.4	150	12.9
		0.02	—	1.231	−4.0	−1.8	−3.7	162	12.9
		0.03	—	1.275	−4.5	−3.3	−4.4	168	12.9
		0.04	—	1.322	−5.1	−4.9	−5.0	174	12.9
		0.05	—	1.373	−5.6	−6.5	−5.7	180	12.9
		0.07	—	1.485	−6.6	−9.6	−7.0	192	12.9

[a] Other parameter values are as follows: (i) $w = 1.0$; (ii) $n = 0.01$; (iii) $T' = 45$; (iv) $T = 55$; (v) $p = 0.9$; and (vi) $\alpha = 0.5$.

there is no mobility or switching between classes (cf. Vaughan (1979)). I have not proved that there is always a two-class solution. In particular, it is possible that under certain conditions (parameter values) the workers savings propensity is so high that they accumulate wealth faster than the capitalists. In this case, the only equilibrium which results is a one-class worker economy.

Third, I have not shown whether the steady-state equilibrium is stable or whether there is convergence to the steady state. This is difficult to prove since the parameters g and r are included in the workers' savings model. If the economy were not in steady-state equilibrium, it is not immediately clear which values of g and r the worker would include in his utility function:

Would the worker anticipate the (unknown) steady-state values of g and r? If not in steady state, would the workers change their consumption level each year depending on how g and r altered? Once reasonable assumptions are made with regard to these issues, it may then be possible to determine the movement of wealth inequality as the economy approaches (if it does) the steady state.

Finally, various factors were adduced which might help to explain the observed reduction in personal wealth inequality over the last 50 years or so. Of these, the increased life expectancy and reduction in work life and hence increase in the number of years of retirement seems the strongest force leading to increased wealth equality. Second, a slowdown in productivity growth and a decline in the profit (or real interest) rate may have led to greater wealth equality. Third, an increasing size of the capitalist class may have contributed to a decline in personal wealth inequality. Fourth, a decline in the rate of return to age or experience on wages may have led to reduced wealth inequality. Fifth, the increase of the social security tax rate from zero% in 1934 to 7% or so today has probably led to increasing wealth inequality.

Notes

1. In other variants of his model, relative wealth inequality remains constant in the steady state.
2. It should be noted that there is a logical contradiction between the assumption that the age of death is known and the assumption that the discount rate is constant over time, particularly as one approaches one's time of death. I maintain these two assumptions to simplify the algebraic derivations.
3. See Pasinetti (1962 and 1974) and Samuelson and Modigliani (1966) for a discussion of the Pasinetti model.
4. I have not shown that the steady-state equilibrium is stable with respect to the savings rate — that is, if the savings rate is perturbed from its steady-state level, will it necessarily return? Nor have I shown that the savings rate will necessarily approach its steady-state level and hence the economy will reach a steady-state equilibrium. Both issues are beyond the scope of the present paper.
5. It is perhaps helpful to contrast the result here of a constant degree of wealth inequality in the steady state with Stiglitz' basic model which predicts declining wealth inequality and eventual perfect equality in the steady state. My result comes from the use of the life cycle savings model, whereas Stiglitz' comes from the use of a linear savings hypothesis. Essentially, Stiglitz assumed that the level of savings is linearly related to income, and the wage is the same for everyone. Though part of income is from the return to capital, in the steady state it is the constant savings out of wages, which is equal across individuals, which dominates household wealth accumulation, eventually leading to perfect equality (see Stiglitz, (1969) 383, eqn. (2.5), and 386, eqn. (2.16)). In the model here, the dominant factor is the different levels of wealth as a function of age, which remains constant over time.

6. In particular, the life cycle savings model implicitly assumes that the economy is in the steady state. In some other models, it is possible to obtain solutions when the model is not in steady state. In Stiglitz' basic model, for example, wealth inequality is found to increase before steady-state equilibrium is reached.
7. Equations. (13), (14), (15), (16), (33), and (34) hold only when $g \neq r$ and $r \neq g + n$. For $g = r$, the following modified forms are used

$$nw_{a_t} = w_t \left[a + \frac{T'(e^{-ga} - 1)}{(1 - e^{-rT})} \right], a \leq T', g = r \tag{33'}$$

$$nw_{a_t} = T'w_t \left[1 + \frac{e^{-ga} - 1}{1 - e^{-rT}} \right], a > T', g = r \tag{34'}$$

This case might occur if n were zero and m equalled unity or n were negative. For $r = g + n$ (or $m = 1$), these forms would be used

$$nw_{a_t} = \frac{w_t}{-n} \left[(1 - e^{an}) + \frac{(1 - e^{-nT'})}{(e^{-rT} - 1)} \cdot (e^{-ga} - e^{na}) \right], a \leq T', r = g + n \tag{33''}$$

$$nw_{a_t} = \frac{w_t}{-n} \left[e^{n(a-T')} - e^{na} + \frac{(1 - e^{-nT'})}{(e^{-rT} - 1)} \cdot (e^{-ga} - e^{na}) \right], a > T', r = g + n \tag{34''}$$

8. When average and hence total net worth is negative, it is not possible to compute the Gini coefficient.
9. For simplicity, it is assumed that the full incidence of the social security tax falls on wages.
10. Basically, the US system uses undiscounted lifetime earnings in the formula to determine social security benefits.
11. If 'social security wealth' were included as part of household wealth, the resulting time trends in wealth inequality would be quite different.

References

Atkinson, A. B., 'The Distribution of Wealth and the Individual Life Cycle', *Oxford Economic Papers* **23** (1971), 239–54.

King, M. A., and L. Dicks-Mireaux, 'Asset Holdings and the Life Cycle', *Economic Journal* **92** (1982), 247–67.

Kotlikoff, L. J. and L. H. Summers, 'The Role of Intergenerational Transfers in Aggregate Capital Accumulation', *Journal of Political Economy* **89** (1981), 706–32.

Modigliani, F. and R. Brumberg, 'Utility Analysis and the Consumption Function: An Interpretation of Cross-Section Data', in K. K. Kurihara (ed.), *Post Keynesian Economics* (Rutgers University Press, New Brunswick, 1954).

Pasinetti, L., 'Rate of Profit and Income Distribution in Relation to the Rate of Economic Growth', *Review of Economic Studies* **29** (1962), 267–79 (Reprinted with additional commentary in Pasinetti (1974)).

—— *Growth and Income Distribution* (Cambridge University Press, London, 1974).

Samuelson P. A. and F. Modigliani, 'The Pasinetti Paradox in Neoclassical and More General Models', *Review of Economic Studies* **33** (1966), 269–301.

Shorrocks, A. F., 'UK Wealth Distribution: Current Evidence and Future Prospects', in E. N. Wolff (ed.), *International Comparisons of the Distribution of Household Wealth* (Oxford University Press, New York, 1987).

Smith, J. D., 'Recent Trends in the Distribution of Wealth: Data, Research Problems and Prospects', in E. N. Wolff (ed.), *International Comparisons of the Distribution of Household Wealth* (Oxford University Press, New York, 1987).

Söderström, L. 'The Life Cycle Hypothesis and Aggregate Household Saving', *American Economic Review* **72** (1982), 590–6.

Solow, R. M., 'A Contribution to the Theory of Economic Growth', *Quarterly Journal of Economics* **70** (1956), 65–94.

Spant, R., 'Wealth Distribution in Sweden, 1920–1983', In E. N. Wolff (ed.), *International Comparisons of the Distribution of Household Wealth* (Oxford University Press, New York, 1987).

Stiglitz, J. E., 'Distribution of Income and Wealth among Individuals', *Econometrica* **37** (1969), 382–97.

Summers, L. H., 'Capital Taxation and Accumulation in a Life Cycle Growth Model', *American Economic Review* **71** (1981), 533–44.

Vaughan, R. N., 'Class Behaviour and the Distribution of Wealth', *The Review of Economic Studies* **46** (1979), 447–65.

White, B. B., 'Empirical Tests of the Life Cycle Hypothesis, *American Economic Review* **68** (1978), 547–60.

Whiteman, T. C., 'Comparisons of the Distribution of Household Wealth from the 1979 ISDP and the 1962 SFCC', mimeo (1984).

Wolff, E. N., 'The Accumulation of Wealth over the Life Cycle: A Microdata Analysis', *Review of Income and Wealth* **27** (1981), 75–96.

—— (ed.), *International Comparisons of the Distribution of Household Wealth* (Oxford University Press, New York, 1987).

Comments on Chapter 10

R. ROBERT RUSSELL
University of California at Riverside

Wolff's paper addresses one of the most interesting questions about the twentieth-century evolution of Western industrialized countries: what is the explanation for the marked downward trend in wealth inequality — a trend that has become increasingly evident as multi-national data have become available? In the tradition of Stiglitz (1969), Wolff's approach to this issue exploits neoclassical growth theory, but he reaches a conclusion about wealth-inequality trends that contrasts sharply with that of Stiglitz (and with the evidence). Stiglitz's basic result is that there is a tendency for convergence to an egalitarian society (so long as the economy converges to a stable steady state), whereas in Wolff's model the steady-state solution is characterized by a constant and, given his parameter values, 'large' amount of wealth inequality. In this comment, I examine the reasons for this contrast, arguing that both conclusions are imbedded quite explicitly in their respective assumptions and that the logical distance from the assumptions to the conclusions is short.

Stiglitz modifies the neoclassical model to allow for differing initial wealth levels among classes, but retains the neoclassical assumptions of an identical wage rate, w, rate of return on capital, r, and marginal propensity to save, m, for each class. To see why the wealth distribution in this economy converges to equality among classes, suppose that the savings function is proportional and that there are two groups: the opulent and the indigent, with per capita wealth levels (capital stocks), k^O and k^I. The ratio of per capita savings of these two groups is

$$s^O/s^I = [m(w + rk^O)]/[m(w + rk^I)] < k^O/k^I,$$

where the inequality follows from the positiveness of mw and the assumption that $k^O/k^I > 1$. Thus,

$$s^O/k^O < s^I/k^I,$$

that is, the rate of accumulation is less for the opulent than for the indigent. Consequently, the wealth levels of the two groups converge to equality in the steady state, where, by the same argument, the rates of accumulation are also equal.

In the case of proportional savings, therefore, the Stiglitz result is a matter of simple arithmetic. To make the problem more interesting, Stiglitz makes the *average* saving rates of groups with different wealth levels unequal by

281

assuming that the (common) savings function has a possibly non-zero intercept, b. In this case, the savings ratio is

$$s^0/s^1 = [b + m(w + rk^0)]/[b + m(w + rk^1)]$$
$$= [b + mw + mrk^0]/[b + mw + mrk^1]$$

Thus,

$$s^0/s^1 < k^0/k^1$$

if and only if

$$b + mw > 0.$$

If $b \geq 0$, the same convergence result obtains. If $b < 0$, the economy converges to an egalitarian steady state so long as the wage rate (which, of course, depends on the capital–labour ratio) is high enough (in a neighborhood of equilibrium) to make savings positive with no capital income. If this condition is not met, the wealth levels diverge. The substantive contribution of Stiglitz's paper is to show that a steady-state equilibrium is stable if and only if $b + mw > 0$ in a neighborhood of the equilibrium.

It is easy to see why this result holds. The equilibrium condition ($\dot{k}/k = 0$) with an affine savings function is

$$b + m \, f(k) = nk.$$

This is illustrated, for the case $b < 0$, in Fig. A. There are two equilibria — one stable (k^{**}) and one unstable (k^*). At k', $b + mw = 0$; if $k < k'$, $b + mw < 0$, and if $k > k'$, $b + mw > 0$. Thus, in a neighborhood of the stable equilibrium, $b + mw > 0$. If the initial k, k^0, is less than k^*, $k \to 0$ and the wealth distribution diverges; if $k^0 = k^*$, k is stuck but the wealth distribution diverges; if $k^0 > k^*$, $k \to k^{**}$ and the wealth distribu-

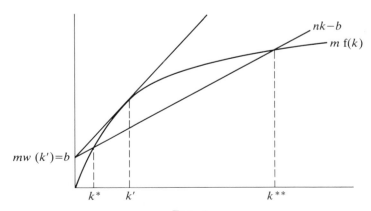

FIG. A

tion converges (though if $k^0 < k'$, it first diverges, then converges after k surpasses k'). Thus, the correspondence principle yields the result that, if the steady-state equilibrium is stable, the wealth levels converge to equality.

The starting point of Wolff's contribution contrasts sharply with that of Stiglitz. Although Stiglitz includes a paragraph on the addition of class savings behaviour to his basic model (p. 395) (with implications that concord with those of Wolff), his starting point is explicitly in stark contrast to the neoclassical growth literature of the day, which emphasized the functional distribution of income (among factors). Wolff's model, on the other hand, is better characterized as a descendant of Pasinetti (1962) and the derivative literature on economic growth and the distribution of income among factors.

The principal distinction between Wolff's model and those in the strict Pasinetti tradition is Wolff's assumption that workers follow the life cycle savings model. Nevertheless, Wolff's conclusions about the size distribution of wealth among individuals is fundamentally a conclusion about the functional distribution of wealth between capitalists and workers that is analogous to the income-distribution implications of Pasinetti-type models.

To see this, first note that the steady-state properties of Wolff's model are identical to those generated by a different institutional set-up: namely, one in which, in a life cycle sense, capitalists own *all* real wealth and workers borrow from (and lend to, or pay back) capitalists in order to smooth out the consumption streams over their lifetimes. This seems to me to be a case in which the understanding of wealth-distribution issues requires a life cycle perspective. In particular, in the steady state, the real wealth of each worker born at time t is the discounted value of his lifetime earnings:

$$W_t^w = \int_t^{t+T'} w_t \, e^{g(\tau-t)} \, e^{-r(\tau-t)} \, d\tau$$

$$= [w_t/(g-r)] \, [e^{(g-r)T'} - 1],$$

where, as in Wolff, T' is the retirement age and g is the steady-state rate of growth of the wage rate. Given Wolff's assumption of a Cobb–Douglas production function, this expression can be written as

$$W_t^w = [\gamma_t(1-\beta) \, k_t^\beta/(g-r)] \, [e^{(g-r)T'} - 1],$$

where γ_t is the technology index and β is the Cobb–Douglas coefficient on capital.

The wealth of capitalists at time t is simply equal to the capital stock or, given the efficient-markets hypothesis, the discounted value of returns to capital,

$$K_t = \int_t^\infty e^{-r(\tau-t)} \, rK_\tau \, d\tau.$$

Per capita wealth of capitalists at time t, therefore, is ρk_t, where ρ is the ratio of the worker population to the capitalist population, which Wolff assumes to be constant. Thus, the ratio of (per capita) capitalist wealth to worker wealth, in the steady state, is

$$W_t^C/W_t^w = \rho k_t/[\gamma_t(1 - \beta)\, k_t^\beta/(g - r)]\, [e^{(g-r)T} - 1]$$
$$= \rho k_t^{1-\beta}(g - r)/[\gamma_t(1 - \beta)]\, [e^{(g-r)T} - 1].$$

In the steady state, $\dot{k}_t/k_t = (\dot{\gamma}_t/\gamma_t)/(1 - \beta)$. Consequently, in the steady state, both the numerator and the denominator of this wealth ratio grow at the rate $\dot{\gamma}_t/\gamma_t$, and the functional distribution of wealth is constant. The aggregate distribution of wealth between capitalists and workers is given by setting $\rho = 1$ in the above equation, and the ratio of per capita wealth levels in the steady state can be set equal to any positive number by a suitable choice of the somewhat arbitrary population ratio, ρ.

Wolff's measure of the wealth of workers is a measure of the cumulative difference between the earnings and consumption paths of workers. As such, it simply reflects the intertemporal reallocation of wealth, determined by intertemporal preferences and the rate of interest, and changes in this measure would appear to have no important welfare implications. Moreover, in the steady state, in which the age distribution is stationary, this wealth concept would also grow at the rate g. Because of the assumption of a homothetic intertemporal utility function, both the consumption stream (equal to a constant under Wolff's assumptions) and the earnings stream grow at the rate g; hence, the cumulative difference between them grows at the same rate, as does the capital stock per capita. This is why the wealth distribution as measured by Wolff is constant in the steady state as well.

To summarize, Wolff essentially builds into his model an impenetrable barrier between capitalists — the holders of all wealth — and workers; in a real (life cycle) sense, there is no possibility of wealth accumulation by the working class. It is, therefore, no less surprising that there is *no* tendency toward the equalization of wealth holdings in Wolff's model than that there *is* such a tendency in the basic Stiglitz model. Wolff's paper focuses on the functional distribution of wealth in a highly structured society in which individuals are either workers (wage earners) or capitalists but never both, whereas Stiglitz studied the distribution of wealth in an economy in which everyone may be both a capitalist and a worker.

In order for Wolff's Pasinetti-type economy to converge to an egalitarian steady state, it would be necessary for the class wealth barrier to break down. One possible way of modeling this phenomenon would be to make savings behaviour endogenous so that, as workers become more affluent, they gradually shift their savings behaviour from the life cycle model to the more acquisitive posture of the capitalists. Of course, Wolff's model is already complicated, and incorporating this kind of savings behaviour might make the analysis insuperable.

Perhaps more to the point, in order to make substantial progress in explaining the important empirical phenomenon of decreasing wealth inequality, it will be necessary to take into account many other factors, including intergenerational redistribution and the effects of institutions that redistribute wealth, such as public pensions, inheritance taxes, and public education. Obtaining clean qualitative results in a model rich enough to accommodate these and other important influences on the distribution of wealth is likely to be virtually impossible. Consequently, simulation techniques — not unlike those being used to model phenomena like tax incidence and trade restrictions in a general-equilibrium context (e.g., Shoven and Whalley (1983) and Harris (1984)) — will probably be required in order to make significant progress in this important area.

References

Harris, R., 'Applied General Economic Analysis of Small Open Economies with Scale Economies and Imperfect Competition', *American Economic Review* **74** (1984), 1016–32.

Pasinetti, L., 'Rate of Profit and Income Distribution in Relation to the Rate of Economic Growth', *Review of Economic Studies* **29** (1962), 267–79.

Shoven, J. and J. Whalley, 'Applied General Economic Models of Taxation and International Trade', mimeo, (1983).

Stiglitz, J.E., 'Distribution of Income and Wealth among Individuals', *Econometrica* **37** (1969), 382–97.

11 Wealth Distributional Consequences of Life Cycle Models

DENIS KESSLER
University of Paris-X

ANDRÉ MASSON
Centre National de la Recherche Scientifique

It is now well established that wealth is very unequally distributed in industrialized countries. The share of the first centile of wealth holders amounts roughly to a quarter of total assets. Moreover wealth for any given age reveals a comparable degree of concentration (Kessler and Masson (1987)).

Atkinson's seminal paper (1971) explores the role played by age in the concentration of wealth. For that purpose, he considers isolated consumers disposing of an identical exogenous non-property income profile, living in a certain world with perfect capital markets, saving only in view of a retirement period of the same duration. In other words, they follow the basic life cycle model under the traditional environmental assumptions. In this so-defined egalitarian society, there is no intra-age wealth inequality, and the inter-age wealth dispersion remains limited.

A possible interpretation of these results is that the major source of actual wealth dispersion is to be found in income and in inheritance distributions. Before jumping to this conclusion, it seems necessary, in the line of Atkinson's approach, to explore the degree of wealth dispersion existing in other egalitarian societies where consumers receive identical amount of resources over the lifetime and still follow some variants of the life cycle model (Modigliani (1975)). However their life durations may differ or their income may be uncertain; capital markets may be imperfect or labour supply may be endogenous . . . In these societies, there are now among consumers other differences than age, leading to intra-age wealth dispersion.

The purpose of this contribution is to study the potential effects on wealth concentration of such specific environments and of such differences between isolated, utility-maximizing consumers having equal initial endowments and opportunities. They may however differ according to their tastes, their abilities (to process information, to value their human capital), or their luck on the various markets.

According to the specific set of assumptions defining each egalitarian society, consumers may hence follow different non-property income profiles. Moreover even if they follow the same income profile, they may adopt various consumption profiles. The dispersion in age–wealth profiles is

287

therefore the combined outcome of the distributions of non-property income stream and of consumption pattern over the life cycle.

More precisely individual age–wealth profiles (A_t) are generated by the non-investment income profiles (Y_t) and the consumption profiles (C_t) with the help of the instantaneous budget relation:

$$\dot{A}_t = rA_t + Y_t - C_t + i_t - b_t \tag{1}$$

where t stands for age, $\dot{A}_t$ is the age derivative of assets A_t, r is the prevailing rate of interest, and i_t (respectively b_t) is the contribution of bequest received (respectively bestowed). Moreover, in a no-bequest world, the following relations hold, where T is (maximum) life duration:

$$A_0 = A_T = 0 \tag{2}$$

Relation (1) implies specific definitions for the different variables. All variables are in real terms, C is consumption of goods and services of durables, r stands for the real rate of interest including both capital gains and income yields but net of taxes and capital depreciation. Moreover A represents net worth (assets including durables minus the discounted sum of future total repayments of debt). Equation (1) holds then even under imperfect capital markets provided that the borrowing rate equals the rate of return (Masson (1986)).

The organization of the paper is as follows; after a brief presentation of the basic life cycle model, section I considers egalitarian societies were all consumers follow the same exogenous and certain non-property income profile. Moreover they do not receive or make any bequest and they live in a stationary world with perfect capital markets. In section II, the effects on wealth dispersion of intracohort income mobility, income uncertainty and capital market imperfections are successively envisaged in societies where consumers are *ex ante* equal as far as they will receive the same expected level of discounted lifetime income. In section III, the effect on wealth inequality of economic growth and (contingent or voluntary) bequest is analysed in a straightforward manner: no attempt is made at modelling bequest behaviour or family relationship. In section IV, the effects on wealth dispersion of the endogeneity of non-property income are studied. This leads to a much broader (and perhaps more debatable) definition of *ex ante* equality between consumers receiving the same 'initial' level of human capital and facing identical opportunities on the relevant markets.

The paper concludes by discussing the difficulty of assessing a potentially high degree of wealth dispersion in egalitarian societies. It is indeed tricky to estimate, even by simulation models, the outcome of complex interactions between non-observable individual parameters (such as preferences) and specific environments (such as market constraints). Moreover the results depend crucially upon the specific assumption adopted for defining 'egalitarian societies': in our view, consumers are considered equal if they have *ex ante* the same level of earnings capacities. Others would prefer to define equality by the same level of utility over the lifetime. In any case, we hope that our analysis will help to design new empirical tests on actual data of the wealth distributional implications of life cycle models.

I Egalitarian societies with identical exogenous, certain age–income profiles and perfect markets

Let us consider a stationary, no-bequest, certain world with a perfect capital market. In this world, isolated consumers earning an exogenous non-property income will behave according to the basic 'elementary' form of the life cycle hypothesis. Equality among individuals is simply defined by identical age–non-property income profile. This concept of equality is only troublesome in the case of different life durations.

In this world, two types of egalitarian societies can be considered. In the first type, all individuals follow the same age–consumption profile, and therefore the same age–wealth profile. However this unique age–wealth profile depends upon institutional arrangements such as social security schemes. In the second type, there may be a noticeable degree of intra-age inequality due for instance to varying life durations or to different time preferences.

1.1 The consumer behaviour: the basic life cycle model

In a world with no bequest and perfect capital market, the budget constraint (1) and (2) can be rewritten in the continuous time case:

$$E_0 = \int_0^T Y_t \, e^{-rt} \, dt = \int_0^T C_t \, e^{-rt} \, dt \tag{3}$$

with E_0 standing for the lifetime discounted income stream (Y_t).

The life cycle hypothesis implies severe restrictions on the intertemporal utility function the consumer maximizes. The proportionality hypothesis implies that preferences are homothetic in consumption and that consumers do not derive present utility from the holding of wealth. The aggregation of all the consumption goods of a given period t into C_t and a forward-looking time-consistent behaviour furthermore imply that preferences are temporally weakly separable and strongly recursive. Homothetic and additive preferences satisfy these requirements. It can then be shown that the utility function U takes the form in continuous time:

$$U = \int_0^T \alpha_t u(C_t) \, dt \tag{4}$$

with an isoelastic instantaneous utility function u:

$$u(C) = C^{1-\gamma}/1 - \gamma \tag{5}$$

where γ is the inverse of the intertemporal elasticity of substitution and α_t reflects both 'impatience' and/or variations of exogenous tastes. Moreover time consistency implies that α_t depends only upon age t (not upon past consumption of wealth), as well as its logarithmic derivative, the rate of time preference (or of tastes variation), δ_t:

$$\delta_t = -\dot{\alpha}_t/\alpha_t = -\hat{\alpha}_t \tag{6}$$

The temporal additivity of the utility function U and the budget constraint (3) imply the well-known relation between marginal utilities:

$$u'(C_t)/u'(C_0) = e^{-(r-\delta_t)t} \tag{7}$$

which means that the consumption profile (C_t) is independent of the income profile (Y_t). Moreover with homothetic preferences, $\hat{C}_t$ equals:

$$\hat{C}_t = g_t = (r - \delta_t)/\gamma \tag{8}$$

for g_t the rate of variation of consumption. Finally, from (8) and (1), the level of initial consumption C_0 verifies:

$$C_0 = k(r, T, \delta_t, \gamma) E_0 \tag{9}$$

In the specific environment of certainty and perfect capital market, this elementary intertemporal model of consumption makes the level and shape of the consumption profile (C_t) depend on five exogenous parameters. Two of them are assumed to be common to all consumers: the rate of interest r and the income profile (Y_t). Three of them may vary among consumers: the life duration T, the time preference α_t and the parameter γ.

When the last three parameters are identical for all consumers, any set of the five parameters leads to a strictly egalitarian society with a unique wealth–age profile. Intra-age wealth inequality appears when T, α_t, or γ vary among consumers.

1.2 Egalitarian societies with equal individual consumption and identical age–income profile

Let us first consider societies where all consumers are identical in all respects apart from age as in Atkinson's (1971) article. They face the same market opportunities and they have the same tastes. They retire and die at the same age. They receive the same income stream which is constant until the age of retirement N and nil afterwards (there is no social security). Let us assume furthermore that the rate of growth of per capita earnings and of population is zero. In this stationary economy all individuals will follow the same consumption profile. This narrow conception of equality will then lead to a con-

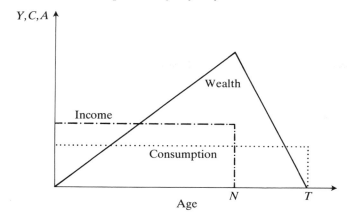

FIG. 11.1. Age–wealth profiles in Atkinson's society (1971).

stant consumption profile with all individuals consuming the same amount equal to E_0/T (this is the case with $\delta_t = \delta = r$, see (7)).

In this stationary society, all consumers follow the same age–wealth profile characterized by a wealth maximum upon retirement. This profile leads to an unequal wealth distribution whose degree is rather small compared to the observed distribution (Fig. 11.1). In one particular case considered by Atkinson (1971) of a zero interest rate, the 10% wealthiest individuals own about 19% of total assets.

For given preferences, the degree of basic wealth inequality depends only upon three factors: the rate of interest, the length of life, and the age of retirement. Therefore, phenomena such as a change in the retirement age, an increase of life duration, or a variation in the long term interest rate exert direct effects on the distribution of wealth.

But this egalitarian society seems . . . a little bit too egalitarian. Alternate egalitarian societies can be envisaged where all consumers are equal but some of them are more equal than the others. The first obvious step in this direction is to consider societies where all individuals follow the same non-investment age–income profile which does not need to be constant before retirement and nil afterwards as in the first society studied.

1.3 An egalitarian society with an income transfer scheme

Let us imagine that there exists an income transfer scheme from the young to the aged similar to the existing pay-as-you-go social security scheme. But for this scheme, all the other characteristics of this new society are identical to the previous ones. Each consumer pays a contribution out of his non-investment

Kessler and Masson

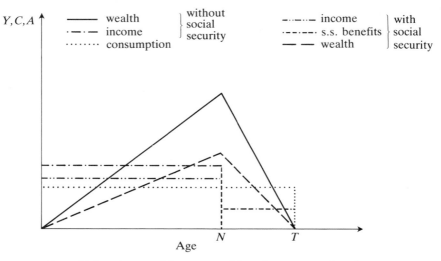

F IG. 11.2.   Age–wealth profiles with an income transfer scheme.

income transferred as benefits to the retirees. The degree of basic wealth inequality vary according to the level of the replacement rate (defined as the ratio: retirement benefits/previous earnings).

In the particular case where the replacement rate is equal to unity, everyone receives the same income at the same age — but the amount of wealth is nil over the whole life cycle. There is neither inter-age nor intra-age wealth inequality. In more realistic cases, there is, for each level of the replacement rate, a specific degree of basic wealth inequality (Fig. 11.2). Therefore, in a given society, there will be some degree of wealth dispersion among consumers having the same total amount of lifetime income, according to the degree of coverage by an income transfer scheme of each consumer.

1.4   Egalitarian societies with different deterministic life durations

Up to this point, all consumers were supposed to die at the same age. This is indeed a very strong hypothesis and one may consider that a dispersion of life spans seems natural in all human societies. Let's assume again that there is no social security scheme. Two definitions of equality among consumers may be envisaged. According to the first definition, all consumers receive when alive the same income Y_t at each age but have different initial non-property discounted incomes E_0. According to the second definition, each consumer has the same E_0, but not the same income Y_t at each age.

According to the first definition of equality, each consumer receives an identical income Y_t when alive. Since life durations differ, consumption profiles and wealth paths will also differ. This leads to an intra-age-wealth

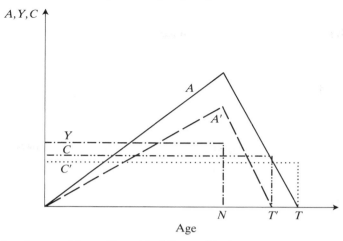

FIG. 11.3. Age–wealth profiles with different life duration. Income *Y*; consumption *C*, *C'*; wealth *A*, *A'*.

dispersion (Fig. 11.3). The introduction of a life duration distribution generates therefore a variety of age–wealth profiles in the egalitarian society considered where everyone receives the same non-investment income at the same age when alive.[1]

According to the second definition of equality, consumers follow the same consumption profile, but have different incomes Y_t at each age. This also generates intra-age wealth inequality.

The choice between the two concepts of equality — same lifetime non-investment income or same consumption at each age — is in fact arbitrary, and corresponds to a specific social welfare function. In the first case (same E_0), as in the second case (same C_t), there is a rather important degree of wealth dispersion.

1.5 Egalitarian societies with different time preferences

Individual consumption behaviour depends upon a temporal horizon, which depends on the life duration and the rate of time preference. Let us assume again that all consumers enjoy identical life duration and examine the specific effects of varying time preferences. In most life cycle models relative to wealth distribution, the rate of time preference δ_t is supposed constant throughout life and unique for all consumers. These two hypotheses restrict the variety of individual accumulation behaviour, even if one assumes positive time preference ($\delta_t > 0$). To assume different time preferences among consumers receiving an identical age–income stream induces different age–consumption profiles.

Recent debates on the consumption function have led to the distinction between myopic or liquidity constrained consumers and lifecyclers. It is obvious that these two different categories of consumers follow distinct consumption paths even if they receive the same income stream. But, even within the framework of the basic life cycle model, specific time preferences may lead to a variety of consumption paths.[2]

Myopic behaviour leads to intertemporally inconsistent choices. On the contrary, lifecyclers will always follow temporally consistent consumption plans whatever their time preferences. According to relation (7), the age–income profile being given, the consumption path followed by life cyclers will depend upon the difference $r - \delta_t$ varying with age (Fig. 11.4). The consumption profile may therefore be non-monotonic. Moreover, this influence is positively correlated with the value of the intertemporal elasticity of substitution $1/\gamma$.

To summarize, if we consider a society where consumers are earning the same non-property income at the same age, and even if those consumers are all lifecyclers, they may follow quite different wealth paths according to their time preferences.

II Egalitarian societies with uncertainties and capital market imperfections

Our quest to find sources of wealth inequality leads us to study more complex societies. As in Section I, we shall still consider isolated individuals in a stationary world without bequest but we shall abandon in turn the assumptions of identical and certain income profiles (Y_t) under perfect capital market. The effect of intracohort income mobility will first be examined in a society where consumers have equal certain lifetime non-property exogenous income. We shall then consider societies where non-property income is uncertain, before studying the effects of capital market imperfections.

The introduction of these new elements has two important consequences: (i) the definition of equality among consumers becomes less and less restrictive since consumers may now receive different lifetime incomes and (ii) the consumption profile (C_t) is in most cases no longer independent of the income profile (Y_t).

2.1 Egalitarian societies with intracohort mobility of income

Within the same environment as in Section I, let us assume that consumers are identical in all respects but for the timing of their non-investment income. In other words, they may have different exogenous and certain (Y_t) profiles but are equal so far as they have the same lifetime income E_0. It follows that they will all choose the same consumption profile (C_t).

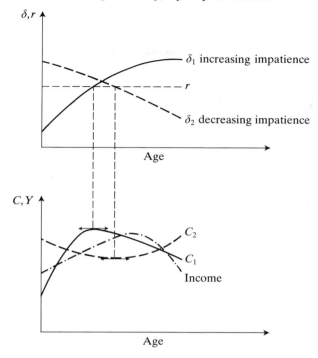

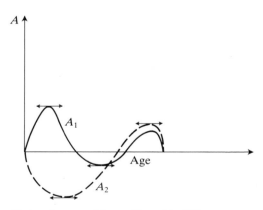

FIG. 11.4.   Age–wealth profiles with different time preferences.

Note then by E_t (respectively K_t) the discounted sum from age t onwards of income Y_t (respectively consumption C_t):

$$E_t = \int_t^T Y_s \, e^{(t-s)r} \, ds \tag{10}$$

$$K_t = \int_t^T C_s \, e^{(t-s)r} \, ds$$

Integration of equation (1) leads then to

$$A_t = K_t - E_t \tag{11}$$

with, by assumption, K_t identical for all consumers. This means that the absolute dispersion in A_t replicates the dispersion in E_t and that the coefficient of variation for wealth, $\mathrm{CV}(A_t)$, is given by:

$$\mathrm{CV}(A_t) = \mathrm{CV}(E_t) \cdot \widetilde{E}_t / \widetilde{A}_t \tag{12}$$

where $\widetilde{E}_t$ and $\widetilde{A}_t$ denote averages over all consumers aged t.

Variation in E_t depends both upon the degree of income inequality at each age and the degree of intracohort mobility.

Suppose for instance that all income profiles are monotonous, comprised between profiles of consumers 1 and 2 and intersect once at age t_0.[3] Then all wealth profiles are also comprised between those for consumers 1 and 2 (Fig. 11.5) and the variance of A_t is maximum around age t_0. If furthermore $T - t_0$ is large, $\mathrm{CV}(A_t)$ is likely to be highly superior to $\mathrm{CV}(E_t)$.

However, imposing the same lifetime income for all individuals and searching for the effects of various income profiles is not a very sensible way to introduce intracohort mobility in an egalitarian society. Indeed in a more realistic world with uncertain resources, this definition of equality — same lifetime income — will appear questionable since it is based on an *ex-post* approach. The effect of random income will now be analysed.

2.2   Egalitarian societies with uncertain income

In a no-bequest stationary world with perfect capital market, the only source of uncertainty may concern the future exogenous non-property income profile. Equal isolated consumers now face the same initial expected distribution of lifetime non-property income. In other words, individuals are *ex ante* equal but may *ex post* be unequal, receiving different lifetime income E_0, according to their luck on the labour market.

More precisely, the degree of dispersion in *ex-post* lifetime income E_0 depends upon the time dependence in the stochastic income process which

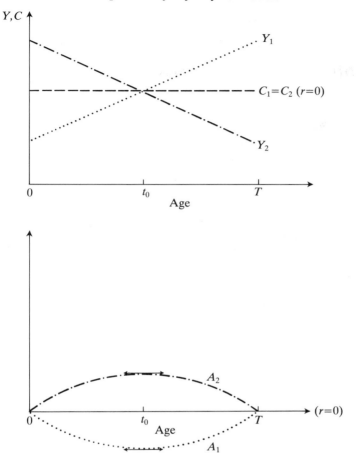

FIG. 11.5. Age–wealth profiles with intra-cohort mobility of income.

characterizes the egalitarian society. Available evidence (Lillard (1977), for instance) reveals a high degree of intra-cohort income mobility: in other words current income autocorrelation is largely inferior to one. However income mobility would be much higher if incomes of different periods were totally independent: the degree of income autocorrelation appears therefore significantly positive but inferior to one.

The higher the autocorrelation in current income Y_t (that is the lower the degree of intracohort mobility), the larger the variance in lifetime income E_0, everything being equal.

Besides generating inequality in actual lifetime income, uncertainty affects accumulation behaviour in two ways: (i) consumers decisions depend upon their level of information (relative notably to their lifetime income). At each period they revise their earlier plans as new information becomes available: this replanning effect depends upon the way they form their expectations; (ii) consumers adopt a specific beháviour towards risk when maximizing their expected utility. We shall examine in turn these two factors.

(i) the replanning effect

To study the replanning effect, it is easier to assume at first certainty equivalence and risk neutrality.[4] Let us consider also the life cycle model in discrete time. Consumers therefore form point expectations about their future income which is generated by the same stochastic process. Unexpected variations are therefore implicitly assumed to be of small size.

The replanning effect can be analysed in the framework of the so-called 'stochastic life cycle theory'. The (positive) temporal dependence in the income process implies that the consumer can learn about his future incomes from the current knowledge of past realizations. Assuming perfect memory, the new information originating from each period is embodied in the current income innovation or surprise, ϵ_t.

Following Deaton's (1983) convention (A_t is the value of assets at the end of period t), the no-bequest discrete version of equation (1) becomes:

$$A_t = (1 + r)A_{t-1} + Y_t - C_t \tag{13}$$

With perfect capital markets and certainty equivalence, total available resources at period t — that is W_t, the sum of human and non-human wealth — equal to:

$$W_t = A_{t-1}(1 + r) + E_t = A_{t-1}(1 + r) + Y_t + E_t' \tag{14}$$

where future income $E_t' = \sum_{t+1}^{T} Y_x(1 + r)^{t-x}$ is unknown at period t. The hypothesis of a temporally additive (or at least strongly recursive) utility function is then crucial to insure that, for given expectations and given preferences, the consumer's new lifecycle programme at age t depends upon past events only through the channel of total wealth W_t.

Homothetic and separable preferences lead to the usual relation of proportionality between consumption and total wealth:

$$C_t = k_t(T, r, \alpha_t, \ldots, \alpha_T) W_t \tag{15}$$

with k_t the marginal propensity to consume lifetime resources W_t at age t, independent of the value of W_t. Since the only random variables is non-property income, k_t is perfectly known and uncertainty is confined to W_t.

The replanning procedure can be described as follows: at period $t-1$, all variables up to $t-1$ are known; the consumer plans his next consumption C_t^{t-1} with expectations from period t onwards of incomes: $Y_t^{t-1} \ldots, Y_T^{t-1}$.

At the beginning of period t, income Y_t becomes known and the consumer reacts to the unexpected variation $Y_t - Y_t^{t-1}$ by choosing C_t which depends upon his new expectations from period $t+1$ onwards of incomes $Y_{t+1}^t, \ldots, Y_T^t$. If income was certain the age–consumption profile would satisfy for an additive isoelastic utility function a discrete time version of equation (8):

$$C_t = (1 + g_t) C_{t-1} \tag{16}$$

with $g_t = ((1 + r)/(1 + \delta_t))^{1/\gamma}$, the rate of growth of consumption.

Let $\Delta X_t = X_t - X_t^{t-1}$ stand for the variation of a variable X generated by the innovation embodied in current income Y_t. The surprise in current income $\epsilon_t = \Delta Y_t$ gives rise to a change of future income expectations $\eta_t' = \Delta E_t'$ and then to a change of total wealth $\Delta W_t = \eta_t = \eta_t' + \epsilon_t$.

Equation (15) shows that the consumer reacts to this variation in total wealth by a change in consumption $\Delta C_t = k_t \eta_t$. Further manipulations lead to the following age–consumption profile:

$$C_t = (1 + g_t) C_{t-1} + k_t \eta_t \tag{17}$$

Consumption fluctuates by $k_t \eta_t$ around its deterministic age profile. Wealth fluctuates around its deterministic profile with the deviation ΔA_t given according to equation (13), by:

$$\Delta A_t = \epsilon_t - k_t \eta_t \tag{18}$$

This replanning effect on the age–wealth profile A_t depends upon the relation between η_t and ϵ_t, that is on the effect of income innovation on expectations of future incomes. This relation depends on two factors: the degree of serial correlation in the stochastic income process and the level of information of the consumer on this income process.

If the stochastic income process is stationary (or at least homogenous) and if information is costless (and immediate) and processed efficiently, then all consumers have the same maximum level of information and adopt 'rational expectations' as in the stochastic life cycle theory.[5] The relation between η_t and ϵ_t is the same for all consumers and may be characterized by the elasticity of expectations linking future to current income. This elasticity is determined by the degree of time dependence in the income process: the higher the degree of income autocorrelation, the larger the response in consumption $k_t \eta_t$ and hence, by relation (18), the smaller the replanning effect on wealth ΔA_t.[6]

The same kind of results will still apply under other forms of expectations: in our egalitarian society there will be a close relation between the basic degree of current wealth inequality and the degree of autocorrelation in income. The higher the degree of autocorrelation in income, the higher the dispersion in actual lifetime income but the lower the degree of intracohort income mobility. This has two opposite effects on current wealth inequality:

it increases wealth dispersion through the higher lifetime income inequality but it decreases wealth inequality through the lower degree of intracohort income mobility. The resulting effect is therefore ambiguous.

(ii) the behaviour towards risk

To study the wealth distributional effects of different attitudes towards risk, let us again consider a society composed of consumers whose non-property age–income profiles are generated by an identical stochastic process. However they now form probability expectations about their income prospects. Consider then the simplest case where all consumers know perfectly the conditional transition probabilities, given their current income Y_t at age t. They benefit at each period from a complete information relative to all the possible future states of the world. *Ex ante* equal consumers will differ *ex post* by the specific state of the world experienced by each of them. They therefore follow an original income path which reflects for instance their luck.

The consumer's accumulation behaviour can be formalized by extending the previous analysis. A similar two-step replanning procedure, from C_{t-1} to C_t^{t-1} and from C_t^{t-1} to C_t takes place in this framework. Planned consumption C_t^{t-1} depends (i) upon the density of probabilities $\phi_t(./Y_{t-1})$ attributed to future income streams from t onwards conditional on the value of income at age $t - 1$ and (ii) on the degree of risk aversion.

In order to analyse consumers' attitudes towards risk, the analysis can be set in the traditional two-period framework with period t standing for the first one and period $(t + 1, T)$ for the second (note however that income Y_t of the first period is also uncertain). If the utility function is additive and isoelastic with instantaneous utility function given by (5), saving decisions are controlled by the value of the parameter γ interpreted here as the constant relative risk aversion.

A higher relative risk aversion increases the income effect in favour of precautionary saving relatively to the substitution effect for increased consumption in period t which is less uncertain.[7] With perfect knowledge of the time dependence in the non-property income process, replanning from C_t^{t-1} to C_t is likely to take place since the consumer acquires through Y_t new information on the state of nature that will finally determine his income stream.

The change in the distribution of probabilities from $\phi_t(./Y_{t-1})$ to $\phi_{t+1}(./Y_t)$ is the equivalent in this general framework to the change η_t in lifetime resources point expectations. A replanning procedure takes place as in the point expectations case and similar conclusions can be drawn on the importance on wealth dispersion of the degree of serial correlation in the non-property income process.[8,9]

2.3 Egalitarian societies with capital market imperfections

In all egalitarian societies considered until now, capital market is assumed to be perfect. On such a market, consumers save and borrow freely at the same rate r; there are no transaction costs and wealth is perfectly divisible.

As a matter of fact, capital market imperfections are likely to play a central role in assets accumulation. Their distributional consequences will be studied in the simple framework of a no-bequest stationary world where life durations are perfectly known and non-property incomes are exogenous. We will assume certainty equivalence and risk neutrality and that expectations are fulfilled.

The sources of capital market imperfections are numerous: heterogeneity of assets relative to their liquidity, divisibility and durability, institutions, taxation, information, uncertainty, etc. Capital market imperfections can be grouped into two categories: (i) constraints limiting the freedom of consumers' choices (liquidity or borrowing constraints, transaction costs, indivisibility, availability of second hand markets, . . .); (ii) capital markets non homogeneities (non linearities of tax schedules, threshold effects on investment, . . .) We will consider successively a borrowing constraint according to which wealth cannot be negative ($A_t \geqslant 0$, $\forall\ t$) and then a specific non homogeneity, namely a correlation between the rate of return and the amount of assets.

How to define equality among consumers in such an imperfect environment? To the previous characteristics, it is possible to add equality of opportunity on the capital market, in the sense that all consumers have equal access to relevant informations on the prices, returns, and other characteristics of assets. It is worth underlining that consumers with different preferences or age-income profiles will not be equally concerned by capital market imperfections. These interactions between preferences, income profiles and capital market imperfections will generate additional variance to the age–consumption profiles.

Let us first examine the effect of a non-negative wealth borrowing constraint in a society with exogenous non-property income. Such borrowing constraints result from lending restrictions from the supply side and concern youths (due to asymmetric information and uncertainty about future resources) or aged consumers (due to an imperfect annuities market). The tastes of some consumers may be such that they will be able actually to achieve their desired consumption path (C_t^*) since its realization does not require any borrowing entailing a zero net wealth. But the constraint will be binding at various degrees for other consumer. More precisely, over a blocked interval, where the constraint is binding, wealth is nil and consumption equals at each age non-property income. Over a free interval, where the constraint is not binding, the consumer can freely allocate his resources.

The segmentation of the population into constrained and unconstrained consumers (or, in Blinder's (1976) terms, into 'reactors' and 'planners'), will depend upon preferences shaping the consumption profile but mostly upon the timing of the non-investment income profile. To take an example, a consumer whose income profile is steadily rising and with a strong time preference is likely to be rationed in the first phase of his lifecourse.

It should be noted that if non-property income is partly endogenous, borrowing constraints exert less effects since consumers can avoid credit rationing by adjusting accordingly their labour supply over the life cycle.

The effect of wealth non-negativity may be estimated for each consumer from the discrepancy between the desired consumption path (C_t^*) and the actual consumption path (C_t). The consequences on wealth distribution of these constraints can be inferred from the difference between the desired (A_t^*) and the actual (A_t) wealth profiles.

Let us consider now another capital market imperfection, namely the dependence between the rate of return r and the level of wealth A in an egalitarian society where non-property income is exogenous. Theoretical preconceptions and empirical evidence conclude to a positive correlation between the two variables, at least when wealth is positive. (see e.g. Shorrocks (1982)).

A generalization of equation (8) for a continuous rate of growth g_t of consumption takes the following form (see Appelbaum and Harris (1978)):

$$g_t = \hat{C}_t = (A_t \partial r / \partial A + r - \delta_t)/\gamma \tag{19}$$

The derivative $\partial r / \partial A$ is presumably of the sign of wealth A (it is probably negative for negative wealth owing to the increasing lack of collateral). It is clear that the age–consumption profile depends now upon the wealth profile and therefore upon the non-investment income profile (Y_t). Moreover the age–consumption profile may be non-monotonic even in the case of a constant rate of time preference. The introduction of increasing returns to wealth may indeed change consumption behaviour: consumers who would have otherwise owned negative wealth over parts of their life cycle will follow steeper consumption profiles in order to benefit from the interesting returns to high positive wealth.

The effects of this imperfection and of the corresponding consumers reactions can once again be estimated by comparing the actual consumption (C_t) or wealth (A_t) profiles with the corresponding desired profiles (C_t^*) and (A_t^*) derived under perfect capital markets (with the average rate of return). However some consumers will benefit from this imperfection, their utility gain being measured by the differences in utilities derived from the actual (C_t) and the reference (C_t^*) consumption profiles.

This distribution of positive and negative gaps between the desired and actual accumulation profiles is yet another potential source of basic wealth inequality in an egalitarian society.

2.4 Multiple sources of age–wealth dispersion

In a stationary world composed of isolated consumers, neither receiving nor leaving bequests, whose lifetimes are certain and non-property income exogenous, wealth dispersion in various egalitarian societies has been examined. Even within this limited framework, not all possible egalitarian societies have been explored. For instance, analysis of uncertainty has been restricted to the case of random non-property income without furthermore considering the differential abilities to search and process information. We have not, in a systematic way, studied combinations of the various sources of uncertainty and capital market imperfections. To give only one example, the results of our analysis of societies with uncertain and exogenous incomes would be altered by the introduction of capital market imperfections, such as the impossibility of holding negative amounts of wealth. The limited analytical tractability of elaborate life cycle models prevents us to examine most of these more realistic cases.

According to our definition, consumers are considered equal when they have the same initial expected distribution of lifetime income, identical access to information and face the same opportunities on the capital market. Inequality in *ex-post* lifetime income in the egalitarian societies we surveyed depends upon the random structure of the stochastic income process and the distribution of life spans.

In order to identify the different factors of wealth inequality, it is preferable to split wealth into two components: A_t^* is the amount of assets owned in case of certainty with perfect capital markets; $A_t - A_t^*$ represents the effect on wealth of market imperfections and uncertainty.

Variance in wealth A_t^* depends mostly on three types of individual parameters: (i) endowments; (ii) preferences; (iii) timing of non-property income. Variance in $A_t - A_t^*$ is attributable to four types of individual factors; (iv) luck; (v) ability to process information; (vi) attitude towards risk; (vii) differential effects of capital market imperfections. If A_t^* is largely under control of the consumer, the difference $A_t - A_t^*$ is largely out of control of most consumers.

The degree of basic wealth inequality is therefore a complex function of the size distribution of various individual factors, the correlations between these distributions and the interactions between behaviours and capital market imperfections. It seems impossible to give a reliable estimate of this basic inequality for two reasons. First, most individual parameters are not observable and their size distribution, and even their mean value, in the population are largely unknown or debatable. Second, most interactions between these factors are likely to be highly non-linear and may generate sizeable discontinuities in the age–wealth profiles.

III Egalitarian societies with economic growth or bequest

We have considered, up to now, stationary societies where lifetimes are certain and where there are no bequests. In this section, these assumptions are relaxed. The introduction of economic growth raises the question of inter-generational equity and leads to the analysis of cohort effects. Uncertain life-times will induce contingent bequests in the case of imperfect annuities market. Finally, the presence of a bequest motive will engender additional variance in wealth accumulation patterns, due notably to the timing of inter-generational transfers.

In tackling some simple effects of these new elements, we keep most of the basic assumptions made until now relative to stationary populations com-posed of isolated consumers.

3.1 Egalitarian societies with economic growth

Life cycle behaviour is compatible with a steady balanced growth, as it has long been acknowledged at least under certainty and perfect capital market. However, even in a no-bequest world with certain lifetime, economic growth is likely to alter the previous conclusions concerning the equality among con-sumers, the average age–wealth profile and the degree of intra-age wealth inequality.

Let n be the constant rate of economic growth (or technical progress) and consider first a society where certainty reigns, where capital markets are per-fect, and where the distributions of individual preferences, endowments (such as life duration), and income profiles are identical from one cohort to another. The population being stationary, the successive cohorts have also the same size.

How to define equality between consumers belonging to different cohorts facing different environments? Equality may be defined by the same amount of discounted lifetime income deflated for growth. In other words, two con-sumers with an age difference of m will be considered equal if the ratio between their discounted lifetime income equals $(1 + n)^m$.

Previous assumptions assure that for each consumer of a cohort born in z, there is a corresponding consumer of the cohort born in $z + m$ with the same preferences, endowments, and homothetic age–income profile. Utility func-tions being homothetic, consumption and wealth profiles of the two con-sumers will also be homothetic with the same ratio of proportionality $(1 + n)^m$.

It follows that steady balanced economic growth exerts no influence on intra-age wealth inequality whenever capital market is perfect under cer-tainty. However inter-age wealth inequality will generally increase when the rate of growth n is positive, although the effect is fairly small (see Atkinson (1971)).

In case of capital market imperfections and uncertainty (with appropriate definition of equality), the effects of a steady growth on wealth accumulation patterns and inequality are less easy to deal with whenever the age–wealth profiles of consumers belonging to different cohorts are not homothetic. To give an example, a positive correlation between the rate of return and the amount of assets is bound to lead to non homothetic profiles and will further modify inter-age wealth inequality.

A non-steady growth leads to cohort effects. Successive cohorts follow specific age–income and age–wealth profiles according to the specific rates of growth they encounter. The outcome on the basic degree of wealth inequality is rather difficult to predict. This is even more the case when environment changes (degree of uncertainty, capital market imperfections, interest rates, . . .) or when cohort effects result from changes between cohorts in preferences or in endowments (such as a steady rise in life expectancy). (On cohort effects, see Kessler and Masson (1985)).

3.2 Egalitarian societies with random lifetimes

Lifetime uncertainty is likely to have an important effect on wealth accumulation patterns since it concerns the length of the consumers behavioural horizon. We shall consider only the more realistic case where no annuities market is available: the consumers have therefore limited means to cope with uncertainty of survival.

Let us first consider an egalitarian society composed of isolated consumers receiving the same certain exogenous non-property income at each age and having the same preferences. Their lifetime is uncertain but they have identical probabilities of survival s_t to age t, correctly anticipated and identical constant relative risk aversion. The capital market is perfect with a rate of interest r except that negative net wealth is forbidden.

The consumer maximizes at the beginning of his life his expected utility function, with T now representing maximum lifetime (see Davies (1981)):

$$U = \int_0^T \alpha_t s_t u(C_t) \, \mathrm{d}t \tag{20}$$

under the constraints (1) and (2) and: $A_t \geqslant 0$, $\forall\ t$. Instantaneous utility is given by (5). On free intervals where the borrowing constraint is not binding, relation (7) is verified with the rate of time preference δ_t increased by $p_t = -\hat{s}_t$, the instantaneous probability of death. With p_t being small relatively to r at younger ages, the optimal consumption profile has a concave shape. It can also be shown that the optimal consumption plan is time consistent: there is therefore no need for replanning.

The age–wealth pattern depends on the value of the relative risk aversion. If it is high, rates of decumulation at older ages are low and the consumer still hold appreciable amounts of wealth later in life which lead to contingent bequests. Since these bequests do not result from any bequest motive, it can be assumed, with no incidence on behaviours, that they are transferred to the State (so that each consumer receives no bequest).

In the egalitarian society just defined, all consumers follow the same age–wealth profile that is truncated at different ages. Hence lifetime uncertainty, for identical life expectancies, decreases the share of top wealth holders (compared to the situation where all consumers have identical maximum lifetime) but does not generate intra-age wealth inequality.

In a more realistic stationary egalitarian society, uncertainty of survival, combined with differences in life expectancy and in risk aversion, is likely to give birth to a sizeable distribution of wealth upon death.

3.3 Egalitarian societies with bequest

We have supposed up to now that there were no bequest either received or left. The accumulation of wealth was therefore a zero-sum game over the life cycle, at least under certain lifetime. We have little to say about egalitarian societies allowing for bequest. Their analysis would require a complete model of intergenerational transfers and relations within the family between at least three generations. We only show that the introduction in a simple way of intergenerational transfers may generate further dispersion in the age–wealth profiles and exert an effect on wealth inequality which appears difficult to measure. For this limited purpose, the previous framework of a stationary world with certain lifetime is perfectly appropriate.

Moreover, it appears quite reasonable in a stationary economy to assume that the rate of return to assets is nil. This restriction has the main advantage of avoiding dealing with the returns to inheritance and gifts received. The status of this specific capital income in 'extended' life cycle models lies indeed at the heart of the debate between F. Modigliani and L. J. Kotlikoff and L. H. Summers (see Chapters 1 and 2 in this volume).

Let us first consider an egalitarian society with bequest where consumers receive the same lump sum amount of inheritance, I, that they have to pass intact to their child at their death. No gifts *inter vivos* are allowed and bequest behaviour is constrained to zero intergenerational accumulation (no difference between bequest left and received) as may be expected in a stationary economy.

These conditions for equality between consumers are in the spirit of Atkinson's contribution (1971). To each of our previously defined societies, there is now a corresponding egalitarian society with bequest.

In the simplest case of perfect capital market, certain and exogenous nonproperty income and with separability of preferences for consumption and bequest, the age–consumption profile is independent of the age–income profile. Moreover, a zero rate of return to assets implies that the consumption profile is identical whether or not there are bequests since the total amount of lifetime resources earmarked for consumption is invariant. Age–wealth profiles are only modified by the presence of inherited wealth from age of reception R until death T.

Change in basic wealth inequality depends then on the relative importance of inheritance and also on the dispersion in ages R which in turn depends on the combined distribution of life duration T and intergenerational age difference $T - R$. Hence, even in this simple case, the distributional consequences of equal inheritance on the degree of wealth inequality are far from being straightforward.

In more realistic cases, intergenerational transfers are likely to influence the consumption profile, generating additional variance in the age–wealth profiles. To take an example, it is clear that consumers who receive their inheritance early in life will be favoured in the presence of capital market imperfections forbidding borrowing with inheritance expectations as collateral.

Let us now envisage an economy where more elaborate bequest behaviours are allowed. Egalitarian societies are composed of consumers who receive the same discounted lifetime income E_0 and the same amount of lifetime receptions, I, but are free to bequeath in two ways. First gifts *inter vivos* are allowed so that the timing of intergenerational transfers is not fixed *a priori* by life duration.[10] Second the total amount of bequest, B, varies according to personal taste. As we allow for some dispersion in the amounts of bequest, we will consider only wealth inequality among the first generations having received equal amounts of bequest.

If we go back to the more tractable simple world first evoked, the consumption–age profile depends only on the amount of lifetime resources devoted to consumption, that is, $E_0 + I - B$, with $B - I$ representing intergenerational accumulation or decumulation. The consumption profile is C_t with the budget constraint:

$$E_0 = \int_0^T C_t \, dt + B - I \tag{21}$$

$$\text{with } B = \int_0^T b_t \, dt \text{ and } I = \int_0^T i_t \, dt$$

with i_t and b_t the instantaneous flows of intergenerational in and outgoing transmissions.

If there were no intergenerational accumulation, he would have chosen a consumption profile C'_t, satisfying:

$$E_0 = \int_0^T C'_t \, dt. \tag{22}$$

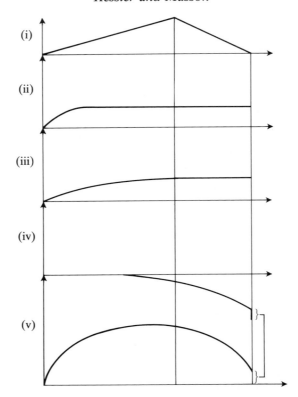

FIG. 11.6.   Age–wealth profiles with bequests: (i) pure lifecycle–wealth profile, (ii) cumulated wealth reception profile, (iii) cumulated intergenerational wealth accumulation profile, (iv) cumulated wealth transmission profile, (v) age–wealth profile.

The difference $d_t = C'_t - C_t$ can be interpreted as the amount that the consumer earmarks at age t for intergenerational wealth accumulation. The difference $f_t = Y_t - C'_t$ is saving for life cycle deferred consumption.

Wealth variation is then given by a reformulation of relation (1):

$$\dot{A}_t = i_t - b_t + f_t + d_t \tag{23}$$

The age–wealth profile (A_t) results therefore from the sum of four profiles (see Fig. 11.6):

(i) the pure life cycle wealth profile,

$$F_t = \int_0^t f_x \, dx$$

with $F(0) = F(T) = 0$;
 (ii) the cumulated wealth reception profile, with flow i_t at age t and terminal value I;
 (iii) the cumulated intergenerational wealth accumulation profile, with flow d_t at age t and terminal value $(B - I)$;
 (iv) the negative of the cumulated wealth transmission profile, with flow $-b_t$ at age t and terminal value $-B$.

Since the four profiles can take various forms according to an important set of parameters, the resulting age–wealth profile may indeed present a large variety of patterns from one consumer to another. Therefore the degree of basic wealth inequality in such egalitarian societies appears unpredictable.

IV Egalitarian societies with endogenous income

In a no-bequest stationary world with perfect capital market, consumers may exert a certain control over the level and timing of their non-property income, which, unless otherwise stated, is assumed to be certain. In all the egalitarian societies studied until now, equality dealt finally only with one variable: consumption power, whether for one's own or one's heir's satisfaction. In the society examined in this section, equality is more broadly defined since the consumer can derive utility not only from consumption but also from leisure. This entails notably two consequences: first, in these societies, lifetime income may display a substantial variance among equal consumers, owing to their specific decisions and, second, wealth looses part of its role, since time can be a substitute to wealth for deriving utility (in the form of leisure).

With no further restrictions on preferences, under perfect capital market and certainty, life cycle models with endogenous income may indeed lead to a great variety of behaviours. For instance, a very high preference for leisure implies very low levels of income, consumption, and wealth. A high rate of impatience generates atypical life cycles beginning with 'retirement', followed by schooling, and ending with work until death (see Blinder and Weiss (1976)).

Let us start by examining briefly the effects of introducing in a simple way the labour–leisure choice before studying the consequences of human capital investment.

4.1 Egalitarian societies with endogenous labour supply

The utility function of the consumers in a society with endogenous labour supply takes a specific form. With additive preferences and instantaneous utility u depending now upon current consumption C_t but also upon leisure time ℓ_t, the consumer maximizes the following taken in continuous time:

$$U = \int_0^T \alpha_t u(C_t, \ell_t) \, dt \tag{24}$$

The budget constraints (1) and (2) still hold. If the maximum amount of time available at t is normalized to unity, non-investment income Y_t is equal to:

$$Y_t = (1 - \ell_t) w_t \tag{25}$$

with w_t the current wage rate assumed to be exogenous.

In addition to the budget and time constraints, the consumer may also be rationed in his labour supply (owing to involuntary unemployment or institutional rules for retirement age or the availability of part time jobs . . .).

In this context, the definition of *ex-ante* equality implies the same amount of potential initial lifetime income V_0, given by:

$$V_0 = \int_0^T w_t e^{-rt} \, dt \tag{26}$$

plus identical opportunities on the labour market.

In such an egalitarian society, inequality in *ex-post* lifetime income E_0 can be attributed to two factors: (i) the variance in life durations, in time preferences and in relative preferences for leisure, leads to a variety of labour–leisure choices and induces a dispersion in unconstrained current income

$$Y_t^* = (1 - \ell_t^*) w_t$$

and in the corresponding lifetime income

$$E_0^* = \int_0^T Y_t^* e^{-rt} \, dt$$

and (ii) the differential effect of labour supply constraints, measured by the difference between the observed demand for leisure ℓ_t with its unrationed counterpart, ℓ_t^*, leads to additional variance through $Y_t^* - Y_t$ and $E_0 - E_0^*$.

The analysis of consumption behaviours must consider two cases according to the form of the instantaneous utility function u. In the first one, leisure is separable from consumption. With the utility form (24) this corresponds to a subutility u additive in leisure and consumption, implying a zero cross-derivative u_{12}:

$$u_{12} = \partial^2 u(C, \ell)/\partial C \partial \ell = 0 \tag{27}$$

The consumption profile remains independent of labour supply decisions and timing of income Y_t as in the case of exogenous and certain income.

However the dispersion in lifetime E_0 will generate additional variance in consumption profiles.

This conclusion does not hold when leisure is not separable from consumption ($u_{12} \neq 0$): the consumption profile will now depend both upon the age–income profile and on the binding constraints which modify the consumption profile from C_t^* to C_t.

In the limit case of purely endogenous income ($\ell_s^* = \ell_s$ for all s) and with a temporally additive utility function (implying that the consumption C_t depends only on labour supply decisions through ℓ_t), the consumption age pattern depends primarily on the sign of u_{12} (see Heckman (1974)). If leisure and consumption are substitutes ($u_{12} < 0$), the consumption stream tends to have a pattern similar to the pattern of the labour supply and hence to the pattern of income. If they are complementary, the consumption profile presents an inverse pattern to labour supply and to income and consequently the resulting age–wealth profile will be steeper than in the substitution case.

Different functions u_{12} can therefore generate additional variance in the wealth profile as Fig. 11.7 illustrates under zero rate of return for consumers with identical endogenous income Y_t, and no time preference.[11]

Note that the introduction of uncertainty, even confined to the wage rate, may noticeably alter the previous analysis. With random wage rates, equality should notably imply identity of expected potential lifetime income, say V_0^*. Moreover inequality in realized lifetime income E_0 would depend on variance in luck ($V_0^* - V_0$), labour–leisure decisions (ℓ_t^*) and constraints ($\ell_t - \ell_t^*$). Finally, consumption behaviour would be more elaborate with complex consequences on wealth dispersion: for instance a consumer with a strong risk aversion and little time preference may be tempted to increase his labour supply early in life, even if the wage rate is not very favourable, in order to accumulate precautionary savings.

4.2 Egalitarian societies with endogenous human capital investment

Suppose now that the wage rate is endogenous and a function of human capital investment and depreciation. Each consumer maximizes a utility of the form (24) but where instantaneous utility u (C_t, ℓ_t, H_t) may also depend upon the human capital stock, whether H_t influences tastes for leisure and consumption or is itself a source of utility (see Heckman (1976)).

There are now two control stock variables: assets A_t, satisfying the budget constraints (1) and (2) and human capital stock H_t, will initial value H_0 and variation:

$$\dot{H}_t = J_t - \sigma H_t \tag{28}$$

σ representing the depreciation rate of human capital. Moreover J_t, the amount of human capital investment is produced from various inputs: time h, market goods q and human capital stock H:

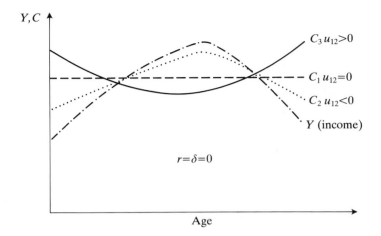

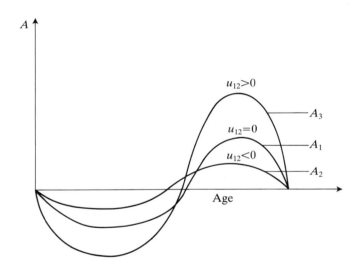

FIG. 11.7.   Age–wealth profiles with endogenous income.

$$J = F(H, h, q). \tag{29}$$

In addition, the time constraint, for a maximum amount of time available at t set to unity, entails a current income equal to:

$$Y_t = (1 - \ell_t - h_t)\, w_t \tag{30}$$

with w_t usually a linear function of human capital:

$$w_t = a\, H_t. \tag{31}$$

Finally, further restrictions on behaviour can be generated by labour supply constraints.

This type of behaviour introduces additional differences among consumers concerning (i) the depreciation rate of human capital, σ; (ii) the capacity and opportunity to value their human capital into wages, which are both represented by the parameter a; (iii), the ability to benefit from human capital investment and the opportunity to invest in this type of capital which are additional parameters of the production function F.

In this framework, *ex-ante* equality among consumers requires first the same initial amount of human capital H_0, but also equality of opportunity on all the different markets. Such a definition of equality is however open to criticism. First it allows for large differences among individuals in their abilities to value their human capital (a) or to benefit from human capital investment (F). This is questionable since intergenerational distributional models have shown that these different abilities depend for a significant part upon family background and discrimination (see Atkinson (1983)). Second the requirement of identical initial stock of human capital H_0 raises the question of the choice of this initial age. After all, in the case where initial age corresponds to birth, all individuals may be considered equal. But one can alternatively consider that initial human capital H_0 is to be estimated at the start of economic life, a convention more in line with the life cycle hypothesis. In such an egalitarian society, there will be a dispersion in current income, in *ex-post* lifetime income, in current wealth, and in age–wealth profiles.

Dispersion in *ex-post* lifetime income E_0 will depend upon a complex set of interacting factors: endowments, abilities, preferences, and constraints on the various markets (educational, labour, . . .).[12] Dispersion in age–wealth profiles in an egalitarian society with endogenous incomes is now the outcome of multiple combinations of two distributions of profiles, namely the income and the consumption profiles,[13] those two profiles resulting from the free choice of equal consumers. In these societies, assets have less importance than in societies with exogenous incomes, but moreover, the distribution of assets is likely to be less equal and more difficult to interpret.

Conclusion

In a speculative way, we tried to evaluate the degree of basic wealth dispersion existing in hypothetical egalitarian societies where isolated consumers, having *ex-ante* equal resources, follow some variant of the life cycle model.

In a stationary world with no bequest and exogenous non-property income, age–wealth profiles result from the complex interactions of a variety of parameters which represent personal characteristics (life expectancy and other endowments, preferences, luck, and income profiles) and properties of the environment (uncertainties and capital market imperfections). In addition, most personal characteristics appear unobservable and for that reason difficult to estimate. Finally, the analytical tractability of models with more realistic environments is quite limited.

Allowing for growth, bequest, or income endogeneity further multiplies the number of parameters and interactions governing the distribution of wealth accumulation profiles and makes even more difficult the analysis of the wealth distribution implications of life cycle models.

These rather negative results have five consequences. First a given accumulation profile can indeed nest a lot of various behaviours and situations, and is therefore difficult to interpret in a life cycle framework. Hence a rich set of longitudinal wealth data is not sufficient to improve our knowledge of accumulation behaviour: other informations relating notably to the consumers' professional and family biography are also necessary.

Second, the degree of wealth dispersion in the more elaborate egalitarian societies does not appear easy to assess. For given distributions of the key parameters and with a simple modelling of capital market imperfections and income expectations, simulation procedures may give some information on the importance of distributional effects. However, owing to data limitations, this approach is only possible in the restricted case of no bequest and exogenous non-property income: data on age–earnings profiles are now available from various empirical studies since Lillard (1977) pioneering work. Also, the results largely depend upon the generally unknown correlations between the various distributions of personal parameters and earnings profiles.

Third, measures of the relative contributions of various factors to wealth inequality are of limited meaning owing to the strength of their interactions. For a given level of resources, the effect of other factors leads to a degree of wealth inequality which depends largely upon the distribution of personal parameters and the characteristics of the environment. This effect is also likely to vary with the level of resources owing to non homogeneities. In a similar way, the role of income and inheritance distributions on wealth inequality may vary largely according to the values given to other parameters and factors. Indeed, the sense of this effect itself cannot always be assessed. The relation between income inequality and wealth inequality operates through a long chain of interacting factors (intracohort income mobility, expectations, attitudes towards risk and replanning, exposure to constraints, . . .) and may lead for these reasons to perverse effects, a decrease in income inequality generating a rise in wealth inequality.

Fourth, given the relative failure of analytical or simulation methods, an estimate of the degree of wealth inequality due to other factors than inequality of resources should be based upon an empirical investigation that would also allow a test of the wealth distributional implications of life cycle models. This test would rely on the relative degree of wealth dispersion for given age and given lifetime resources. Related procedures have already been used by Diamond and Hausman (1984), Hubbard (1984) and King and Dicks-Mireaux (1982).

The weak explanatory power of age on wealth inequality cannot be claimed as clear evidence against the life cycle hypothesis. On the other hand, a weak explanatory power of age and lifetime resources combined would be more troublesome for the theory. It means either that the theory is inappropriate or that the principal factors of wealth inequality are exogenously given in its models.[14]

Fifth given the existence of a lifetime income (or consumption) tax, a wealth tax may have little justification in a life cycle framework, at least as far as well-being inequality is concerned. If the explanatory power on wealth inequality of age and lifetime resources combined is high, it may be preferable to reduce wealth dispersion through a tax on lifetime income. Also, a wealth tax can only be based upon the unknown part of assets, $A - A^*$, which is partly out of control of the consumer, not on the endogenous part A^*.

Notes

1. An empirical estimate of this effect can be inferred from the degree of dispersion of life durations at the normal age of retirement, that is at age sixty in France: the Gini coefficient amounts to 0.26 (using French mortality tables 1979–80).
2. Landsberger (1970) explored some consequences of a variable δ_t according to age and proved that certain patterns of time preference may actually induce a decrease of the marginal propensity to consume with age in the life cycle framework. This happens when the positive effect of the diminishing length of remaining lifetime is overcompensated by the negative effect of a strong decrease in time discounting.
3. This is a stylization of the 'overtaking' age at which observed earnings are equal to average annual equivalent earnings for the discounted lifetime profile. This overtaking age is assumed to show relatively small dispersion among individuals of the same cohort (see Welch (1975)).
4. This procedure allows treatment of the complex case of probability expectations while extrapolating results derived under risk neutrality. Indeed extended analysis of life cycle models with random time dependent income is very rare in the literature. Among the few exceptions are Bewley (1977) and Levikson and Rabinovitch (1983) who also allow for liquidity constraints.
5. See Flavin (1981) or Hall and Mishkin (1982) for instance: the consumer is assumed to know the stable coefficients of the ARMA process generating income or rather its deviation from a given trend.
6. To take two polar cases: if incomes (Y_t) follow a random walk, each surprise ϵ_t is interpreted as a variation in permanent income, leading to a change in consumption approximatively equal to $\Delta C_t = \epsilon_t$. There is in this case no effect on the age–wealth profile followed by the consumer. If current income Y_t is independent

of previous incomes, the surprise ϵ_t is viewed as purely transitory and induces no effect on future income expectations. The replanning effect on wealth $\Delta A_t = \epsilon_t (1 - k_t)$ is then likely to be large, since k_t, the annuity value of wealth is typically small, of the order of the inverse of the horizon length $(1/T-t)$.

7. A troublesome feature of the literature on life cycle models is due to the large variance of estimates of the average value of relative risk aversion from 0.75 or even less to 4 or 5.

8. An interesting variant of the replanning effect under risk has been modelled by Nagatani (1972) in the case of fulfilled expectations. Since uncertainty about future income is gradually removed as the consumer ages (see Eden and Pakes (1981)), realization at each age of previous expectations — call this a confirmation effect — will lead risk adverse consumers to continual replanning, equivalent to an increasing rate of time depreciation with age.

9. Uncertainty in variables other than non-property income leads to more complex models. Random tastes require state-dependent utility functions. On the other hand, uncertainty of rates of return is often viewed as an important contributor to wealth inequality (see notably Russell (1978)). To assess the effect of this factor one needs to model portfolio decisions that depend upon the relation between the relative risk aversion and the amount of assets held. Note that empirical estimates of this relation are based upon the observed share of risky assets in total portfolio, an *ex post* measure that is therefore likely to be biased (see Shorrocks (1982)).

10. Recall data for France collected by a sample survey carried in 1975 show large individual variations in the timing of wealth receptions even among homogenous groups. The ratio: already received wealth/already received wealth + inheritance expectations shows substantial variance for given age and occupational group (see Kessler and Masson (1979)).

11. To appreciate the potential variability in wealth profiles created by this factor, we need to have an idea of the dispersion in u_{12} within the population. We are far from this since authors don't seem to agree even on the sign of u_{12}. Some, like Blinder (1976), will argue that leisure and consumption are presumably complementary (since consumption takes time or leisure demands goods), while Heckman (1974) explains the concavity of the consumption profile with age by the substitution between leisure and consumption.

12. This dispersion could be assessed from the corresponding lifetime income inequality in the real world by eliminating all the differences in opportunities. In the real world, most authors would agree that the principal contributor to lifetime income inequality is the distribution of wages (Blinder (1974)). This latter distribution depends in turn primarily on the respective effects of the distributions of abilities and opportunities relevant to earning power. The key parameter to assess income inequality in our egalitarian society is therefore the relative contribution of different opportunities in actual wage inequality (see Becker (1975) and Atkinson (1983)).

13. . . . with furthermore non-separability of human capital decisions.

14. Using the Theil index to decompose inequality, the relative contribution of age (in 12 groups) to wealth inequality amounts to 10.9% estimated on French data coming from a household survey (C R E P 1980) and to 12.5% in the Canadian survey studied by King and Dicks-Mireaux (1982) who graciously gave us the

data. The combined contribution to inequality of age and permanent income (in decile) is 26.2% in the Canadian survey but 44.3% in the French survey, using current income as a proxy for permanent income.

References

Appelbaum, E. and R. Harris, 'Imperfect Capital Markets and Life Cycle Savings', *Canadian Journal of Economics* **11** (1978), 319–24.

Atkinson, A. B., 'The Distribution of Wealth and the Individual Life Cycle', *Oxford Economic Papers* **23** (1971), 239–54.

—— 'Income Distribution and Inequality of Opportunity', in *Social Justice and Public Policy* (Wheatsheaf Books Ltd, London, 1983), 77–92.

Becker, G. S., *Human Capital: a Theoretical and Empirical Analysis with Special Relevance to Education* (2nd edition), (NBER, New York, 1975).

Bewley, T., 'The Permanent Income Hypothesis: A Theoretical Formulation', *Journal of Economic Theory* **16** (1977), 252–92.

Blinder, A. S., *Toward an Economic Theory of Income Distribution* (MIT Press, Cambridge, Ma., 1974).

—— 'Intergenerational Transfers and Life Cycle Consumption', *Papers and Proceedings of the American Economic Review* **66** (1976), 87–93.

—— and Y. Weiss, 'Human Capital and Labor Supply: A Synthesis', *Journal of Political Economy* **84** (1976), 449–72.

Davies, J. B., 'Uncertain Lifetime, Consumption and Dissaving in Retirement', *Journal of Political Economy* **89** (1981), 561–77.

Deaton, A. S. and J. Muellbauer, *Economics and Consumer Behaviour* (Cambridge University Press, London, 1980).

Deaton, A. S., 'Savings and Inflation: Theory and British Evidence' in F. Modigliani and R. Hemming (eds), *The Determinants of National Saving and Wealth* (MacMillan, New York, 1983), 125–39.

Diamond P. A. and J. A. Hausman, 'Individual Retirement and Saving Behaviour', *Journal of Public Economics* **23** (1984), 81–114.

Eden, B. and A. Pakes, 'On Measuring the Variance-Age Profile of Lifetime Earnings', *Review of Economic Studies* **48** (1981), 385–94.

Feldstein, M. S., 'Social Security and the Distribution of Wealth', *The Journal of American Statistical Association* **71** (1976), 800–7.

Flavin, M. A., 'The Adjustment of Consumption to Changing Expectations about Future Income', *Journal of Political Economy* **89** (1981), 974–1009.

Hall, R. E. and F. S. Mishkin, 'The Sensitivity of Consumption to Transitory Income: Estimates from Panel Data on Households', *Econometrica* **50** (1982), 461–81.

Heckman, J., 'Life Cycle Consumption and Labor Supply: an Explanation of the Relationship between Income and Consumption over the Life Cycle', *American Economic Review* **64** (1976a), 188–94.

—— 'A Life Cycle Model of Earning, Learning and Consumption', *Journal of Political Economy* **84** Part 2, (1976b), S11–S44.

Hubbard R. G., 'Do IRAs and Keoghs Increase Saving?', *National Tax Journal* **37** (1984), 43–54.

Kessler, D. and A. Masson, 'Les transferts intergénérationnels: l'aide, la donation, l'héritage', Rapport A T P Modes de vie, mimeo, (1979).

Kessler, D. and A. Masson, 'Petit guide pour décomposer l'évolution d'un phénomène en termes d'effets d'âge, de génération et de moment', in D. Kessler and A. Masson (eds.), *Cycles de Vie et Générations* (Economica, Paris, 1985).

—— and ——, 'Personal Wealth Distribution in France: Cross-Sectional Evidence and Extensions', in E. N. Wolff (ed.), *International Comparisons of the Distribution of Household Wealth*, (Oxford University Press, New York, 1987).

King, M. A. and L. Dicks-Mireaux, 'Asset Holdings and the Life Cycle', *Economic Journal* **92** (1982), 247–67.

Landsberger, M., 'The Life Cycle Hypothesis: a Reinterpretation and Empirical Test', *American Economic Review* **60** (1970), 175–83.

Levikson, B. and R. Rabinovitch, 'Optimal Consumption-Saving Decisions with Uncertain but Dependent Incomes', *International Economic Review* **24** (1983), 341–60.

Lillard, L., 'Inequality: Earnings vs. Human Wealth', *American Economic Review* **67** (1977), 42–53.

Masson, A., 'A Cohort Analysis of Age-Wealth Profiles Generated by a Simulation Model in France (1949–1975)', *Economic Journal* **96** (1986), 173–190.

Modigliani, F., 'The Life Cycle Hypothesis of Saving Twenty Years Later', in M. Parkin and A. R. Nobay (eds.), *Contemporary Issues in Economics* (Manchester University Press, Manchester, 1975).

Nagatani, K., 'Life Cycle Saving: Theory and Fact', *American Economic Review* **62** (1972), 344–53.

Russell, T., 'The Share of Top Wealth Holders: the Life Cycle, Inheritance and Efficient Markets', *Annales de l'INSEE* **33–34** (1978), 159–80.

Shorrocks, A. F., 'The Portfolio Composition of Assets Holdings in the United Kingdom', *Economic Journal* **92** (1982), 268–84.

Welch, F., 'Human Capital Theory: Education, Discrimination and Life Cycles', *Papers and Proceedings of the American Economic Review* **65** (1975), 63–73.

Comments on Chapter 11

DANIEL FEASTER
University of Miami

SHELDON DANZIGER
University of Wisconsin

Kessler and Masson catalogue numerous reasons why a society in which consumers begin with equal endowments may have an unequal distribution of wealth. They use a life-cycle consumption model and an *ex-ante* definition of equality to trace out the effect of variations in market conditions and consumer preferences and behaviours on wealth inequality. The paper is motivated by Atkinson's (1971) paper which demonstrated that the extent of wealth inequality could not be generated solely by the age distribution (that is, otherwise equal individuals at different points in the life cycle with differing stocks of wealth accumulated for retirement). As Kessler and Masson note, most work since Atkinson has explored the effect of intergenerational transfers on observed wealth dispersion. While they provide a comprehensive evaluation of how a dozen different factors contribute to inequality, they do not provide a method for deciding whether the magnitudes of the derived effects are quantitatively important. As a result, the next step is to parameterize the relationships they evaluate either through direct estimation or simulation strategies.

We begin by reviewing their underlying model. We then comment on several of the issues they cover and offer some suggestions for further research.

Kessler and Masson assume individuals maximize a homothetic time-additive lifetime utility function defined over a composite consumption good. This type of specification is common to many analyses of the life cycle hypothesis. However, as the authors state, the life cycle hypothesis merely requires an individual to maximize a lifetime utility function subject to a lifetime budget constraint. Also, the aggregation of consumption to one consumption good has no implication for the temporal separability or recursive nature of the utility function. While these assumptions on the utility function are common, they are not required by the factors the authors indicate.

The authors define an egalitarian society as one in which individuals have (1) equal endowments including equal initial human capital and (2) equal access to markets and information. This definition has the advantage of avoiding interpersonal utility comparisons that a definition based on equal lifetime utility would require. Given their assumptions about life cycle utility maximization in this egalitarian society, Kessler and Masson demonstrate that many factors might cause individuals of the same age to hold differing amounts of wealth.

Kessler and Masson consider a simplified (perfect certainty world) life-cycle framework: The age distribution generates an unequal distribution of wealth at any particular point in time, even though the egalitarian assumptions imply that the lifetime wealth of each individual is the same. They then show that a social security type transfer scheme would decrease this dispersion by reducing the accumulation at every age necessary to finance retirement. They also demonstrate that differing (but certain) life durations would lead to intra-age wealth inequality and that differing time preferences can generate a myriad of age–wealth profiles.

While any investigation of the relative importance of these various factors in explaining observed wealth inequality in any society will have to account for the effect of social security, the only plausible explanation of wealth inequality in this section is differing time preferences. Life duration is not certain, so as Kessler and Masson consider in Section III, the differing dates of death do generate differences in wealth at death (regardless of a bequest motive). However, if bequests are fully taxed by the state, then uncertain survival needn't generate additional wealth inequality unless coupled with some other deviation from the general model.

In the second section the effects of an uncertain income stream (or more exactly a random path with known, equal expected value over the life cycle) and capital market imperfections are considered. However, there is no discussion of the effect of a redistributive tax-transfer scheme even though it seems appropriate in this case. Intuitively the effect of such a scheme would be to decrease wealth dispersion since the income and, therefore the accumulation for those with a large income realization must decrease to fund the present consumption of those with an unlucky income realization (who would not be saving at that particular point in time).

Also, while the authors do consider two forms of capital market imperfections (borrowing constraints and a positive relationship between interest rates and amount invested) other well-documented aspects of the capital market may have important effects. For example, if the rate of return is positively related to the level of risk and if different individuals have varying tastes for risk, then the savings of risk-takers will grow faster than those who are risk-average, and wealth inequality will increase. Likewise if investment instruments of different maturities have different rates of return, and if individuals with different time preferences purchase different maturities, wealth inequality will also rise.

While Kessler and Masson extensively list factors which can generate (in particular intra-age) wealth inequality, the applicability of their conclusions to public policy is limited by their analysis of an egalitarian economy. Any empirical investigation must deal with a non-egalitarian world and consider how differing endowments, particularly human capital, and differing degrees of access to markets and information affect inequality. In the case of human capital there is ample room for individual differentiation of accumulation and depreciation functions which could be additional causes of wealth inequality. In fact, our subjective judgement is that none of the causes considered can generate the amount of inequality actually observed.

Kessler and Masson note that the theoretical models quickly get very complicated as more assumptions are dropped and more possible sources of wealth inequality are considered. The problem is only compounded when estimation is contemplated. For this reason it would seem that a simulation strategy to assess the potential relative importance of the various factors may be advised. In that case complicating factors that can not account for much inequality can be assumed away.

We feel that the more simple certain world life cycle model, combined with endogenous labour supply should be specified as a simulation model. The predicted wealth distributions derived from varying time preferences, taste for leisure, and tax-transfer schemes could then be compared. Our preference for emphasizing labour supply issues rather than capital market issues stems in part from our interest in income inequality but also from the greater availability of previous micro-research from which to pull consensus parameter estimates. While this exercise undoubtedly would not explain the existing wealth distribution, it would give a better understanding of the possible magnitudes involved. As well it would allow the examination of both differing definitions of egalitarian and deviations from these egalitarian norms. While we are willing to accept their definition of an egalitarian society, as they note, there are other possible definitions. More important (in our opinion) would be the comparison of the simulated egalitarian outcomes to the non-egalitarian ones.

In sum, Kessler and Masson extend Atkinson's work and show that some wealth inequality will occur even in an egalitarian economy. They show how changing assumptions on life cycle models will generate intra-age wealth inequality. Unfortunately, we still do not know how much.

Conclusion: Modelling the Accumulation and Distribution of Wealth — An Overview and a Point of View

ROBERT H. HAVEMAN
University of Wisconsin

'Modelling the Accumulation and Distribution of Wealth' is a title broad enough to encompass a wide variety of papers on the wealth phenomenon. And, indeed, the Conference from which this volume is drawn contains that variety. The papers presented ranged from very straightforward reports on the contents and descriptive statistics of wealth-oriented micro-data sets to exceedingly complex, indeed arcane, theoretical models. By and large, the papers were theoretical, but some empirical results were also reported. While one had the sense that the Conference objective was to report on theoretical work, in fact some of the most important findings stemmed from the empirical papers.

The Conference papers in this volume emphasize both theoretical work on issues surrounding the upper tail of the income or wealth distribution, and papers whose contribution can be understood only with the background of the prior literature in the field. These comments, however, are prepared by a non-theorist, whose primary interest is in the bottom tail of the distribution, and with substantially less than full familiarity with the prior literature in the area. That disjointness is, perhaps, both their strength and their weakness.

In these reflections, I will first attempt to identify the primary questions which motivate economic research in the wealth accumulation/distribution area, and the relationship of the Conference papers to these questions. Then, I will offer a very personal appraisal of the nature and magnitude of the contributions which the papers and this volume make to the field. Finally, I contrast the content of this Conference volume to what I envision would be the content of a Conference volume which displayed current economic research on the bottom tail of the income distribution — the poor.

The literature on the accumulation and distribution of wealth is not voluminous, and has concentrated on a limited set of basic questions. The papers at this Conference have a clear tie to this earlier literature, and many have been clearly motivated by it. As I perceive that literature, the primary questions to which it is addressed are the following:

What can economic theory tell us about the basic motivations for saving and wealth accumulation, and what does this theory indicate regarding the individual and aggregate patterns of individual and aggregate wealth holding? Does the life cycle hypothesis explain these wealth-holding patterns or do bequest motives or insurance motives or market imperfections or power motives or entrepreneurial motives dominate?

Several Conference papers touched on this issue in some way. It is the central focus of the Modigliani paper, and of the heated Modigliani–Kotlikoff debate that enlivened the Conference. Unfortunately, no written record can preserve such intense and unique moments. And, it was this topic that underlies the Kotlikoff–Summers paper. The contribution by Vaughan directly explores the nature of the life cycle hypothesis and its distributional implications, while those by Tomes analyse the implications of family behaviour on patterns of asset accumulation across generations.

Does the available empirical evidence support the life cycle hypothesis in general, or does it seem to explain behaviour for only particular portions of the population? Are life cycle motivations consistent with individual asset decumulation patterns, or with patterns of asset and liability holdings across the population?

This was, perhaps, the dominant concern at the Conference. The paper by Modigliani is directly concerned with shedding empirical light on this issue, and Blinder's comment on the Modigliani paper stimulated the most lively discussion at the Conference.

If the life cycle hypothesis is true or if bequest motives dominate behaviour, what are the implications for the distribution of wealth over time? Do these hypotheses suggest intergenerational regression to the mean for wealth holdings, or do they imply increasing intergenerational wealth inequality?

The theoretical papers by Vaughan and Wolff address this issue directly, and those by Davies and Kuhn and Cremer and Pestieau indirectly deal with the underlying determinants of wealth inequality. The evidence brought forward by Menchik and the models discussed by Tomes are directly relevant to appraising the intergenerational effects of bequest behaviour.

What is the level of inequality in the distribution of aggregate personal wealth, and what is the trend over time in wealth inequality? To what extent are changes in the determinants of the distribution of wealth holdings over time — productivity, life expectancy, bequest behaviour, the return on investments, fertility, household structure — associated with changes in the intertemporal distribution?

Within the context of an intertemporal, two-class model, Wolff explored these relationships using simulations over time. And the papers by Tomes deal explicitly with those parameter and behaviours which determine the intergenerational patterns of wealth and income inequality.

In appraising the degree of wealth inequality, what is the appropriate egalitarian norm? What factors — life cycle wealth, distributions of longevity, time preference, uncertainty — should be considered as 'natural' or exogenously determined in making this appraisal? Given some definition of natural wealth inequality, how should inequality in the actual distribution be measured, given interactions among factors and the decomposition characteristics of inequality measures?

While no papers at the Conference addressed the issue of empirically measuring the egalitarian distribution of wealth, that by Kessler and Masson extensively explored the implications of accepting a variety of exogenous factors in defining a 'natural' or egalitarian distribution of wealth.

To what extent do policy or institutional changes — in particular, Social Security or income transfer systems — alter both aggregate personal wealth holdings and their distribution, both in the short and long runs? Do public policies — e.g., Social Security systems — equalize or disequalize the distribution of wealth holdings in both the short and long runs; in particular does the interaction of these policies with changes in fertility patterns, bequests, or the uncertainty of longevity affect the distribution of wealth holdings over time?

This most relevant of the issues in this field was addressed explicitly by only two of the Conference papers — those by Davies and Kuhn, and Cremer and Pestieau. In both cases, the analysis was at a theoretical-simulation level, and no empirical evidence of governments' effect on wealth accumulation or its distribution was brought forward.

What is the nature of bequest behaviour? Is it best characterized by game theoretic approaches to the relationship of parents to children, or is pure selfishness or pure altruism a more accurate representation? Or is equal distribution of bequests the rule, and if so, why?

At the Conference, all of these perspectives were addressed: the papers by Kotlikoff and Summers, and Tomes appeared to rest on views of the nature of bequest motivation which were at substantial variance with the evidence of equal distribution presented by Menchik.

These, then, appear to me to be the central questions in the field, and the linkage of the contributions of the Conference papers included in this volume to these questions. Were contributions made by these papers to understanding the accumulation and distribution of personal wealth? If so, of what did they consist, and on which questions were the primary contributions made? Any attempt to answer this question must be idiosyncratic, and thus open to criticism. What follows reflects my own reading of the literature and the papers, and my own tastes.

As in the existant literature, there was some empirical support for the life cycle hypothesis (primarily in the Modigliani paper), and some evidence suggesting the absence of 'hump' saving and wealth holding. On balance, the evidence presented did little to shake belief in the hypothesis, and in fact lent a tenuous credence to it especially for non-highest wealth class units.

Progress was made in resolving the enormous disparity in the empirical estimates of the relative contributions of life cycle behaviour and bequests to aggregate wealth holdings. The paper by Modigliani and the discussion by Blinder were important in this process. As Blinder pointed out in his discussion, further resolution of this issue requires empirical estimates of behavioural responses — e.g., labour supply responses to wealth holdings. Participants appeared to agree that the true value of the contribution of bequests lies closer to the 20% figure suggested by several analyses in the literature than it does to the estimate of 80% discussed in Kotlikoff–Summers. ·

Little progress was made in setting an empirical norm for an egalitarian distribution of wealth holdings. However, the paper by Kessler and Masson highlights the complexity of this issue and revealed the many phenomena which have some claim to being both 'natural' (exogenous) and determinants of measured wealth inequality.

Similarly, little progress was made in understanding the magnitude of the contribution of the determinants of inequality in the distribution of wealth holdings to observed levels of inequality and changes in them over time. Vaughan's model was seen as too complex and unrealistic to be revealing; Wolff's too limited. In both cases, however, the papers pointed to the parameters which have to be considered, and whose effects and interactions need to be understood, in order to model the process by which wealth inequality is established and changed. As Malinvaud put it in his discussion, the papers 'helped us to think clearly' about the problem.

The paper by Kotlikoff and Summers made an important contribution in emphasizing the potential of insurance and capital market imperfections in explaining private saving behaviour and aggregate wealth holdings. Further, it was shown that under symmetrical bargaining conditions, families may themselves provide substantial insurance against the uncertainty of longevity, hence reducing the demand for private saving and wealth. From this, it follows that the insurance-based welfare gains often attributed to Social Security systems are small if such self-insuring by families is the rule. The Conference participants, however, appeared to be unconvinced that symmetrical bargaining exists between parents and children, or that parents and children actually undertake such insurance-based transactions to any substantial extent.

The Conference produced few contributions to the question of the effect of government policy — in particular, social security policy — on savings behaviour and wealth holding. While this has been a long-standing and central area of dispute in the saving-wealth literature, the only Conference papers directed to this subject were the theoretical-simulation analyses by Davies and Kuhn, and Cremer and Pestieau. The counter-intuitive wealth disequalizing effect of Social Security emphasized by Davies-Kuhn was viewed as an interesting insight.

Evidence on estate division patterns provided by Menchik suggested the overwhelming predominance of an equal distribution pattern. These results called into question the unequal distribution implications of a variety of models suggesting selfish, altruistic, or gaming behaviours among parents and children, such as those presented by Kotlikoff and Tomes at the Conference. Menchik's challenge was for a theory which would explain equal division.

Finally, the Conference produced an interesting start toward the incorporation of entrepreneurial activity in a model of the accumulation of large — very large — wealth stocks. The Shorrocks' paper seemed quite consistent with a number of aspects of entrepreneurial behaviour — single item portfolios for low budget entrepreneurial activities, and diverse portfolios for high budget activities, and the non-participation of some individuals in entrepreneurial activity.

For a single Conference and volume, these contributions are noteworthy and surely make the enterprise a worthwhile one. Yet, this area of economic inquiry is quite different from many others in the discipline, both in terms of the questions asked and the tools brought to bear. A heavy emphasis on rather complex theoretical models is perhaps required by the intergenerational nature of the wealth transmission problem. Yet one is distressed by some of the rather extreme — indeed, bizarre — assumptions which drive a number of models; assumptions, for example, regarding gaming or selfish behaviour of parents and children toward each other. Findings, especially counter-intuitive findings, from these models are taken by some as 'knowledge,' when in fact there is little or no correspondence of the presumed behaviour to reality. Moreover, the merits of theoretical inquiries with no conceivable tie to empirical validification need to the questioned. Perhaps their main contribution is to pedagogy — identifying relevant relationships and encouraging straight and comprehensive thinking — rather than to knowledge.

The basic reason for this relative concentration on theory in the wealth-saving area is not difficult to identify. Micro-data — and aggregate data — on saving and wealth are among the most scarce and unreliable of those on which any sub-field in economics relies. And, given the intertemporal nature of the process of wealth accumulation, manipulation of the required data is particularly difficult.

In this regard, an interesting comparison may be made between research on issues relating to the bottom of the income distribution — the poor — and the research presented at this Conference and in this volume. How would the content of what one might envision a contemporary poverty research conference differ from that of this Conference and volume? Several differences seem clear:

Research on the economics of poverty rests on by and large accepted definitions of income, living unit, and accounting period. Disagreement on these matters in the wealth-saving field is wider, as witnessed by the Modigliani-Blinder-Kotlikoff discussion. Long experience with the analysis of micro-data perhaps explains the smaller divergence of viewpoints in the poverty research area.

Again, for reasons of data availability, a conference on poverty economics would contain many more empirical contributions in the line of those by Menchik presented here. These, as well as theory-simulation research, are described by the term 'modelling,' used in the title of this Conference and volume.

The hypothetical poverty research conference would have a high concentration of studies designed to estimate the impact of government on the lower tail of the distribution, and the behavioural responses of those in that tail to the incentives implicit in policy measures. Such labour supply, migration, family structure, consumption decisions have been made substantially more endogenous in the poverty area than in research on wealth. Again, data availability may explain the difference.

Finally, poverty research has emphasized the process of mobility into and out of the tail far more than has research in the wealth area. Again, the explanation may be data.

All would probably agree that data — especially micro and longitudinal data — are required to move a field of inquiry from theory toward estimated parameter values describing those relationships relevant to understanding the world, and changing it. It is the lack of such data that has constrained wealth research, and encouraged the intensive development of complex and arcane theoretical modelling techniques which now characterize the field. However, the other half of his half-empty glass contains some fine wine. One senses that researchers in the wealth area are a good deal more sensitive to the complexities of the process by which wealth creation and distribution occur than are their counterparts in the poverty research area to the equally complex process of poverty creation and income distribution. This sensitivity to complex interactions on the part of wealth researchers no doubt stems from the theoretical development which data constraints have induced. While the mindless dash to the computer which characterizes too much poverty research is absent among wealth researchers, more data on and empirical analysis of existing wealth distributions, and more micro-econometric estimates of crucial wealth-related behavioural parameters, would surely leaven what is now a severely constrained field of inquiry.

Author Index

Subject Index

DATE DUE
